DEBORAH REMINGTON

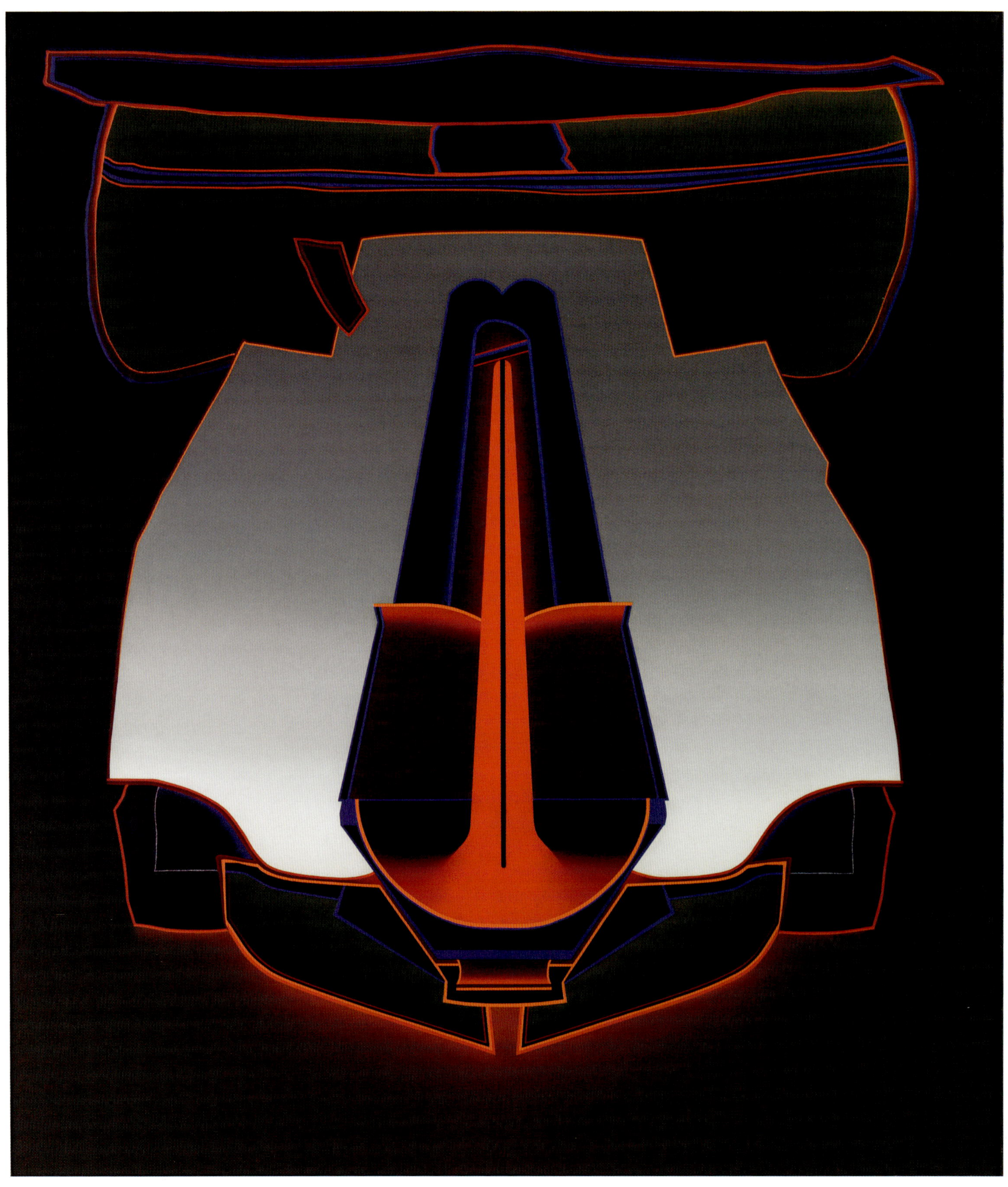

DEBORAH REMINGTON

EDITED BY

Margaret Mathews Berenson

Nancy Lim

WITH CONTRIBUTIONS BY

Carroll Dunham

Stephanie M. Hohlios

Suzanne Hudson

Anna Katz

Kevin Killian

Paul Schimmel

Rizzoli Electa

CONTENTS

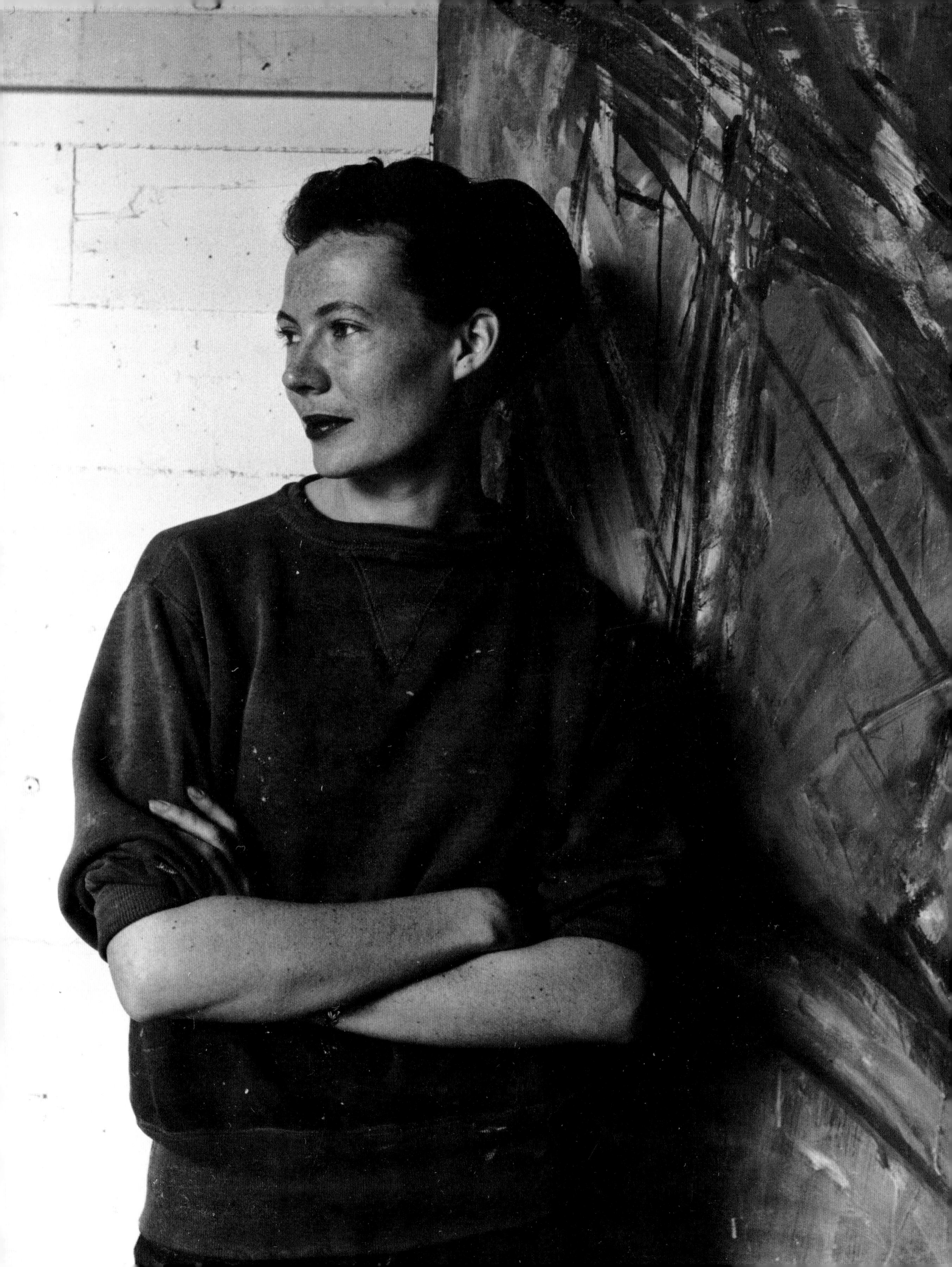

Foreword

MARGARET MATHEWS BERENSON

I have always clung to the belief that painting is a moral enterprise, a process of discovery, a mode of inquiry, a passionate and exuberant . . . struggle to give form to one's experience and relate it to one's culture. Using abstract imagery, I attempt to portray and examine some of the complexities of the human experience. . . . My work is guided by these thoughts.

—DEBORAH REMINGTON, 1995

As director of the Deborah Remington Charitable Trust for the Visual Arts for the past fourteen years, I have learned something new about the artist nearly every day. Although we were friends for over two decades before her death in 2010, I had only known the most basic facts about her rich and productive life. For instance, I discovered that she was an early member of the Beat generation and cofounder of one of San Francisco's first artist-run spaces, and that she was passionate about jazz, played the bongos, and dated the first drummer in Dave Brubeck's jazz band. She also enjoyed a brief career as an actress while living in Japan in the late 1950s before finally settling in New York in 1965—a move she was convinced would advance her career. Self-confident and independent throughout her life, she was proud of being different—doing the unexpected, making work that did not always fit easily into the art world canon, and constantly striving to change as her own maverick sense of self dictated rather than as accepted tastemakers proclaimed.

More details of the artist's life would soon unfold as the team of intimate friends and family she appointed to the Remington Trust began working together to assess and protect her legacy: a duty she entrusted to a group of four individuals, including her cousin, Craig Remington, executor of the estate and sole trustee of the Remington Trust; Cheri Smith, a cherished friend and devoted studio assistant who cared for her in her final days; and Phyllis Landau, the attorney who expertly helped her formulate the trust's mission and has advised us on every legal matter since.

Collectively, we became dedicated stewards of her work as we tended to the basic tasks of cataloguing, photographing, storing, preserving, and promoting. We gained intimate knowledge of every phase of her career: one that spanned six decades from the early 1950s to the mid-2000s, as the work evolved from Abstract Expressionism to a luminous hard-edge geometry and, in the last two decades of her life, returned to gesture, which suited the increasingly emotional content of her drawings and paintings. There is a bewildering strangeness to every period of Remington's practice. Asked to explain, she often referred to an affinity for

Remington in her studio at the California School of Fine Arts, San Francisco, 1955 paradoxes, contradictions, and absurdities that left viewers struggling to make sense of the work. It was perhaps her passion for science during the space age (she was an avid reader of *Scientific American*) that contributed to the unearthly glowing shapes in her signature geometric paintings from the 1970s and 1980s. They are perfectly in tune with the digital generation for whom her edgy, vibrating, kaleidoscopic shapes do not seem at all alien.

This book is the first comprehensive study of Remington's work in over four decades—a twenty-year survey curated by Paul Schimmel debuted at the Newport Harbor Art Museum (now the Orange County Museum of Art) in 1983—making this the most detailed unfolding of the Deborah Remington story to date. The authors of this new monograph have had access to hundreds of reviews, articles, documents, interviews, and personal correspondence, which the artist collected and preserved throughout her lifetime and is now housed in the Special Collections and University Archives at Rutgers University Libraries in New Brunswick, New Jersey. Remington kept meticulous records documenting her life and created a detailed database of the work she made from the time she was a college student to the last paintings she completed shortly before her death. "The most important thing in my life . . . is the fact that I am a painter," she wrote in an autobiography for an English class at the California School of Fine Arts in San Francisco in 1955.

Among the unusual discoveries in the Rutgers Archives is a series of black-and-white photographs of the artist in the early 1950s posing, costumed and made-up, much like in the images artist Cindy Sherman conceived of more than twenty-five years later in her groundbreaking series *Untitled Film Stills* (1977–80). Unlike Sherman, Deborah had a rather antic sense of humor and a penchant for comic acting evident in these images. Also included in the archives are letters to special friends and colleagues (most likely the artist asked for them to be returned to her for safekeeping). These letters, as well as her diaries from Japan, have provided us with her intimate recollections of daily life in Tokyo in the mid-1950s—a time when few foreigners, and certainly not many young, single American women, lived there. Although her notations are brief, they are nonetheless informative. Her experiences in Japan and later travels throughout Southeast Asia and India had a lasting impact on her life and artistic practice, as the writers acknowledge in this volume.

Shortly after the artist's death, the Remington Trust embarked on an oral history project with video interviews of friends, critics, artists, gallerists, and curators whom she knew at various stages of her life, among them Dore Ashton, Patricia Hamilton, Klaus Kertess, Mary McChesney, David Simpson, and Judith Solodkin. These interviews not only added to our knowledge of the artist's life but also would lead to greater visibility and new audiences for her work over time. The interview with New York–based gallerist and independent curator Jay Gorney resulted in solo exhibitions at Wallspace Gallery in New York in 2015 and at Kimmerich Galerie in Berlin in 2016 and 2018. Many key works from these exhibitions made their way into significant museum and private collections, and critical reviews appeared in the *New Yorker*, *Art in America*, and other publications.

However, it was perhaps a timely group show that contributed most significantly to raising public awareness of Remington's life and work in the years since the Remington Trust was established. *Women of Abstract Expressionism*, organized by Gwen Chanzit at the Denver Art Museum in 2016, was a catalyst that not only brought critical attention to Remington's work but highlighted the role of women in one of the most influential art movements of the twentieth century. Among the artists included in this groundbreaking exhibition was Jay DeFeo, a member of Remington's intimate group of friends in the Bay Area, where she lived from 1949 to 1965. Knowing that Deborah yearned for her own work to be rediscovered like that of DeFeo, whose monumental painting *The Rose* (1966) is now considered iconic, I reached out to Leah Levy, executive director of the Jay DeFeo Foundation, whose advice proved invaluable. In addition to sharing her wisdom and experience about managing an artist's estate, she introduced us to the Aspen Institute's Artist-Endowed Foundations Initiative and its Leadership Forum, which fosters networking opportunities among artist-endowed foundations, trusts, and estates and has established standards of practice that now guide our vision and mission.

As coeditor of this volume, curator Nancy Lim has been a devoted partner and inspiration throughout the gestation of the project and during our many conversations at least six years before the book was conceived. Her vision, intelligence, and commitment have added immeasurably to ensuring that Deborah Remington's life and work will not be forgotten. Nancy organized a major solo exhibition for the artist slated to open in 2020 at the di Rosa Center for Contemporary Art in Napa, California. Sadly, this was one of countless exhibitions worldwide to be canceled due to the global pandemic. Nonetheless, Remington's work was showcased the following year in concurrent solo exhibitions at Bortolami Gallery and Craig Starr Gallery in New York. The fortunate convergence of these two shows resulted in a great deal of press at a time when audiences were eager to once again experience art in person, and galleries were perhaps more receptive to considering a woman artist with historical gravitas whose work had not been widely seen.

In addition to exhibiting, preserving, and promoting her work, the Remington Trust, in accordance with the artist's wishes, is committed to creating opportunities for artists and nonprofit groups to further their creative goals. The trust has made over a dozen grants to individual artists and nonprofit institutions, including the San Francisco Art Institute, The Cooper Union (New York, NY), the Miriam Schapiro Archives on Women Artists at Rutgers (New Brunswick, NJ), and the University of New Mexico Foundation/Tamarind Institute (Albuquerque), among others. Throughout her life, the artist supported herself through teaching, to which she was almost as dedicated as to her own work, writing in 1995, "In school, I was fortunate enough to have a number of outstanding teachers who made a meaningful difference in my life at an important stage. I teach in order to give something back, to create the same stimulating and productive learning experience for my students as I had."

The Remington Trust has been grateful to make connections through an ever-expanding network of critics, curators, and friends, as well as through serendipitous events that brought people together through an appreciation of Remington's work. We look forward to many more opportunities for the artist's paintings and drawings to be studied and seen. Yet to be explored, for example, are her own writings, which remain largely untapped. She wrote terse, often humorous verses of Beat poetry and recorded her thoughts about painting in countless lectures, interviews, and unpublished letters. Artist, beatnik, adventurer, and independent spirit, Deborah Remington left a legacy we hope will continue to gain relevance for future generations. Her work reverberates with an idiosyncratic, crackling energy uniquely its own. To me, she will always remain very much alive—her voice strong, unfaltering, and compelling.

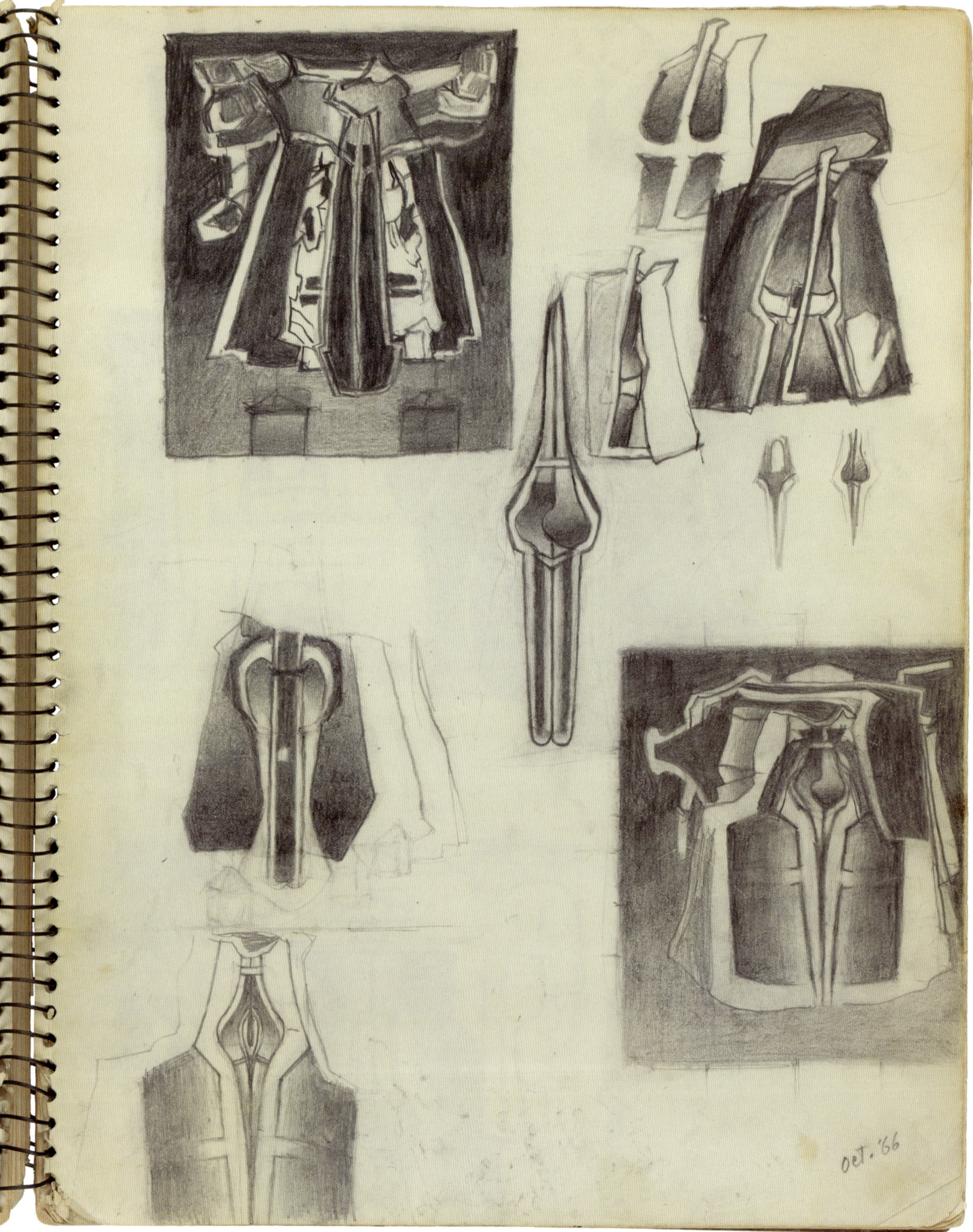
Oct. '66

Introduction: A Luminous Vision

NANCY LIM

Deborah Remington's career spanned six eventful decades, from her beatnik days in San Francisco during the 1950s to her death in New Jersey in 2010. An artist whose volume of paintings, drawings, and prints exceeds thousands, she experienced the art world's loftier echelons, as well as episodes of unsteady critical and commercial visibility. But vagaries regardless, she upheld a clarity of vision that gusted her to the end. Through scholarly essays, remembrances, and newly unearthed archives, *Deborah Remington* is the first publication to examine the breadth of the artist's career. Starting with her early efforts as an art student in the aftermath of World War II, progressing to her iconic paintings and drawings, and concluding with works whose highly embellished imagery crowns her last two decades of life, these periods of form and sensibility may appear neatly correspondent with concurrent developments, such as Light and Space in California and Minimalism in New York. Yet her artworks reveal a language distinctly her own, one whose evolution demonstrates the vibrant interplay of experimentation and constancy that animated the heart of her creative practice.

Prior to New York, Remington was an art student at the California School of Fine Arts (CSFA; later the San Francisco Art Institute). Quickly recognized by faculty for her talent, she produced dynamic paintings and prints that embrace a postwar spirit of urgency, and these works are inflected by the spontaneity and reactiveness of modern jazz, which was continuously playing in her studio. Following graduation, the artist spent two formative years in Japan, where she undertook intensive training in classical Chinese and Japanese calligraphy. As she practiced brushwork in black ink on white paper, she delighted in the tonal richness of grays, and upon her return to California in 1958, she briefly continued in these chromatic parameters, better able to focus on the quality of her line, form, and composition absent color's distractions. Her palette slowly expanded as she reincorporated color in modest doses; simultaneously, she began pulling her strokes away from the edge and into the center, her works marching steadily toward the consolidated, iconic forms that she would later call "portraits of shapes."[1]

Relatively scant attention has been paid to these years before the mid-1960s. Remington is instead best known for the auratic paintings that materialized following her move from

Page from Remington's sketchbook, October 1966

San Francisco to New York in 1965, where she quickly gained attention. Making good on her hopes, she was offered numerous exhibition opportunities, first at the 1965 Whitney Annual, which led to her inclusion in the collection of the Whitney Museum of American Art.[2] She also became affiliated with high-profile galleries both at home and abroad: New York's Bykert Gallery, run by an ambitious Klaus Kertess, whose roster included Dorothea Rockburne and Brice Marden; and the eponymous Galerie Darthea Speyer in Paris that introduced Remington's work to European collectors and institutions. Today, these archetypal paintings—such as *Haddonfield* (1965), *Dorset* (1972), and *Saratoga* (1972)—remain her primary legacy.

Perfected in her SoHo studio throughout the 1970s, these proto-digital creations abandoned the gestural, topographic drama of her Bay Area works. They now embraced licked surfaces and precise lines and hues, including electric blue and cadmium red articulated in lush, gradated sweeps—formal decisions that heightened the strangeness of her compositions. Each painting is a union of extremes: at once spare and maximal, cold and libidinal, and, most curiously, abstract and allusive with resemblances to mirrors, spaceships, and car grilles. When asked to reveal specific references, Remington demurred, preferring to describe herself more broadly as "a great IBM machine of some sort, a great computer, because all the stuff just gets fed in."[3] Sketchbooks and related sources confirm at least some concrete origins at play in her work, from steel beams and pocket watches to the landscapes around her, together with New York's skyscrapers and the deserts along the banks of the Nile. Contemporary geopolitical events also influenced Remington, such as the space race, which inspired her to develop artworks that push beyond an earthbound vision in search of other worlds.

It was the medium of drawing, however, that held a singular status in Remington's practice. Its functions and pleasures were manifold, and over the course of her life she made thousands of works on paper. While some served as preparatory sketches, others were finished pieces unto themselves, and yet others were hybrids of the two: stand-alone works that became key to advancing her paintings. Indeed, from the beginning, drawing was Remington's most prescient medium, often predicting her paintings' future course. "In drawing, I can think and not be encumbered by color," she once said. "I get a more instant feedback."[4] As a result, drawing cultivated an openness, offering a freedom of gesture and improvisation, all qualities that encouraged the artist to explore new ways of thinking that became the primary guidepost for her works on canvas.

In the final stretch of her career from the mid-1980s to 2007, Remington faded from critical glare. During these years, she returned to her San Francisco–era works, creating paintings that reengaged the canvas edges and revived a dramatic, eventful facture. But the renewed visibility of her hand held an emotional valence, one she had never allowed in her work to such a personal degree. In the early 1980s, she had been treated for breast cancer, and starting in the 1990s came a steady stream of further illnesses, resulting in hospitalizations every few years. The subtle allusions in her early imagery—to inanimate objects, for example—now gave way to more evocative representation: of rib cages and bones, lungs and hearts, as Remington attended to her ailing body. The shapes in these later works are less airtight and self-contained, with fragments that begin to disperse, poignantly evoking an ever-dissolving form.

Remington passed away in 2010. She remained active nearly to the end, persisting through a series of health concerns and struggling with feelings of irrelevance in the art world, particularly as her career became increasingly dormant after her significant twenty-year survey at the Newport Harbor Art Museum (now the Orange County Museum of Art) in 1983. Given the whims of critical attention, the existing literature is slim, and this monograph is the first major assessment to be published on the artist. It aims to contribute scholarship that is not only substantial and new but also illuminates the whole of her career rather than the narrow slices more common in criticism on Remington, which are likely due to the seemingly episodic nature of her practice. We also hope to bring the artist into fuller context alongside her peers, even as she positioned herself as a singular artist who contributed, inadvertently, to her own disappearance.

Organized chronologically, the essays in *Deborah Remington* begin with my examination of her foundational years in San Francisco, including her immersion in CSFA's heady milieu and the city's thriving Beat and jazz spheres. This period encompassed the artist's influential two-year stay in Japan, which Stephanie M. Hohlios examines through newly unearthed archival research, illuminating a critical period in Remington's life until now enshrouded in mystery. Anna Katz positions the artist's most iconic years—the late 1960s and 1970s, inaugurated by her decisive move to New York—in a trenchant and wide-ranging context to the practices of peers, such as Lee Bontecou and Miriam Schapiro. Carroll Dunham offers a similar comparative framework but filtered through personal memories of Remington's work at Bykert Gallery in the 1970s. Finally, Suzanne Hudson examines the last few decades of Remington's life, taking the 1983 survey at the Newport Harbor Art Museum as this period's originating moment, one that was simultaneously a landmark event in the artist's career as well as the start of a diminished visibility that would persist until her death. An interview with Paul Schimmel, who organized this significant survey, recalls its successes and complications, and assesses her artistic paths in the years that followed. A memorial text by the late poet Kevin Killian, written shortly after Remington's passing in 2010, concludes the essays, and an extensive illustrated chronology closes this volume.

The essays draw from recently available resources, including the artist's archives, a rich trove that was long maintained by Remington, who was a scrupulous recordkeeper. These archives became publicly accessible in 2014 after entering the Rutgers University Libraries' Special Collections and University Archives. Ultimately this publication serves as the start of a redress, one that illuminates new avenues of curiosity and research for art historians, curators, and the broader public. And indeed, featured now in a growing range of historical and contemporary exhibitions, her works have recently been undergoing a steady rediscovery. Even her best-known works from the 1970s are experiencing a renaissance particularly apt for the cultural currents of today; their proto-digital qualities, seamed into forms that appear to alight from another world, suffuse her paintings and works on paper with an ineluctability. Remington's imagery has long felt mysterious, but beyond that, it has felt prescient, as the works draw us closer and closer, and then wait patiently for us to catch on.

1949–1965

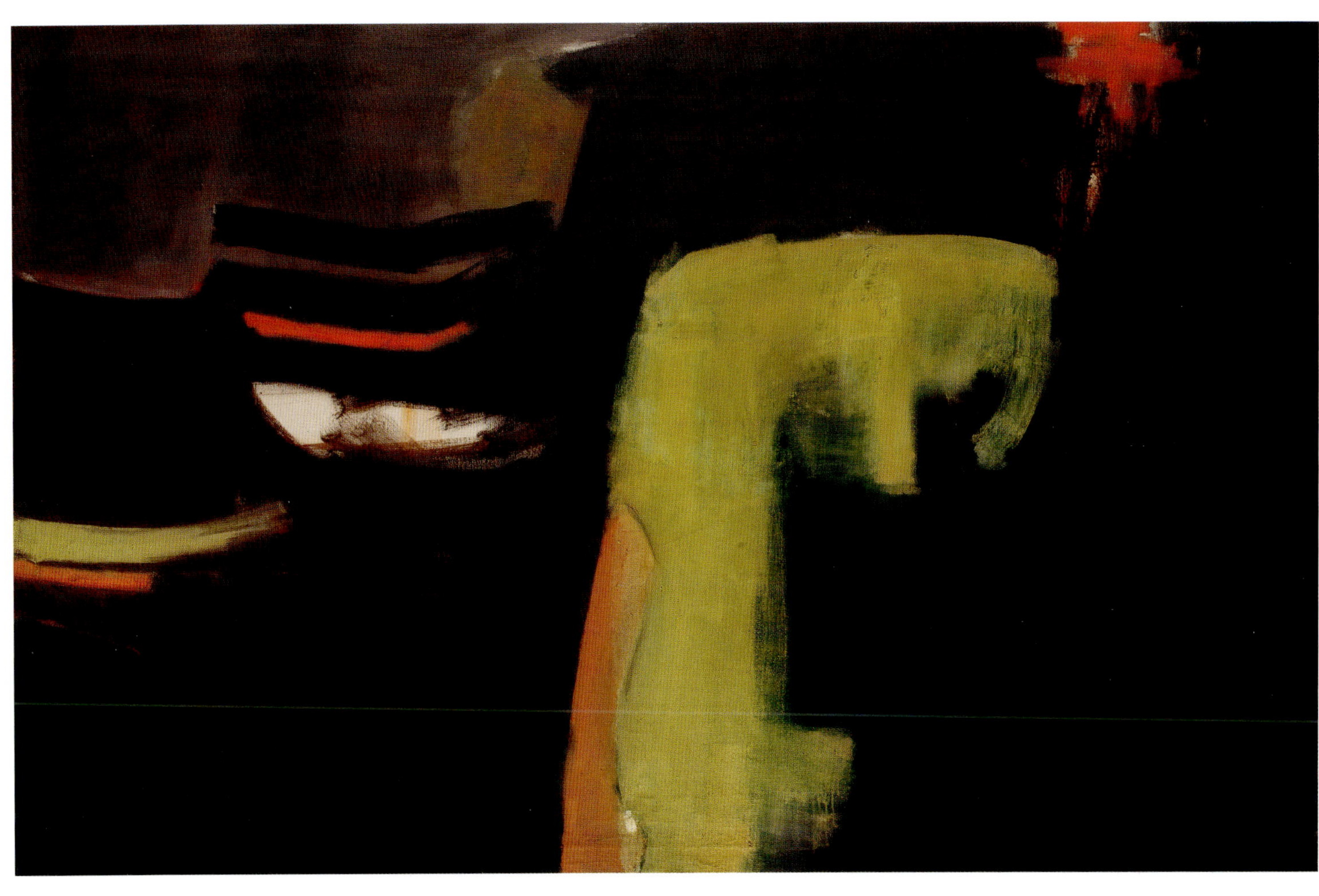

Eleusian, 1951. Oil on canvas, 43 1/4 × 71 1/2 in. (109.9 × 181.6 cm)
The Levett Collection

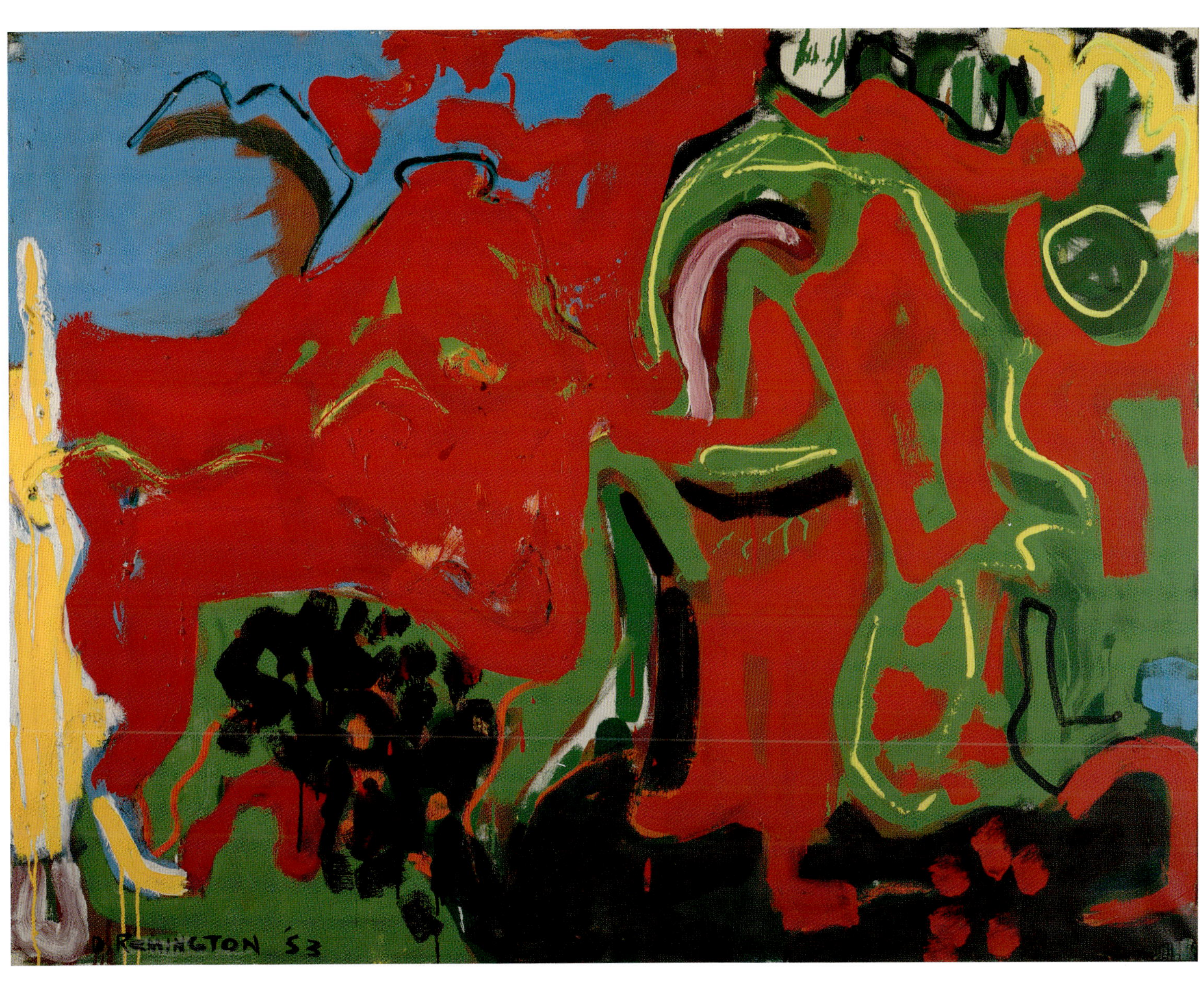

Untitled or *Apropos*, 1953. Oil on canvas, 39 × 51 in. (99 × 129.5 cm)
Denver Art Museum, Colorado. Vance H. Kirkland Acquisition Fund

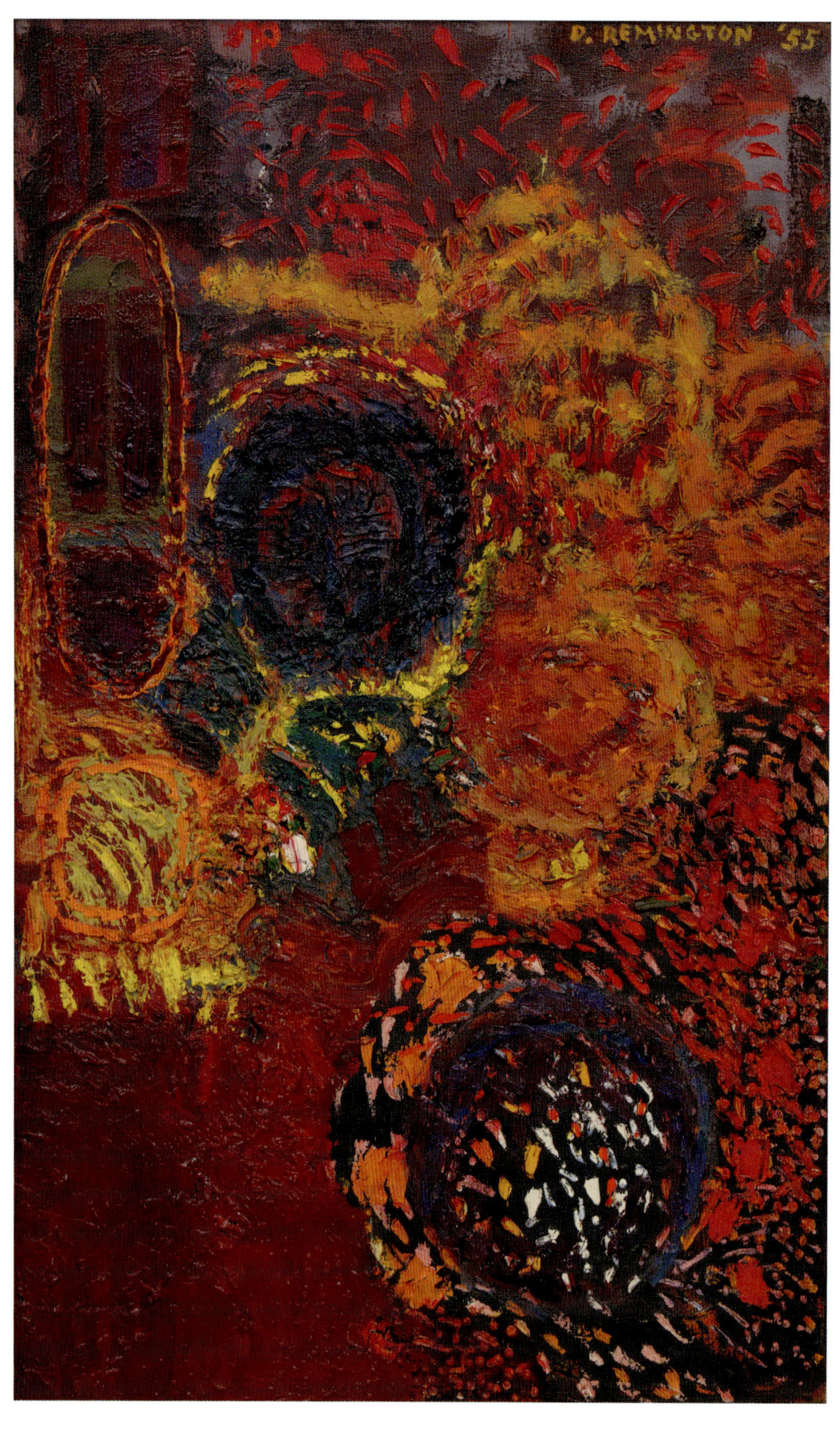

Untitled, 1955. Oil on canvas, 36 × $21\frac{3}{4}$ in. (91.5 × 55.3 cm)
Deborah Remington Charitable Trust for the Visual Arts

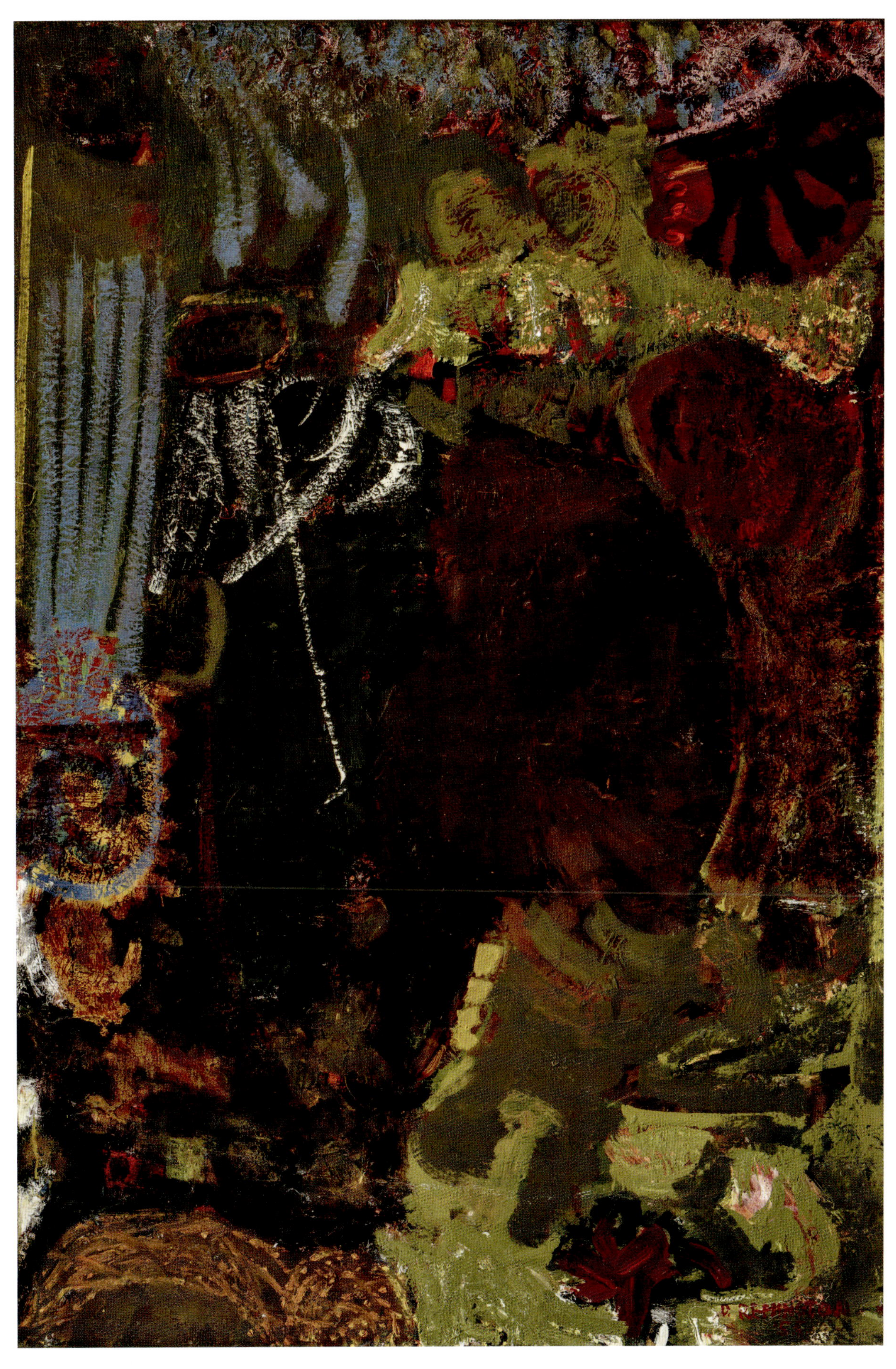

Gopher Baroque, 1955. Oil on canvas, 58 × 40 in. (147.3 × 101.6 cm)
Private collection

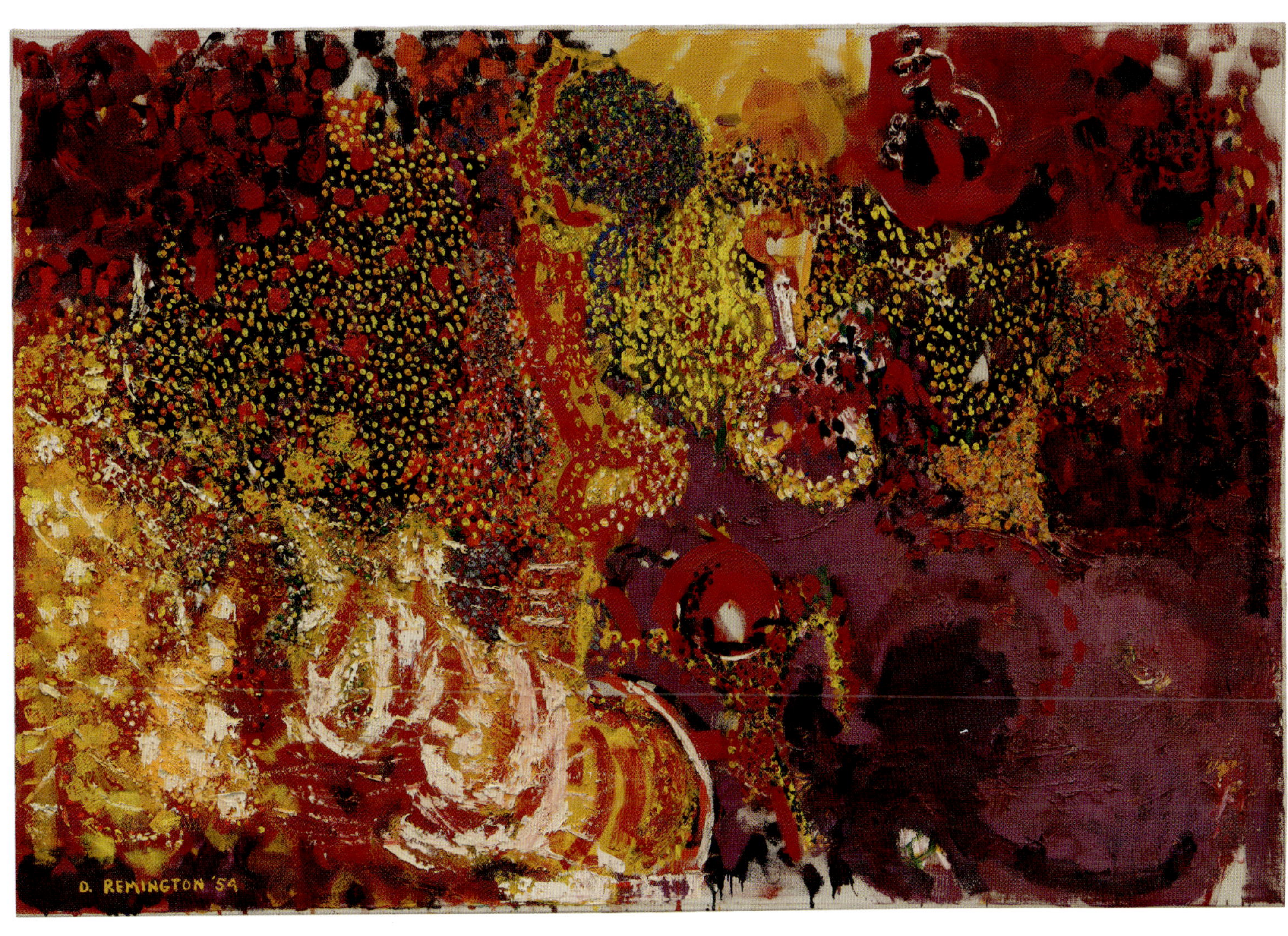

Untitled, 1954. Oil on canvas, 48 × 70 in. (122 × 178 cm)
Private collection

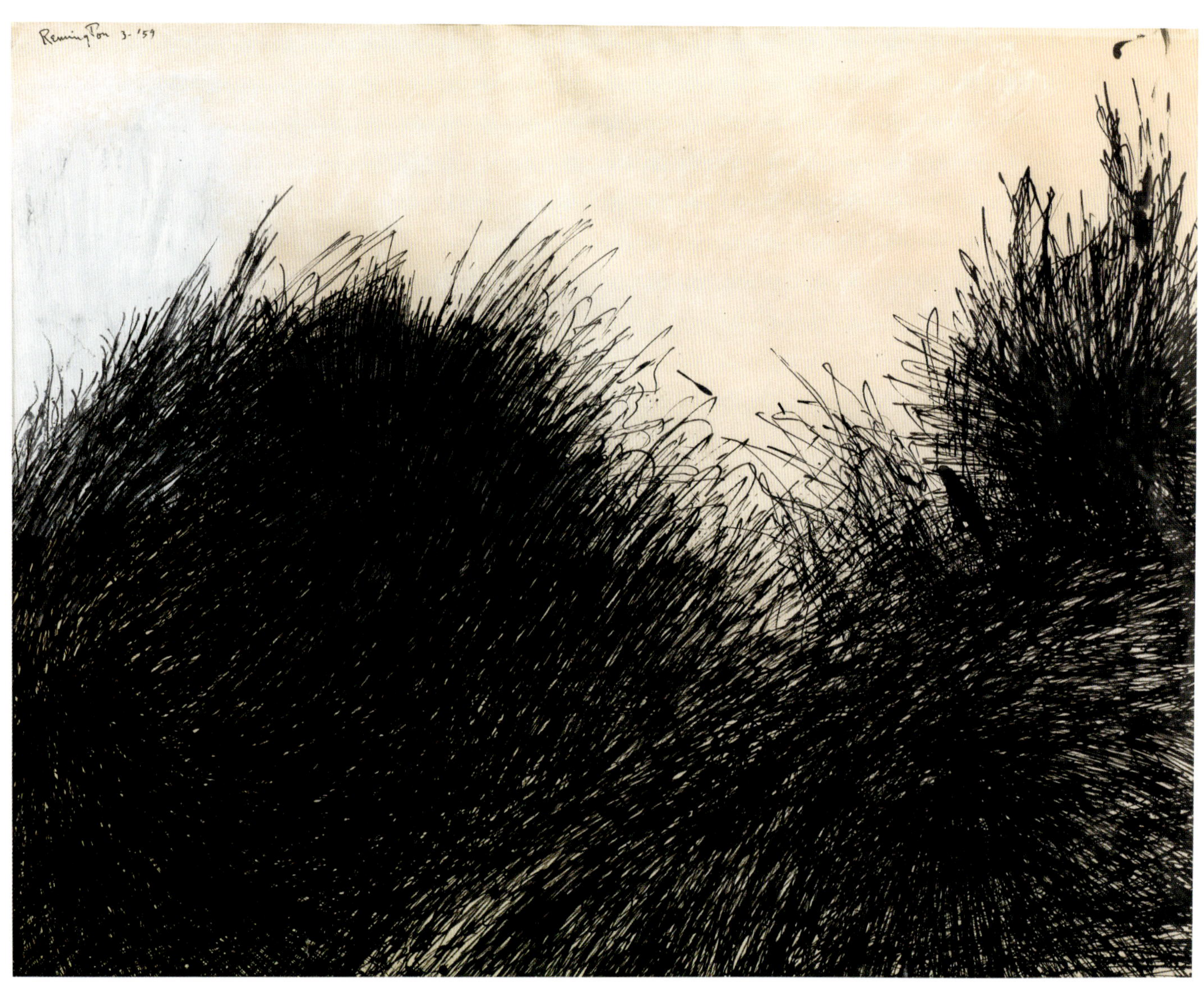

Untitled, 1959. Ink on paper, 18 1/4 × 22 1/2 in. (46.4 × 57.1 cm)
Collection of Beth Rudin DeWoody

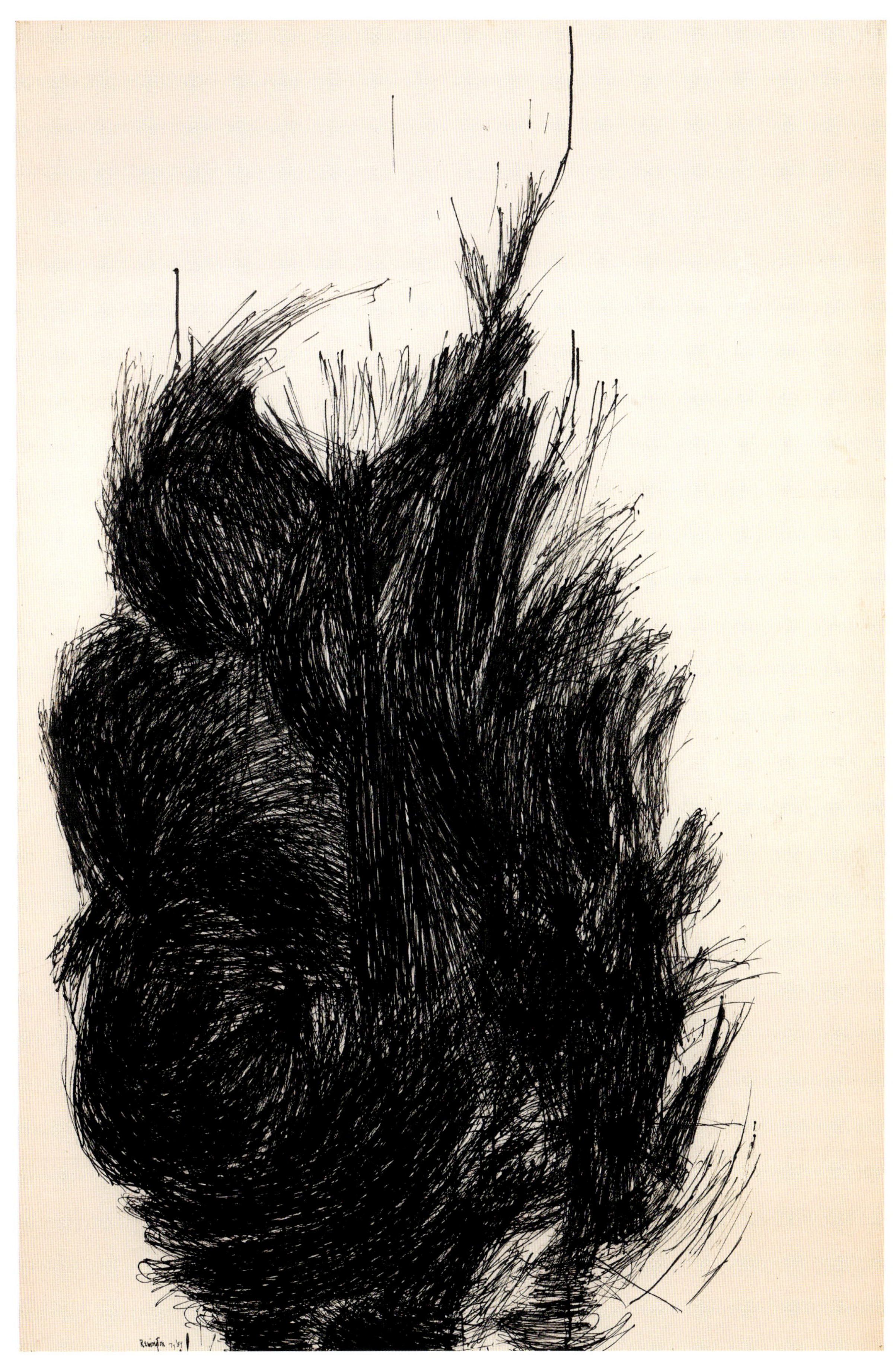

Untitled, 1959. Ink on paper, $59\,^1/_2$ × 44 in. (151.1 × 111.8 cm)
Deborah Remington Charitable Trust for the Visual Arts

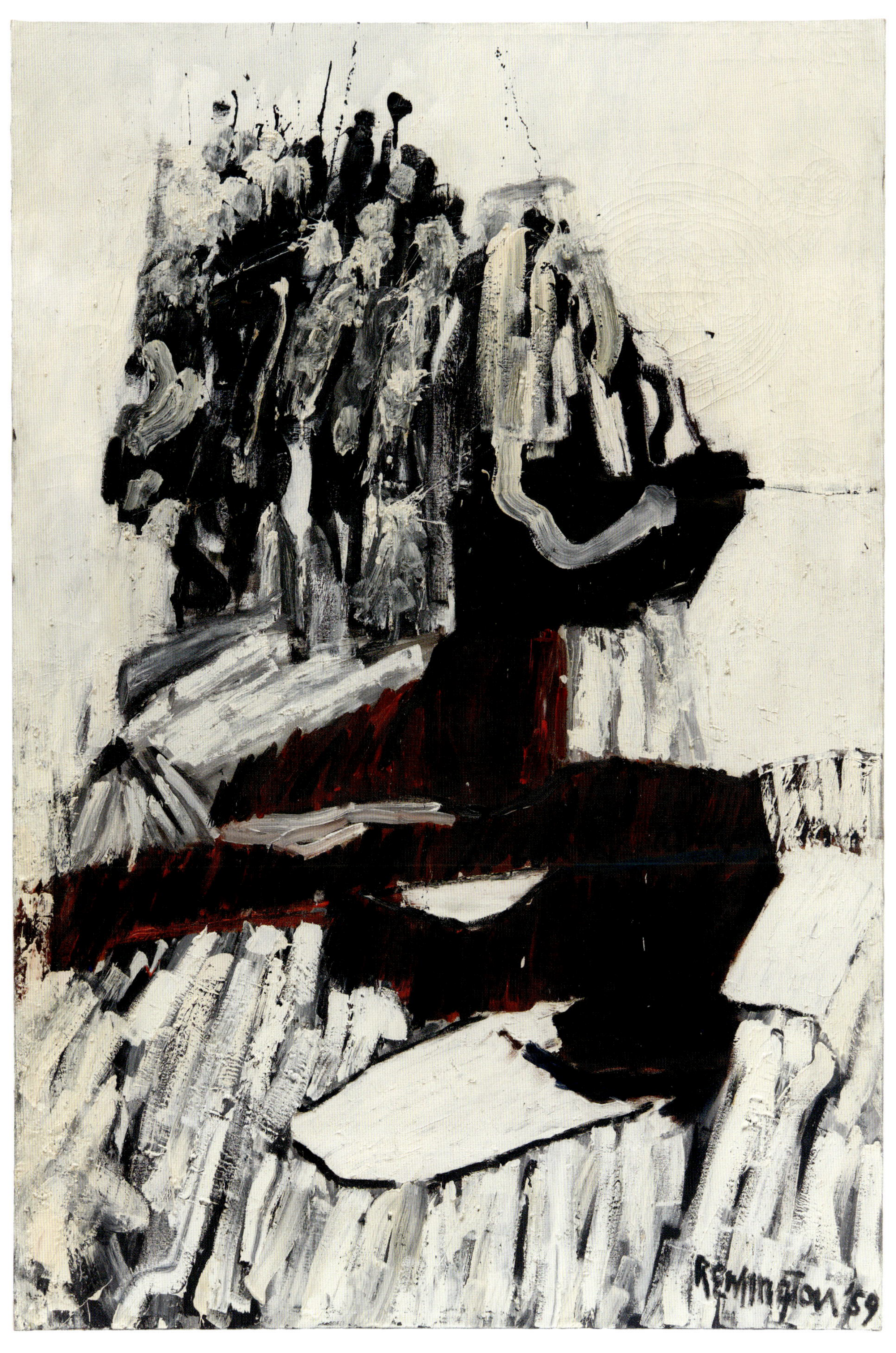

Elevation, 1959. Oil on canvas, $69\frac{1}{4} \times 47\frac{1}{2}$ in. (176 × 120.5 cm)
Private collection

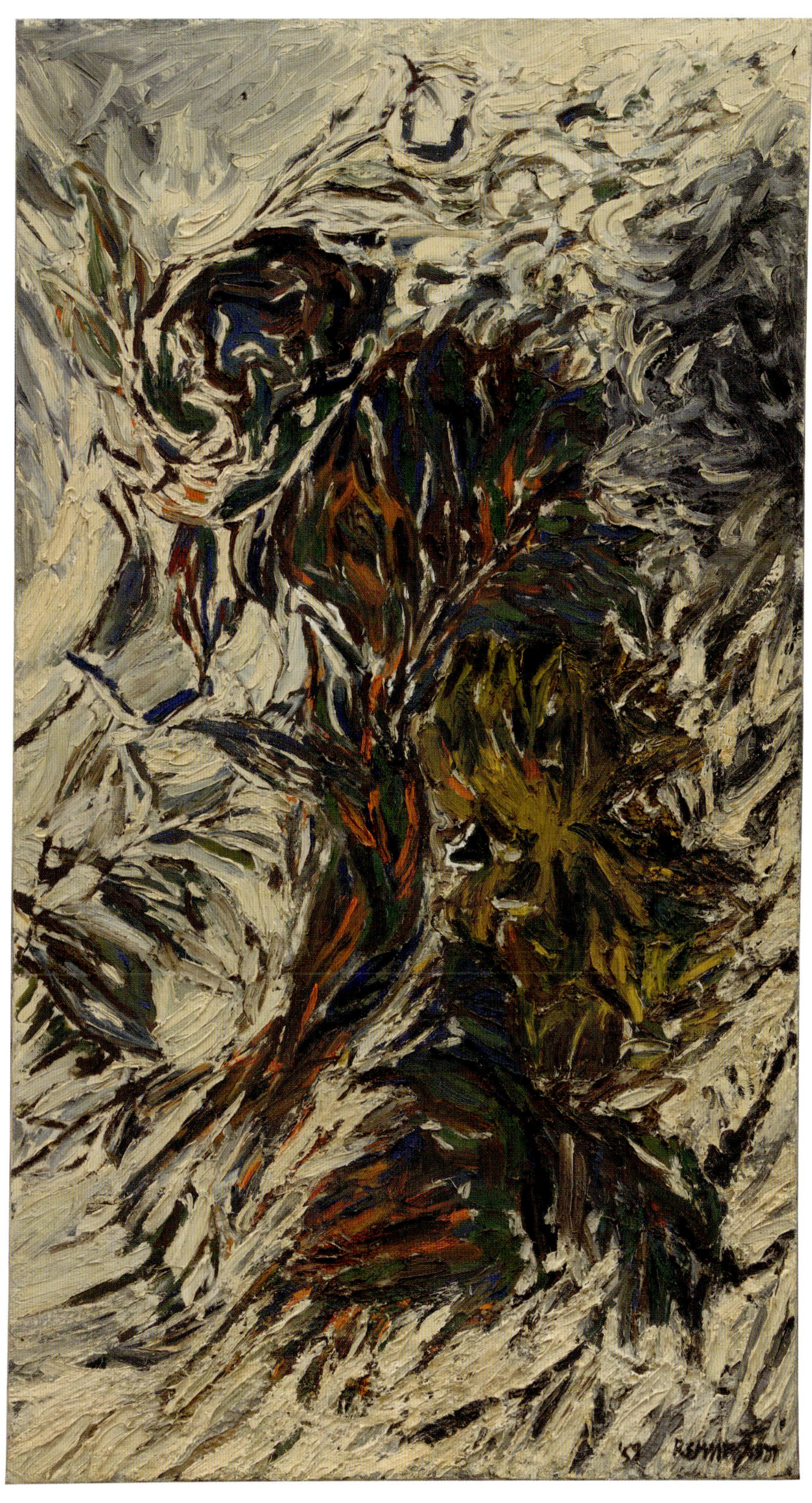

Irreparable, 1959. Oil on canvas, 84 × 48 in. (213.5 × 122 cm)
Private collection

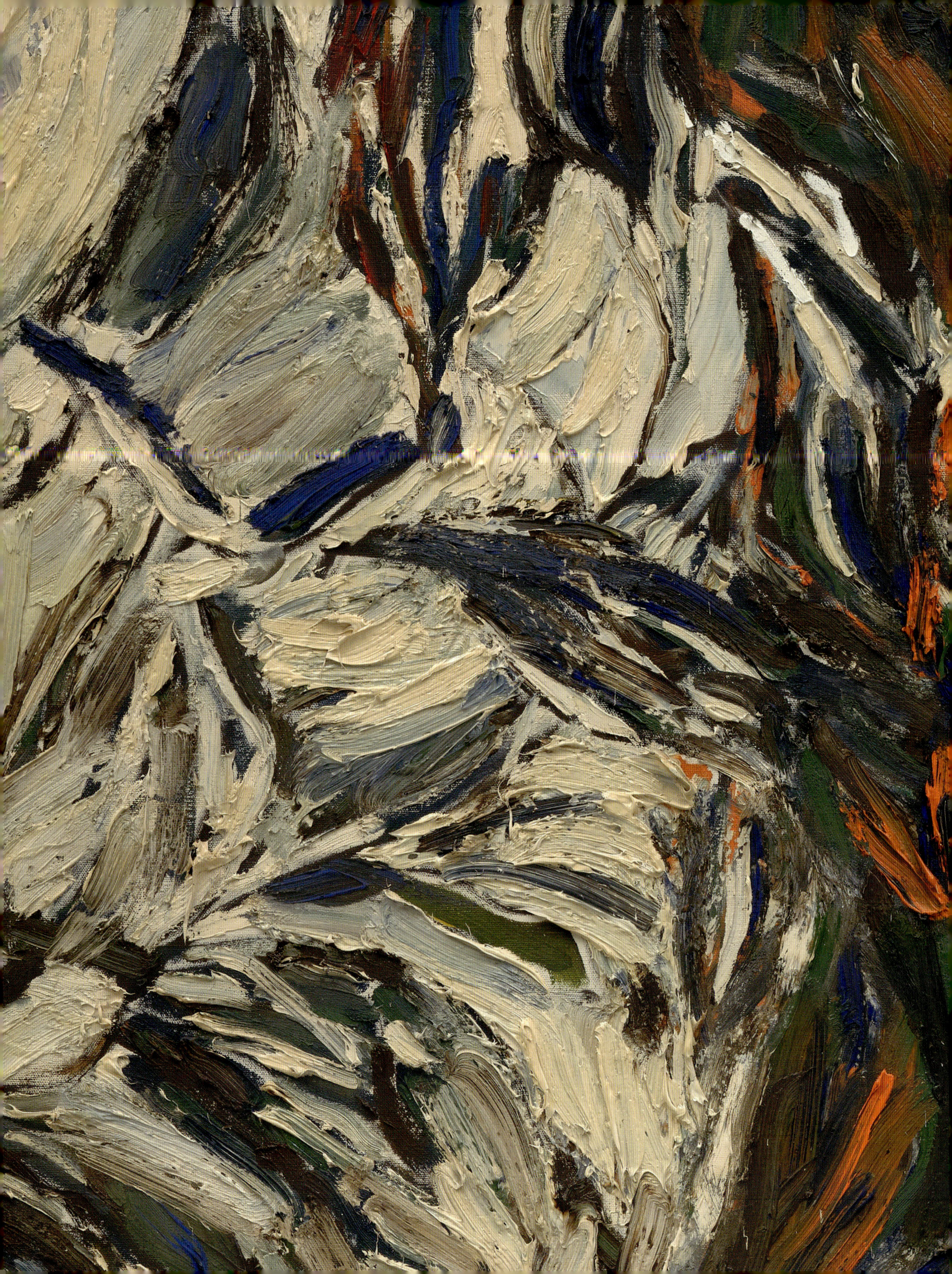

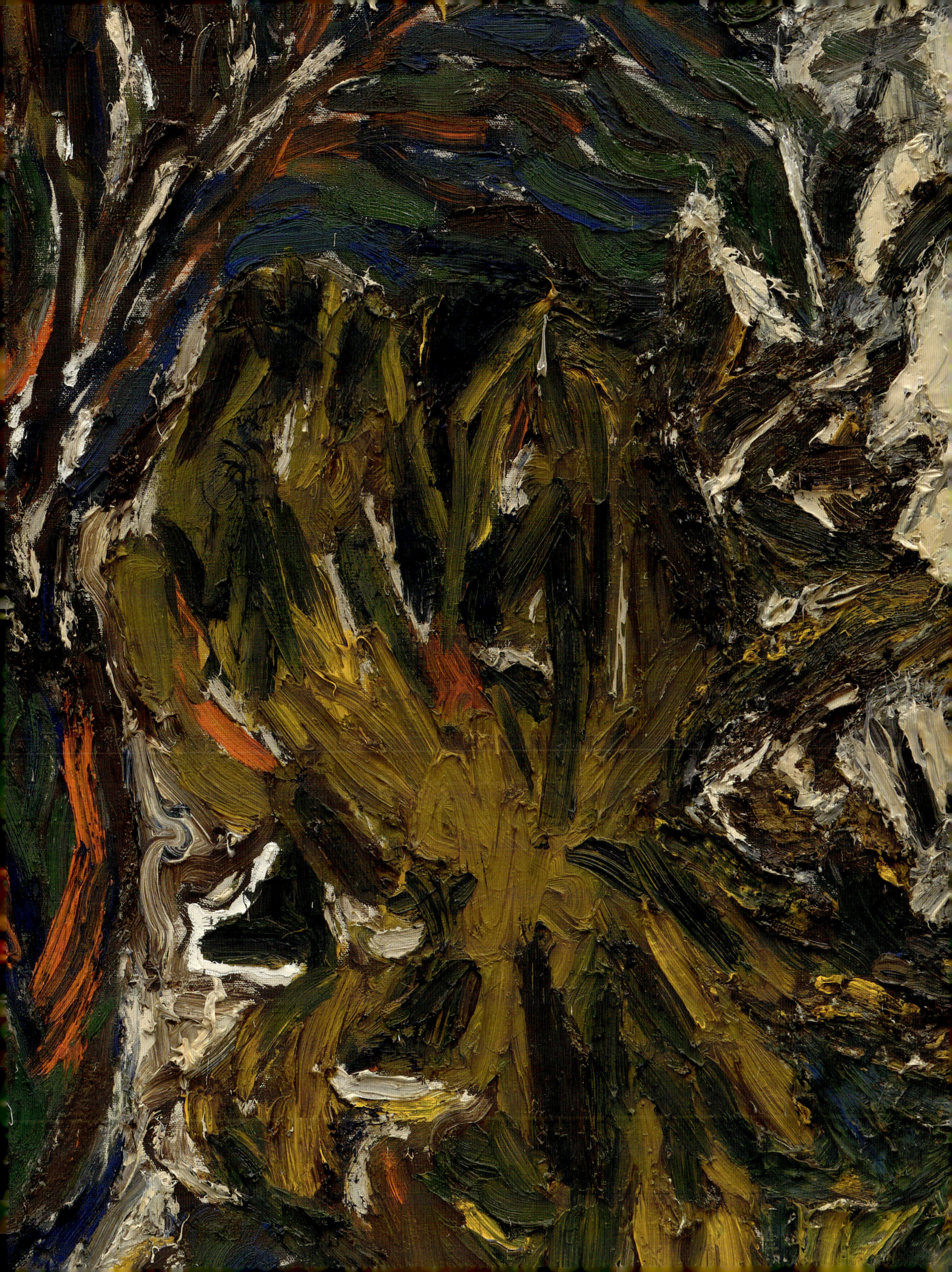

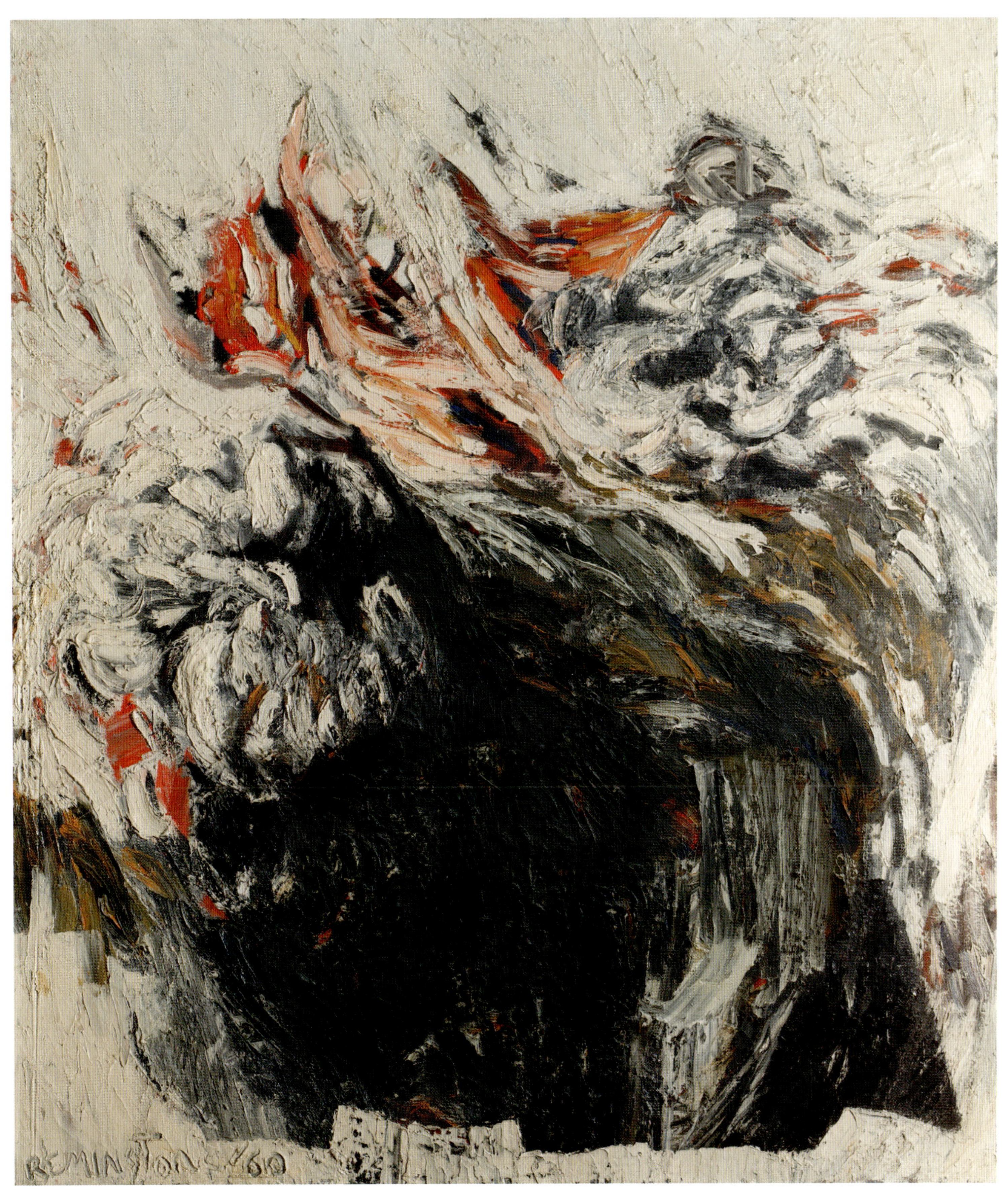

Exodus, 1960. Oil on canvas, 69 × 63 in. (175.3 × 160 cm)
Private collection

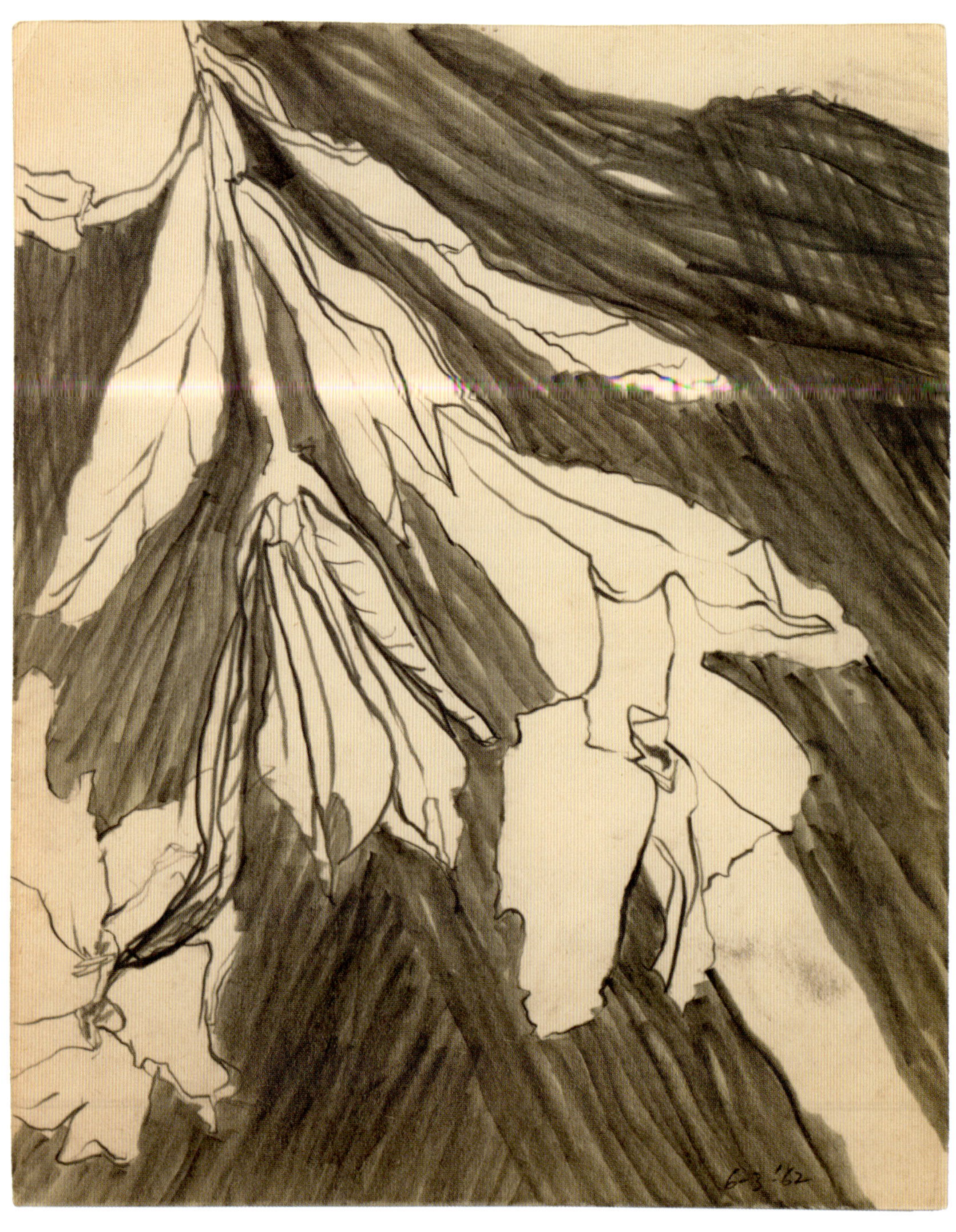

Untitled, 1962. Graphite on paper, 13 × 11 in. (33 × 27.9 cm)
Deborah Remington Charitable Trust for the Visual Arts

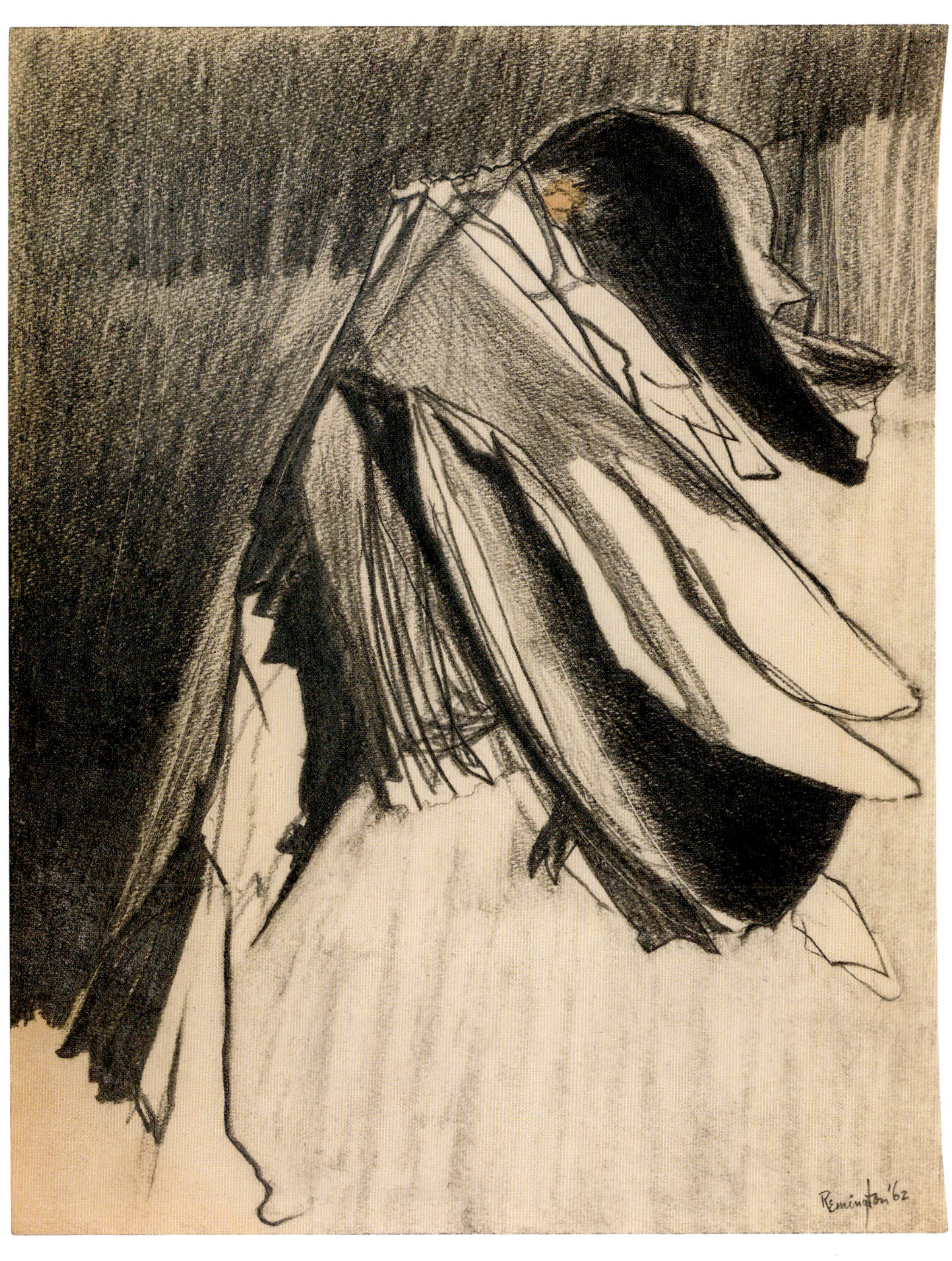

Untitled, 1962. Graphite and crayon on paper, 17 × 14 in. (43.2 × 35.6 cm)
Deborah Remington Charitable Trust for the Visual Arts

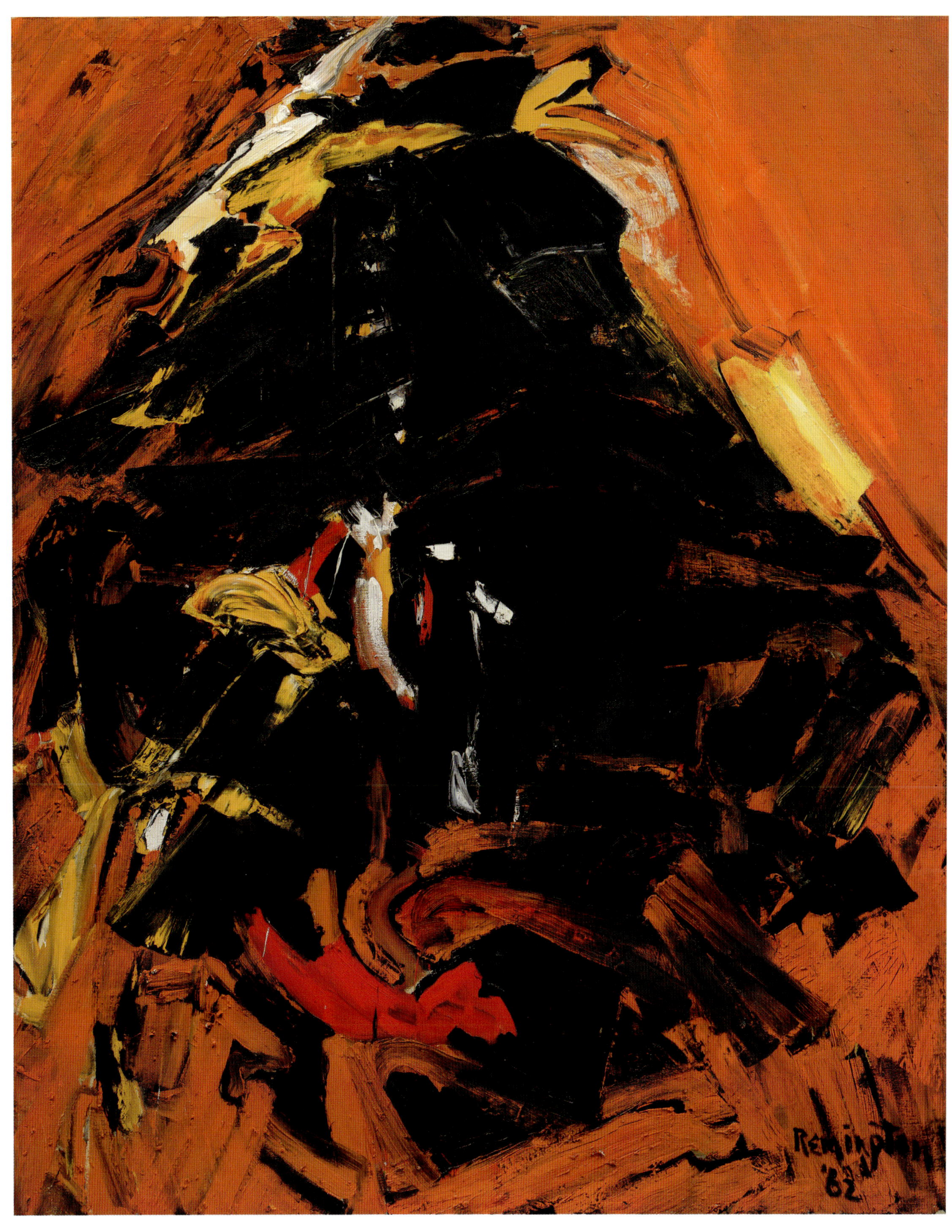

Last One, 1962. Oil on canvas, 84 1/2 × 68 3/4 in. (214.6 × 174.6 cm)
Collection of Timothy C. Headington

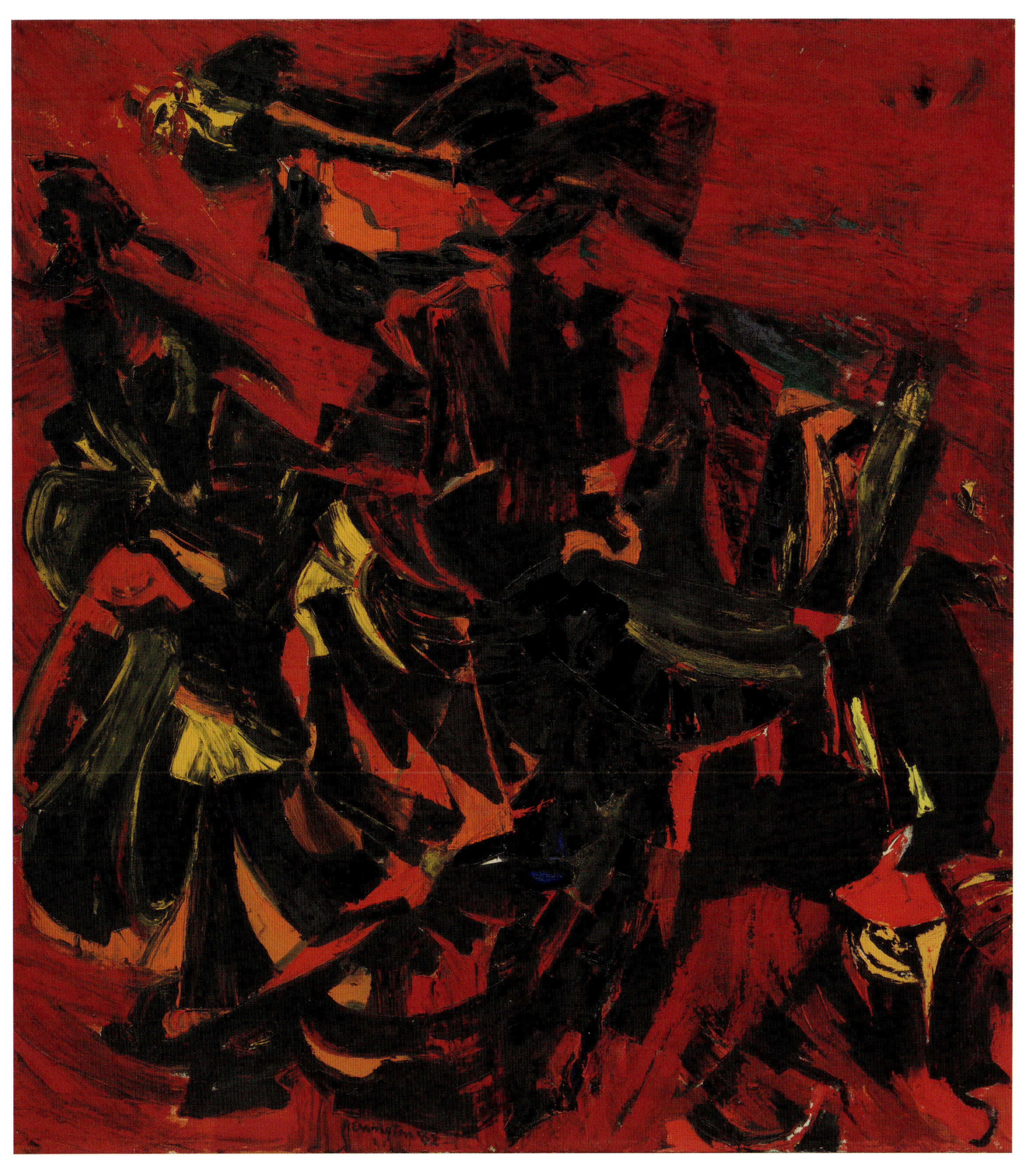

Big Red, 1962. Oil on canvas, 75 × 69 in. (190.5 × 175.3 cm)
Private collection

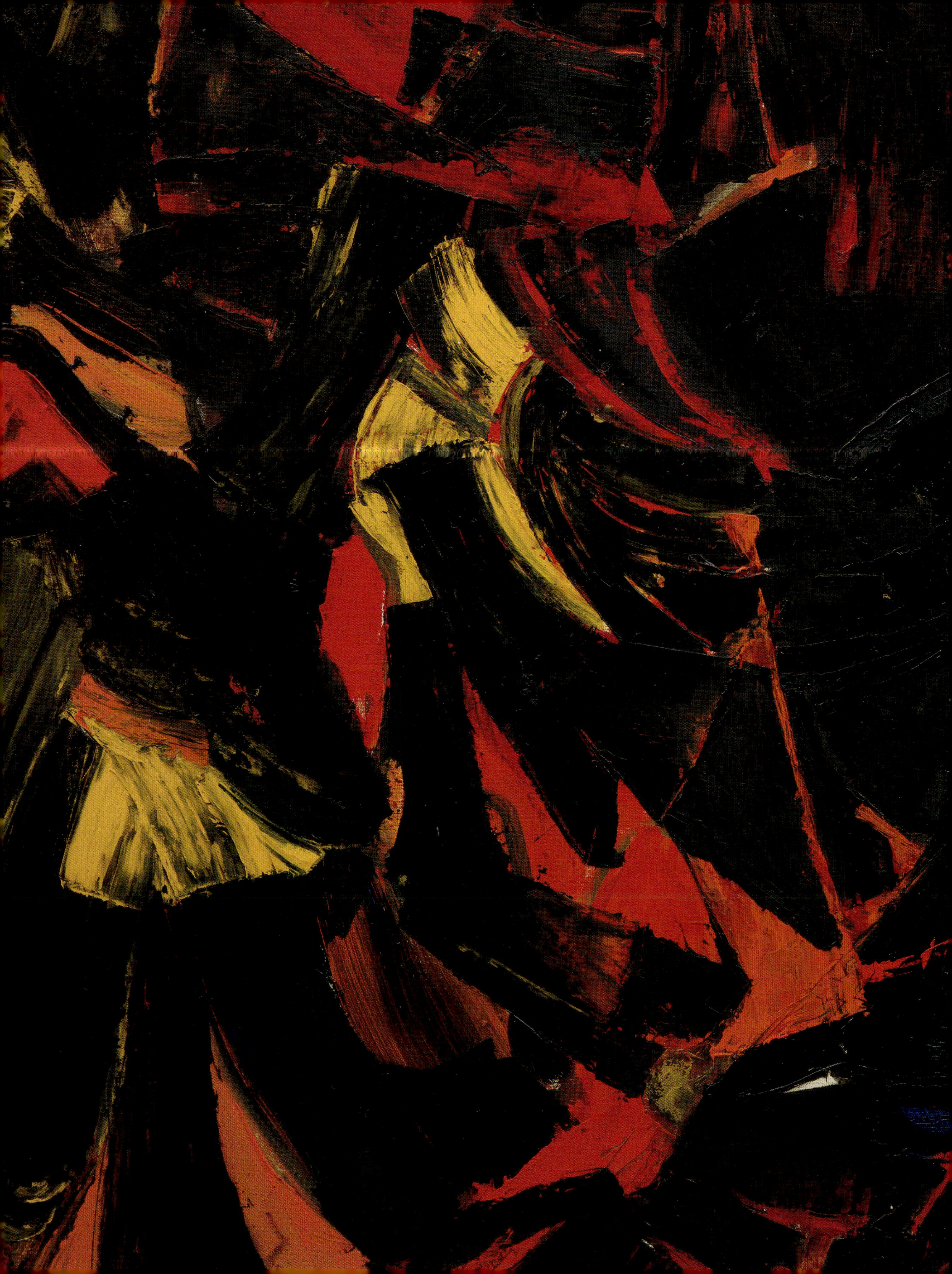

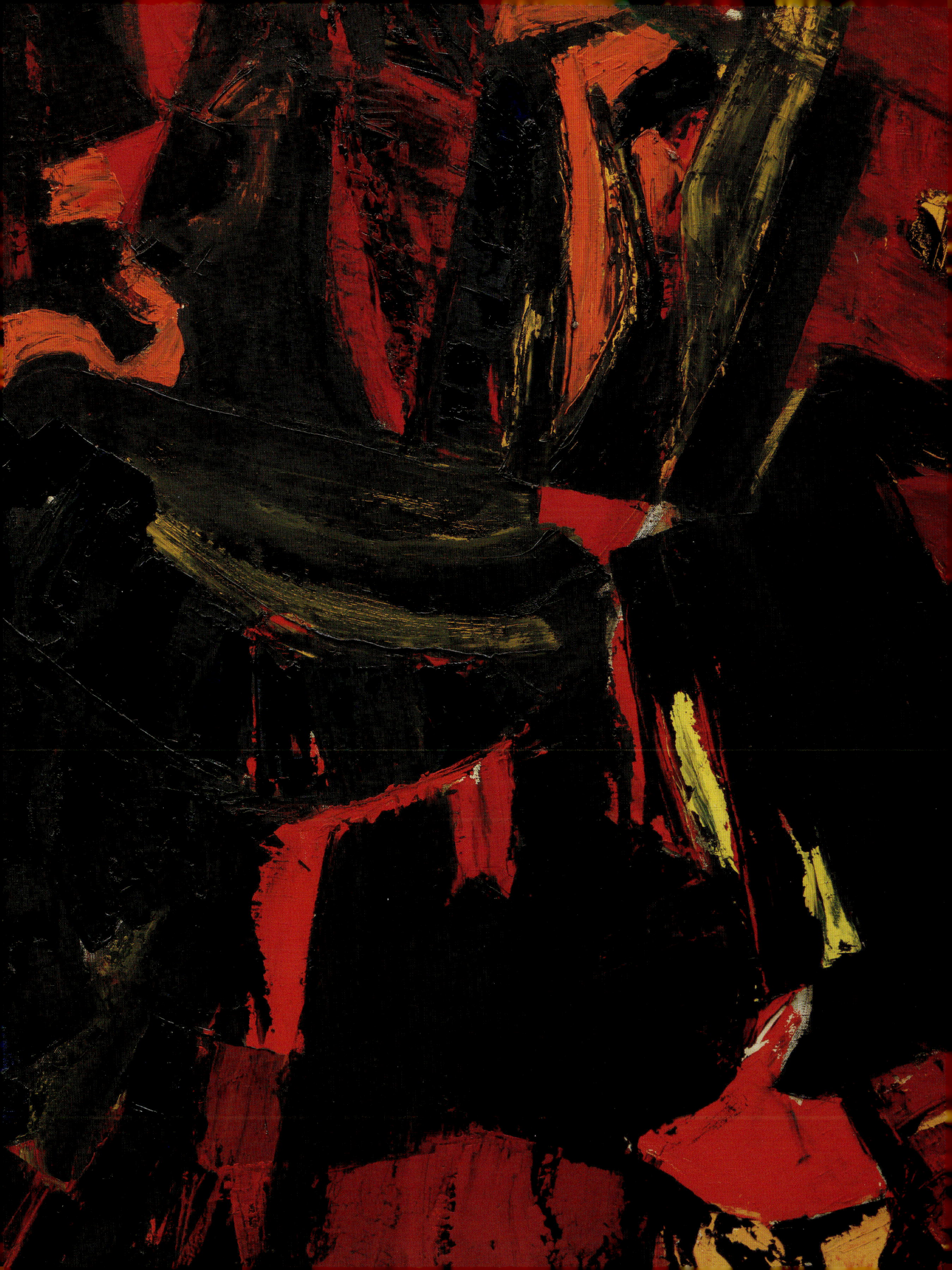

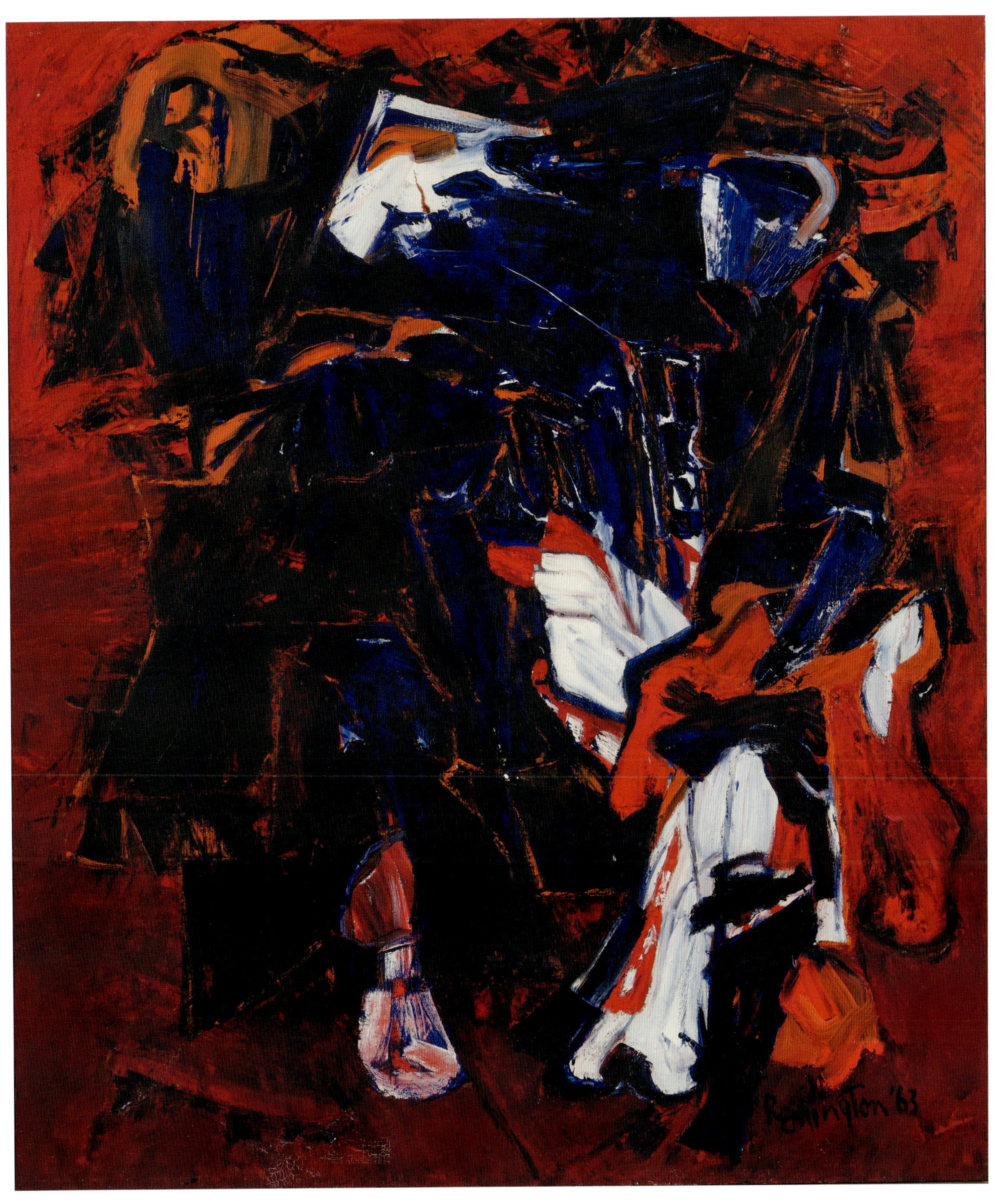

Winter '63, 1963. Oil on canvas, 70 × 60 in. (177.8 × 152.4 cm)
ASOM Collection

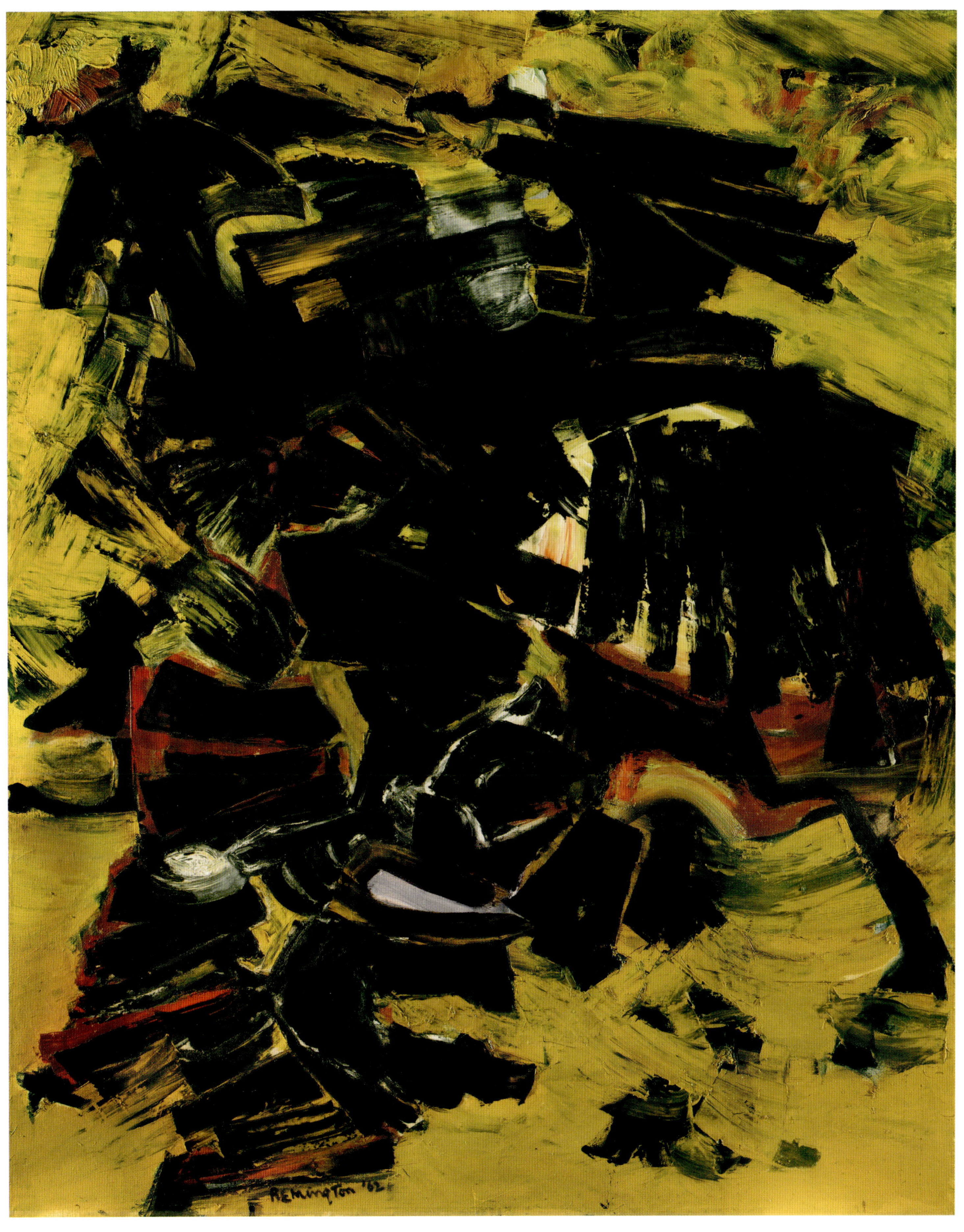

Dr. S, 1962. Oil on canvas, 84 × 67 3/4 in. (213.4 × 172.1 cm)
The Levett Collection

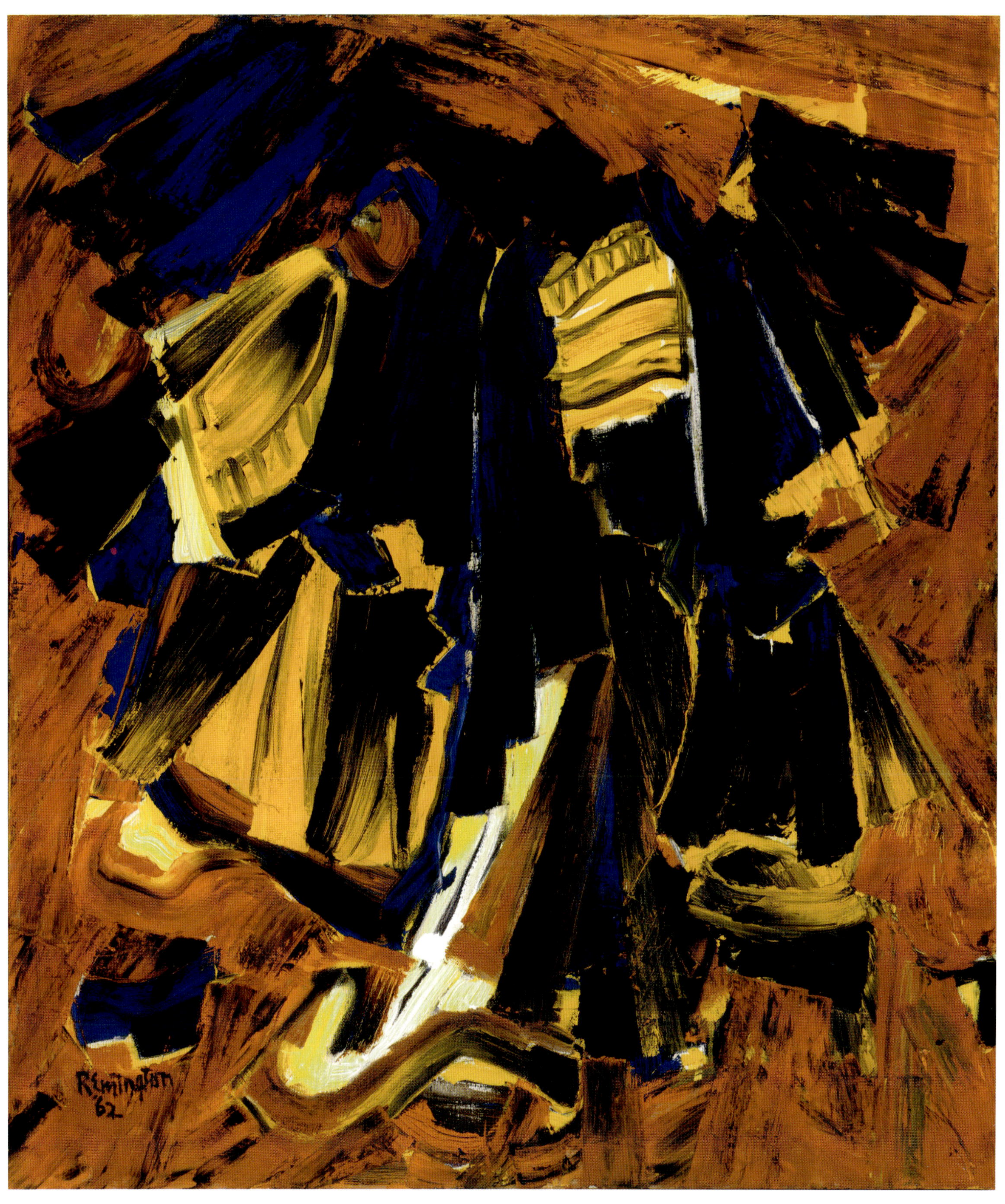

For H.M., 1962. Oil on canvas, $72\frac{1}{2} \times 62\frac{1}{4}$ in. (184.2 × 158.1 cm)
Oakland Museum of California. Gift of Harry Hunt

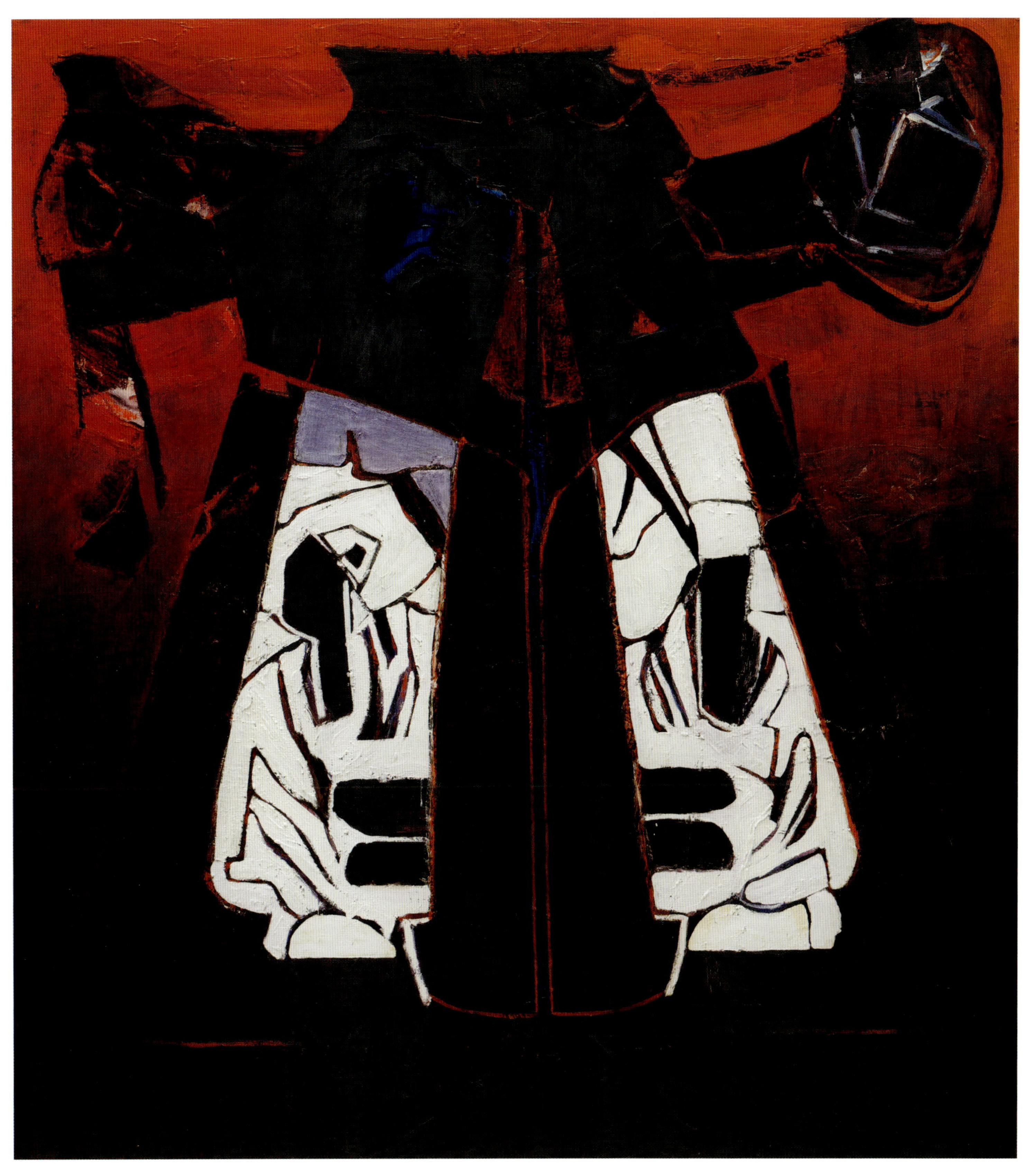

Statement, 1963. Oil on canvas, 76 5/8 × 70 in. (194.6 × 177.8 cm)
San Francisco Museum of Modern Art, California. Gift of the First Savings and Loan Association

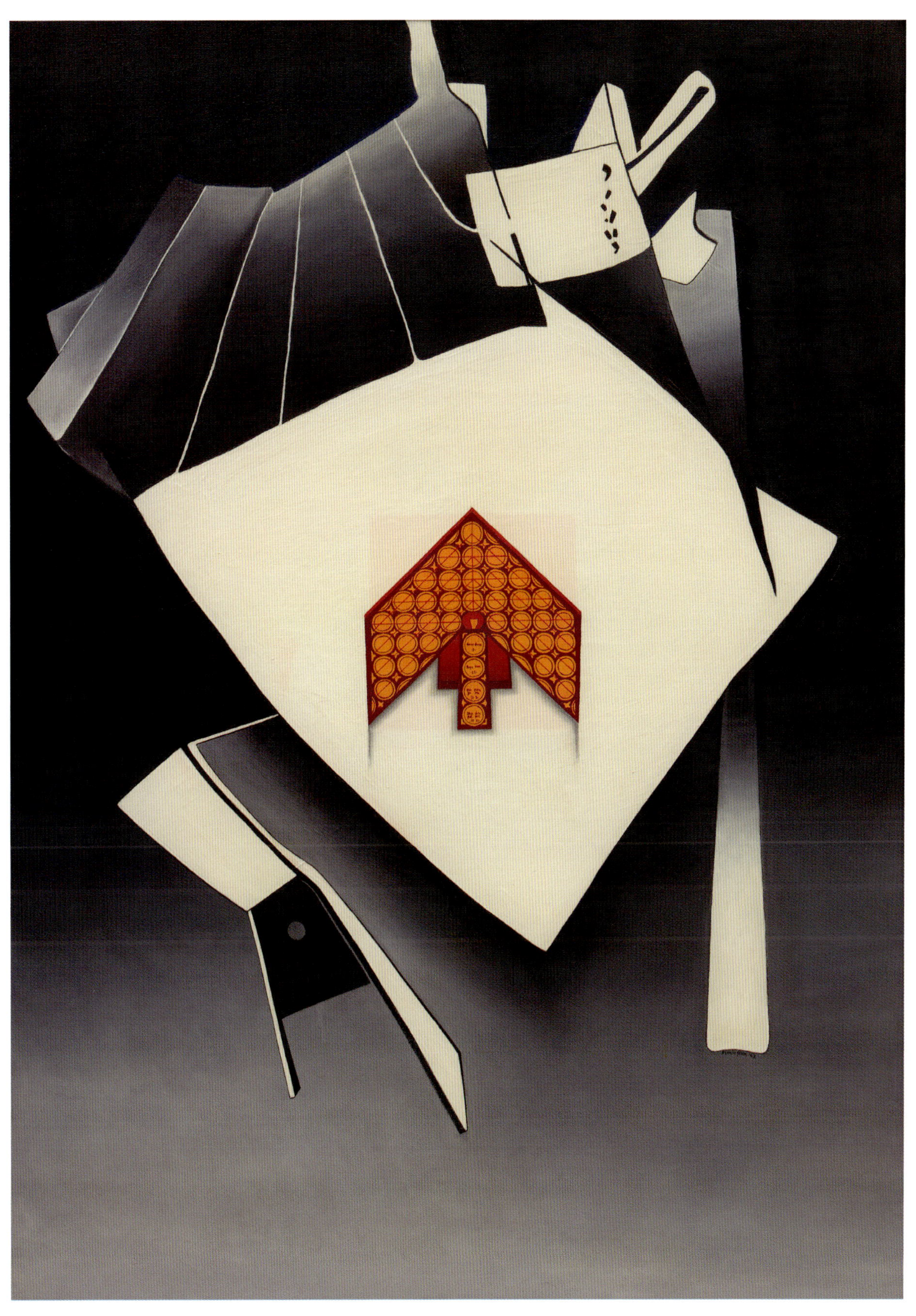

G.B. II, 1963. Oil on canvas, 50 × 36 in. (127 × 91.5 cm)
Hood Museum of Art, Dartmouth College, Hanover, New Hampshire. Purchased through Evelyn A. and William B. Jaffe 2015 Fund

Soot Series 1, 1963. Soot and crayon on muslin, 20 3/4 × 17 in. (52.7 × 43.2 cm)
Private collection, New York

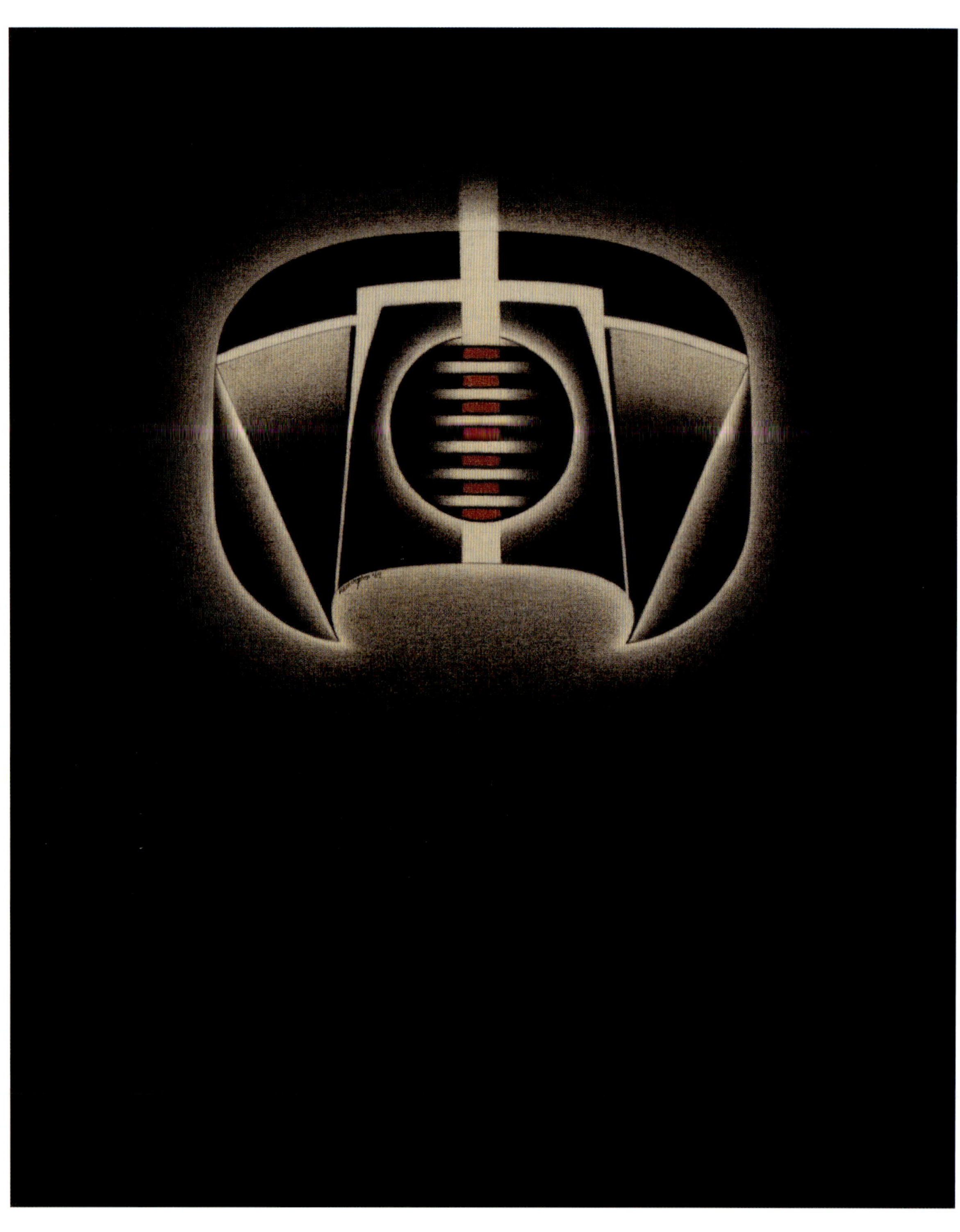

Soot Series, 1964. Soot and crayon on muslin, 22 1/4 × 18 1/4 in. (56.5 × 46.5 cm)
Collection of Marc Selwyn

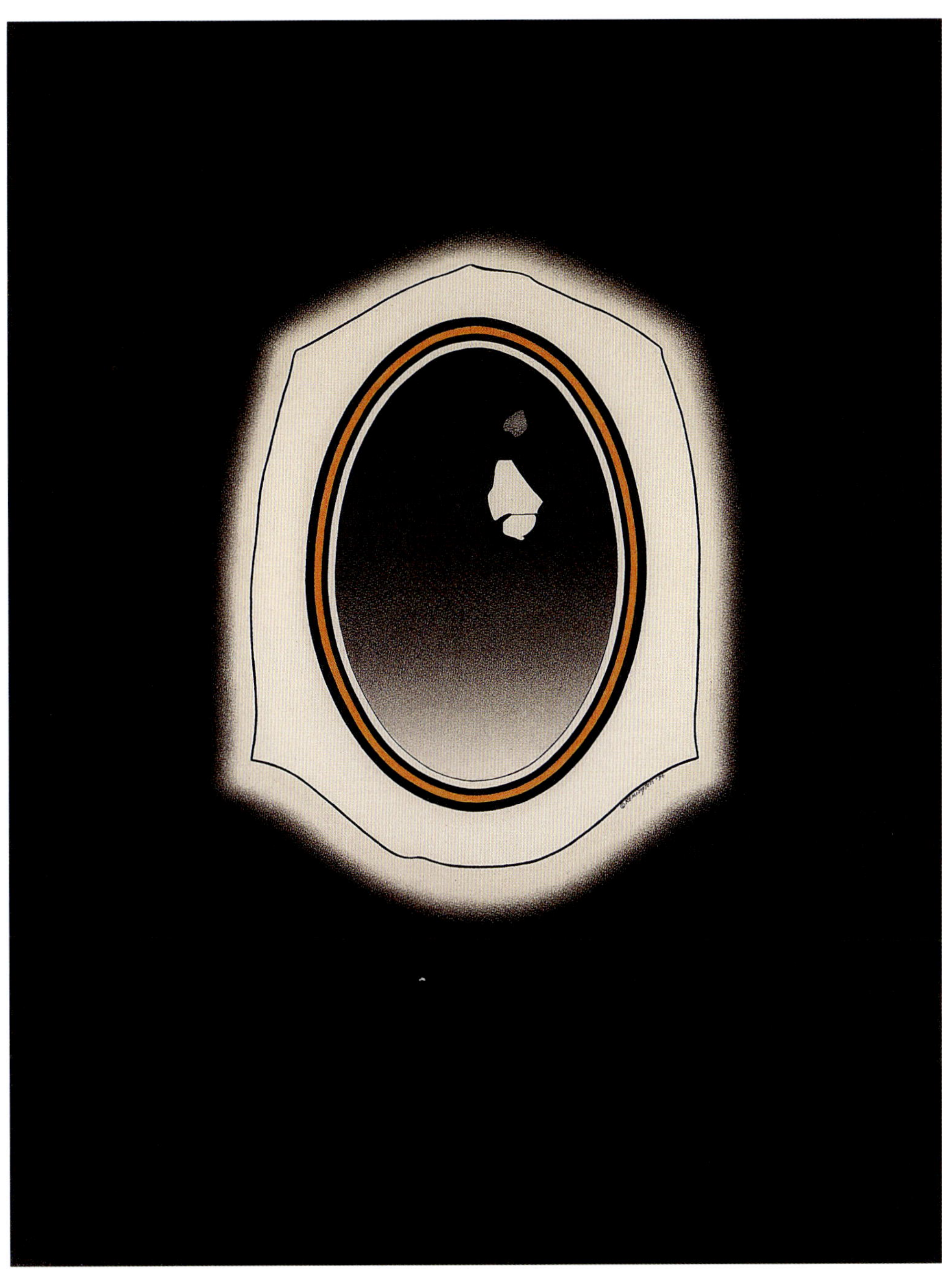

Soot Series 11, 1976. Soot and colored pencil on paper, 25 1/2 × 19 3/4 in. (64.8 × 50.2 cm)
Private collection

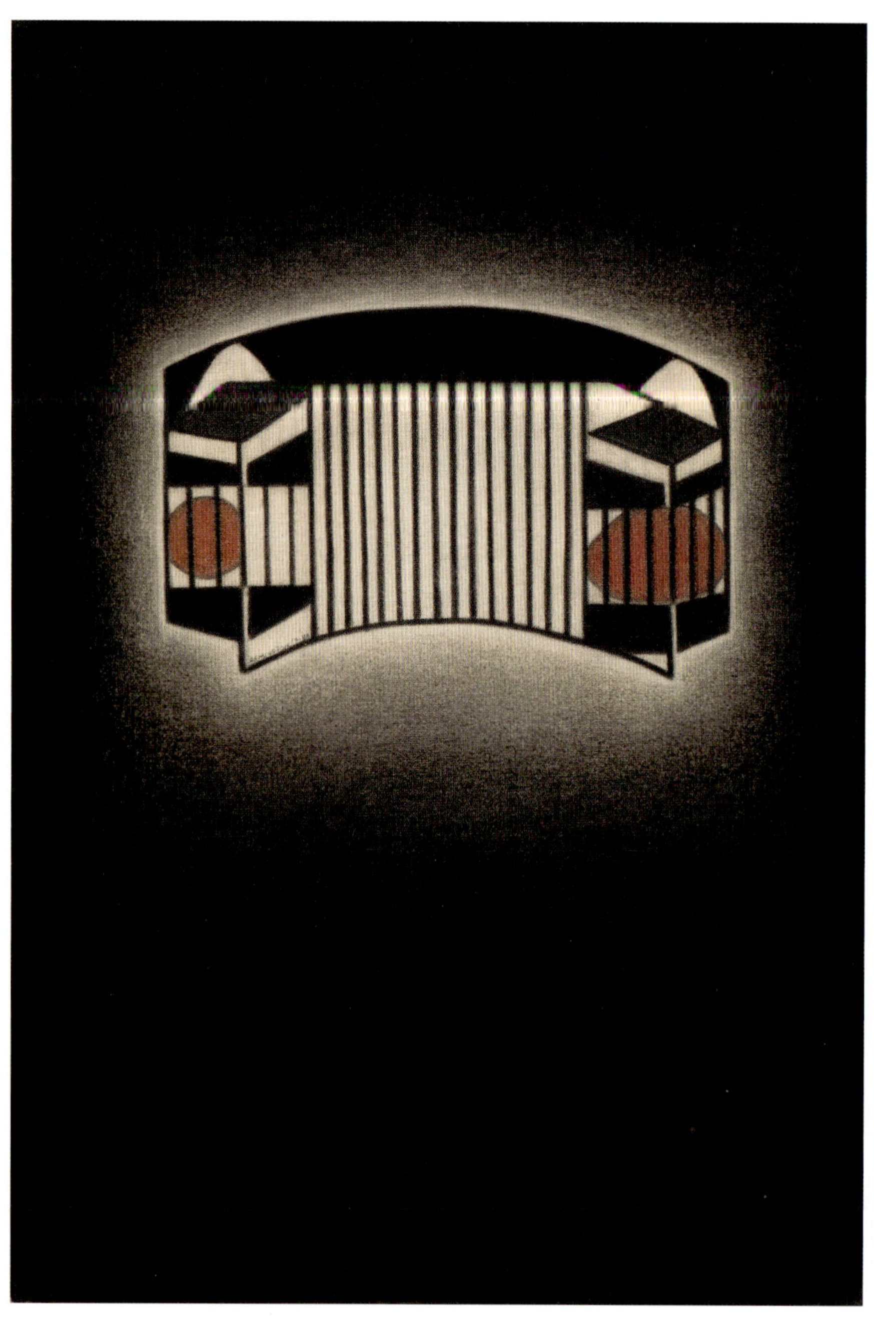

Soot Series 2, 1963. Soot and crayon on muslin, 18 1/2 × 13 in. (47 × 33 cm)
Collection of Beth Rudin DeWoody

Soot Series 4, 1969. Soot, charcoal, and crayon on muslin, 22 × 18 in. (55.9 × 45.7 cm)
Private collection

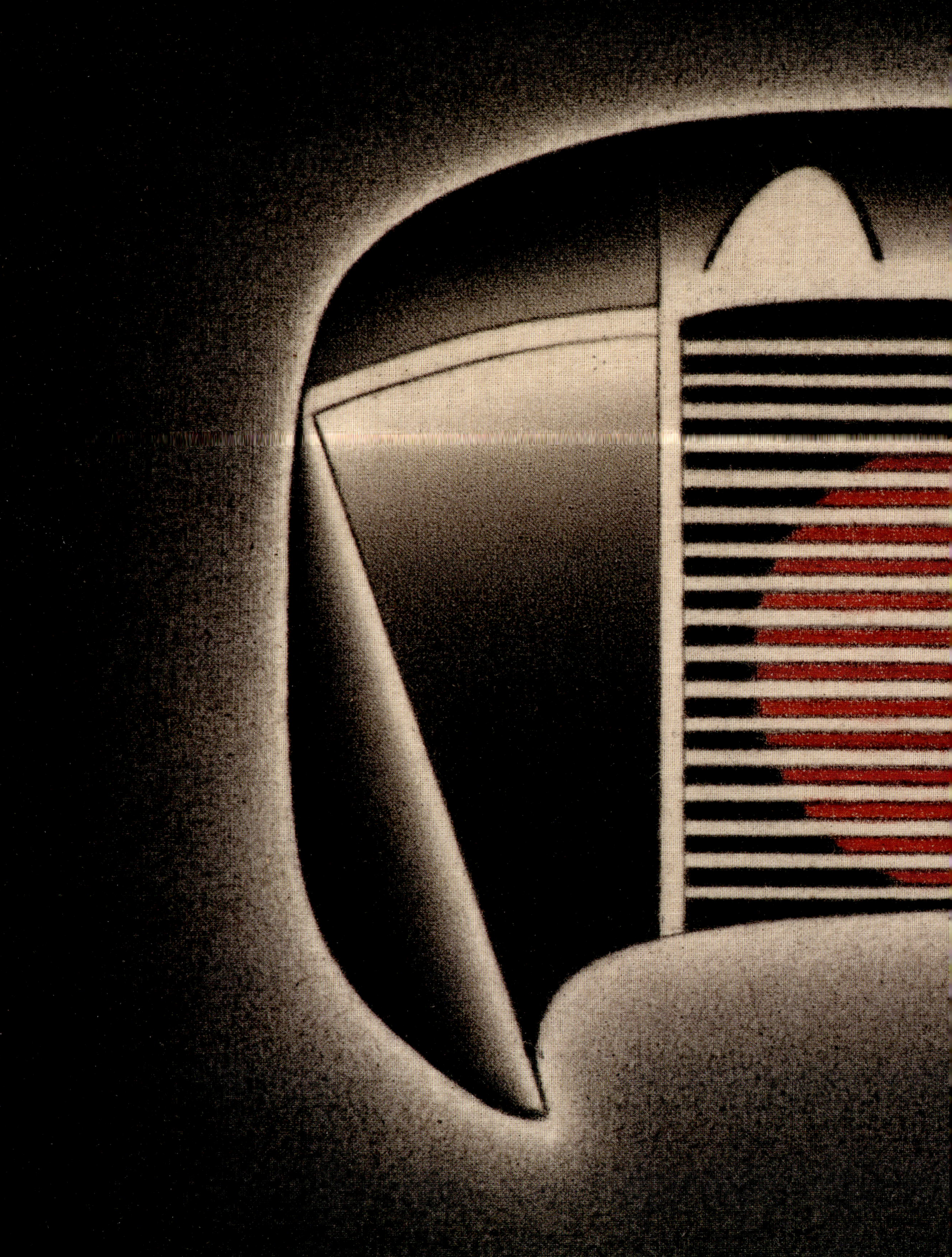

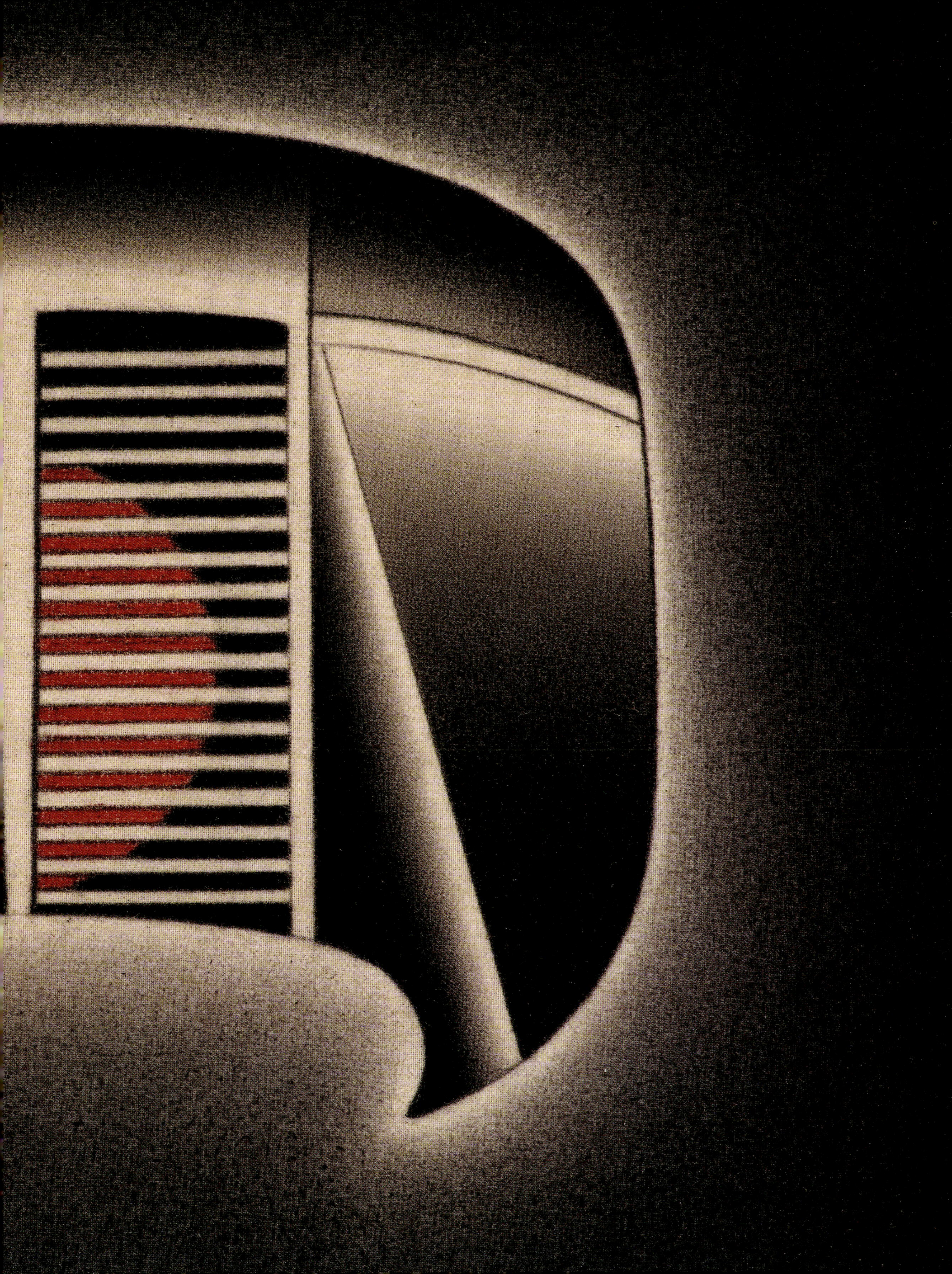

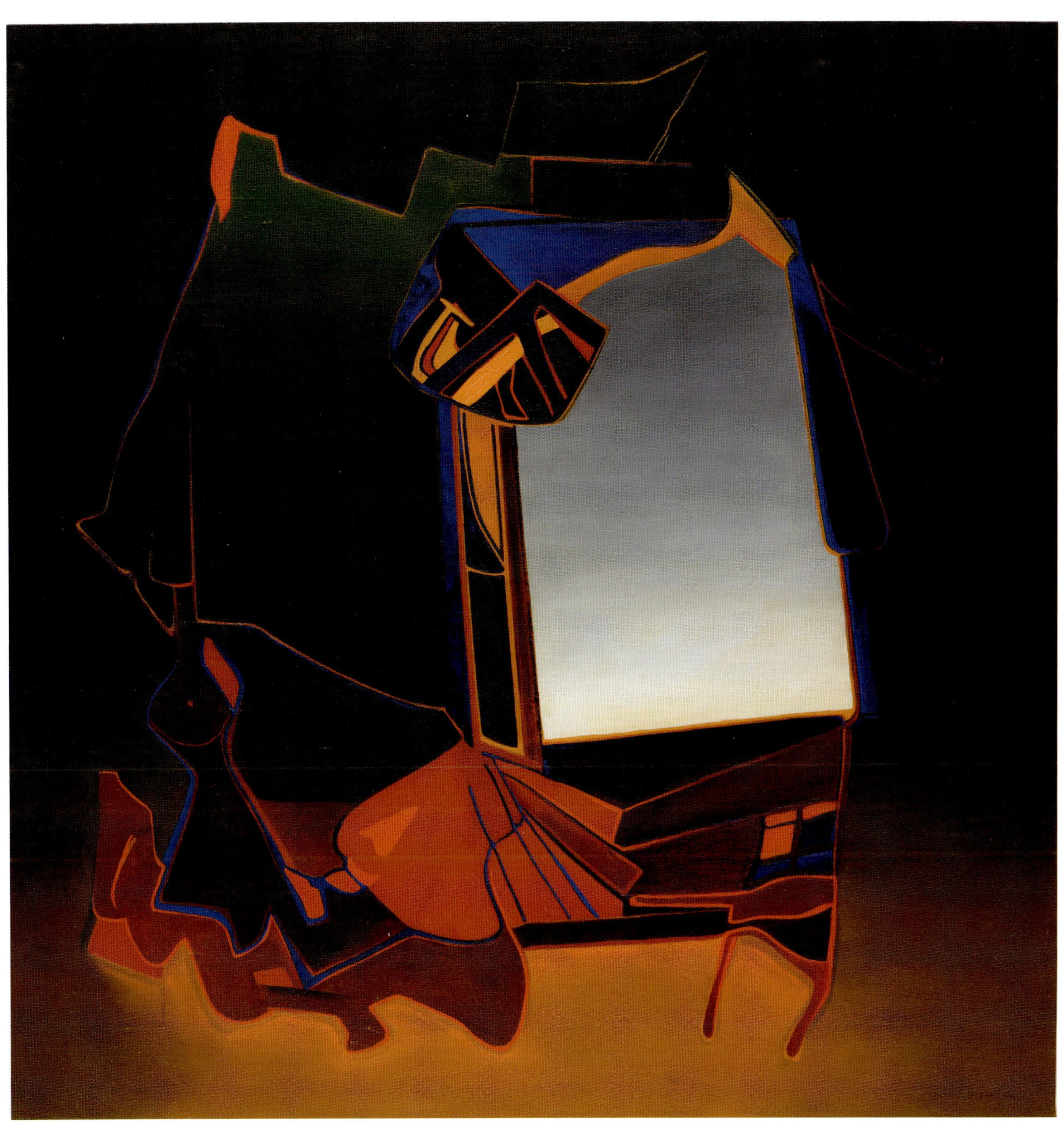

Emanon, 1964. Oil on canvas, 71 × 70 in. (180.3 × 177.8 cm)
San Francisco Museum of Modern Art, California. Gift of Sarah Sterling

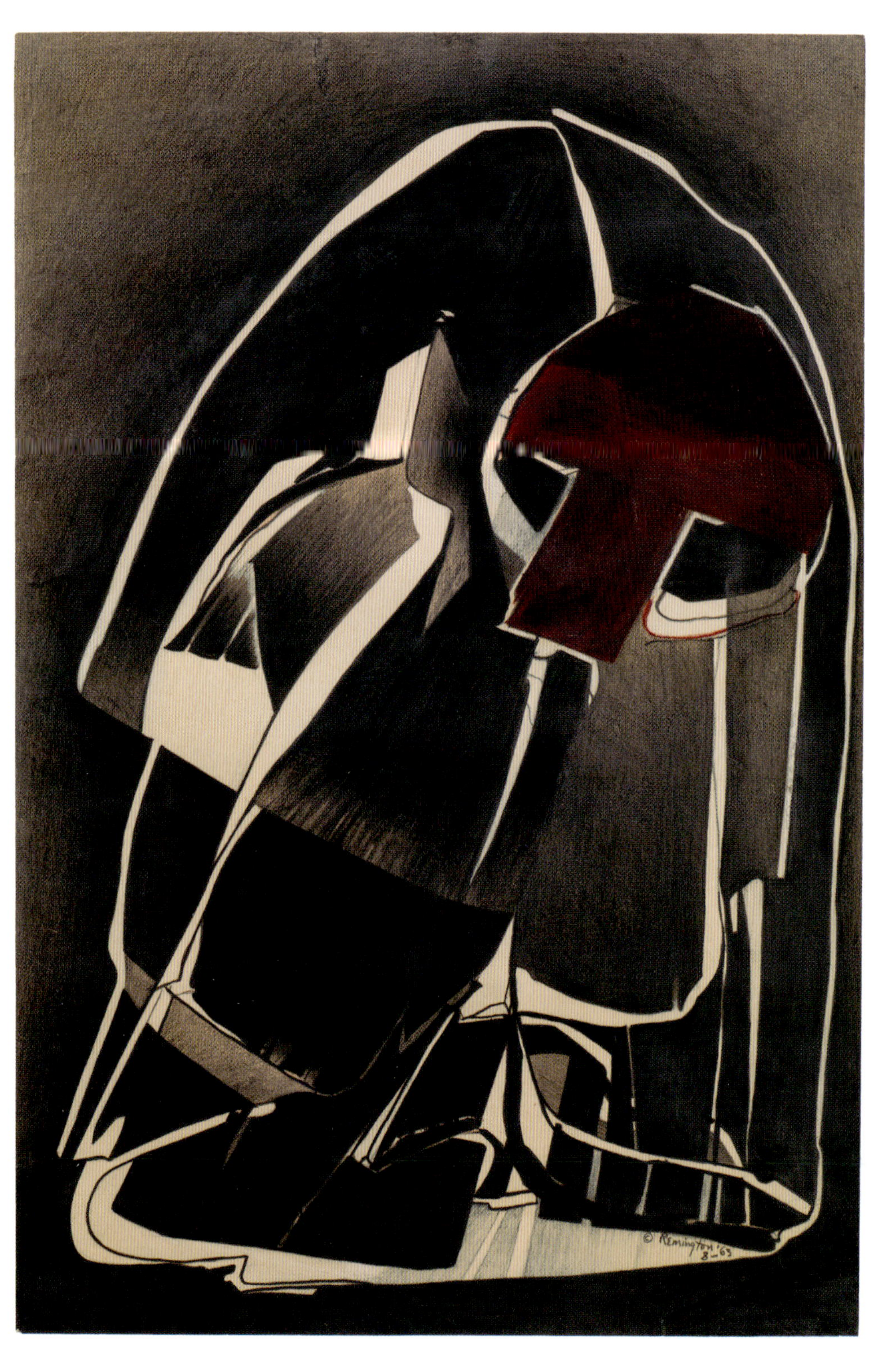

Untitled (Adelphi Series), 1963. Graphite and crayon on paper, 18 × 12 in. (45.7 × 30.5 cm)
Deborah Remington Charitable Trust for the Visual Arts

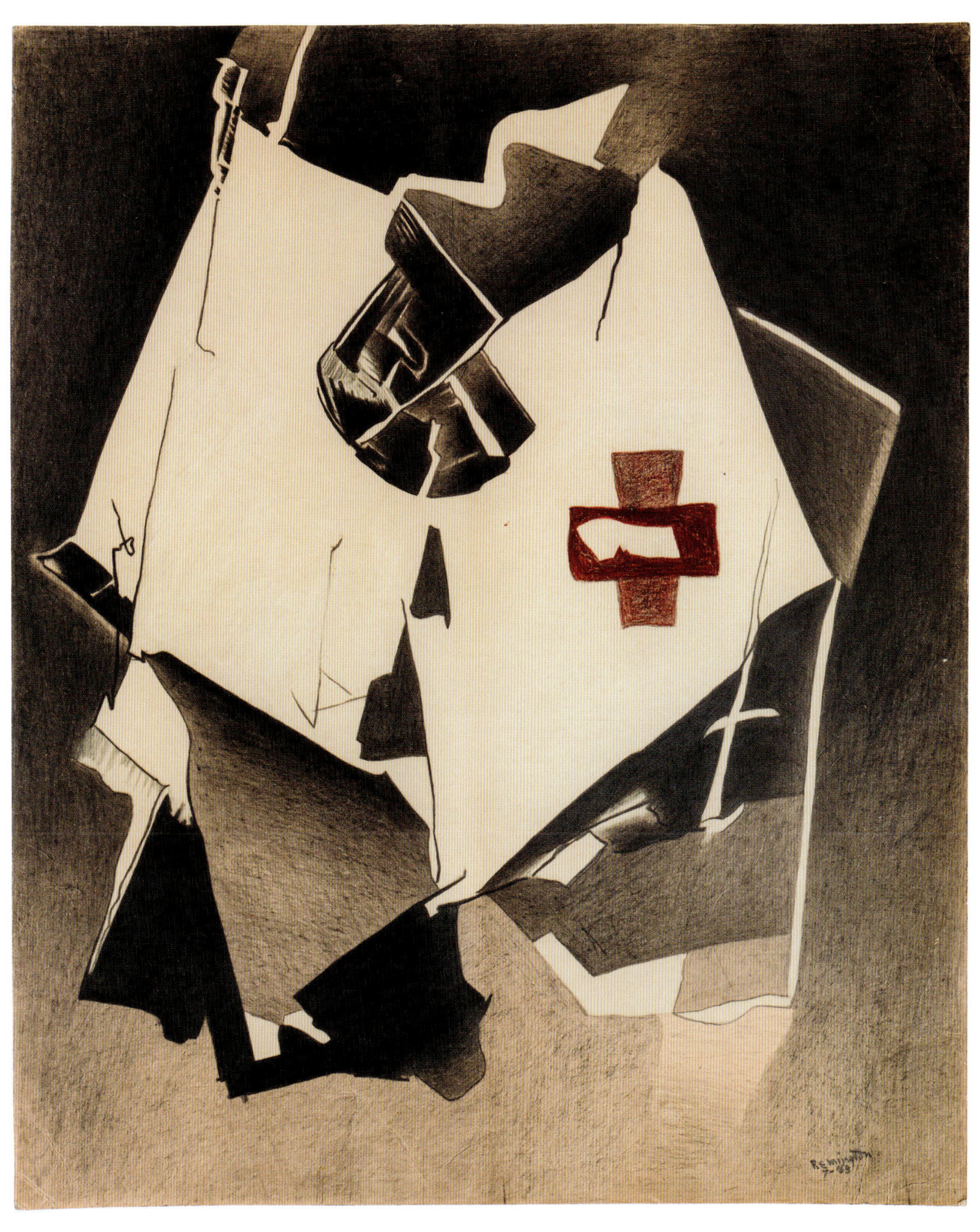

Untitled (Adelphi Series), 1963. Graphite and crayon on paper, $18\frac{1}{2} \times 15\frac{1}{2}$ in. (47 × 39.4 cm)
Collection of Marc Selwyn

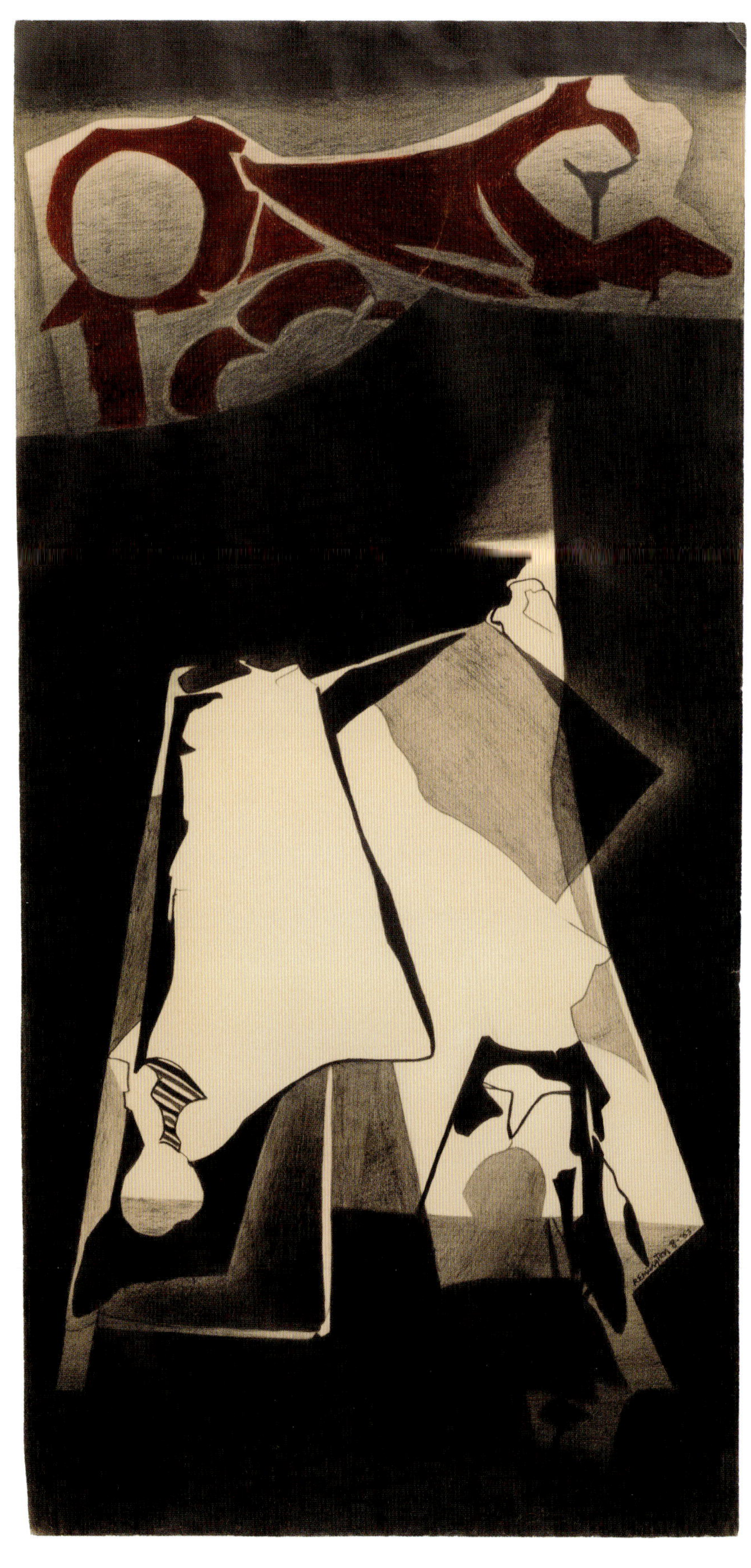

Early Adelphi Series, 1963. Graphite and crayon on paper, $25^{1}/_{2} \times 12^{1}/_{2}$ in. (64.8 × 31.8 cm)
Collection of Marc Selwyn

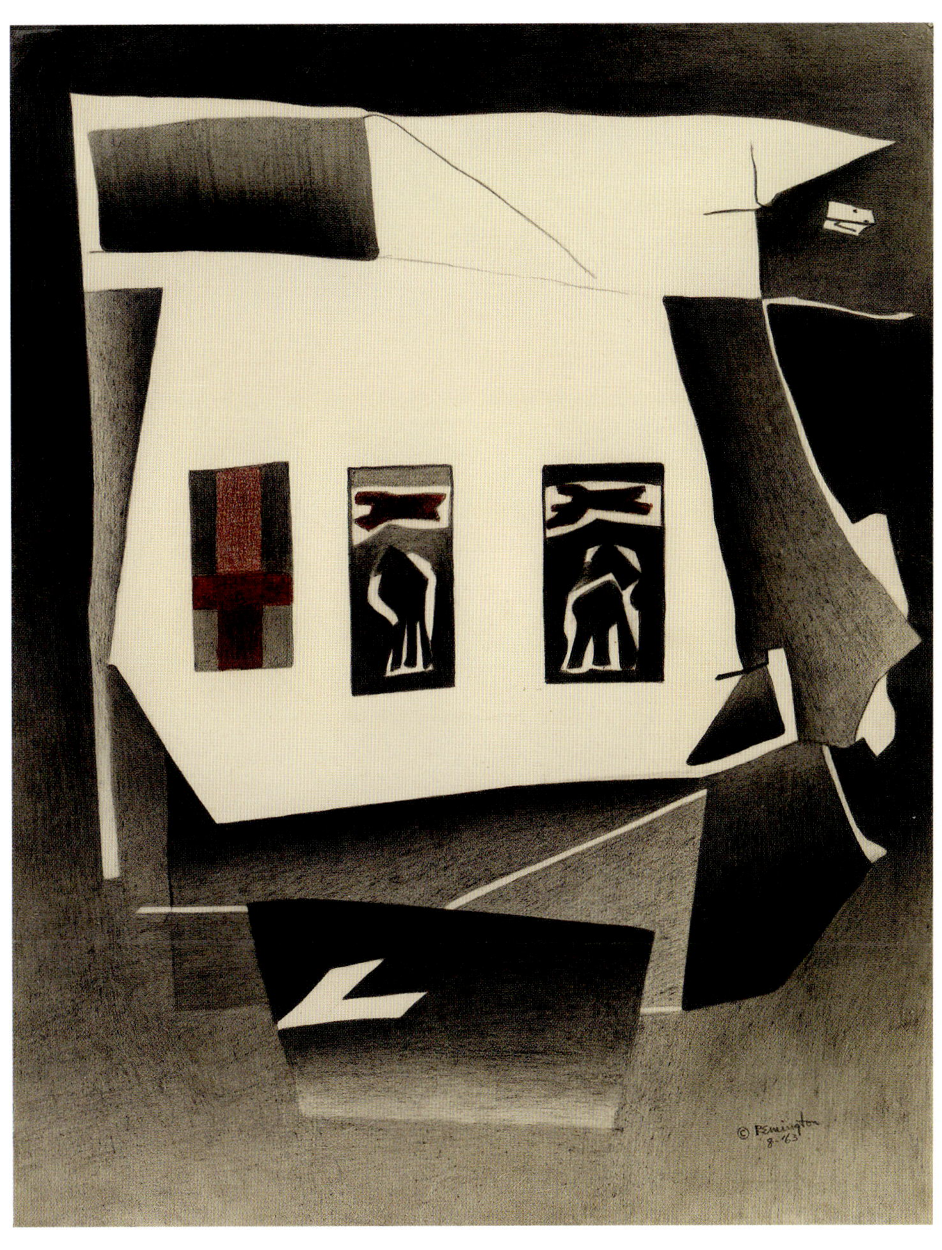

Untitled (Adelphi Series), 1963. Graphite and crayon on paper, $14^{3}/_{4} \times 11^{1}/_{2}$ in. (37.5 × 29.2 cm)
Collection of Beth Rudin DeWoody

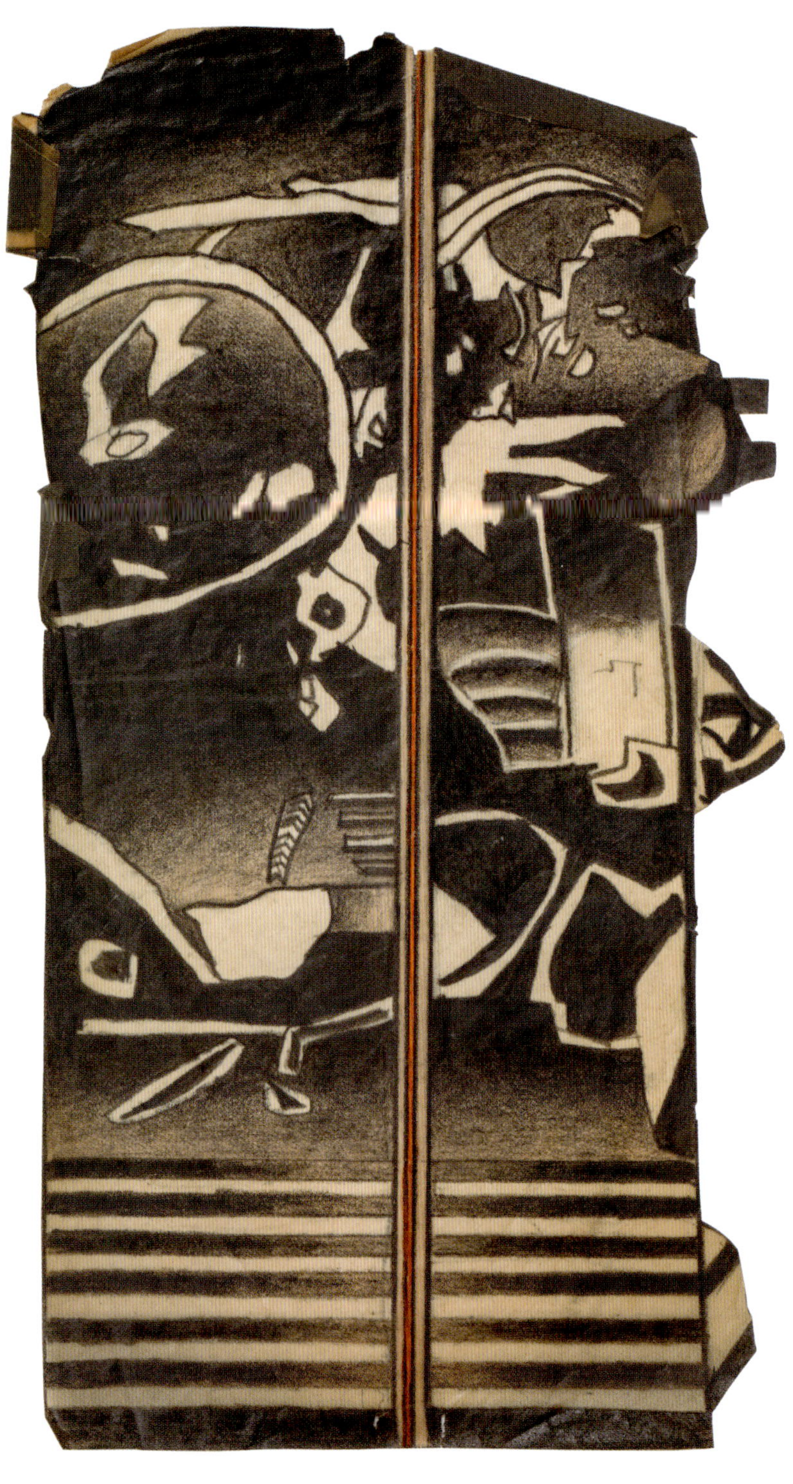

Untitled, 1965. Graphite and crayon on paper, 9 × 5 1/4 in. (22.9 × 13.3 cm)
Collection of Marc Selwyn

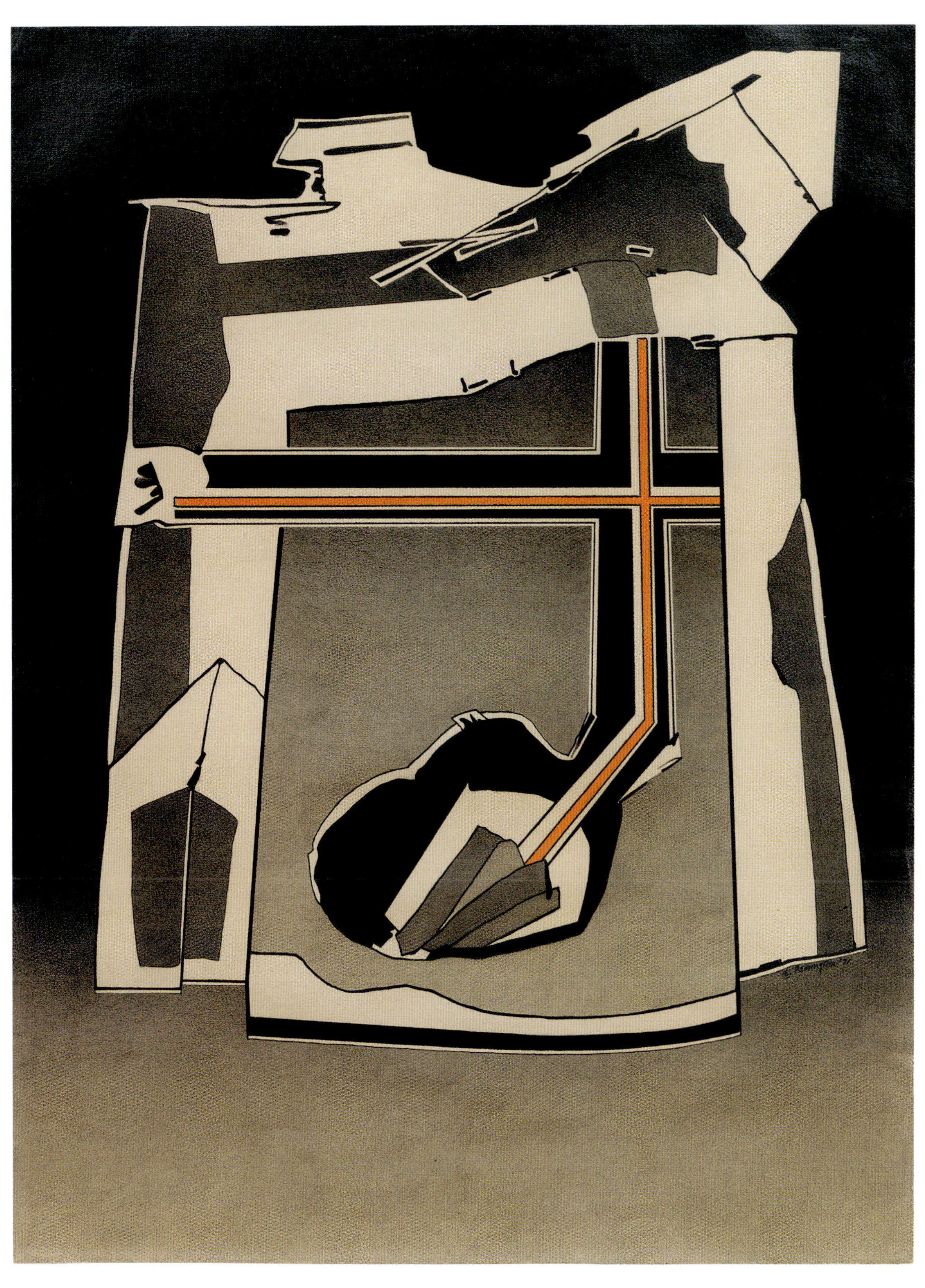

Adelphi Series 13, 1967–71. Graphite and crayon on paper, 24 × 18 in. (61 × 45.7 cm)
Collection of Jane Hait and Justin Beal

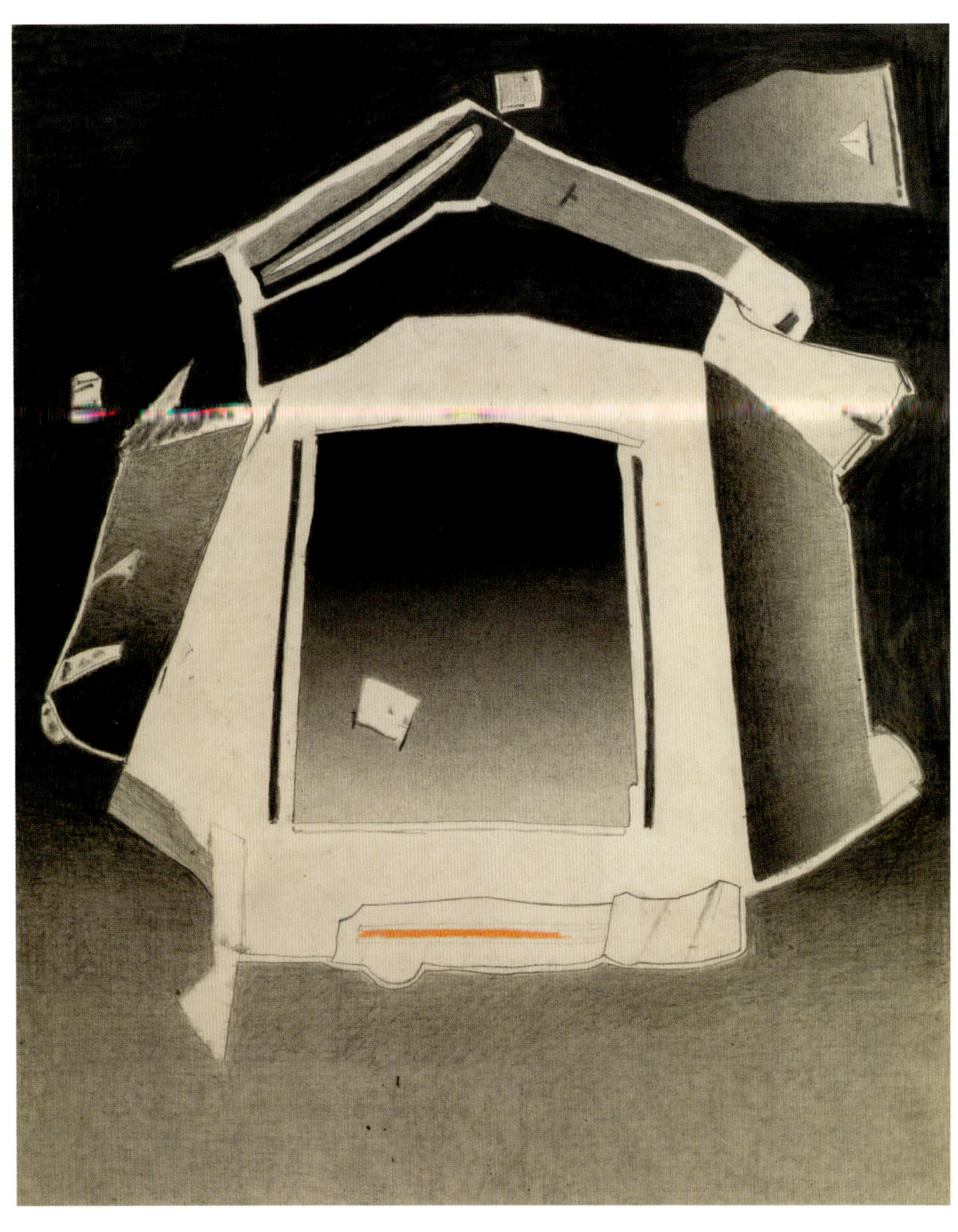

Untitled (Adelphi Series), 1983. Graphite and colored pencil on paper, 14 1/2 × 11 1/2 in. (36.8 × 29.2 cm)
Collection of Beth Rudin DeWoody

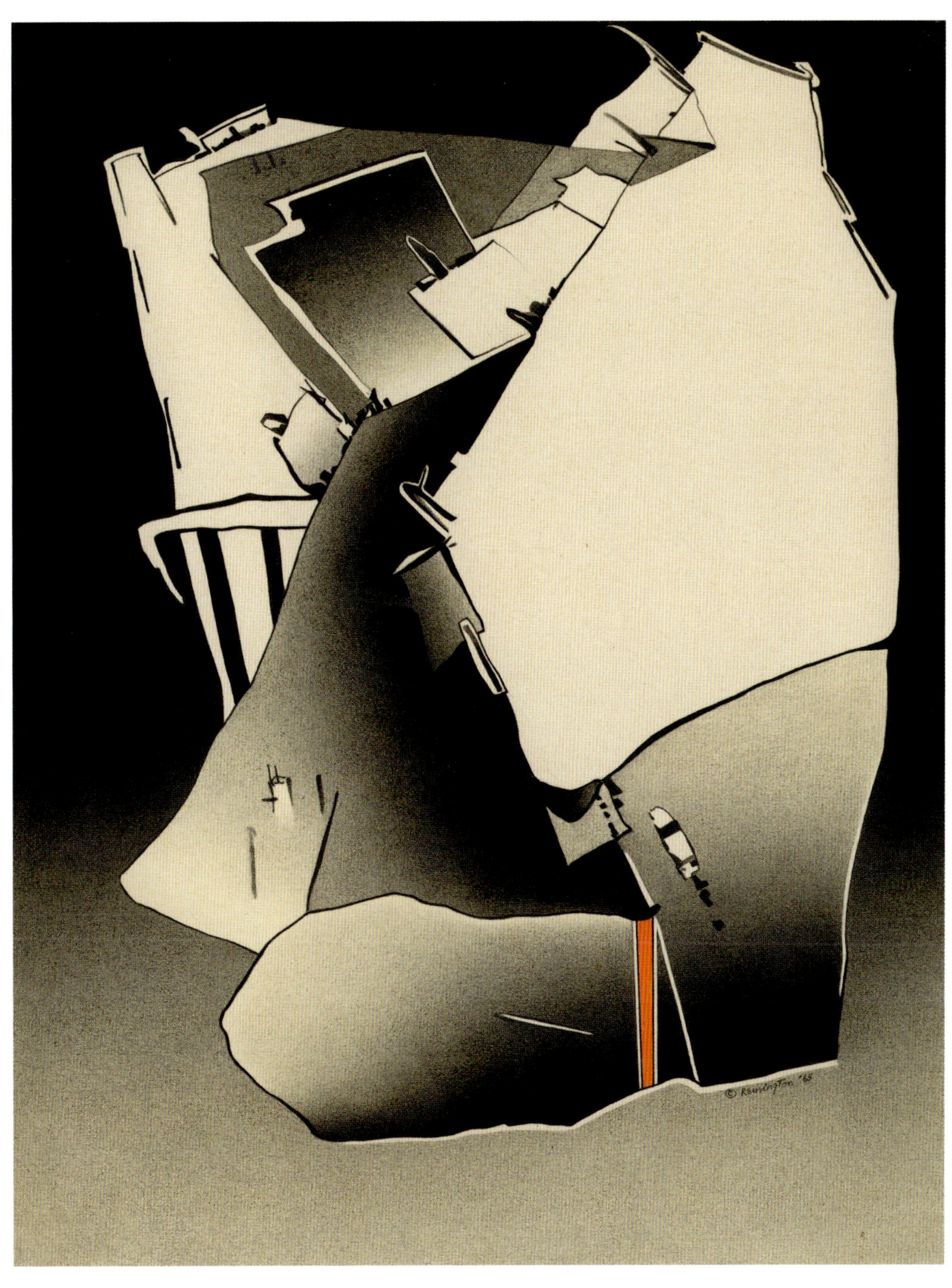

Adelphi Series 11, 1965. Graphite and crayon on paper, 14 × 10 3/4 in. (35.6 × 27.3 cm)
Whitney Museum of American Art, New York. Purchase, with funds from the Drawing Committee

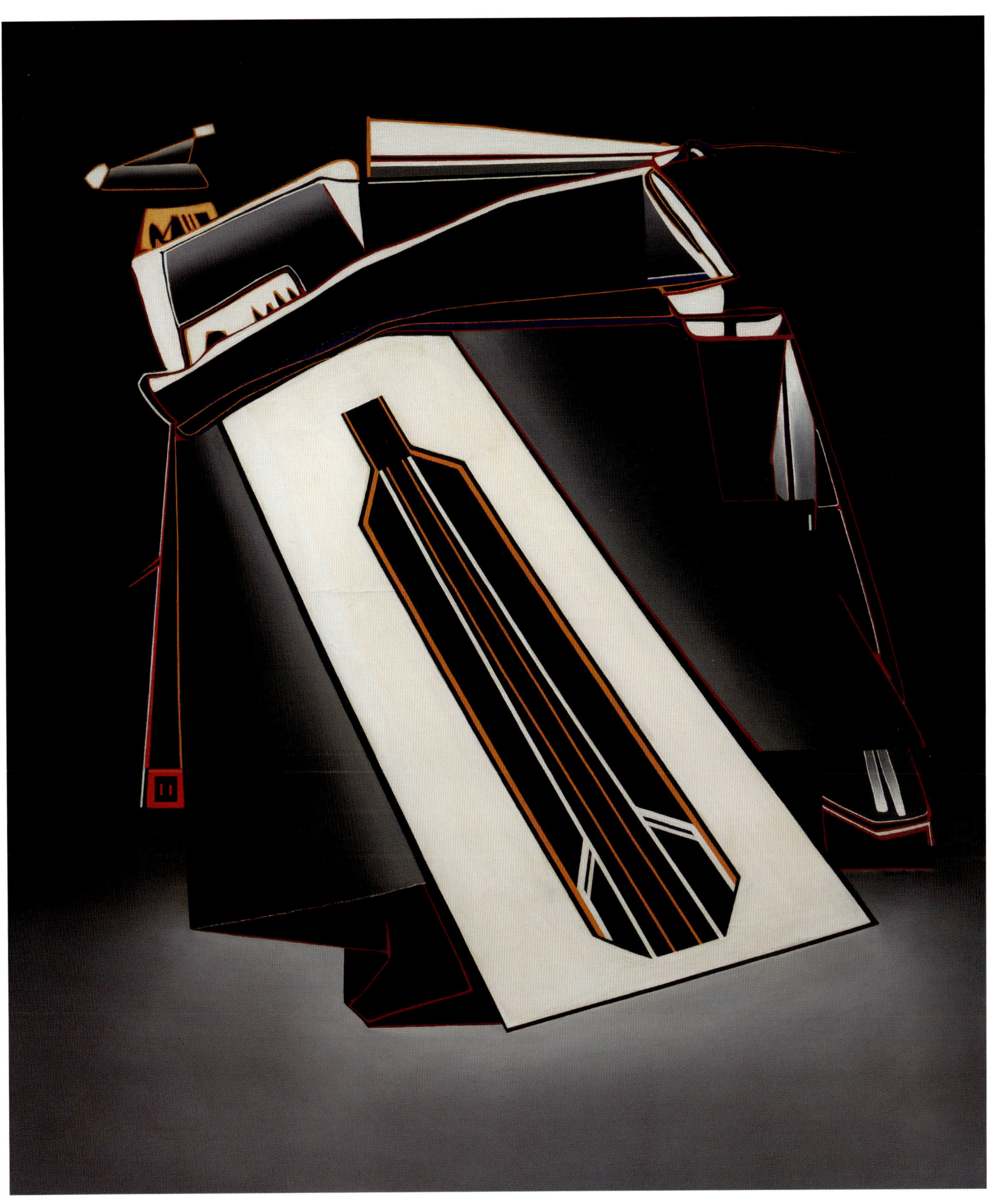

March, 1964. Oil on canvas, 57 1/4 × 49 1/2 in. (145.5 × 125.5 cm)
Private collection

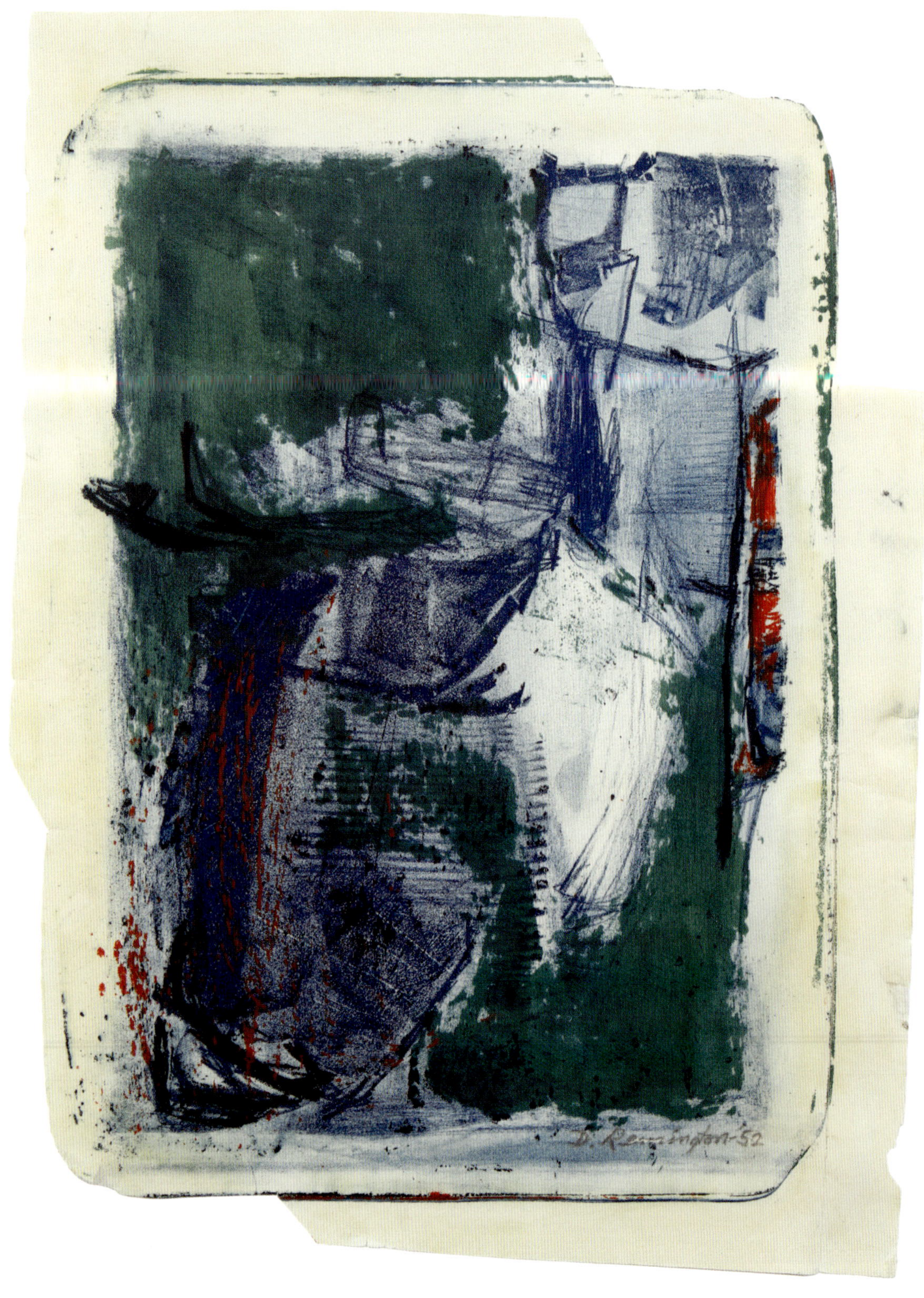
D. Remington '52

Deborah Remington's Early Years

NANCY LIM

Deborah Remington's artistic path was set at age fourteen, when she joined a cohort of precocious creative minds at Pasadena Junior College, a progressive high school in Pasadena, California. Her early childhood had been spent in Haddonfield, a New Jersey suburb near Philadelphia, but in 1945, a year after her father's death, she and her mother moved to the Los Angeles area. At her new school, Remington experienced a remarkable social serendipity: she encountered Wally Hedrick, Hayward King, and David Simpson, all of whom would also become artists and would remain her close friends. After graduation, following a disappointing semester at Otis Art Institute (now Otis College of Art and Design) in Los Angeles, the group decided to enroll together at the most experimental art college on the West Coast: San Francisco's California School of Fine Arts (CSFA; later the San Francisco Art Institute).[1]

When they arrived on campus in 1949, CSFA was in the grip of an Abstract Expressionism craze. The San Francisco Museum of Art (SFMA; now the San Francisco Museum of Modern Art) had presented a Jackson Pollock solo exhibition in 1945, followed the next year by a solo presentation of Mark Rothko, who solidified his influence in the Bay Area through summer teaching sessions at CSFA in 1947 and 1949. "[William] Baziotes, [Adolph] Gottlieb, [Jackson] Pollock, of course. . . . It was . . . an osmosis," recalled Elmer Bischoff, an influential painting professor at CSFA. "These ideas were just there, they were in the air and they infiltrated and took hold."[2] For Remington, who had only ever explored figuration, nonobjective compositions delivered a whiplash of intrigue and disorientation. "Right straight smack in the face," she later recalled. "It fascinated me. I loved it. I hated it. It interested me all in the first impact. . . . It was like a step into another world all of a sudden."[3] She embraced this new language quickly and definitively, infusing even her representational works—still lifes and renderings of the live models from her occasional figure drawing and portraiture courses—with strong lines and eddies of color, influenced by professors such as Rothko, Bischoff, Clyfford Still, Hassel Smith, and David Park.[4] At this time, Park was making the opposite turn as Remington, literally tossing his nonobjective paintings into a Berkeley dump, inaugurating the Bay Area Figurative movement.[5] Nevertheless, Remington counted Park as a significant teacher, absorbing from him lessons in complicating figure and ground to create startling

Deborah Remington
Swinging, 1952
Lithograph
13 1/4 × 9 1/4 in
(33.7 × 23.5 cm)
Deborah Remington Charitable Trust for the Visual Arts

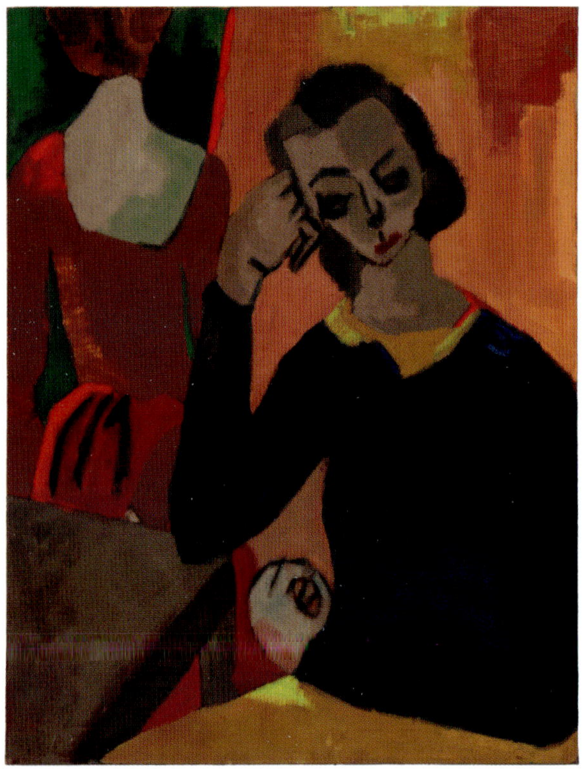

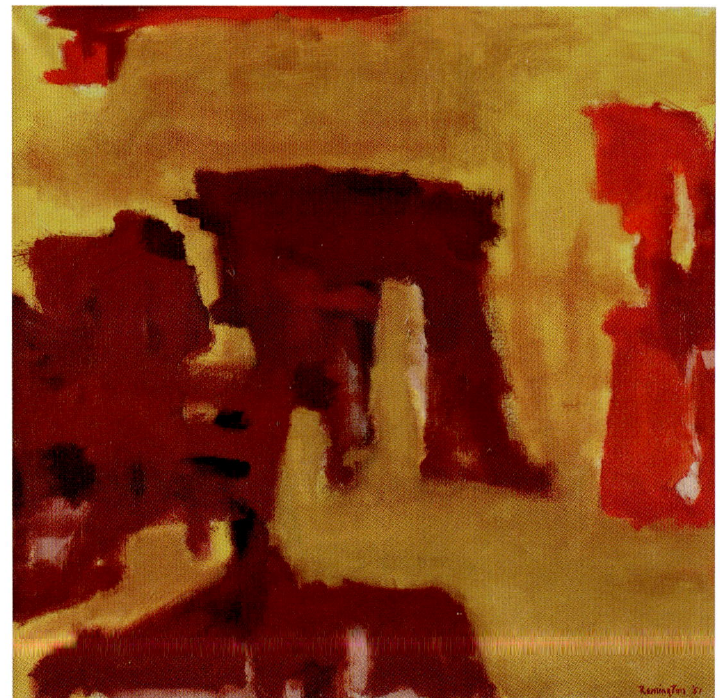

FIG. 1 [LEFT]
Deborah Remington
Untitled, 1950
Oil on canvas
35 3/4 × 28 in.
(90.8 × 71.1 cm)
Deborah Remington Charitable Trust for the Visual Arts

FIG. 2 [RIGHT]
Deborah Remington
Untitled, 1951
Oil on canvas
28 × 30 in.
(71.1 × 76.2 cm)
di Rosa Center for Contemporary Art, Napa, California

compositions (1950; **FIG. 1**), a strategy that ultimately helped her develop—across her career, in fact—an abstraction informed at turns by objective imagery. Within a few years she would delve into abstraction exclusively, running jagged patches of red along palimpsests of yellow hues in an echo of Still's painterly maneuvers (1951; **FIG. 2**). She also adopted Smith's intricate mark making, characterized during this period by interplays between sharp curves and lush fields of color—especially evident in the more ornate works she produced as her training at CSFA progressed (1953; **PAGE 19**). "I definitely remember doing Hassel Smith paintings," she once recalled. "I think one did paintings of everybody. . . . You worked your way through it. You got out of it what you wanted, let's say, that would relate to your own work, and that was the end of it."[6]

A number of these professors—including Bischoff, Still, and Rothko—had been recently hired by Douglas MacAgy, who himself had been installed as CSFA's director in 1945. Although his tenure ended in the summer of 1950, less than two years after Remington began coursework, she experienced the revitalized school that MacAgy had dedicated himself to creating, particularly through the visiting and permanent instructors he recruited to the faculty. These new hires energized the curriculum and catalyzed a fresh dynamic between teachers and students that valued open dialogue and expansive artistic approaches. Additionally, many members of the campus community were veterans of World War II, and this supercharged the school's intensity. "There was a conflict of feeling," Remington remembered. "A hard, serious, knuckled-in feeling about painting—[but] also the feeling that you didn't care what you did today because tomorrow you might not be alive . . . that kind of hangover from the war."[7] It was in this environment that her painting practice took form. Hunkered down in the school's studios, Remington mixed her paints in used tuna cans and carefully applied them to her canvases. Through trial and error she taught herself chemistry and conservation, and she developed a reputation as an avid technician at a time when her CSFA peers tended toward more feverish output in a drive to express ideas as quickly as possible—regardless of whether the physical artwork they created would even last beyond a day.

This same intensity permeated the 6 Gallery, an experimental space Remington cofounded in 1954 with five CSFA colleagues: the poet and professor Jack Spicer and fellow students Wally Hedrick, Hayward King, John Ryan, and David Simpson, most of whom she had first befriended in Pasadena. Located at 3119 Fillmore Street, a former auto repair shop and the onetime site of the short-lived King Ubu Gallery (1952–53), the 6 was a scrappy, high-spirited response to the dim commercial and institutional interest that its founders and their peers faced in San Francisco. It "[inherited] the light fixtures as well as a stage that had been built for poetry readings by the Ubu poets,"[8] Remington later recounted, and hosted raucous openings for artists whose works spanned dance, experimental sound, photography, painting, and poetry. Its program, guided by a democratic selection process, included exhibitions by professors, students, and other local art world denizens, from Richard Diebenkorn and Joan Brown to Leo Valledor, Jay DeFeo, and Sonia Gechtoff, whose mother would soon open East & West Gallery across the street. It was at the 6 that Allen Ginsberg and five other poets infamously debuted his poem "Howl," now considered the moment that ushered in the Beat generation. "[We were] presenting ideas as fast as we could get them down," artist Manuel Neri recalled. "[We] would paint a whole show the night before it opened. The immediacy was exciting even if the work was raw and incoherent. . . . The excitement was in having all these ideas coming at you at once from all directions."[9]

The early 1950s were heady years for Remington. In addition to her activities at the 6, she lived in the Fillmore District, known then as the West Coast epicenter of jazz, and she passed countless evenings in the Beat generation's home base of North Beach, which abutted CSFA in nearby Russian Hill. Remington embraced the porousness between the studio and the cultural vitality beyond campus, socializing with musicians and Beat poets and incessantly chasing down albums and live performances of modern jazz. Her painting *23° North by 82° West* (1954; **FIG. 3**) took its title from a 1952 recording by the Stan Kenton Orchestra, while the lithograph *Well You Needn't* (1953–54; **FIG. 4**) was named after the Thelonious Monk song from 1944. The genre's qualities of improvisation and sociability also infused Remington's compositions themselves as jazz became a potent imaginative force behind her works and pushed them deeper into more experimental abstraction.

This proved especially true in her printmaking. Remington created dozens of prints while at CSFA, borrowing lithographic stones from the school—one of which she rotated repeatedly, evident from the telltale notch on the sheets—to explore mark making and color overlays. She noted, "In my more expressionist period where if the register was off a little bit that was even more marvelous, and you never knew what you were going to get."[10] Remington reveled in printmaking's variability and surprise, and she also found that in comparison to painting, the medium encouraged in her a wilder hand and greater freedom of gesture, as well as unexpected palettes that hummed with dissonant energy. Her prolific engagement with lithography and etching during her student years led to awards and exhibitions as well as to the stubborn misconception among many of her classmates that Remington was a

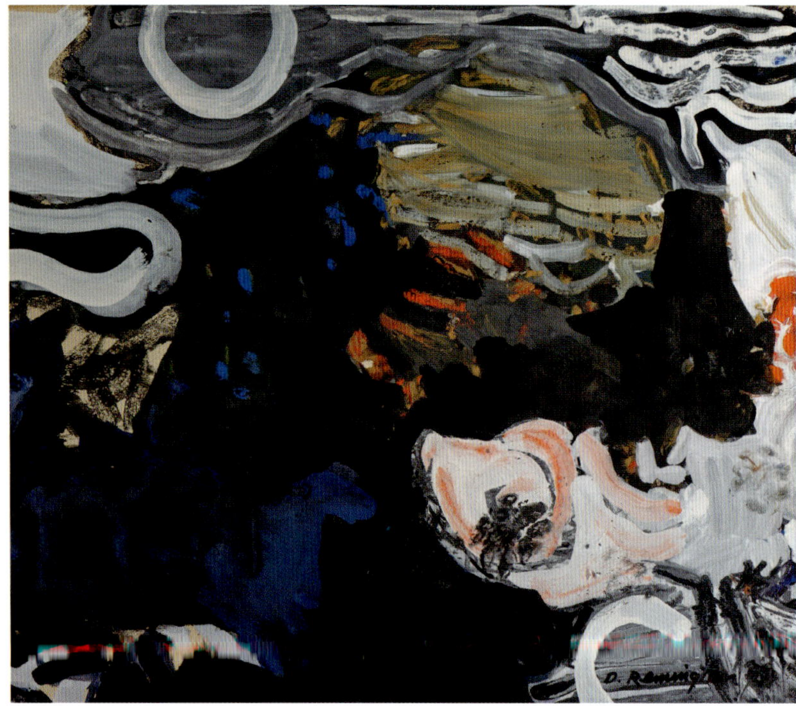

printmaker, even long after her activities in the medium had waned.[11] She would reengage it only sporadically after graduating from CSFA in 1955, although each return proved important; printmaking, like drawing, was a sure way to loosen her hand and clear her mind. Thus, while her works on paper were separate from her paintings—equivalent to them, not preparatory—they would repeatedly serve as stepping stones from one body of paintings to the next and from one way of thinking to another.

Although Remington's paintings were more controlled, their compositions more orderly and the forms more discrete, they nevertheless shared with her works on paper a rootedness in jazz and Beat culture. Compositions such as *Phunky* (1956; **FIG. 5**), for instance, quickly telegraph their origins in conversations happening in the Bay Area art scene.[12] "I remember it being spelt P-H-U-N-K-Y," fellow artist William Wiley recalled, mystified. "I said, 'What's this word mean, phunky?'" Upon hearing that it was a New Orleans blues term meaning "down-home" and soulful, he realized the intuitive sense this made to him, despite his meager knowledge of jazz. "But then the next time I remember hearing it was just around the school, it [was] being used in relationship to something homemade-looking," he continued. "No bullshit. A lot of heart."[13] This sensibility ushered in the Northern California aesthetic from the late 1950s and early 1960s that curator Peter Selz would identify—with notorious resistance from artists—as "funk" in his 1967 exhibition by that title at Berkeley's University Art Museum (now Berkeley Art Museum and Pacific Film Archive). In the catalogue, Selz described funk as the antithesis of "New York 'primary structures' or the 'Fetish finish' sculpture which prevails in Southern California. Funk art is hot rather than cool; it is committed rather than disengaged; it is bizarre rather than formal; it is sensuous; and frequently it is quite ugly and ungainly."[14] Indeed, although Remington was not included in the show, *Phunky* embodies Selz's description. The work handily rejects finesse: a scratched, saw-toothed mass of paint occupies the lower left corner, from which a brain-like form emerges. It is at once obdurate and

FIG. 3 [LEFT]
Deborah Remington
23° North By 82° West, 1954
Tempera on paper
12 1/2 × 14 1/2 in.
(31.8 × 36.8 cm)
Denver Art Museum, Colorado. Gift of the Deborah Remington Charitable Trust for the Visual Arts

FIG. 4 [RIGHT]
Deborah Remington
Well You Needn't, 1953–54
Lithograph
21 1/4 × 14 3/4 in.
(54 × 37.5 cm)
Deborah Remington Charitable Trust for the Visual Arts

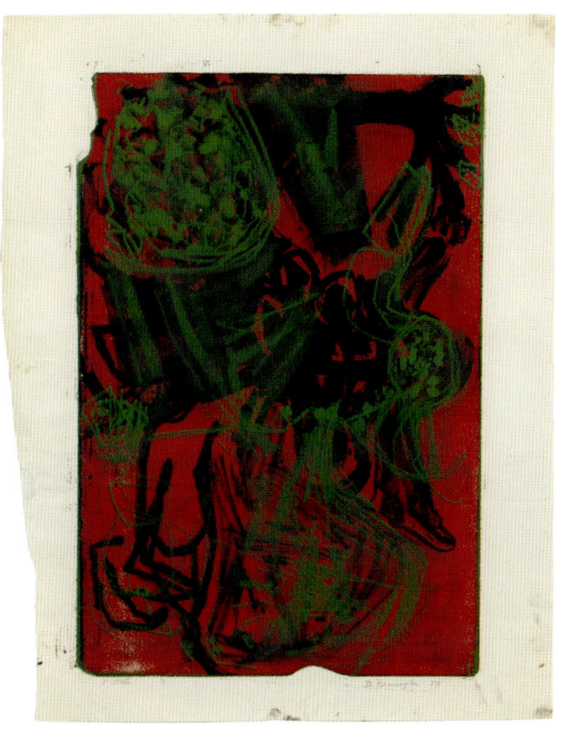

alive, declaring itself an object to reckon with even as the question of what thing this is remains stubbornly unanswered—a sign without a referent, whose uncanny associations to the material world are forever elusive.

* * *

In 1956, the same year she completed *Phunky*, Remington departed for Tokyo. She would live there for nearly two years, setting aside her studio practice and focusing instead on intensive coursework in Japanese and Chinese calligraphy. She entered a "marvelous sort of gray world,"[15] as she later recounted, one with surprisingly rich chromatic possibilities that helped exact the welcome consequence of sharpening her mark making. "Nothing can be dead in a stroke—it has to have a certain spring to it like a twig," she reflected. "This is the way I was taught calligraphy and from this I got a lot of feeling for a certain movement of line and for the angles of relationships of lines."[16] After returning to California in 1958, she continued working within these formal parameters for several months, creating drawings of the tufted grasses that swayed along the shorelines of the San Francisco Bay (1959; **PAGES 24–25**). With a Speedball ink pen typically used for Western calligraphy, she pulled wet lines across the page, imbuing them with the gestural energy she had learned, and learned to harness, not from Abstract Expressionism in the United States but from calligraphy in Japan. In some of these drawings her mark making is so kinetic it verges on feral, seemingly belying her rigorous training. But as much as this line work registers her intense focus on the pressure and motion of the pen, it also reveals the disciplined dexterity she had developed, one informed by the rich histories of the calligraphic traditions she had studied.[17] The result is a body of drawings that is at once influenced by—and a rupture from—her training, like two sides of a spinning coin.

Remington never made works quite like these ink drawings again, so it is tempting to see them as outliers. However, despite how distant they appear from her future output, they were in fact

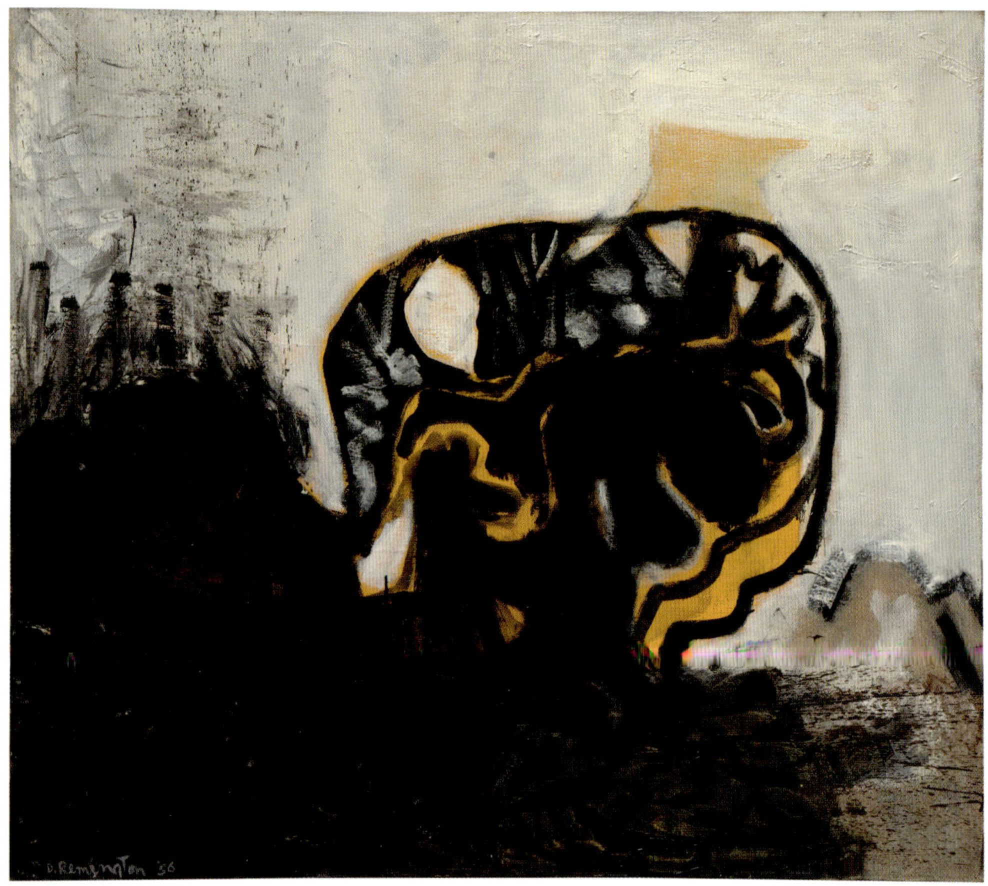

FIG. 5
Deborah Remington
Phunky or *Dacia*, 1956
Oil on canvas
40 × 46 in.
(101.6 × 116.8 cm)
Private collection

foundational, providing the compositional logic for *Irreparable* (1959; **PAGES 29–31**), *Exodus* (1960; **PAGE 33**), and her other paintings from the late 1950s and early 1960s—a lineage evident in their windswept lines that collide and decouple exuberantly. Remington created these works as a wave of gestural expressionism engulfed the Bay Area, conjoining learnings from her training in Japan with the San Francisco milieu she had reentered. Unlike the drawings of grasses, though, she now embraced monumentality, scaling up to five or six feet tall, dimensions she felt could bear the energetic application of thick paint with which she formed these canvases' roiling topographies—a style not uncommon within certain CSFA circles during those years. On this count she was especially proud of *Exodus*, a "big thing" that hung in the boardroom of the San Francisco–based paper conglomerate Crown Zellerbach. "[It's] a hell of a mother strong painting & will probably scare the shit out of the Board bored members plus sending a few screeming [*sic*] secretaries off to the booby hatch,"[18] she gleefully wrote to a friend. For Remington, *Exodus*—and her other large, loud paintings from these years, such as *Big Red* (1962; **PAGES 39–41**), *For H.M.* (1962, **PAGE 47**), and *Dr. S* (1962; **PAGE 45**)—was a declaration. These works embodied a new sense of conviction with a deepened set of stakes, and that attitude would infuse her practice going forward.

In early 1963, Remington completed *Winter '63*, the last such painting (1963; **PAGE 43**). Its background was distinct from any she had previously made; it featured a sweep of vermilion that unfurled from the top and faded gently into black. A few months later, she began two series of drawings—*Soot* (1963–76; **PAGES 53–59**) and *Adelphi* (1963–83; **PAGES 62–69**)—that definitively extended this experiment in gradation. For the former, she applied ethereal layers of fireplace soot to a muslin support, while the latter used soft graphite sticks, orange crayon, and pencil.[19] Ranging from a velvety surface to a diffuse particulate, these works possessed a textural breadth that helped Remington refine her technical precision. She developed soft fades and quick switches, as well as slow burns that creep through the sheet—and she applied these throughout the compositions rather than solely to the background, as in *Winter '63*. In *Adelphi*, the gradations appear within and around the myriad forms, creating panoplies of positive and negative space. They flow into each other, aided by interrupted outlines that leave some shapes exposed, and Remington extends the spatial complexities by untethering many of the central forms from the edges of their sheets. In her paintings from this period, such as *Exodus*, the shapes had yet to fully disengage, but in most *Adelphi* works—and all of *Soot*—Remington at last jettisoned Bischoff's dictates. "You can't have things floating around in the air. You have to have a ground plane for them to stand on," he had advised.[20] With their hovering imagery, her *Soot* and *Adelphi* drawings explore the infinite dimensions of indeterminate space, using line, luminosity, and flickers of allusion as their primary tools. Through these explorations, Remington cemented the defining characteristics of her artistic practice.

Remington's project of translating this new direction into painting began in late 1963. Achieving it in this medium would be a different proposition. Compared to what she could advance and solve through her drawings, her paintings tended to attain her aims belatedly. "My drawings [were] the wellspring of my imagination in terms of the imagery,"[21] she said, explaining their primacy. Her painting *Statement* (1963; **PAGE 49**), which she called her breakthrough piece, incorporates many of the refinements of the *Adelphi* and *Soot* drawings, including a crisp, tensely balanced form with slight asymmetries to confuse the eye, a smoother topography that abandoned what she now referred to as her "agonized surface,"[22] and a portentous luminosity. Although her paintings from this period allowed her to extend her experimentation, it is her drawings—and the *Adelphi* series, in particular—that were the essential bridge.

In 1964 she debuted *Statement* in an exhibition at SFMA. Viewers, disinclined toward evolutions in her painting practice, were "absolutely dumbfounded," Remington recalled. "I thought people were going to have heart attacks over this. I mean, I got phone calls in the middle of night from friends saying, well, I'm very upset. I saw your work, and I don't understand it. What do you think you're doing?"[23] The art dealer Jim Newman, however, was among the few enthusiasts. Already a supporter, he had featured Remington in previous exhibitions at Dilexi Gallery, and he now invited her to open its new San Francisco location on Clay Street with a solo show. She happily obliged, but the exhibition, which opened in September 1965, would be her last involvement with the gallery for many years. Remington had decided that the Bay Area offered too little to artists, and she planned to move east.[24] "I was really about at the top of where one could go in San Francisco professionally, and that means that you level off, you top out, and you get yourself a university job," she explained. "You settle into a comfortable chair for the rest of your life, and I didn't want to do this."[25] With a few sales from the Dilexi show lining her pockets, she left for New York in a secondhand Porsche and settled into an apartment on Canal Street in SoHo. There she swiftly set herself on a path to create the astonishing paintings for which she would soon become known, compositions defined by icon-like morphologies whose foundations had been laid in San Francisco.

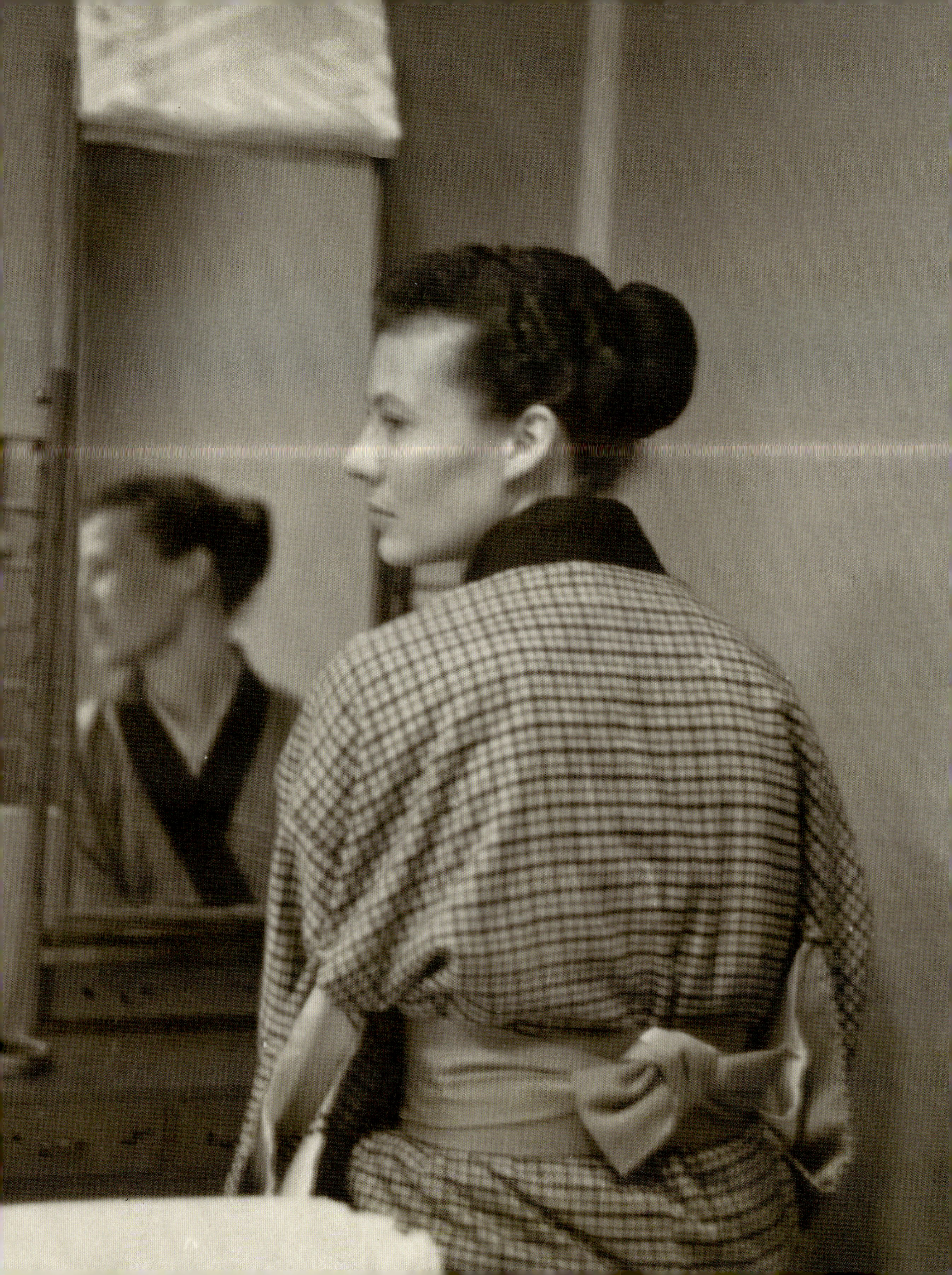

Framing the Self, Seeing the Other: Deborah Remington in Japan, 1956–58

STEPHANIE M. HOHLIOS

After Deborah Remington's almost three-year sojourn to Japan from 1956 to 1958, with time spent in India, Tibet, Nepal, and Southeast Asia, her artwork evoked notions of "the Orient" for U.S. critics, especially notions of Japan and the poetic modes of expression to be encountered there. Writing for *Artforum* in 1966, art critic Knute Stiles even attributes Remington's focus on symmetrical forms to her time spent in Japan, and identifies an "expressive mystery" in her use of black pigment as a medium.[1] Considering early abstract compositions from Remington's *Soot Series* (1963–76), artworks produced with chimney soot from the fireplace in her Bay Area studio, Stiles identifies a common element in these works on muslin that call to mind the shape of a Japanese fan. In a drawing from the series, the shapes and planes layer, abut, and interact (*Soot Series 1*, 1963; **PAGE 53**). A form, perhaps evocative of the silhouette of an extended accordion-style paper fan of the sort common in Japan, is set within the frame of the largest element, seemingly behind the most central, smaller ones. Stiles sees this fanlike element and the "machine-like" forms[2]—shapes suggestive of batteries, pumps, or tanks—that pervade the *Soot Series* as examples of how the artist might, as Remington puts it, "clock images of everyday life . . . notice it, store it and somehow it emerges, somewhat modified, somewhere in the work."[3]

However, Remington frequently rejected the identification of Japanese elements in her artwork.[4] What her study of East Asian calligraphy and *sumi-e* (Japanese ink painting) while living in Japan did provide her with, she says, is a renewed interest in issues of balance, support, and the quality of a brushstroke.[5] By way of letters to friends, notes taken during her Japanese-language lessons, photographs, daily schedules, and daybooks from this time period, we understand that Remington also sought an immersive cultural experience, mutual exchange, and encounters with new methods for expression.

Remington in Japan, 1957

Remington's interest in Japanese culture began with the Japanese woodblock prints that her mother collected and displayed on the walls of their home.[6] Later, when she was in college, she

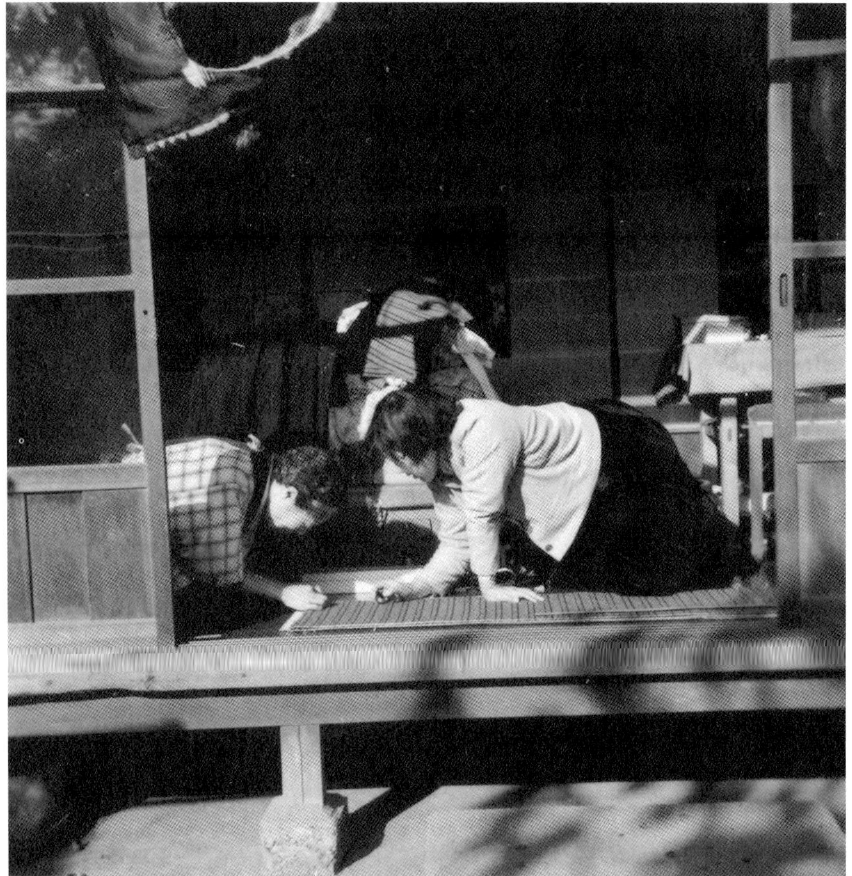

FIG. 1
Mrs. Tamura and her daughter, Tokyo, c. 1957. Photograph by Deborah Remington

befriended two women of Japanese heritage. In 1954, she began to formally study the Japanese language at the Galileo Adult School in San Francisco, also enrolling in a Chinese-language class the following year.[7] Once in Japan, Remington learned the language by speaking with her host family, the Tamuras, who spoke almost no English, and recounts in her journal that she learned Japanese in the same manner "as a child learns one's native . . . language. . . . They would just repeat . . . sentences until I understood."[8] Her host family also educated Remington in the cultural practices considered proper for a young Japanese woman. She studied flower arranging (*ikebana*), tea (*chanoyu*), Japanese cuisine (*washoku*), and how to move appropriately in Japanese dress by observing contemporary practices in civility and manners. Instead of making painting her primary focus, Remington's preoccupation with entering into a completely foreign habitus afforded her clarity regarding her own culture, biases, and perspective.[9]

A photograph taken by Remington shows Mrs. Tamura and her daughter "making kimono," as the inscription on the back reads (**FIG. 1**). Indeed, they appear to be engaged in constructing traditional garments by chalking out a pattern for cutting directly on a bolt of fabric while in the setting of their traditional wood-constructed home. One might read Remington's abstract composition *Statement* (1963; **PAGE 49**), which includes a form evocative of a splayed-out silk kimono with full sleeves, high-contrast printed pattern, and contrasting lapel trim, as a momentary return (even if subconscious or unintended) to experiences like this one or to the forms the artist would have encountered in Japan.

Uprooting herself from the familiar and immersing herself in Japanese life afforded Remington a perspective on how gender's construction relates to other cultural formations: What is it to be "American," "Japanese," and, in particular, a woman in either of these contexts? Remington occasionally donned Japanese garments when the occasion called for it, such as on vacation at a hot spring retreat (*ryokan*) in Hakone. In a photograph from 1957, Remington wears a padded cotton garment (*tanzen*) tied at the waist with a sash (*obi*) and a traditional overcoat (*haori*). We can deduce from the arrangement of her upper body that she sits demurely with her back to the viewer in the "correct" or "true" sitting (*seiza*), with one's shins tucked beneath the thighs on the tatami mat floor. With her head turned to the left, the vanity mirror in front reflects her image back to the viewer. As Remington performs her knowledge of Japanese etiquette and customs within the setting of the *ryokan*, her composure before the mirror recalls the modern European painting trope from the late nineteenth century of the beautiful woman at her toilette—notably the female form as a subject to be regarded and desired.[10]

Remington's time spent navigating social frameworks in Japan prepared her for the roles she assumed in Japanese television and film as a comedienne or villainess. Citing the conservative rules of the Tamuras' household, which Remington felt to be stifling, and a desire to expand her experiences in Japan, Remington departed for Kyoto in 1957 with some new friends. Upon returning to Tokyo, she elected to move in with them in December 1957 "instead of returning to the clutches" of her host family, as she phrases it in a letter to a friend in the United States.[11] Her roommates were actors, and the woman starred in the television comedy series *The Busy Housewife*, in which Remington later appeared as "the funny lady."[12] "And naturally, I'm too tall, so I would hit my head on the door . . . I was the biggest ham, I tell you."[13] This gag plays to the stereotype of the foreigner in Japanese popular culture—typically a white foreigner of Euro-American background (like Remington) who appears frequently on variety television shows, and whose comic appeal lies in how their habits or expectations depart from those of Japanese people.[14] As a woman, however, Remington was in the minority; most comedy stars in Japan were (and still are) men.[15]

Remington dabbled in B movie acting, where she played, as she describes it, "the parts that white ladies get to play . . . the reverse roles that the dragon lady Oriental, mysterious woman played in the mysteries of the '30s and '40s in America."[16] As a white foreigner in Japan, she was limited to roles of the comedic, exotic, or terrifying variety, but she seized the opportunity to better understand cultural expectations and consumer desires by immersing herself in the role of the outsider. We can view her acting work in television and film as part of her personal rubric for cultural exchange, one that held for her a parity with her more formal learning in calligraphy and painting, for example.

According to her daybook from 1957, Remington took classes in both Chinese and Japanese calligraphy, as well as ink painting.[17] Through calligraphy, Remington engaged with seventh- and eighth-century literary works as examples in her calligraphy practice and which piqued her interest in translation.[18] In her datebook, Remington inscribes the *Iroha Poem* (eighth century or later) in the blank space for the week of March 3, 1957: "Iro wa nioedo chiri nuru o" ("Colors are fragrant, but they will eventually scatter"). This poem is often used in calligraphy practice because the full poem includes every component of the Japanese syllabary.

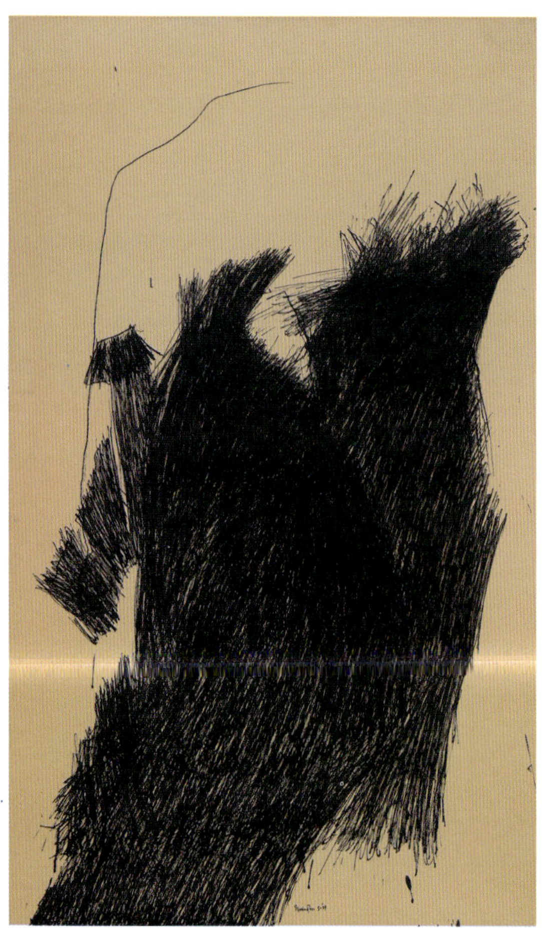

FIG. 2 [LEFT]
Deborah Remington
May Drawing, 1959
Ink on paper
50 1/4 × 30 1/2 in. (127.6 × 76.8 cm)
Deborah Remington Charitable Trust for the Visual Arts

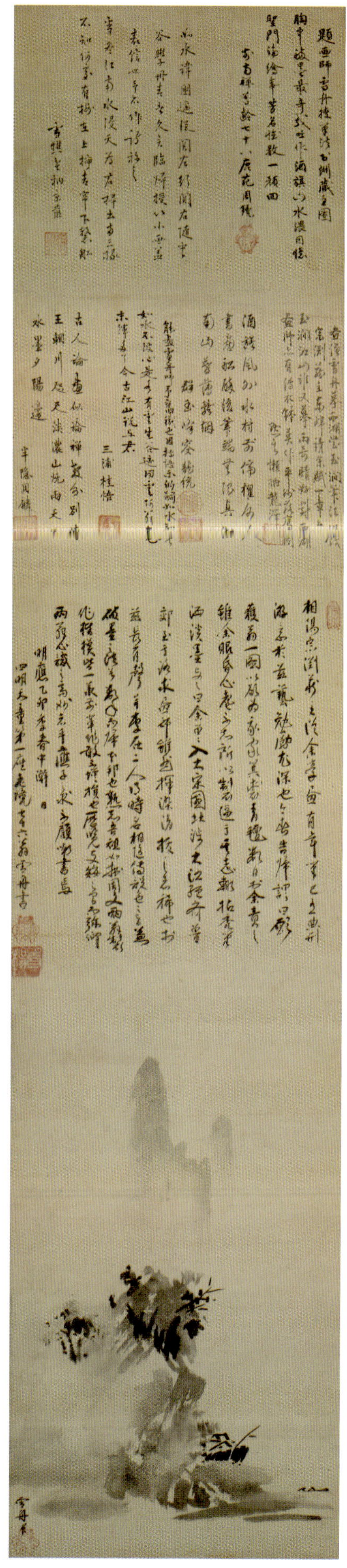

FIG. 3 [RIGHT]
Sesshū Tōyō, with inscriptions by Tōyō and six monks
Haboku sansui (*Broken Ink Landscape*), 1495
Ink on paper
58 1/2 × 12 4/5 in.
(148.6 × 32.5 cm)
National Treasure,
Tokyo National Museum

While she lived in Japan, Remington's training in ink painting would have exposed her to the compositions and techniques of canonical masters, such as the medieval Japanese Zen Buddhist monk-painter Sesshū Tōyō (1420–1506?), whose body of work represents the consolidation of transnational modes of ink painting, including the Chinese Song Dynasty artists Ma Yuan (active c. 1160–1225), and Ruofen Yujian (active c. 1250).[19] Remington quickly tired of her ink painting classes because the instructor relied too heavily, in her opinion, on the copying and rote memorization of canonical examples, probably of artists like those previously mentioned.[20] Even so, Remington's relationship to East Asian ink painting is evident in her work after she returned to the United States in 1958.

Between that year and 1960, Remington taught East Asian calligraphy at the California School of Fine Arts (CSFA; later the San Francisco Art Institute) and produced several monochrome pen-and-ink drawings of flowers and marsh grasses that grow near the coastal inlets of San Francisco Bay. These are studies in line, saturation, composition, and volume that verge on representation. Some of these drawings seem to traffic in the splashed-ink aesthetic associated with Sesshū and Yujian.[21] In *May Drawing* (1959; **FIG 2**), the abstract vertical composition suggests the flow of tufts of grass up a steep hill face, patches bowing uniformly in one direction then shifting direction as though caught by the wind. Yet the dominant theme of tight, parallel lines finds a counterpoint here in the seemingly uncontrolled—perhaps unintended or impromptu—splashed and dragged blots of ink that hover around the bottom right and top left of the composition. A seemingly runaway line also tracks upward from the left side and snakes toward the right—the suggestion of a second hill in the distance perhaps, or else the pen allowed to move freely without the artist's conscious thought. Evocative of the splashed-ink blots that produce fronds and gnarled tree branches in Sesshū's painting in the Yujian mode *Haboku sansui* (*Broken Ink Landscape*, 1495; **FIG. 3**), Remington's saturated pools of ink pull and smear along the right vertical border of the grass composition. Translucent, watery streaks of black reveal the paper ground beneath in a manner evocative of the "flying white" (*feibai* in Chinese) style of calligraphy stroke, where pressure on the brush fans out the bristles, leaving streaks of white ground visible underneath tracks of black ink. And dancing above the upper left of the central mass, there are small specks and larger splats of ink—accidental or purposeful?—with tendrils jumping outward that are produced on impact with the paper surface and appear almost like water droplets

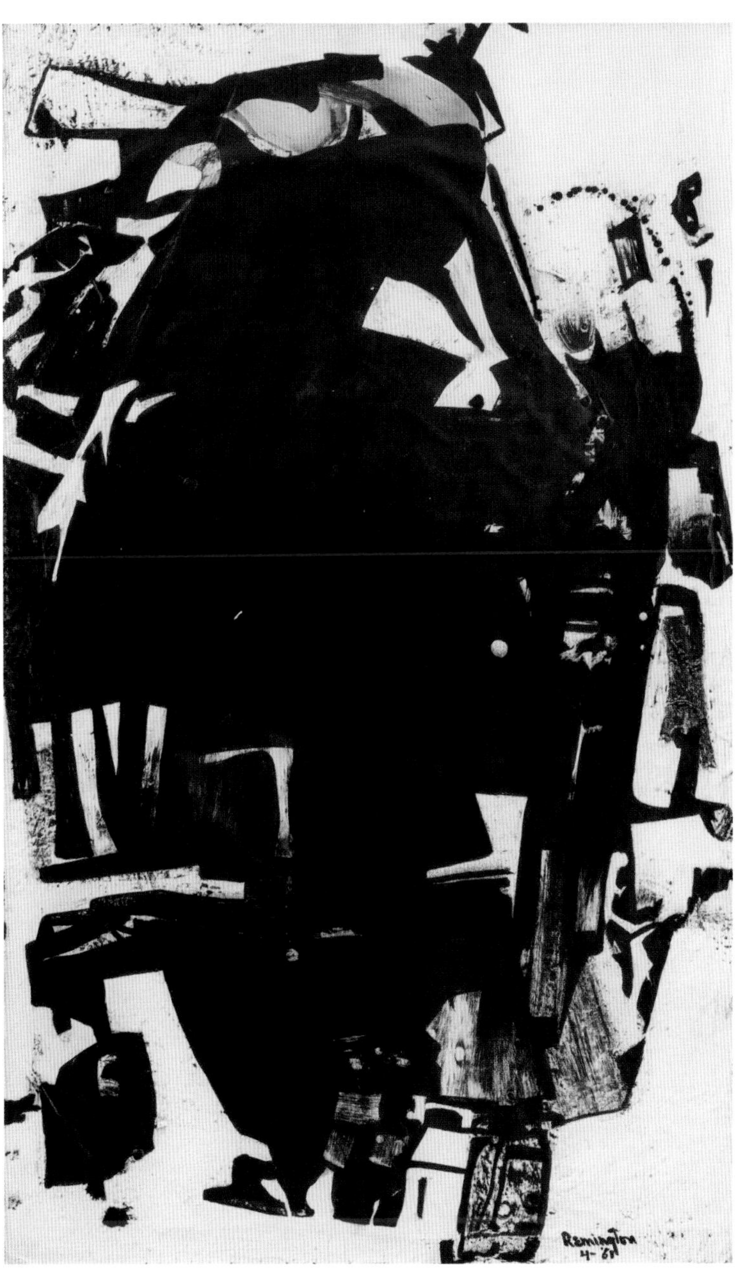

FIG. 4
Deborah Remington
Ancestor, 1961
Ink and gouache on paper
25 × 15 in. (64.5 × 38.7 cm)
Deborah Remington Charitable Trust for the Visual Arts

FIG. 5
Franz Kline
Meryon, 1960–61
Oil on canvas
93 × 77 in. (235.9 × 195.6 cm)
Tate Gallery, London

set loose from the grass blades by a gust of wind. Her composition veers close to the realm of stylistic homage, evoking modes of ink-based expression associated with historical masters of ink painting.

Remington's *Ancestor* (1961; FIG. 4) likewise grapples with issues of saturation and color bleed that she explored in her lessons in ink painting and calligraphy, albeit in a manner consistent with Franz Kline's synthesis of East Asian aesthetics. Kline, like Remington, was associated with Abstract Expressionism in the United States, and also, like Remington, studied East Asian calligraphy and ink painting. His black-and-white compositions, such as *Meryon* (1960–61; FIG. 5), were similar in form to Remington's *Ancestor*: bold black strokes of diverse texture and quality on a white ground.[22] But Remington did not wish to be received as another Abstract Expressionist painter prone to appropriating Asian aesthetics. This phase of her painting career was short-lived, perhaps precisely because it bound her work to the trend of American Abstract Expressionists who were synthesizing East Asian ink aesthetics.

After Remington's return to the United States, critics and curators, including Stiles, frequently identified in her compositions elements that seemed to them authentically Japanese. In a review of Remington's exhibition at Zolla / Lieberman Gallery in Chicago in 1976,[23] critic Devonna Pieszak writes,

> There is beyond the precision a vulnerability to movement and escape which comes as you slip into . . . an undefined, decontrolled space. The paintings have the aura of

> another place and time. There is a strong oriental quality to her work which I felt before I knew that she spent two years in Japan studying calligraphy, which, though there are no specific formal influences, certainly established some of her methods of working.[24]

Remington's artwork functions for the critic as a conduit for experiencing the unfamiliar—here, Japan—even as, Pieszak remarks, "there are no specific formal influences" denoting Japan-based training or Japanese imagery in her composition. Indeed, paintings in the Chicago exhibition, including *Maranon* (1975), which was a central image in the show and reproduced in the brochure, present a near-total erasure of the hand and brush from the finished composition by precluding any identification of calligraphic aesthetics that might otherwise denote "Japan." Instead, Remington's abstraction seems an ideal armature onto which the critic drapes affective description and personal expectation.

Remington's abstractions frequently speak of "Japan" to viewers, critics, and scholars of her artwork even if the artist did not always see a Japanese influence in her compositions. And beginning in the late 1960s, the more easily traceable elements denoting Japan (like the ink textures evocative of Sesshū's or Yujian's "broken ink" in her 1959 drawing or the kimono-like form in *Statement*) seem to disappear. Remington's training in East Asian ink painting and calligraphy visually persists but only as part of a holistic approach to issues of line, texture, and contrast. In a recent oral history, longtime supporter and dealer Daniel Lienau identifies a "calligraphic nature" in the structure and linear quality of Remington's compositions from the 1970s and 1980s, and he labels it a fusion of gesture with control or "studied spontaneity."[25] Yet if we take the artist at her word—that her abstract imagery is a consolidation of personal history—then we may indeed expect to find "Japan" someplace therein.[26]

For Remington, Japan was an opportunity to empathize with a cultural position entirely different from her American upbringing and to challenge herself linguistically and artistically. Her travels facilitated an engagement with categories of gender and race as a woman and foreigner. We can understand her time in Japan as one of total immersion in new perspectives, a new habitus, and a new way of being understood or received. The depth of her connection with Japan catalyzed the desire of American audiences to learn about Japan from Remington and to see "Japan" in her artwork. In addition to teaching East Asian calligraphy at CSFA, Remington gave numerous public talks on Japan and its art. In a letter to a friend, Remington mentions a particular lecture that she gave on the country to a group of men who "don't know their *Naniwas* [a name for modern-day Osaka] from their hooplas . . ." but indicates that, despite a paucity of shared knowledge and interest, she was able to connect with her audience and to even entertain.[27] The artist's sensitivity as a student of Japanese practices also saddled her with a burden to translate her newfound understandings once she returned to the United States.

1965–1983

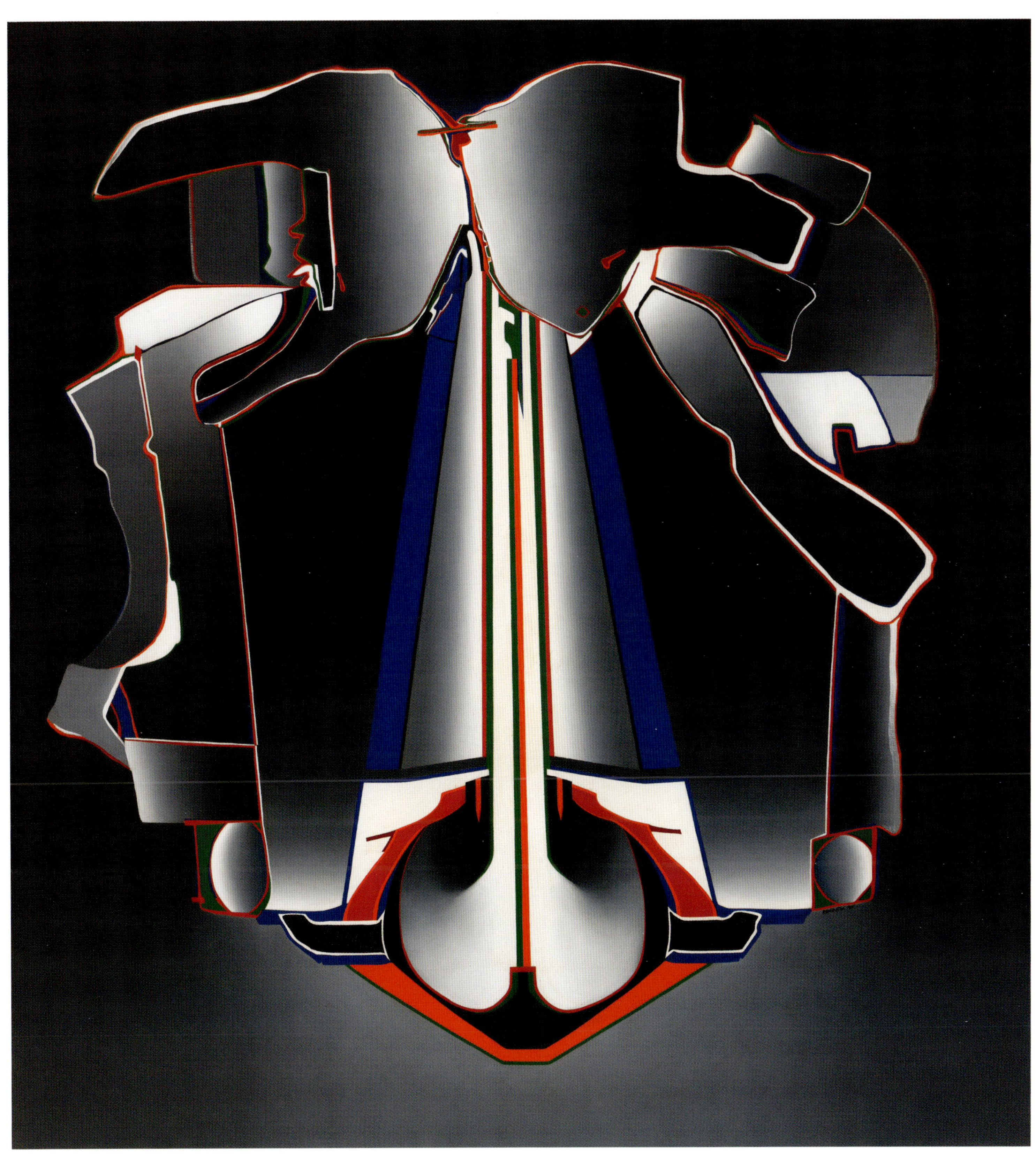

Haddonfield, 1965. Oil on canvas, 74 × 69 in. (188.3 × 175.3 cm)
Whitney Museum of American Art, New York.
Purchase, with funds from the Friends of the Whitney Museum of American Art

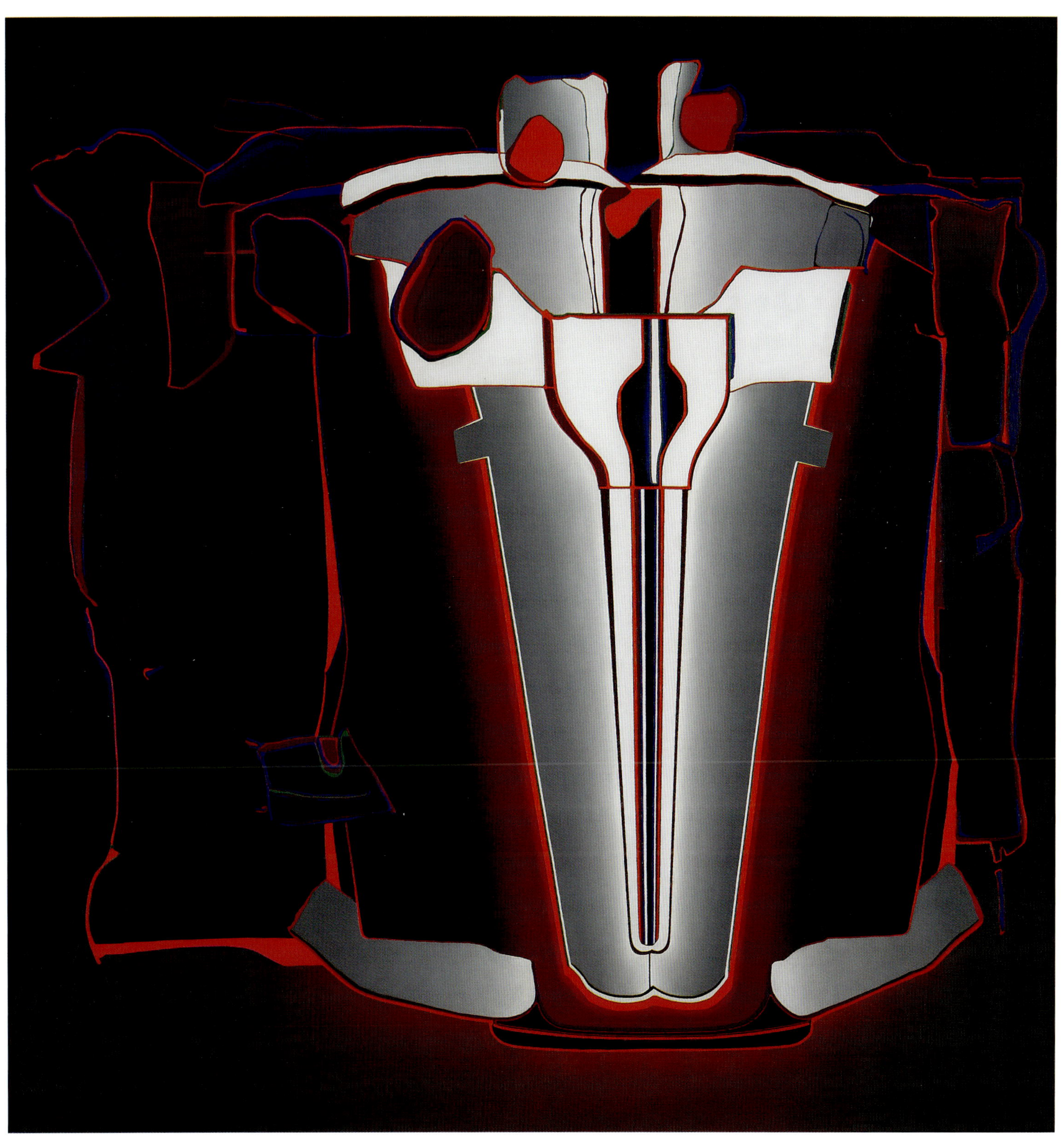

Merthyr, 1966. Oil on canvas, 72 × 70 in. (182.9 × 177.8 cm)
Centre national des arts plastiques, Paris, France

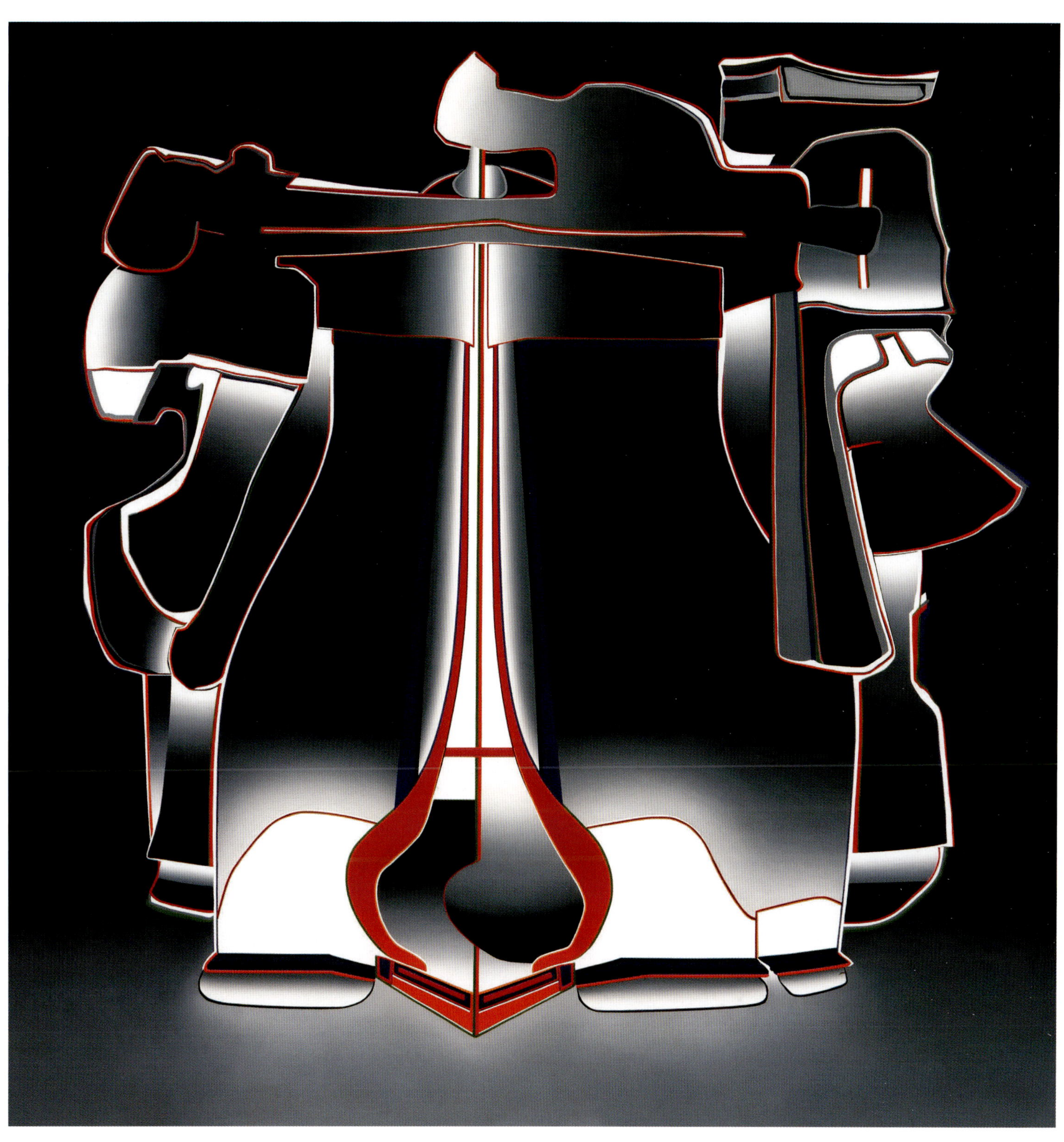

Saxon, 1966–67. Oil on canvas, 72 7/8 × 70 7/8 in. (185.1 × 180 cm)
Smithsonian American Art Museum, Washington, D.C. Gift of Flora M. Biddle

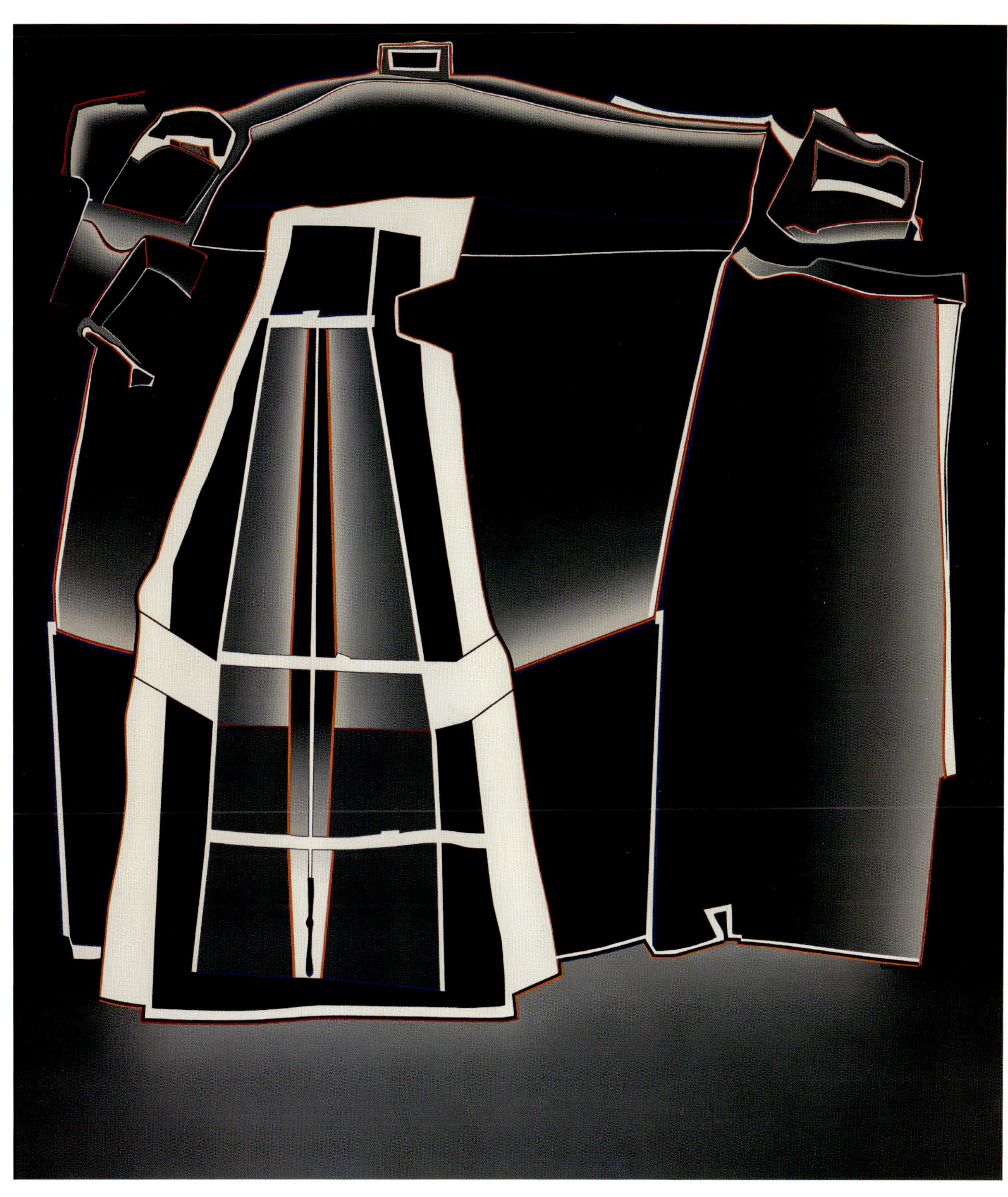

Moultrie, 1967. Oil on canvas, 60 × 53 in. (152.4 × 134.6 cm)
Indianapolis Museum of Art at Newfields, Indiana. Gift of the Contemporary Art Society

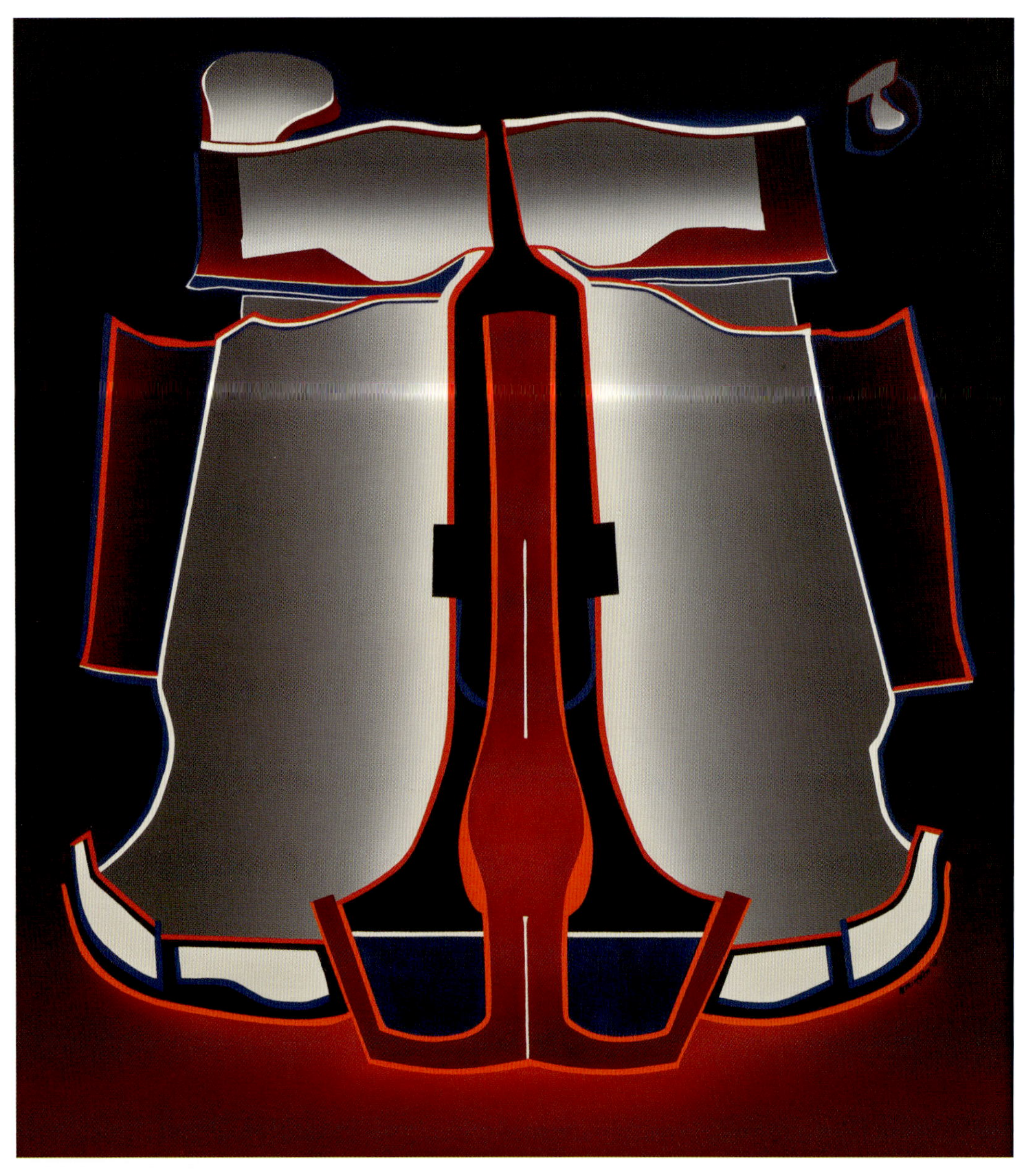

Untitled No. 4, 1969. Oil on canvas, 20 × 18 in. (50.8 × 45.7 cm)
Wadsworth Atheneum Museum of Art, Hartford, Connecticut. Gift of Mr. Herrick Jackson

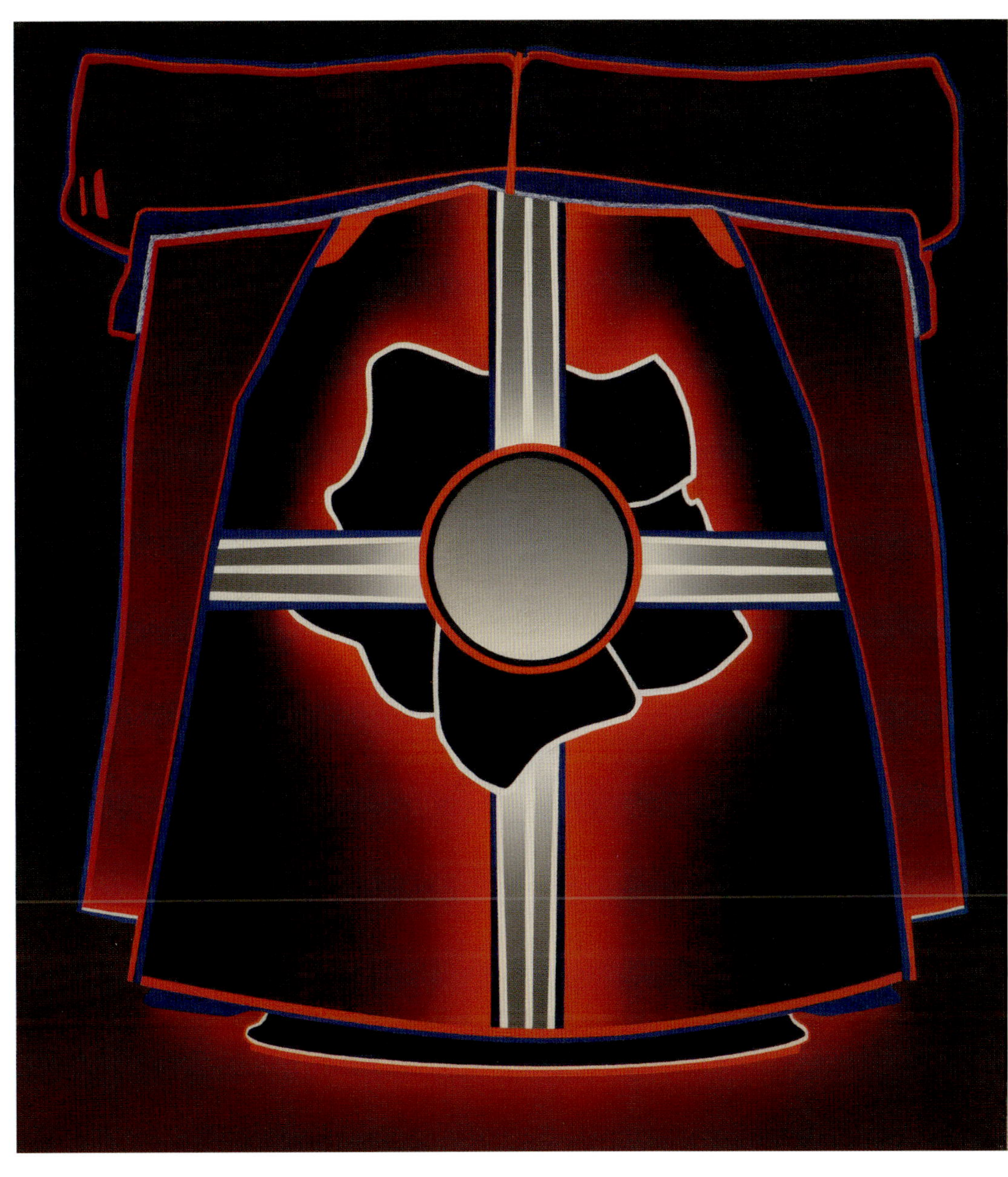

Couronne, 1969. Oil on canvas, 20 × 18 in. (50.8 × 45.7 cm)
Private collection

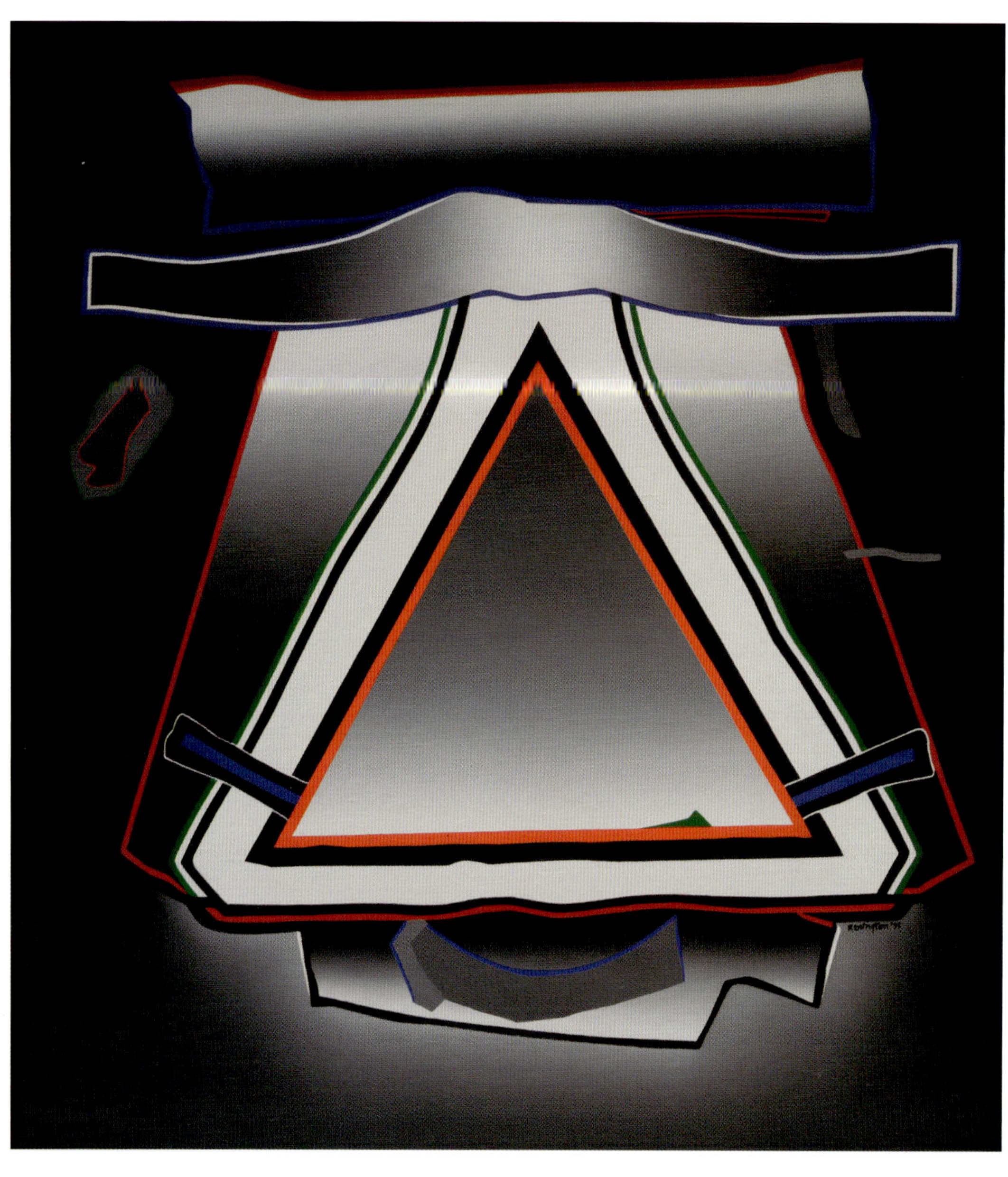

Daen, 1971. Oil on linen, 20 × 18 in. (50.8 × 45.7 cm)
Collection of Sasha and Charlie Sealy

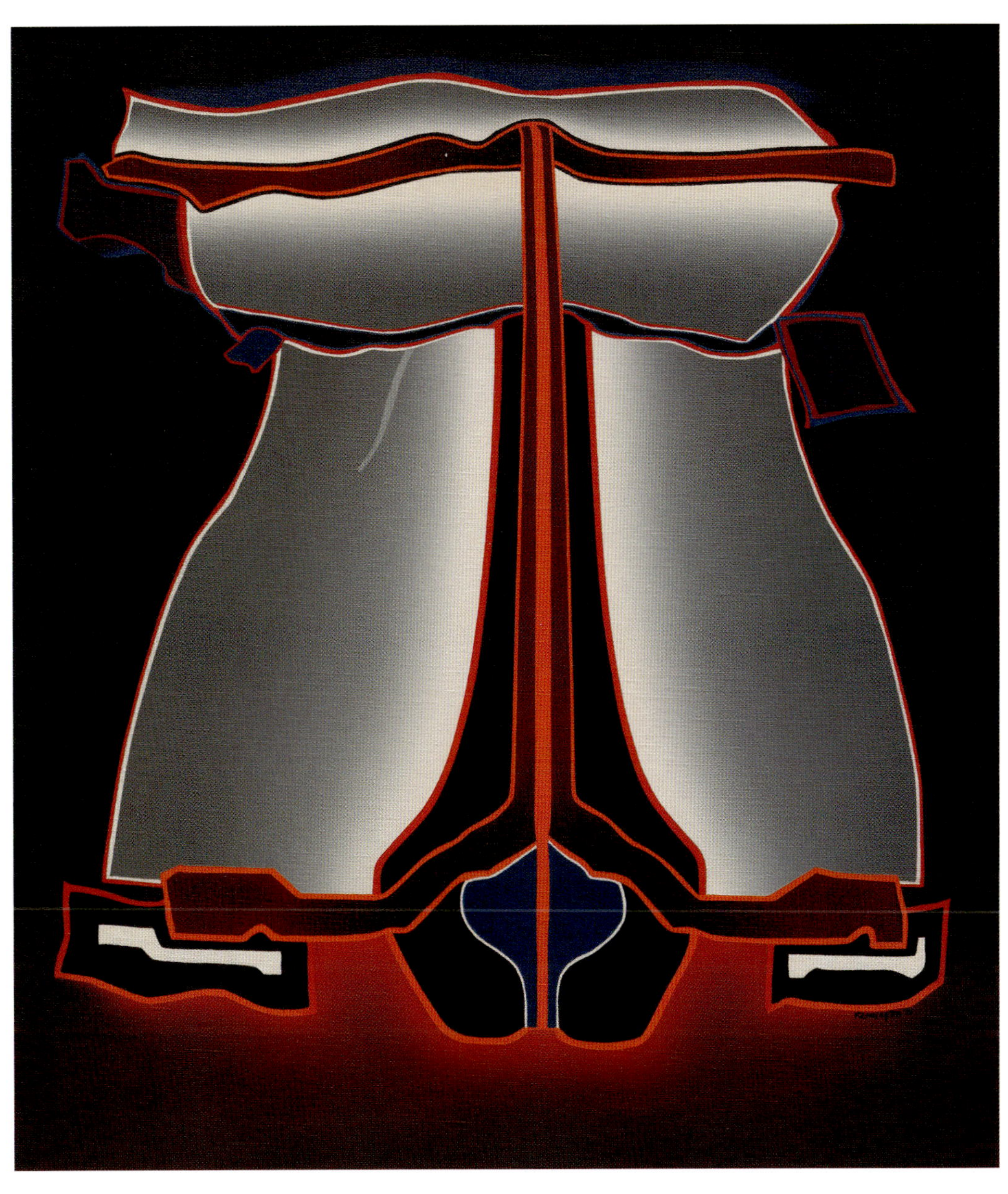

Alar, 1971. Oil on linen, 20 × 18 in. (50.8 × 45.7 cm)
Yale University Art Gallery, New Haven, Connecticut. Richard Brown Baker, B.A. 1935, Collection

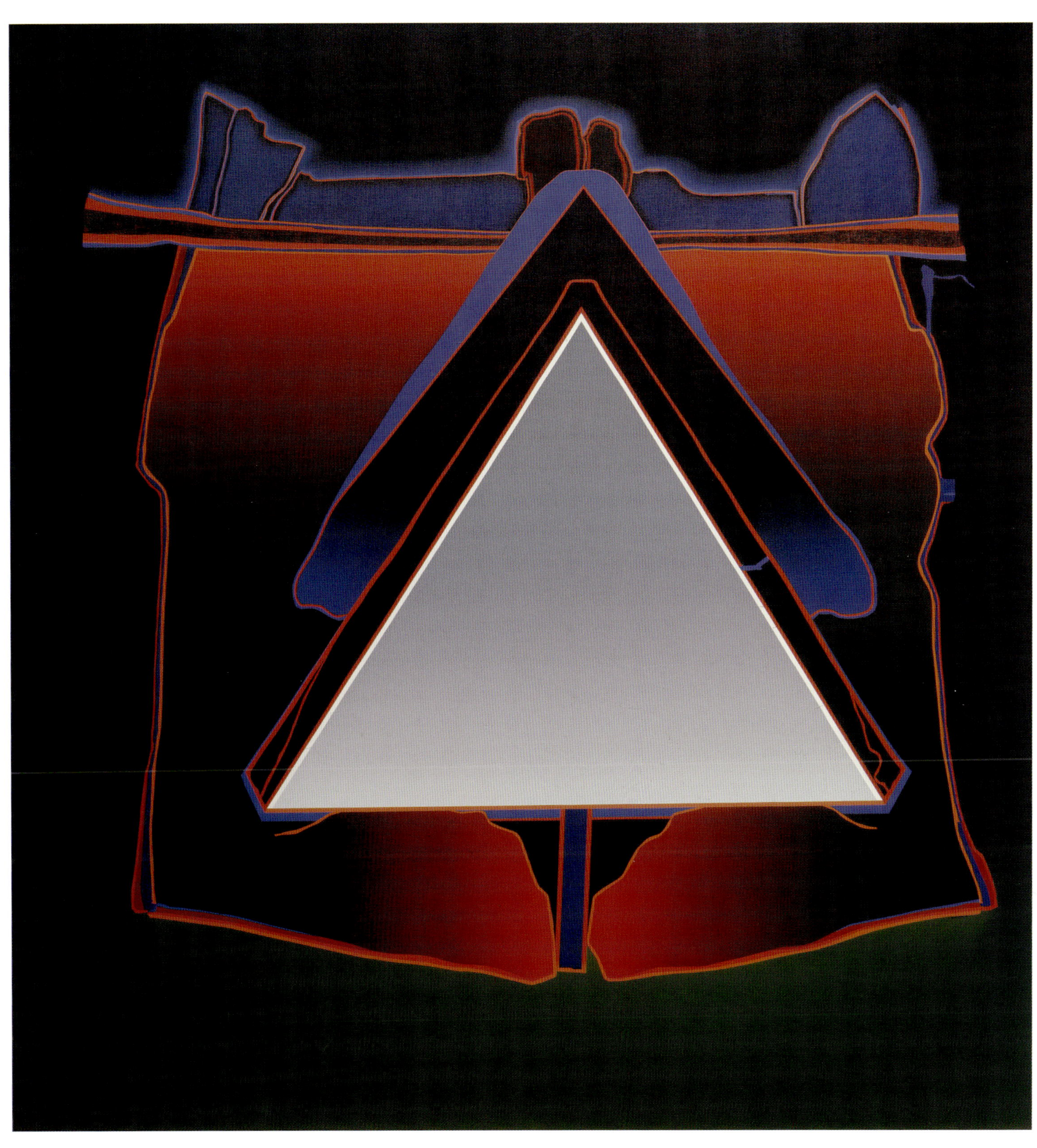

Axios, 1971. Oil on canvas, 95 × 92 in. (241.3 × 233.7 cm)
Addison Gallery of American Art, Phillips Academy, Andover, Massachusetts. Museum purchase

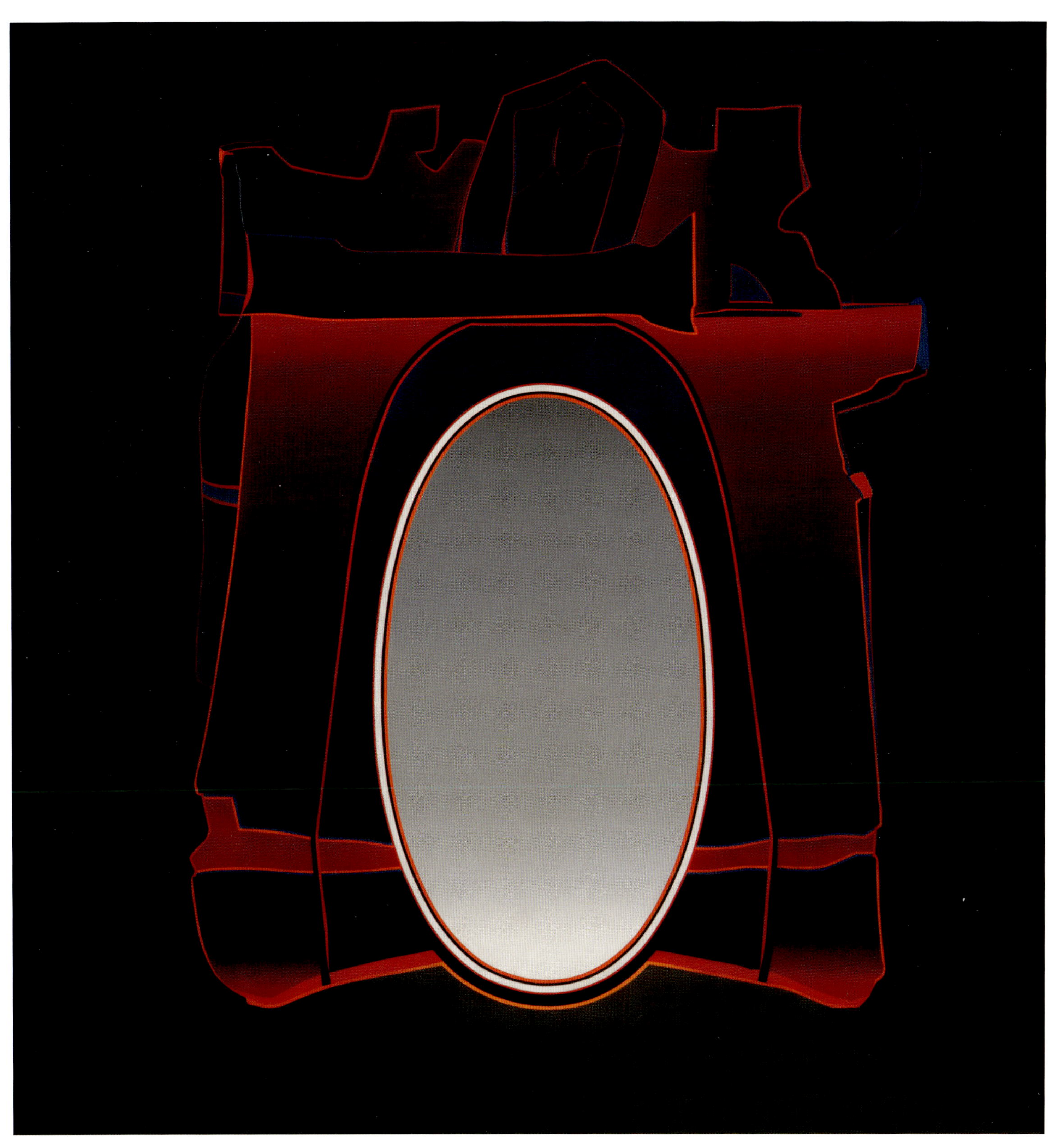

Devon, 1969. Oil on canvas, 73 × 71 in. (185.4 × 180.3 cm)
Collection of Mark Rosman

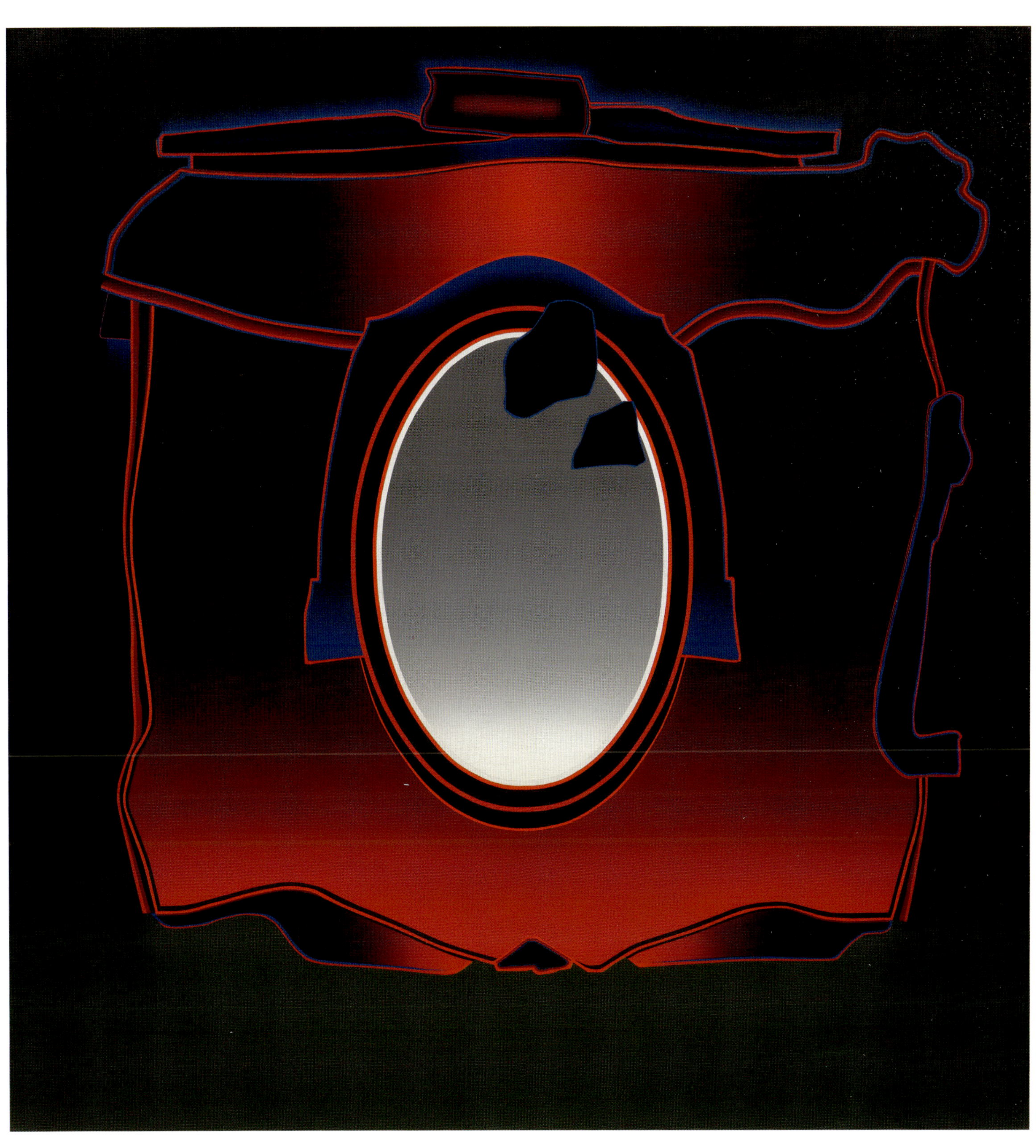

Dorset, 1972. Oil on canvas, 91 × 87 in. (231 × 221 cm)
Shah Garg Collection

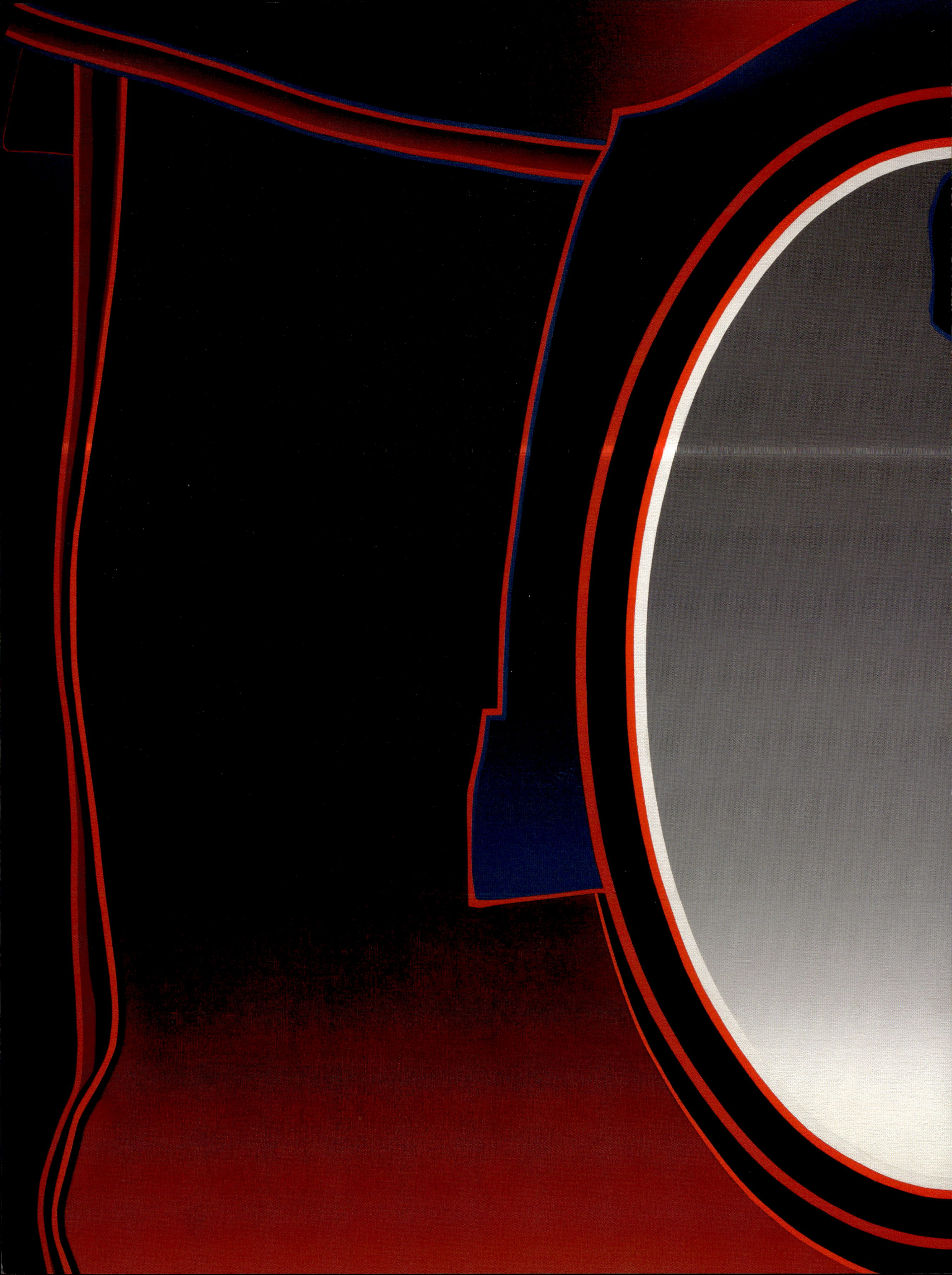

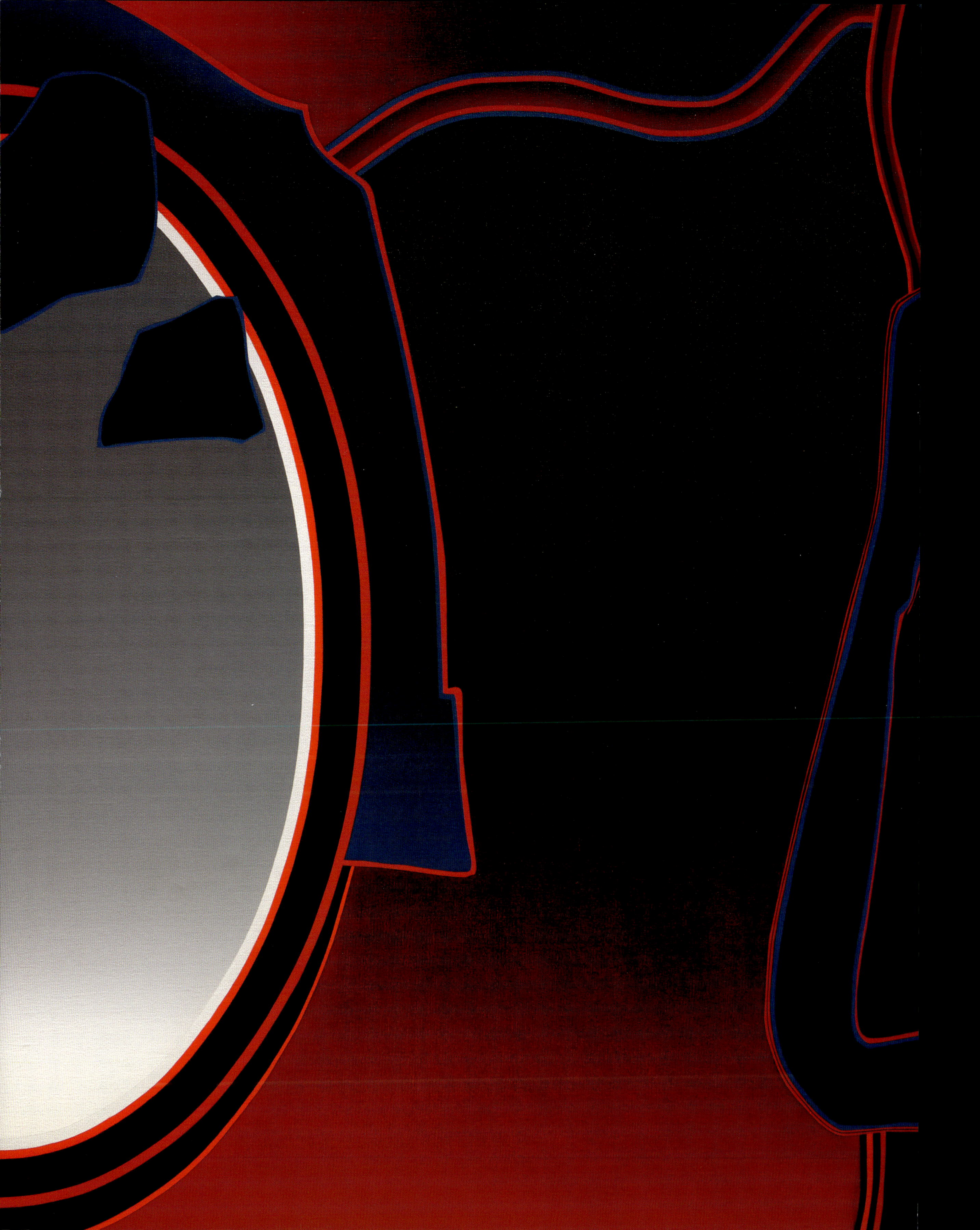

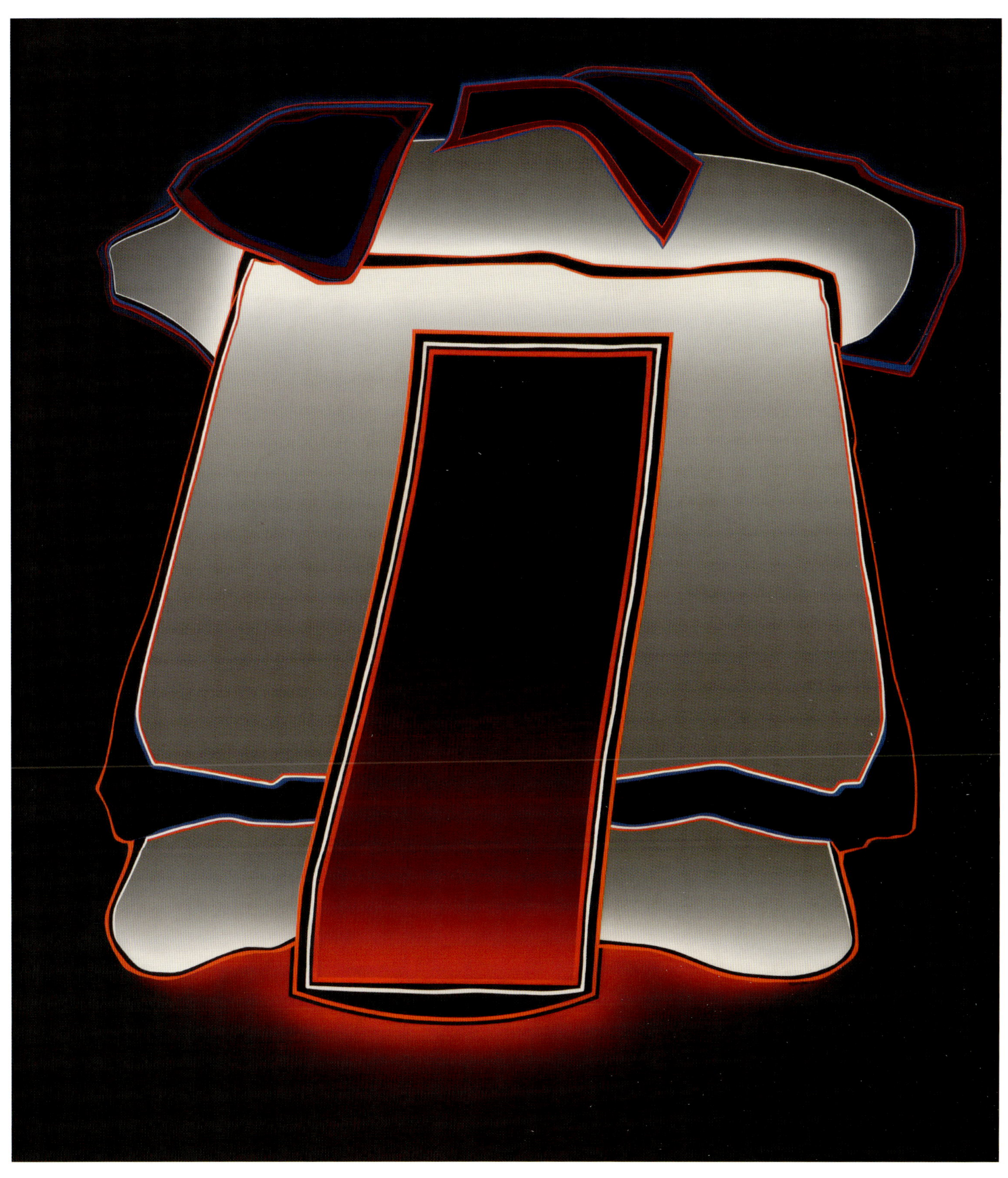

Regent, 1971. Oil on linen, 56 × 50 in. (142 × 127 cm)
Collection of John Raimondi, Palm Beach Gardens, Florida

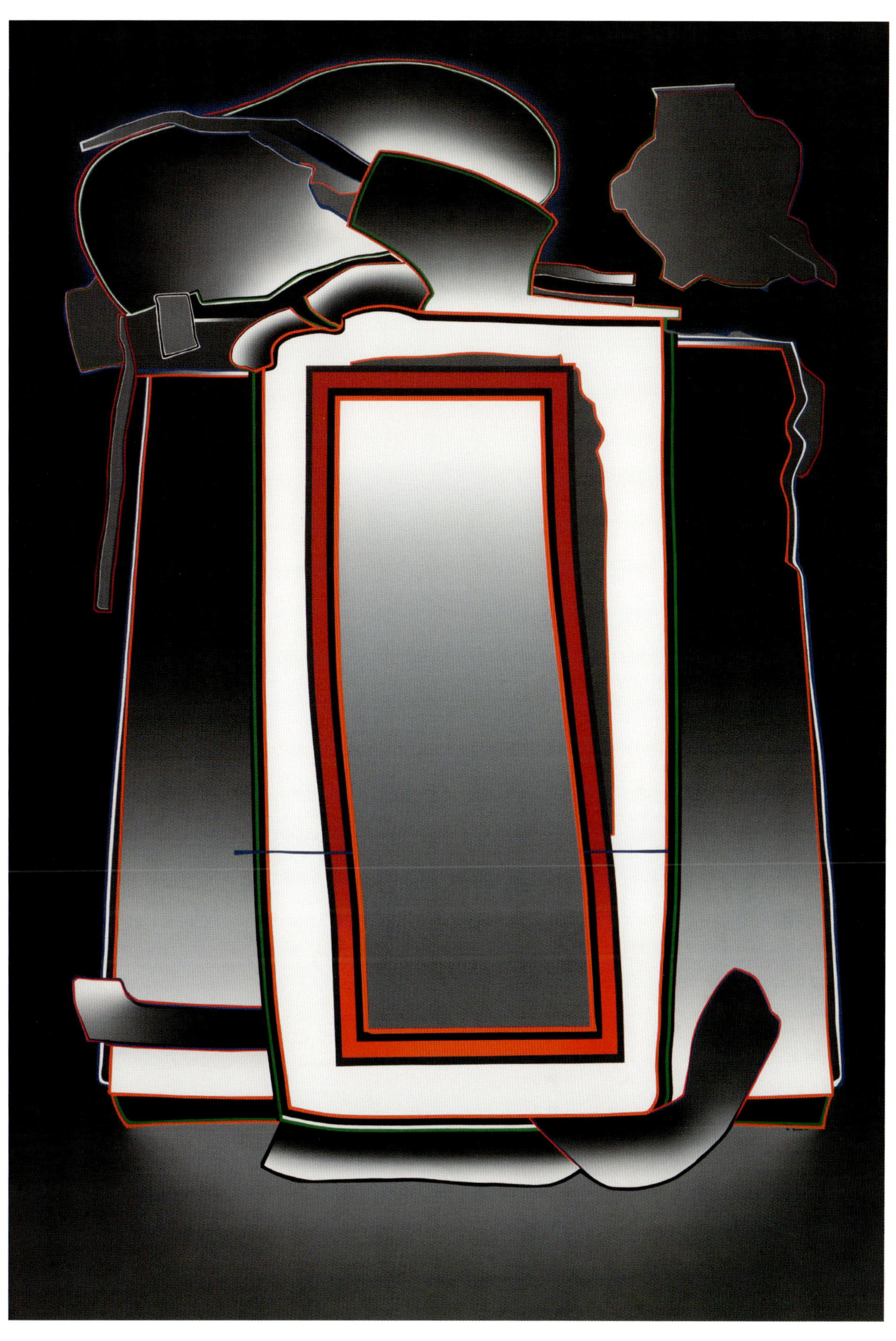

Essex, 1972. Oil on linen, 95 × 66 in. (241.3 × 167.6 cm)
Collection of Gaby and Wilhelm Schürmann, Herzogenrath, Germany

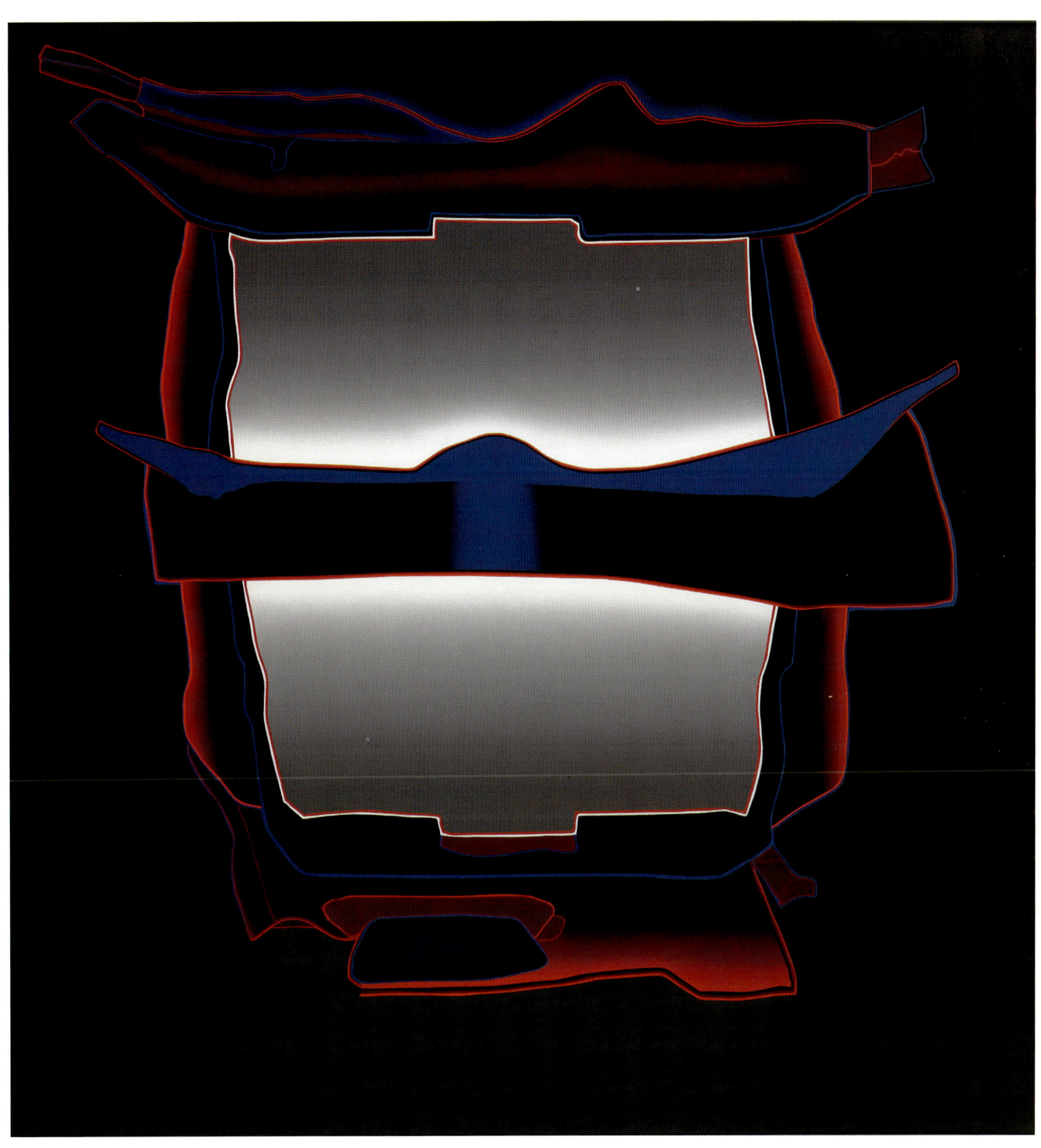

Saratoga, 1972. Oil on linen, 91 × 87 in. (231 × 221 cm)
The Alfond Collection of Contemporary Art, Rollins Museum of Art, Winter Park, Florida

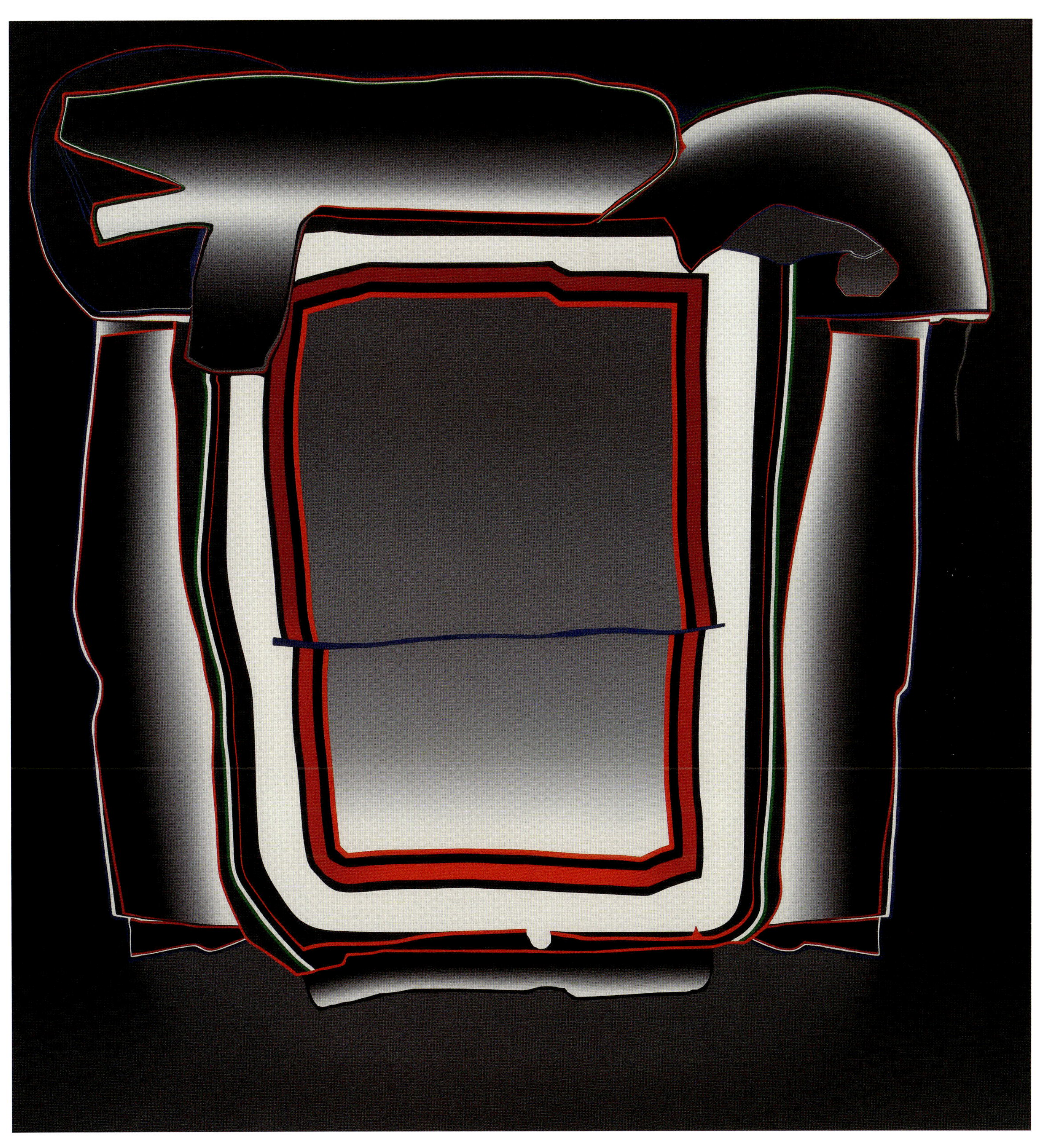

Trent, 1973. Oil on canvas, 78 × 74 in. (198 × 188 cm)
Collection of Timothy C. Headington

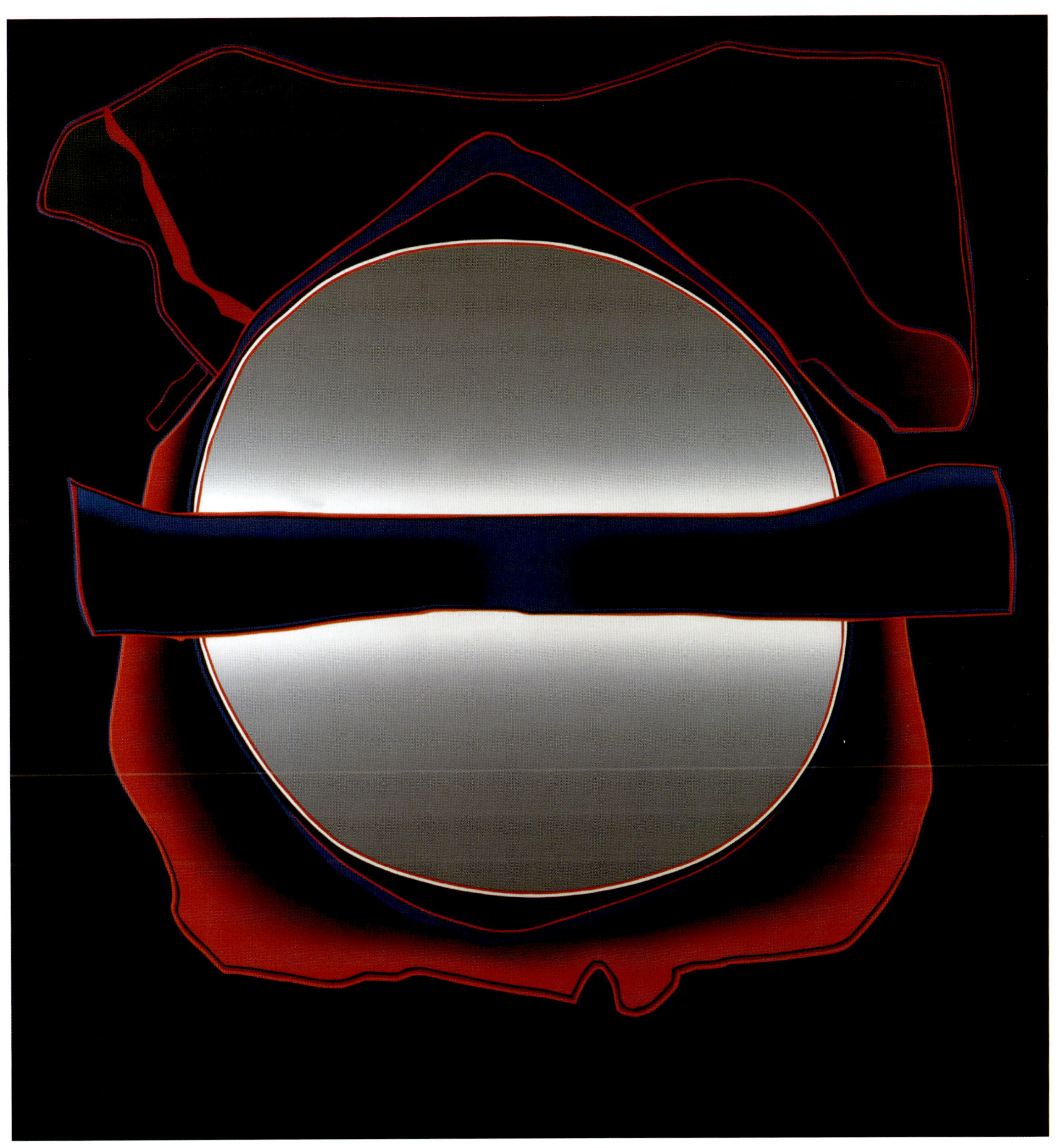

Chatham, 1973. Oil on canvas, 78 × 74 in. (198.1 × 188 cm)
Toledo Museum of Art, Ohio. National Endowment for the Arts Purchase Plan Program and an anonymous donor

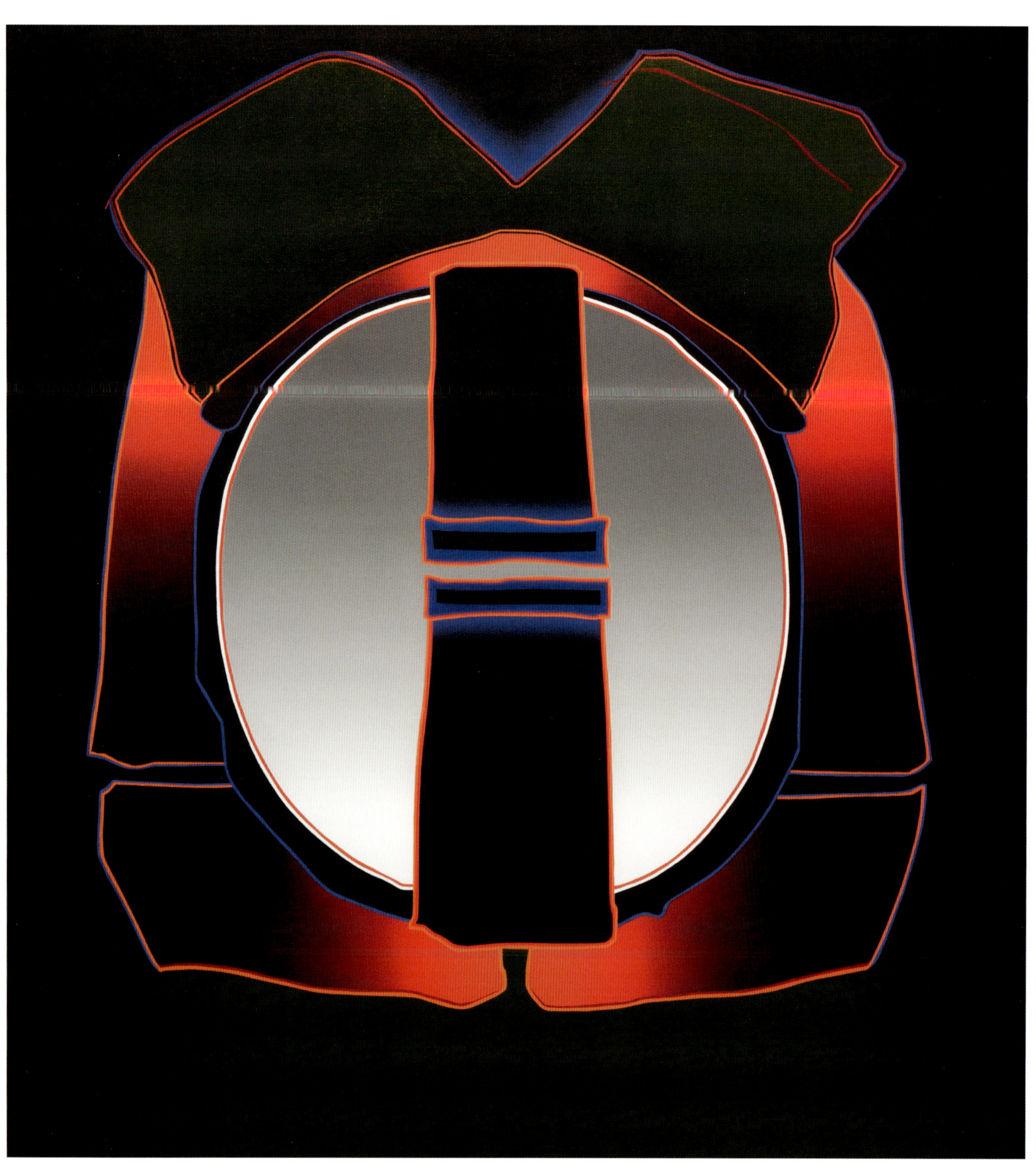

Dalton, 1974. Oil on canvas, 56 × 52 in. (142.2 × 132.1 cm)
Carnegie Museum of Art, Pittsburgh, Pennsylvania. Gift of Michael and Sherle Berger

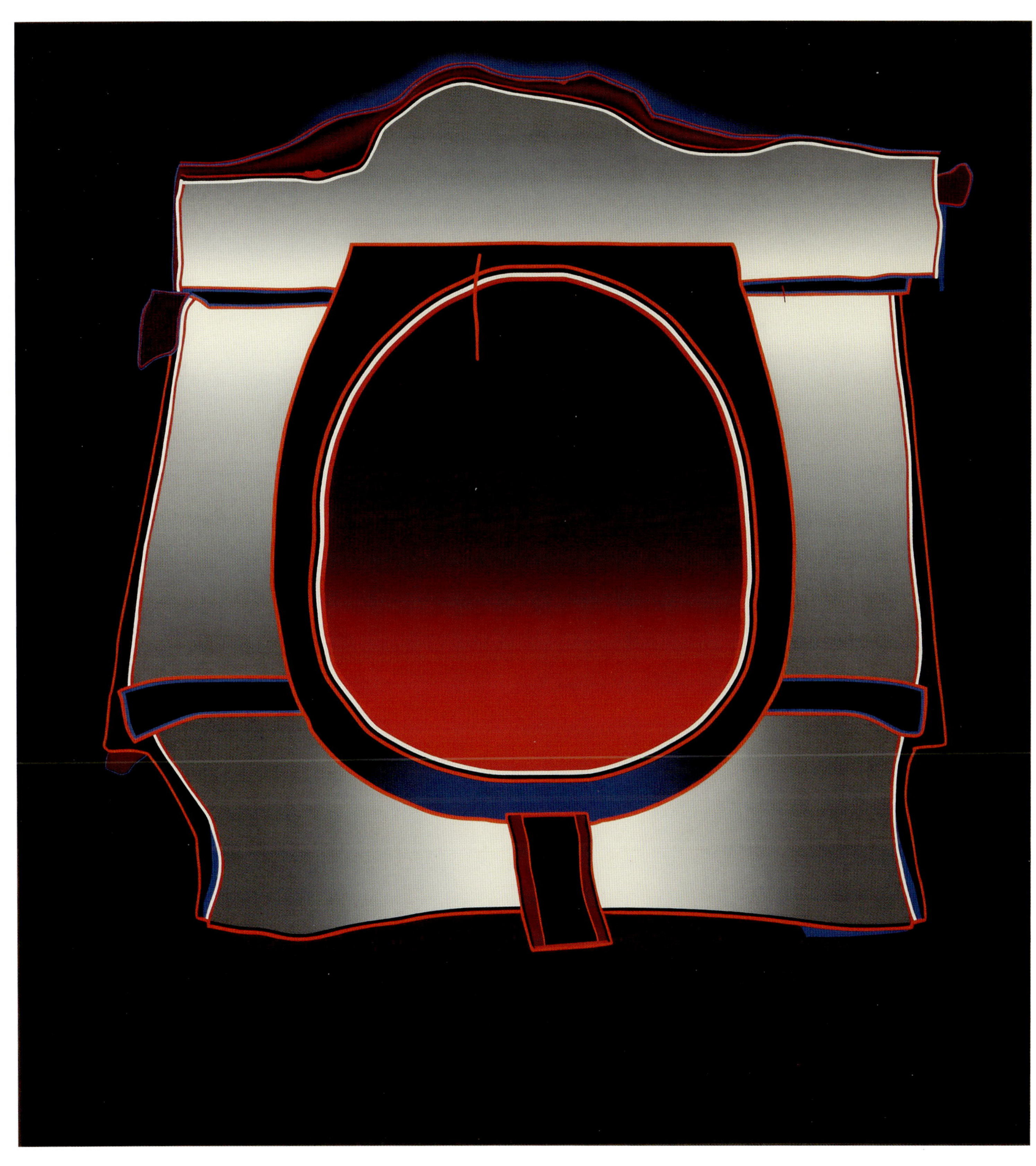

Elyria, 1975. Oil on canvas, 56 × 52 in. (142.2 × 132 cm)
Private collection

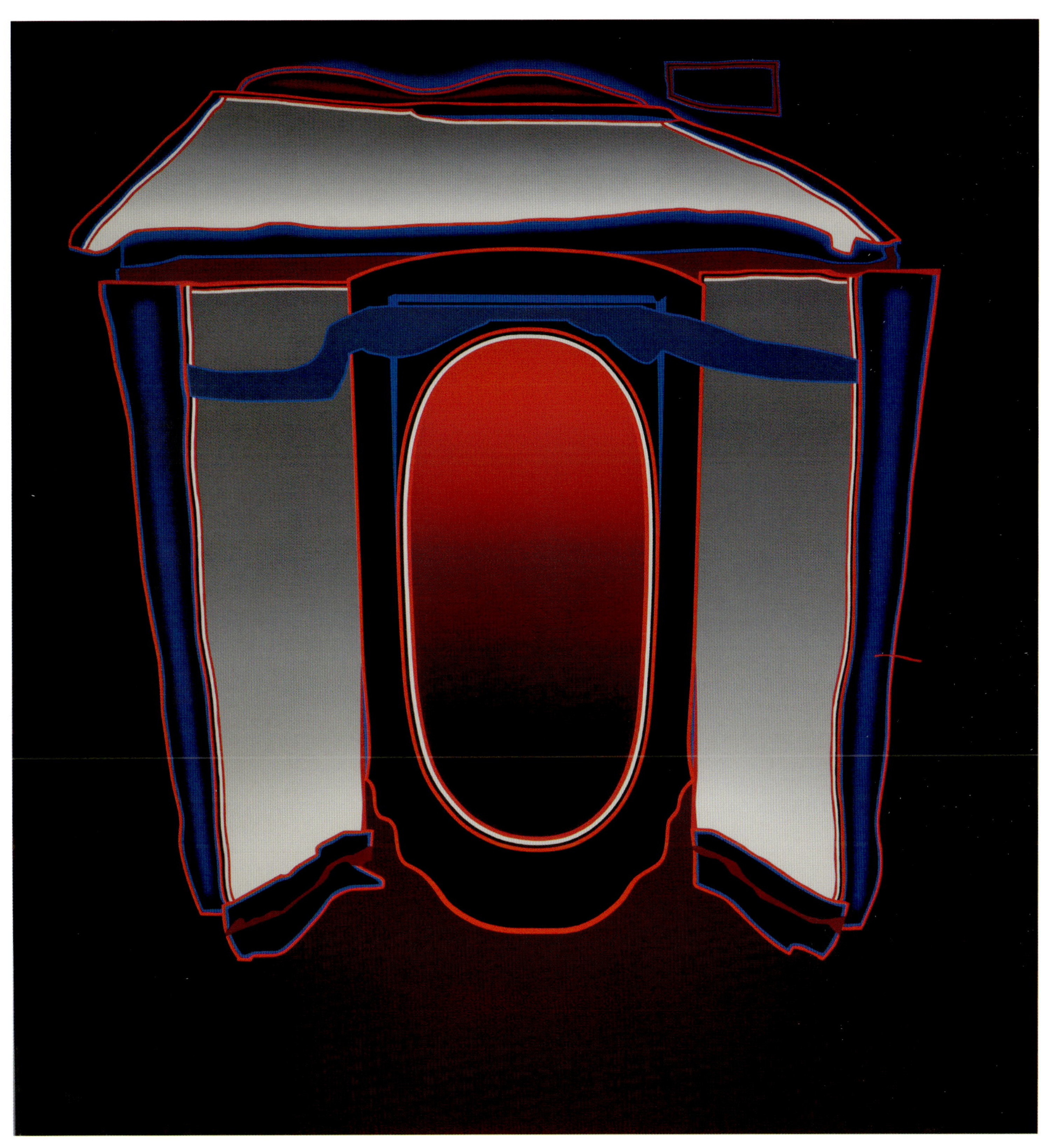

Dover, 1975. Oil on canvas, 78 × 74 in. (198 × 188 cm)
Phoenix Art Museum, Arizona. Gift of Mrs. Leonard M. Haddad

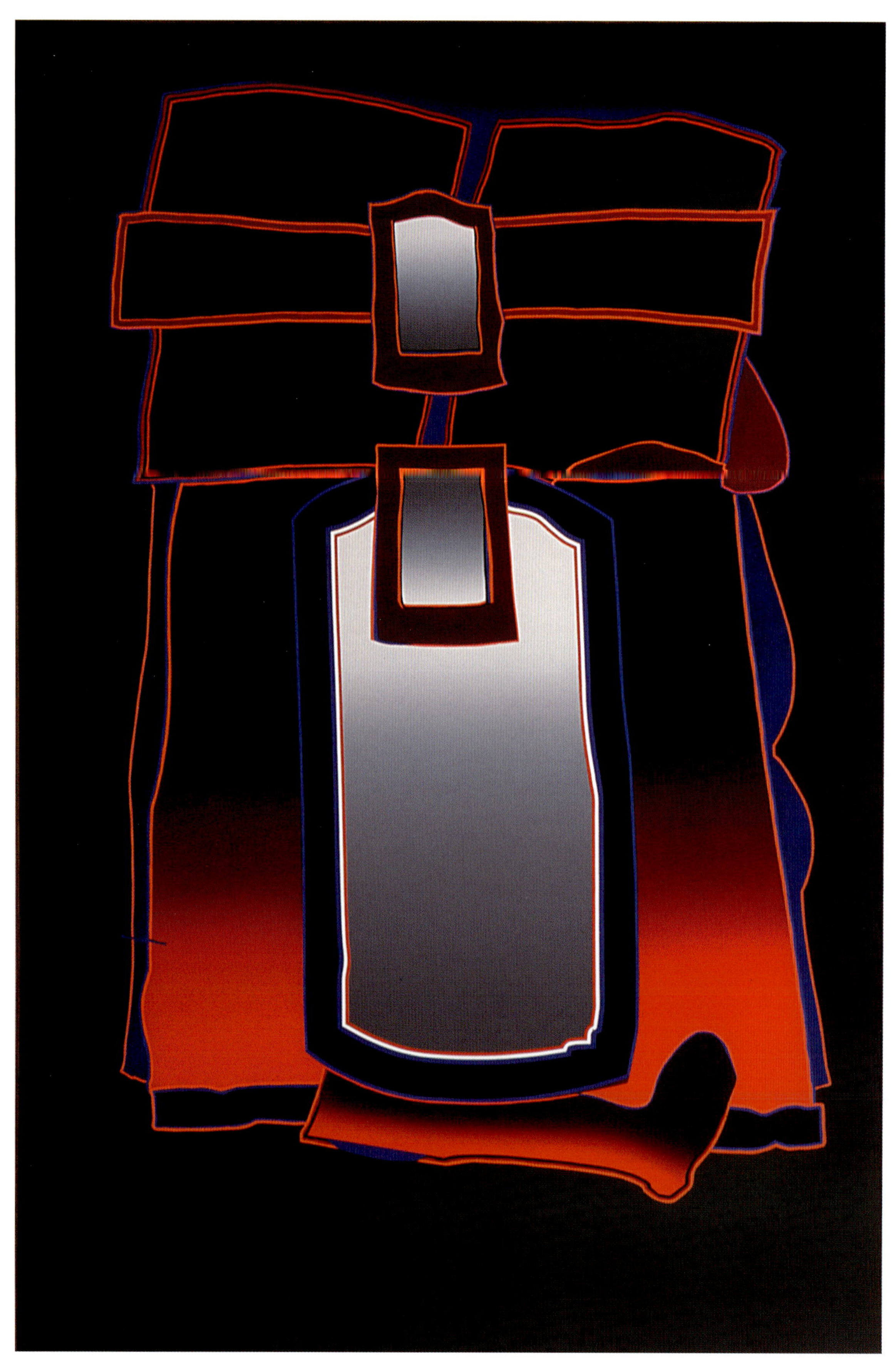

Eton, 1977. Oil on canvas, $74\frac{1}{2} \times 50\frac{1}{2}$ in. (189 × 128 cm)
CU Art Museum, University of Colorado Boulder. Gift of Mr. and Mrs. Cecil M. Hernandez

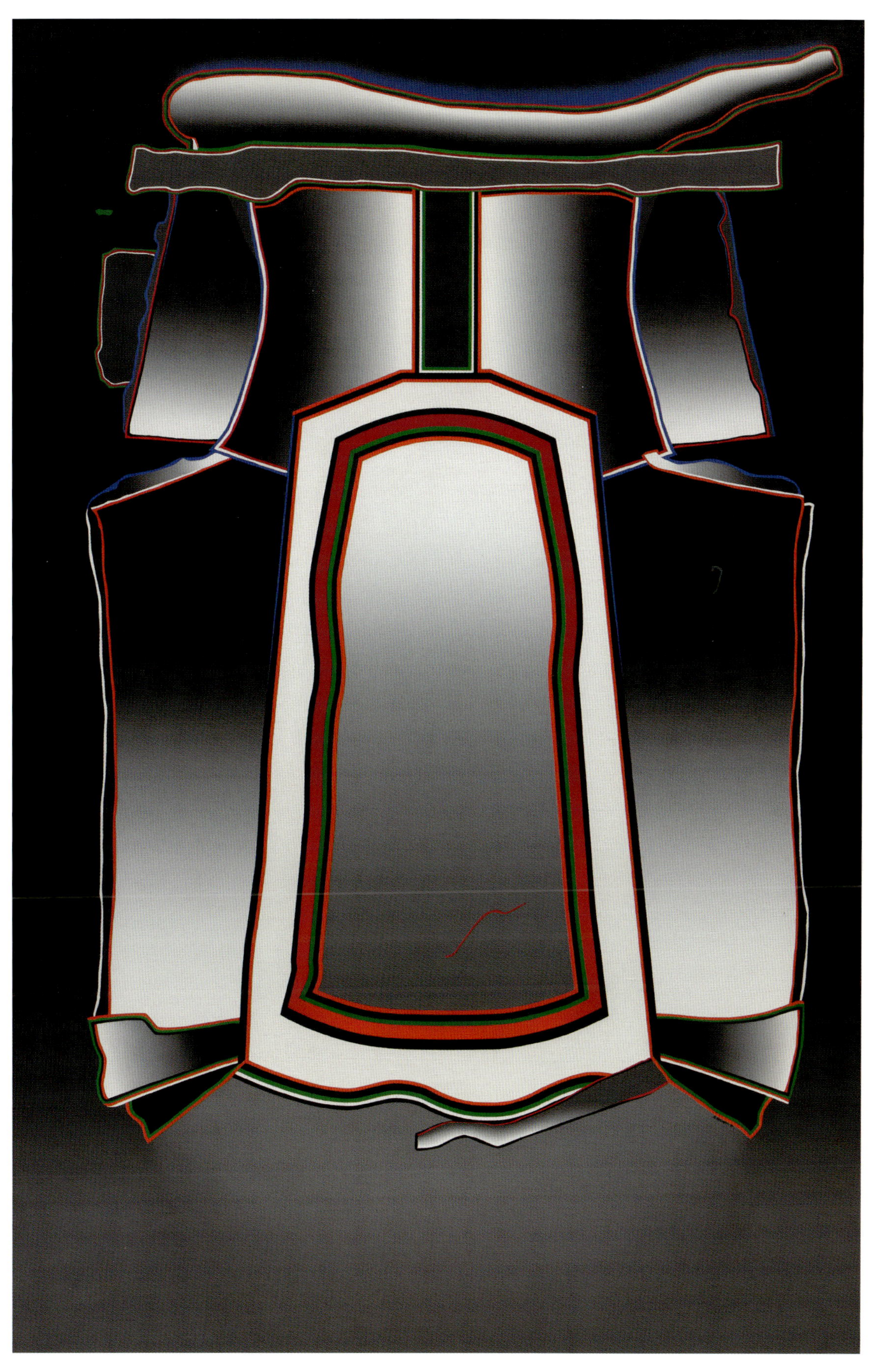

Sussex, 1976. Oil on canvas, 75 1/2 × 49 1/2 in. (192 × 126 cm)
Private collection

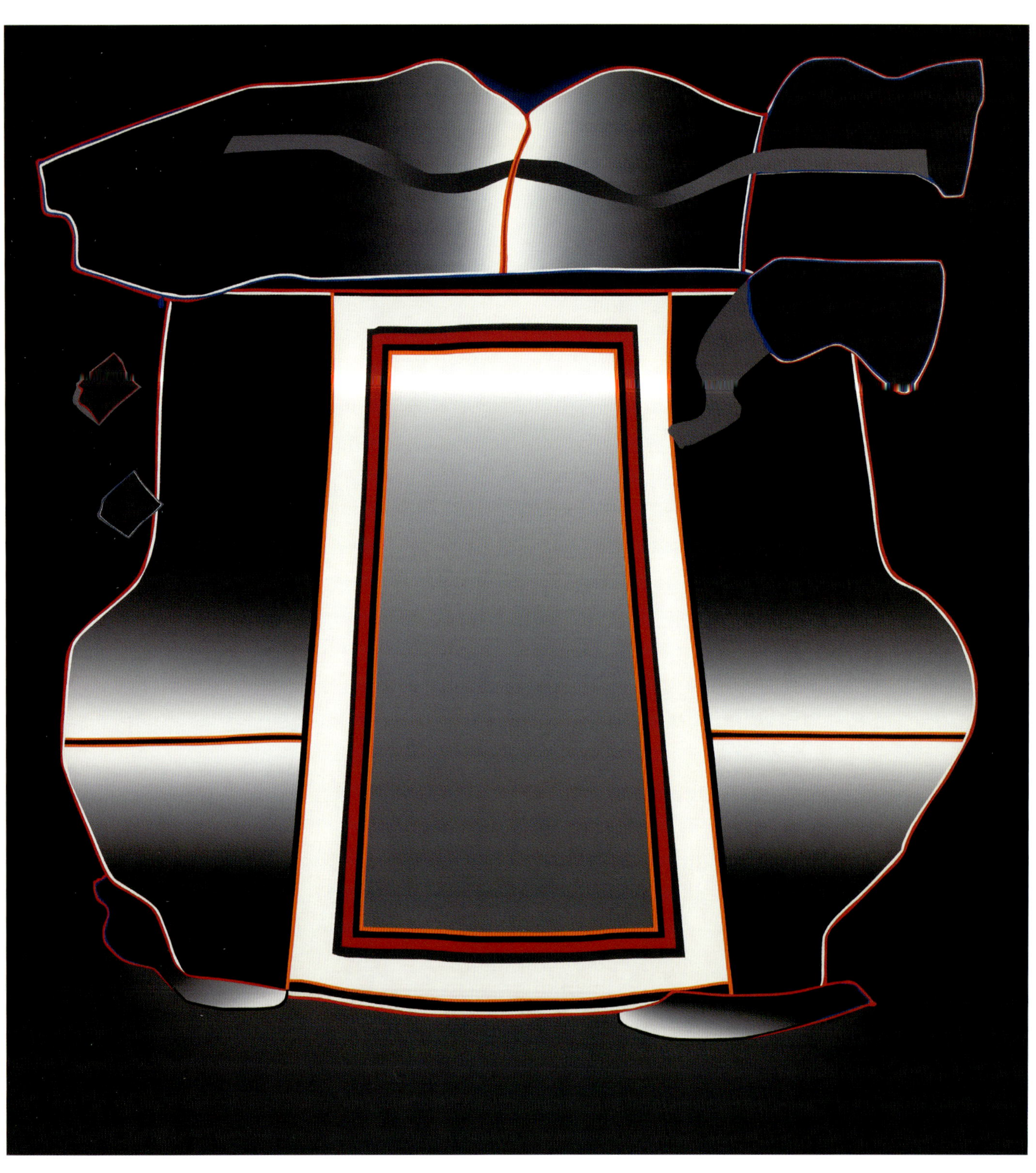

Aldwych, 1973. Oil on canvas, 56 × 52 in. (142.2 × 132.1 cm)
Private collection

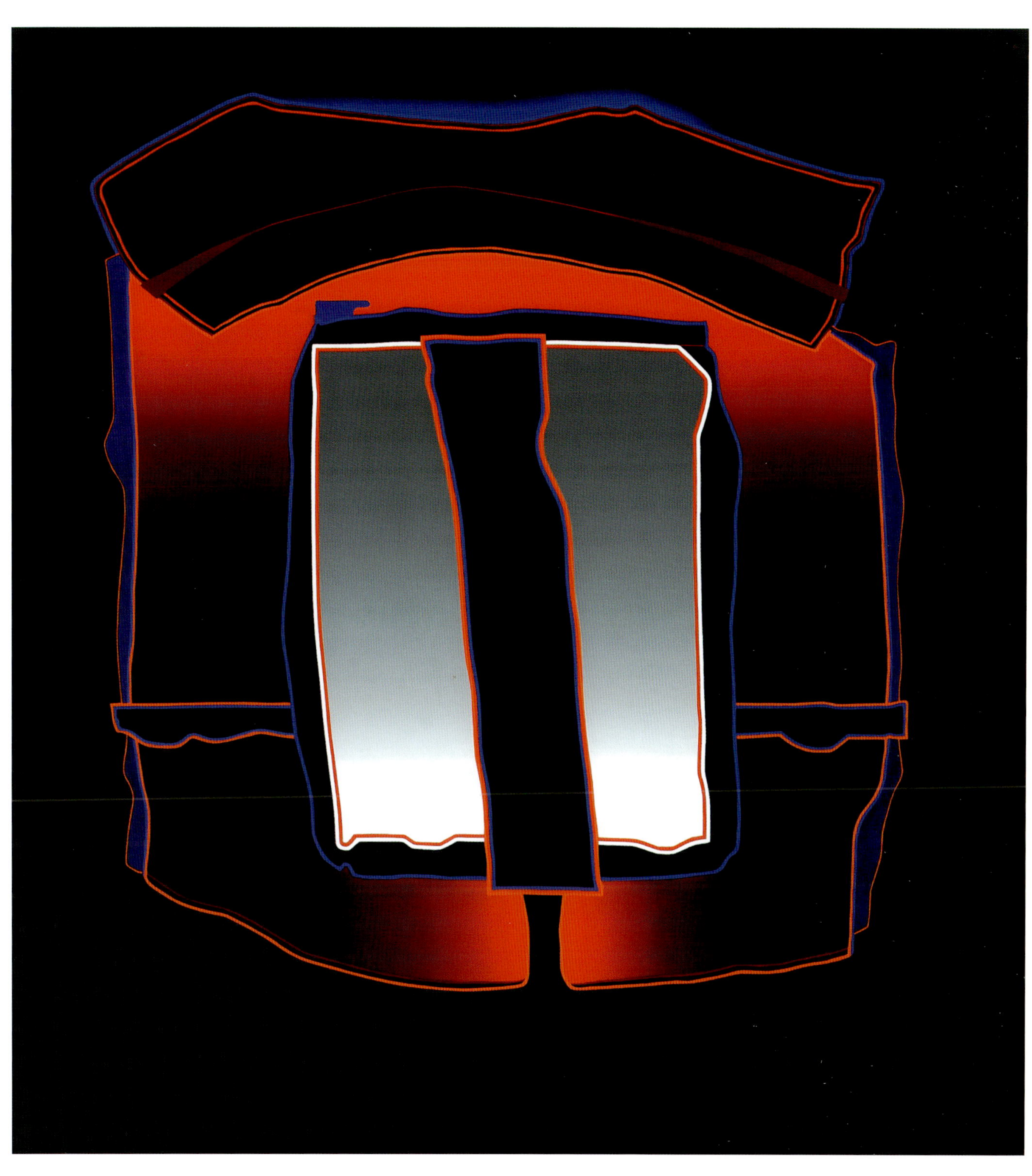

Rashin, 1976. Oil on canvas, 56 × 52 in. (142.2 × 132.1 cm)
Private collection

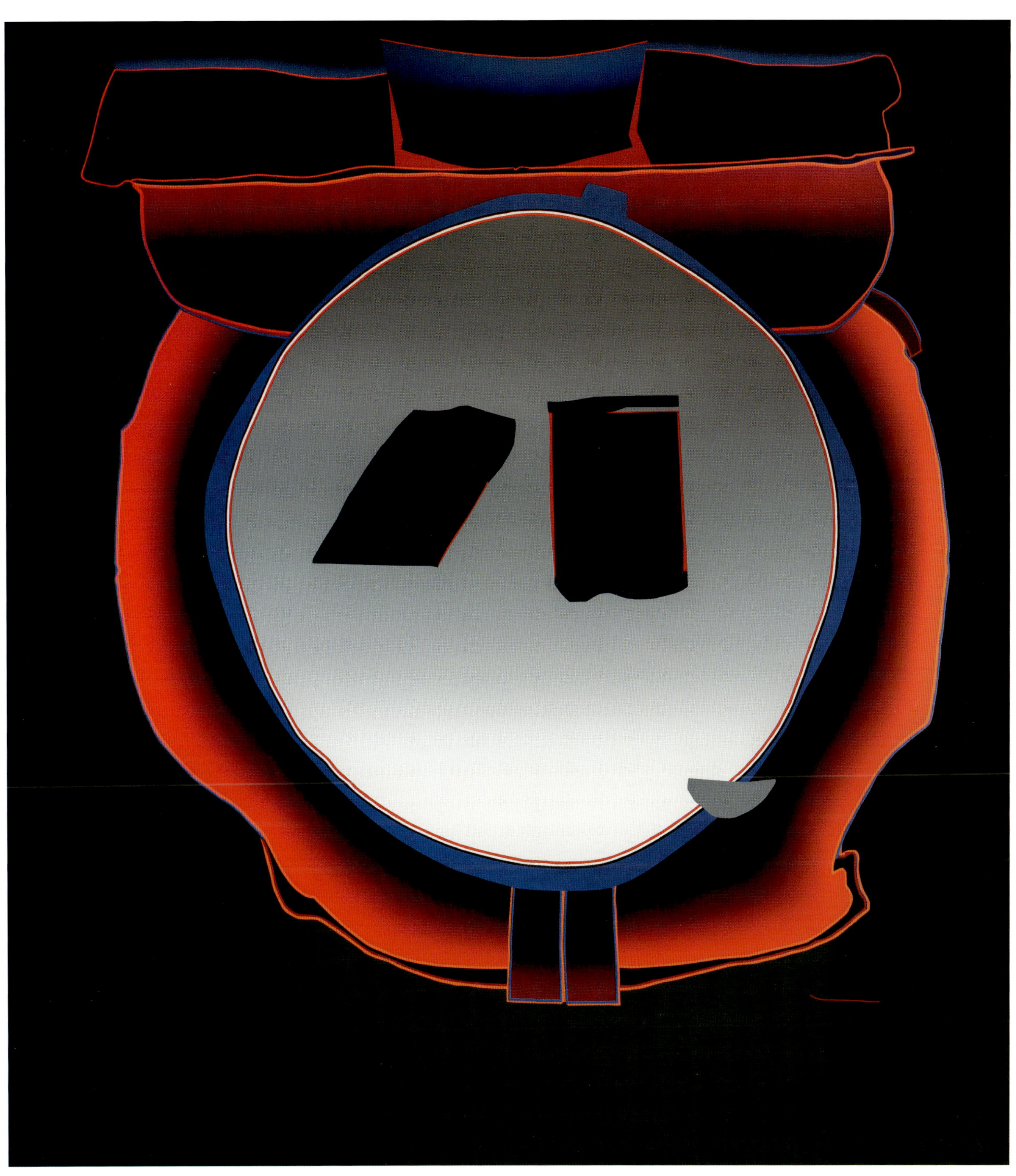

Omina, 1978. Oil on canvas, 74 × 67 in. (188 × 170 cm)
San Antonio Museum of Art, Texas. Gift of the Deborah Remington Charitable Trust for the Visual Arts

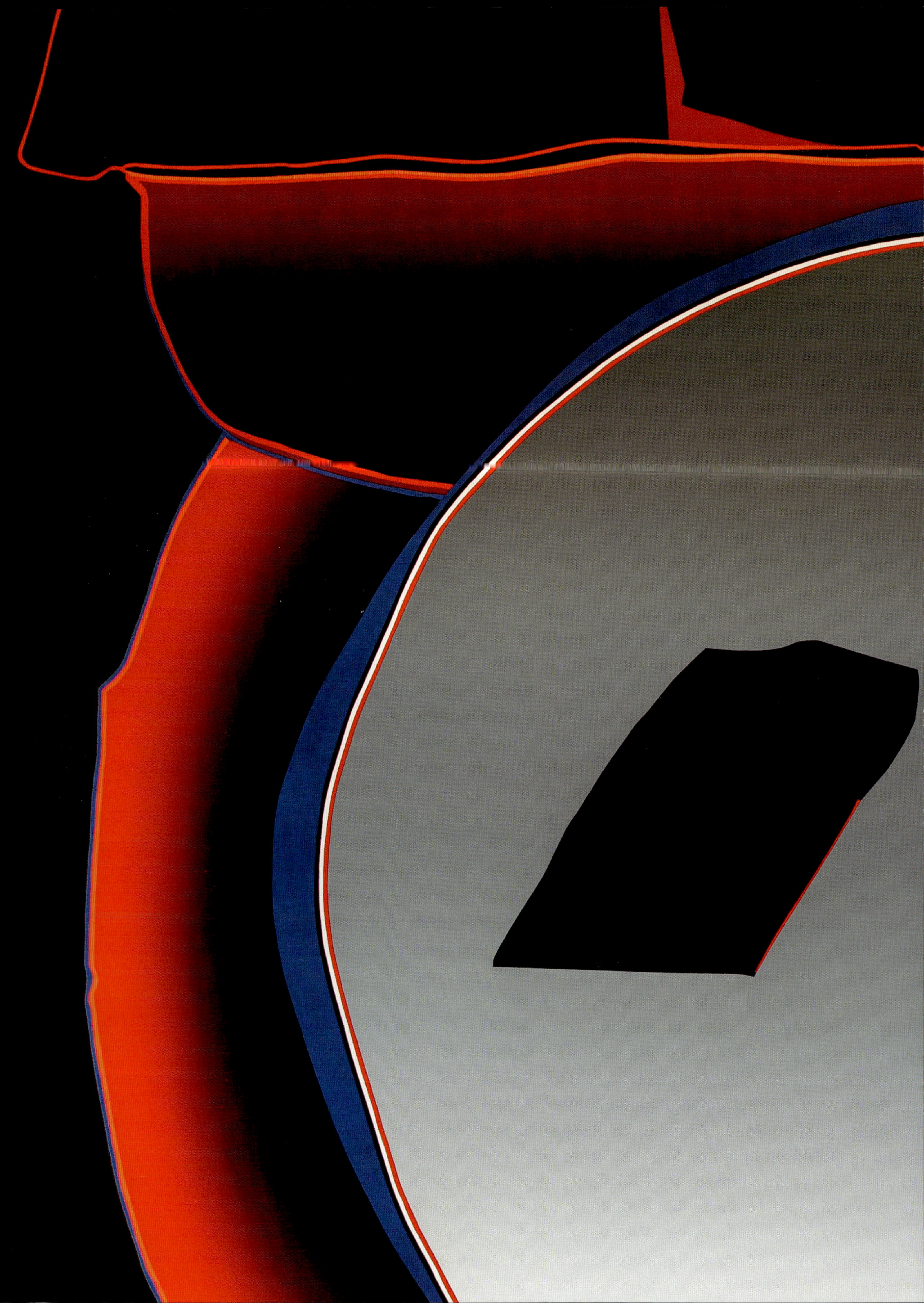

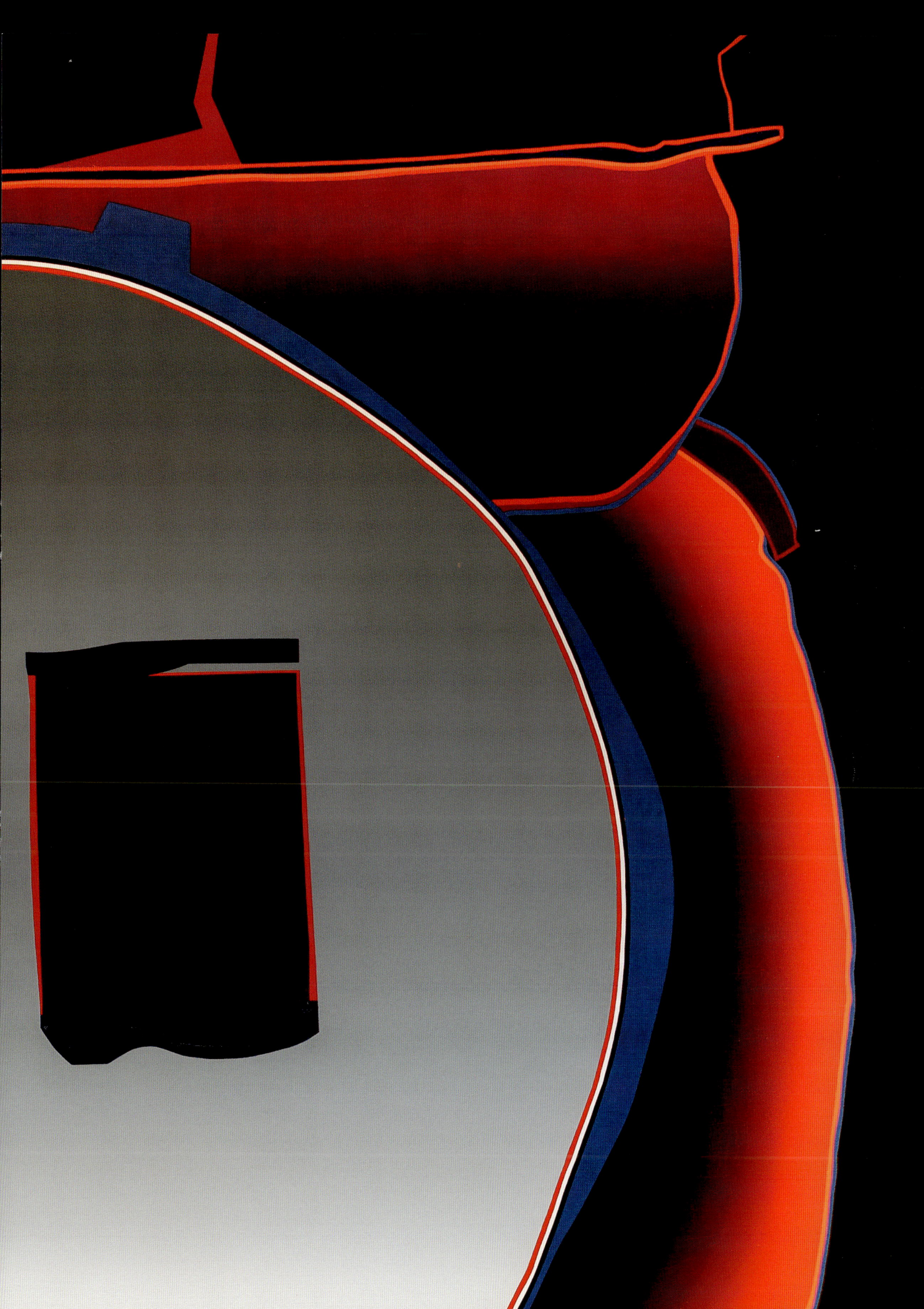

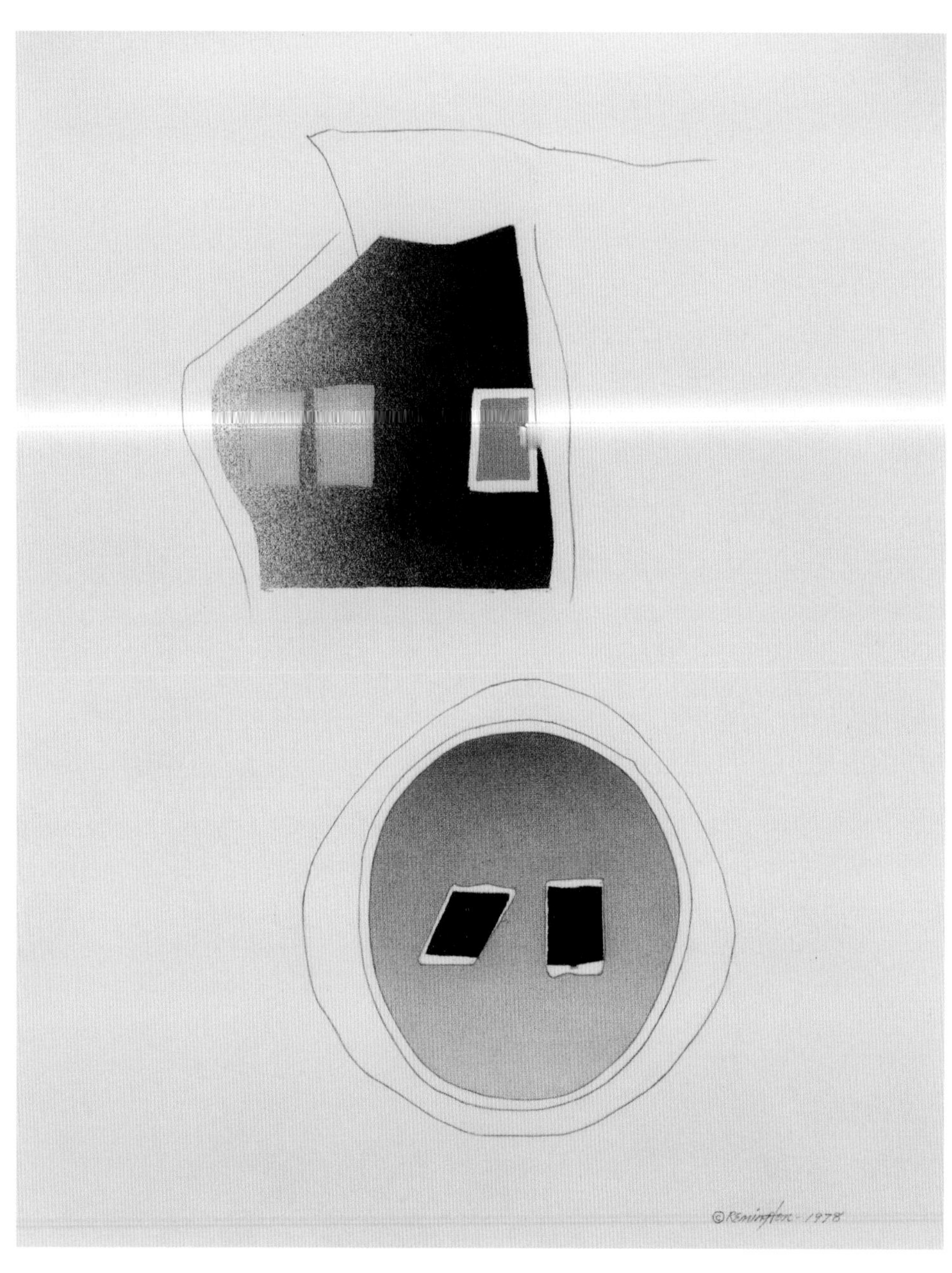

Trace Series 1, 1978. Spray paint and graphite on paper, 14 × 11 in. (35.6 × 27.9 cm)
Deborah Remington Charitable Trust for the Visual Arts

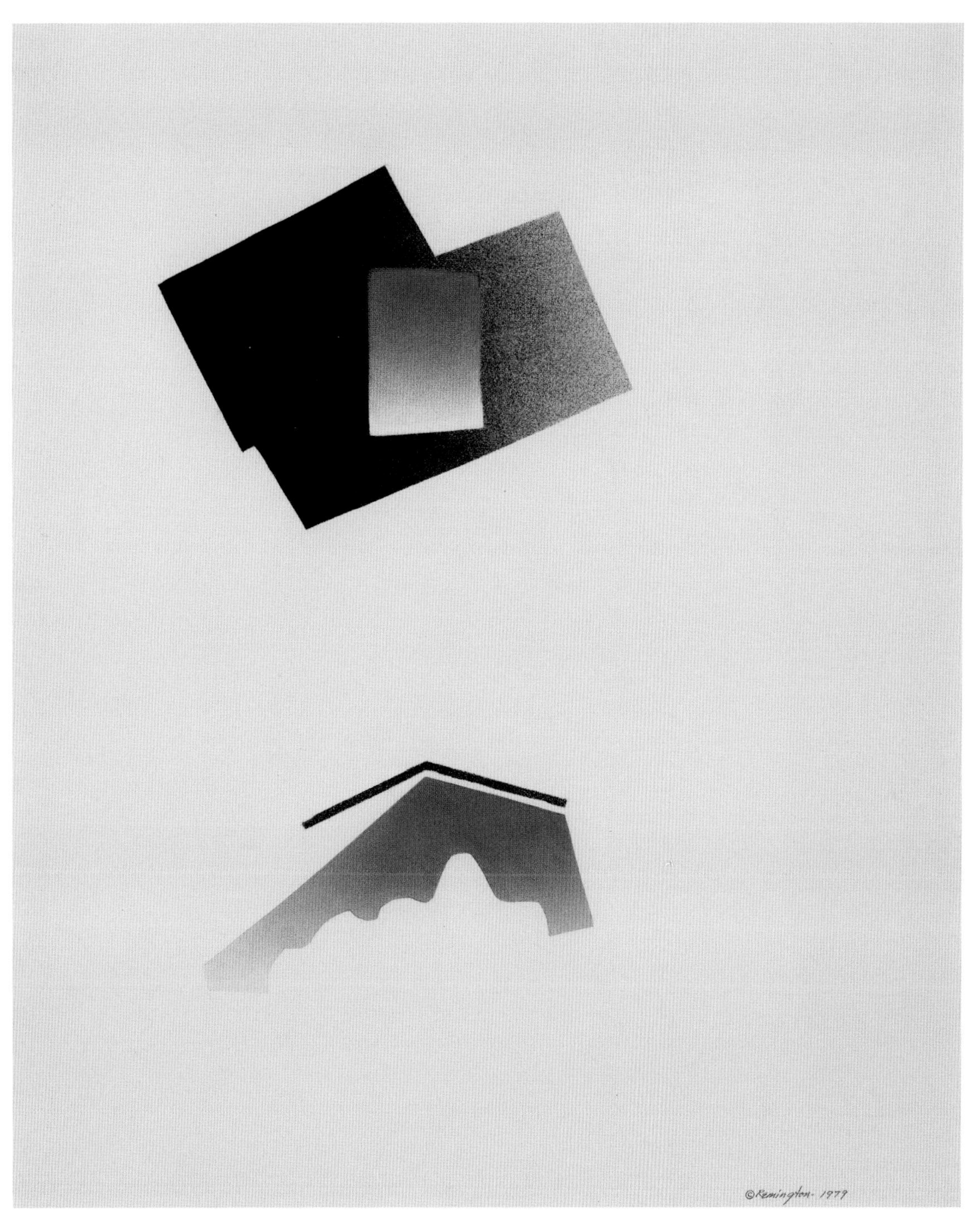

Trace Series 8 (1), 1979. Spray paint and graphite on paper, 17 1/8 × 14 in. (43.5 × 35.6 cm)
Whitney Museum of American Art, New York. Gift of the Deborah Remington Charitable Trust for the Visual Arts

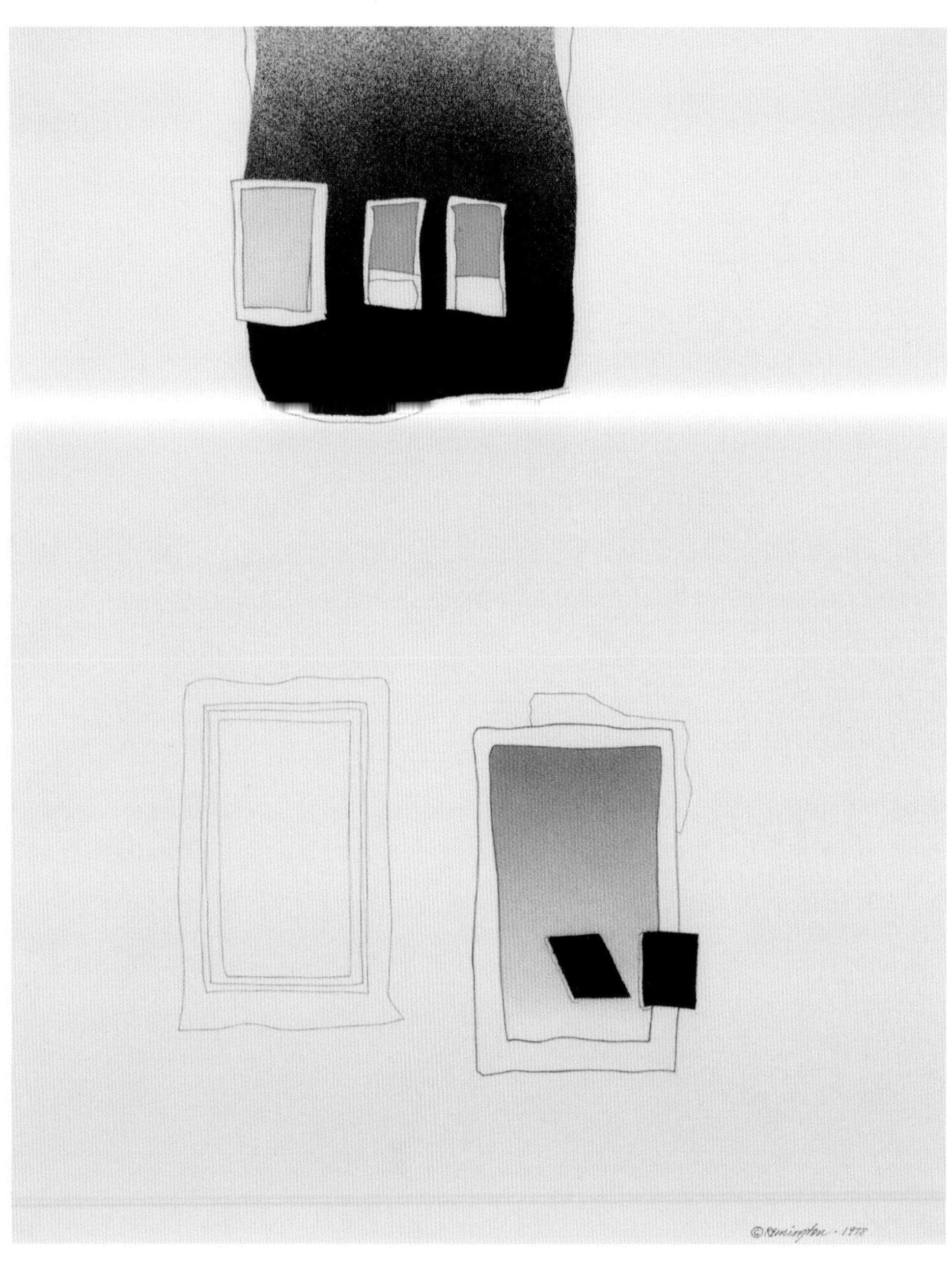

Trace Series 3, 1978. Spray paint and graphite on paper, 14 × 11 in. (35.6 × 27.9 cm)
Collection of Mark Rosman

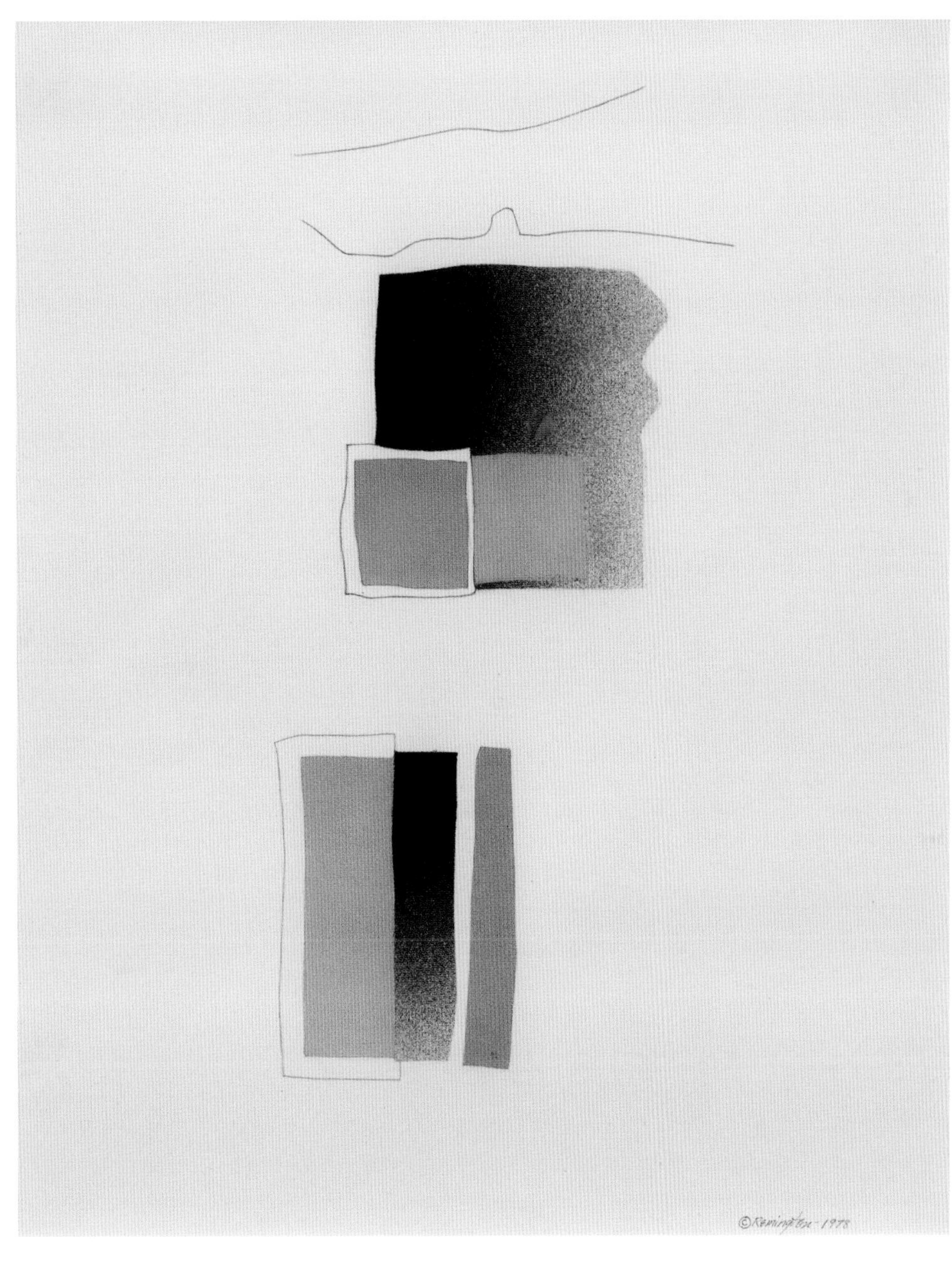

Trace Series 4, 1978. Spray paint and graphite on paper, 14 × 11 in. (35.6 × 27.9 cm)
Deborah Remington Charitable Trust for the Visual Arts

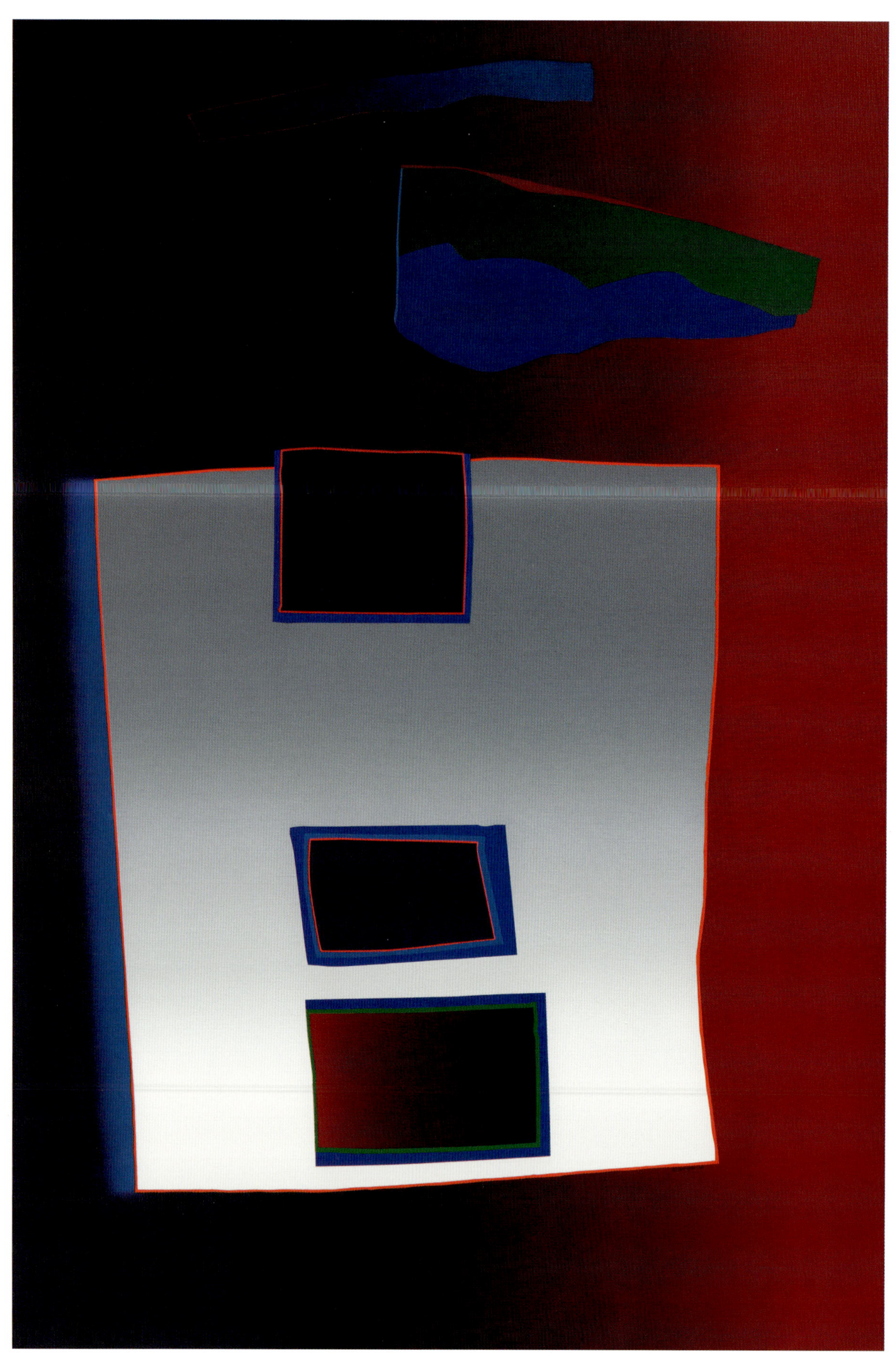

Auriga, 1980. Oil on canvas, 74 × 50 in. (188 × 127 cm)
Private collection

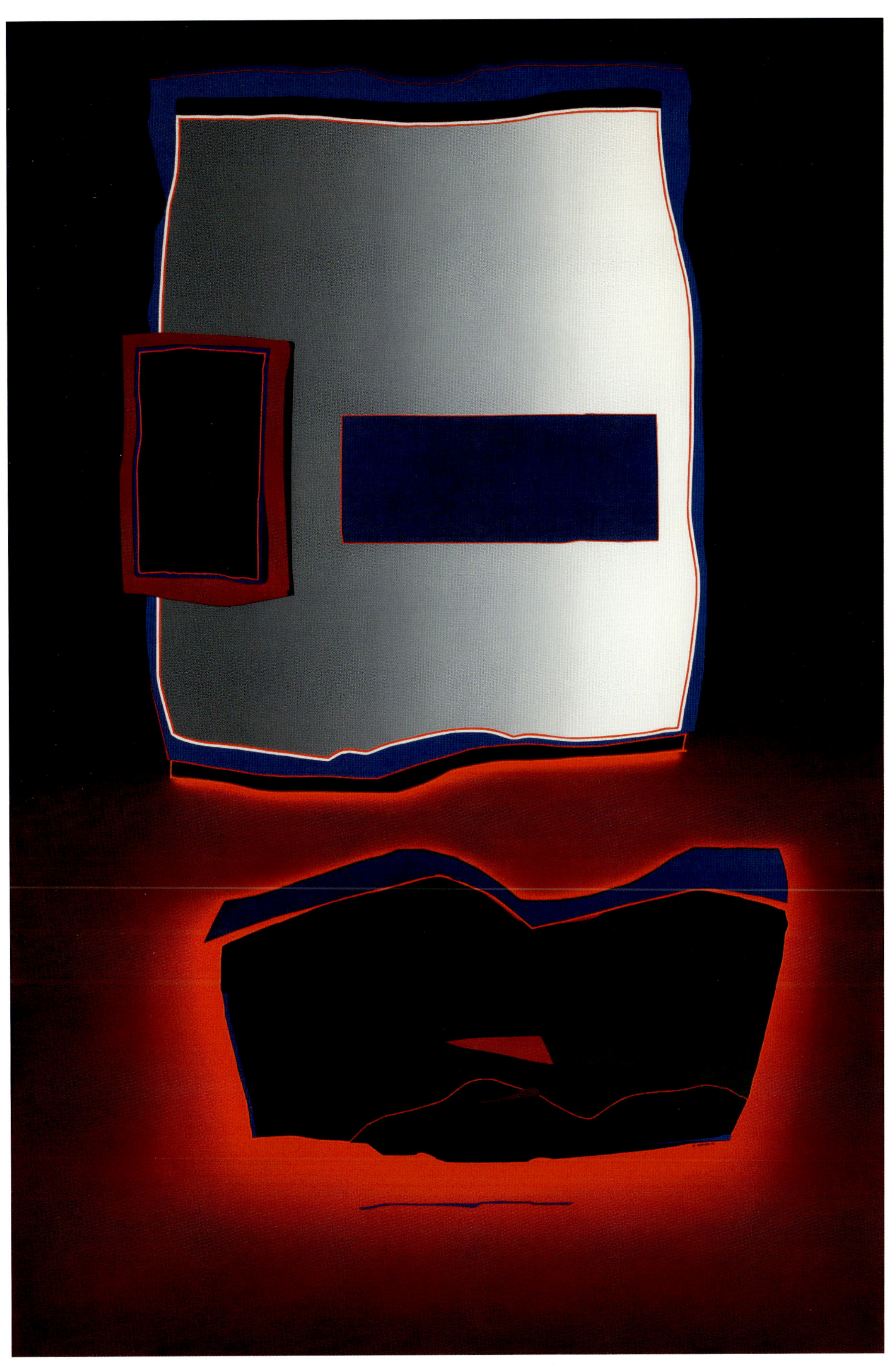

Aryx, 1982. Oil on canvas, 74 × 50 in. (188 × 127 cm)
Worcester Art Museum, Massachusetts. Gift of Mr. and Mrs. William Block

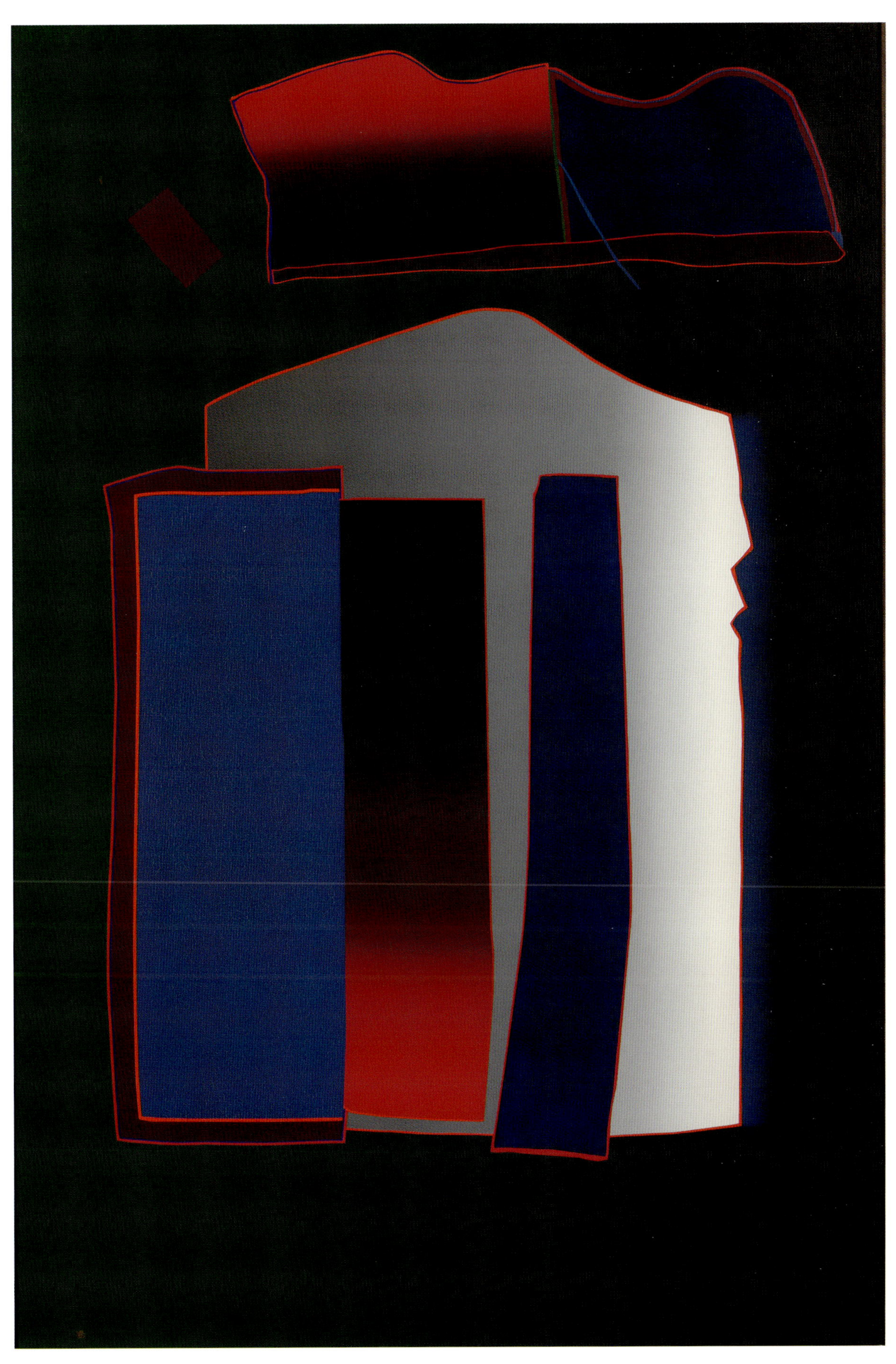

Kamerun, 1979. Oil on canvas, 74 × 50 in. (188 × 127 cm)
National Gallery of Art, Washington, D.C. Pepita Milmore Memorial Fund and
Gift of Funds from Lio Malca, Isaac Malca, Eric Gertler, and Brett Shaheen

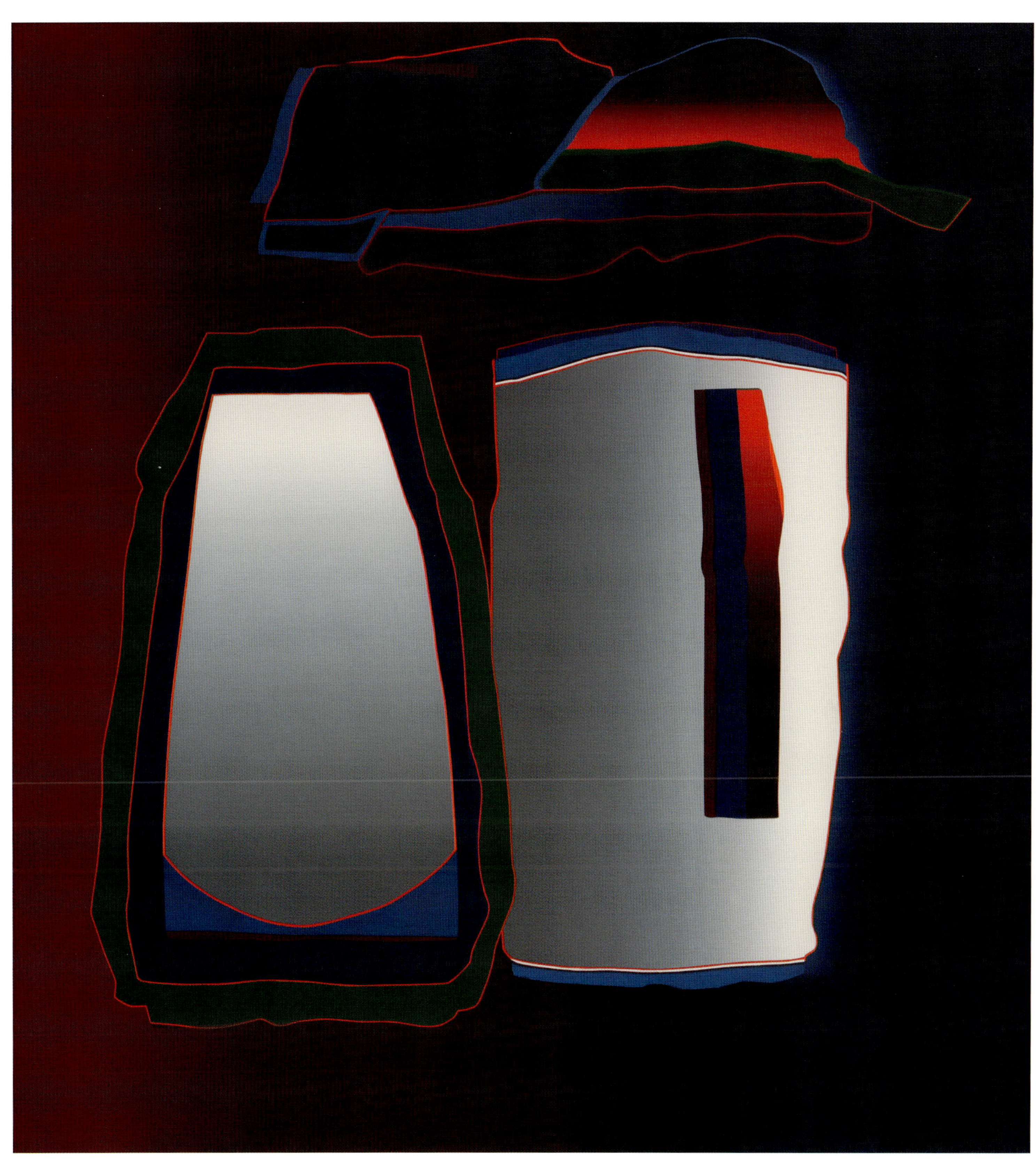

Elatea, 1981. Oil on canvas, 56 × 52 in. (142.2 × 132.1 cm)
Collection of Gaby and Wilhelm Schürmann, Herzogenrath, Germany

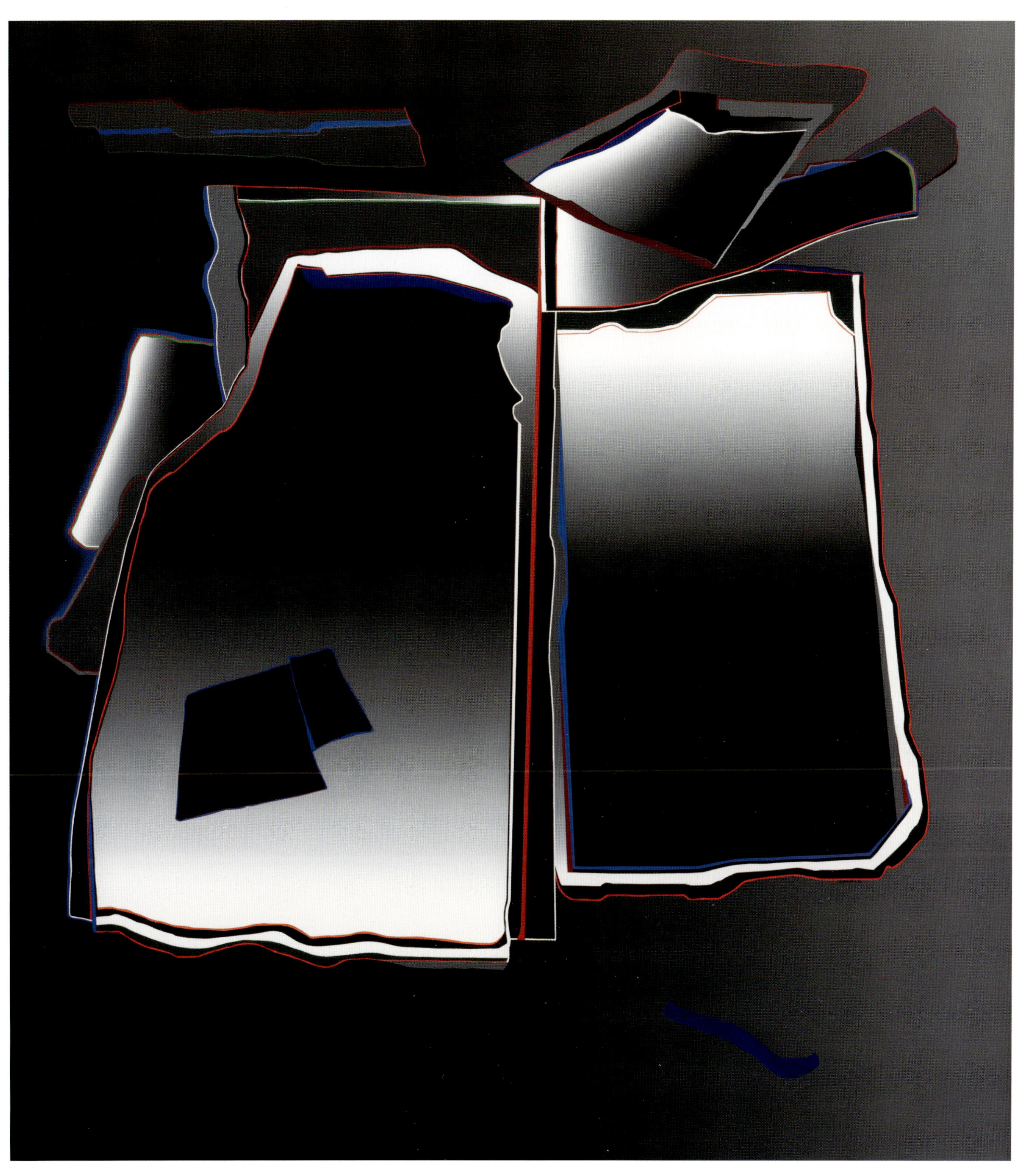

Zanthus, 1983. Oil on canvas, 74 × 67 in. (188 × 170.2 cm)
Private collection

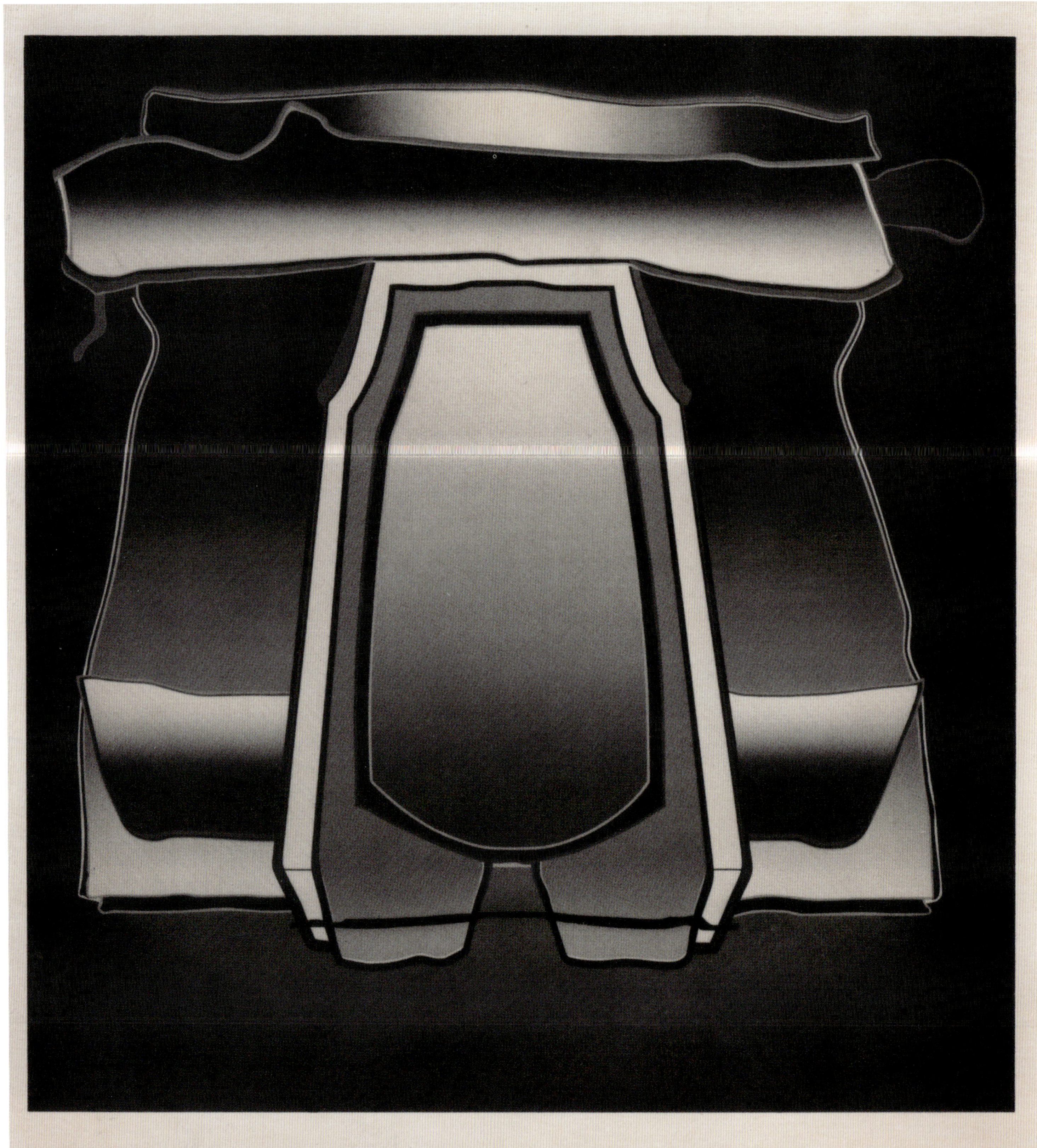
Deborah Remington September 7 through September 26, 1974
Bykert Gallery 24 East 81/New York

Deborah Remington, Cutting-Edge Artist

ANNA KATZ

Beginning in the 1960s in San Francisco and then moving to New York, Deborah Remington made abstract paintings, the place of which in art history has come to be defined by their lack of place. Having cycled through various modes of Abstract Expressionist painting in the course of her formal art education in the 1950s and having cultivated her draftsmanship through independent study of Japanese calligraphy during extensive travels in Japan and Asia, Remington produced her signature works by 1964: oil paintings typically described by the hard edges and polysemous imagery of a central, frontal, and bilaterally symmetrical form—both crustacean and grille, hot rod car and kimono, medieval heraldry and spaceship, cyborg and fossil—suspended in an indeterminate and enigmatic spatial field. The ambiguity, even mystery, of imagery is matched only by the precision of technique manifested in her paintings' polished surfaces; exacting gradients; crisp lines; and restricted palette of black, white, a range of smokey and silvery grays deployed tonally, and saturated reds, oranges, greens, and blues. She would develop these elements for the next two decades.

Haddonfield (1965; **PAGE 91**) is a stellar, if frequently cited, example in part because it changed Remington's career. Upon its acquisition by the Whitney Museum of American Art in 1966, the calls from art dealers rolled in and Remington's phone "rang constantly for six weeks," and soon she was represented by Bykert Gallery in New York.[1] Scaled to the body at 74 1⁄8 by 69 inches, the painting is nearly square, much as the imposing composition is nearly symmetrical. Its forms fold and unfurl around a central metallic cone that is flanked by flat stripes of blue. The cone gapes open at the bottom, where it is ringed by a red too orange to be bloody and pulled apart by two black tabs. Within this nonsensical orifice or aperture, a form recalling a pelvis doubles back on itself; that which evokes cold metal in the cone here suggests the colorless mechanical vision of an X-ray machine. At the top and sides of this cone, areas of jagged-edged, paper-thin layered forms outlined in elegant fine strips of blue, red, and green are treated with tonal gradations of silvery grays that shine like chrome steel. While there is a sense of revelation—of layers scraped away, corners pulled up, surfaces punctured—there is little sense of motion or any principles of physics, really, because the form is suspended, looming and still, in a nondescript field of deep black. A light, apparently located behind this form, shines against the black, but it exposes nothing, only rendering the bottom portion of the canvas gray.

Exhibition poster for *Deborah Remington*, Bykert Gallery, New York, 1974

What kind of strange, self-assured painting is this? In keeping with modernist protocols, *Haddonfield* is abstract, flat, immediate, and stripped down to a handful of elements, yet it is not an all-over composition nor is it gestural or necessarily self-referential; even more incriminating, it traffics in illusionism. In fact, it is a kind of sampler of the tricks of illusionism, and in the manner of Op art, *Haddonfield* deploys geometric forms to optical effect. Still, the experience is not primarily retinal, given the rich range of visual references and social associations the work summons. Similar to realist painting, *Haddonfield* operates as a picture—a portrait or still life perhaps—however, not a humanist window onto the world. Its composition shares the hard edges of Minimalist painting, which likewise eschewed the presence of the hand by eliminating brushstrokes, but Remington's forms are irregular in shape and illogical in conception. Indeed, there is little literalism or object-ness here; rather Remington's central forms are bathed in an auratic glow suggestive of narrative or metaphor. *Haddonfield* contains some of Pop art's slickness and its reliance on the icon but lacks Pop art's obsession with mass culture subjects (again, it is abstract). There is some of the surrealism of the Chicago Imagists—Christina Ramberg's palette and gradients are highly relevant (*Vertical Amnesia*, 1980; **FIG. 1**)—but without the emphasis on the figure. And similarly, the eccentricity of Bay Area Funk is apposite; however, the cartoonish, garish, purposefully vulgar qualities are absent.

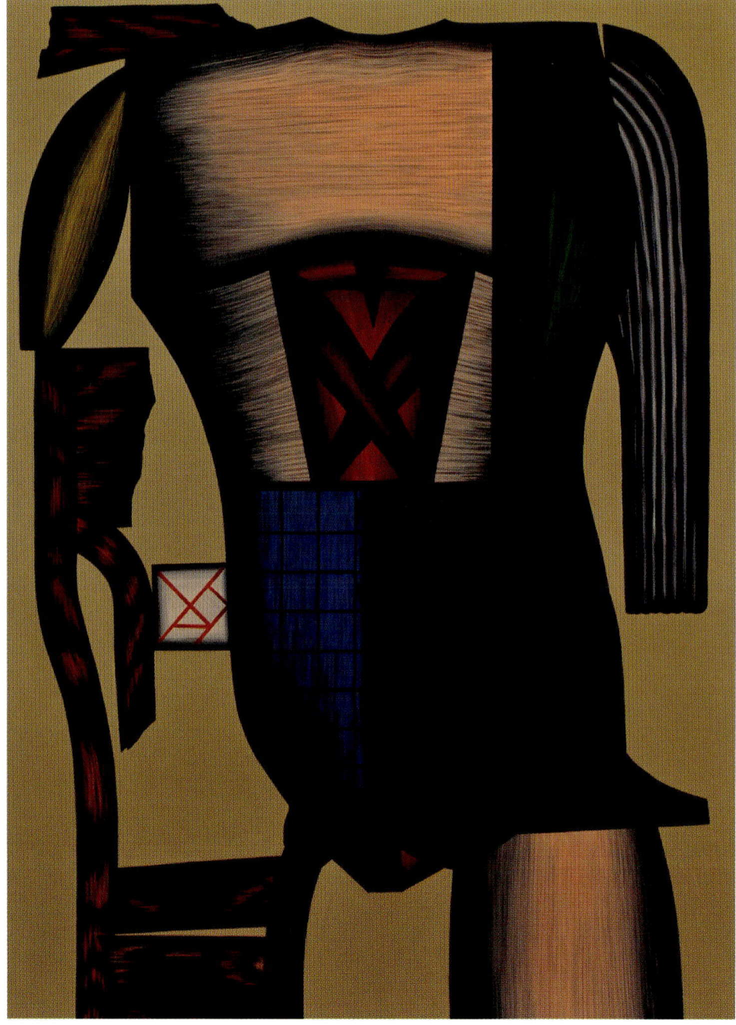

FIG. 1
Christina Ramberg
Vertical Amnesia, 1980
Acrylic on Masonite
49 1/4 × 37 1/4 in. (125.1 × 94.6 cm)
Madison Museum of Contemporary Art, Wisconsin. Museum purchase, through funds from George and Sally Johnson and the Rudolph and Louise Langer Fund

Remington wore her paintings' place/nonplace in the field of contemporary art as a badge of distinction, her self-professed individualism equally allied with Abstract Expressionist notions of freedom, buffeted by Beat antiauthoritarianism, and strategically calculated for artists who were women in this period. "The language is my own," she averred in 1965.[2] And later: "Nobody paints like me, and I don't paint like anyone else."[3] This constituted something of a refrain: "I belong to no school of painting. No school of painting belongs to me."[4] Remington was, by her own account, a formalist at heart, interested in and motivated by "visual conflicts, visual incongruities," the "unexpected," in putting "things that don't work together," together.[5] She strove in her work to create a "tense balance" of elements simultaneously attracting and repelling each other.[6] These elements included masculine and feminine, hot and cold, order and chance, dissonance and harmony, color and line, organic and mechanical.

Indeed, as Remington professed, a driving question was, "How do you marry the organic and the mechanic?" Because, she continued, "Our world today is clearly made up of both. It's everything that goes into making up the human being in conjunction with, and at times against, the whole mechanistic world which we have very carefully and quickly built up around us. . . . I suppose somewhat subconsciously I attempt to make some sense out of this."[7] Fittingly, the terms of the organic and mechanical comprise the central trope of the critical literature, right out of the gate. Critics understood Remington's imagery to confound the organic and mechanical: "The image suggests a machine which is coming to life, or perhaps a life which is becoming a machine,"[8] or, "Are these paintings of organic machines or of machine-like organs?"[9]; to waver between them: ". . . allusions which are sometimes organic, sometimes mechanic"[10]; or to meld them: "Organic shapes are married to mechanistic forms; there is a deliberate mystery of opposites that resists metaphorical analysis."[11]

It is tempting to read Remington's organic-mechanical forms as an attempt to render a figure—to refuse the Greenbergian requirement of jettisoning the figure in total favor of ground—but one that is not yet a woman specifically or even a human generally. Consider Miriam Schapiro, an artist close in age to Remington who similarly passed through the crucible of Abstract Expressionism to emerge in the 1960s as a hard-edge painter, and whose aesthetic strategies artist and writer Mira Schor helpfully characterized as a "feminist détournement of formalism."[12] In the computer-assisted orange, silver, and pink acrylic *Big Ox* (1967; **FIG. 2**), Schapiro smuggled in the image of a sexual female body through the guise of geometry and cloaked in the armor of references to industrial fabrication, lacquers, and plastics, later admitting that the letter *O* superimposed on the letter *X* was actually a pink labial interior (following her own feminist awakening, Schapiro retrospectively identified the "central core" imagery of her geometric abstract paintings). Thus, with Schapiro, what is organic (vaginal, feminine) cannot be disentangled from what is mechanical (abstract, masculine)—in fact, the latter constitutes the former.

Whereas with Remington, who seeks a tense balance, these terms can often still be pulled apart on the basis of the distinction between shape and surface. For instance, her painting *Saxon* (1966–67; **PAGE 95**) suggests the body: its feet are planted on the ground; its red, black, and white bulbous form recalls testicles or some bodily cavity enclosed in a membrane; and at the upper right, a horizontal shape protrudes like an outstretched arm and its fist grips a white stick or perhaps pulls on a white handle. Though the orientation, form, and gesture of the figure of *Saxon*

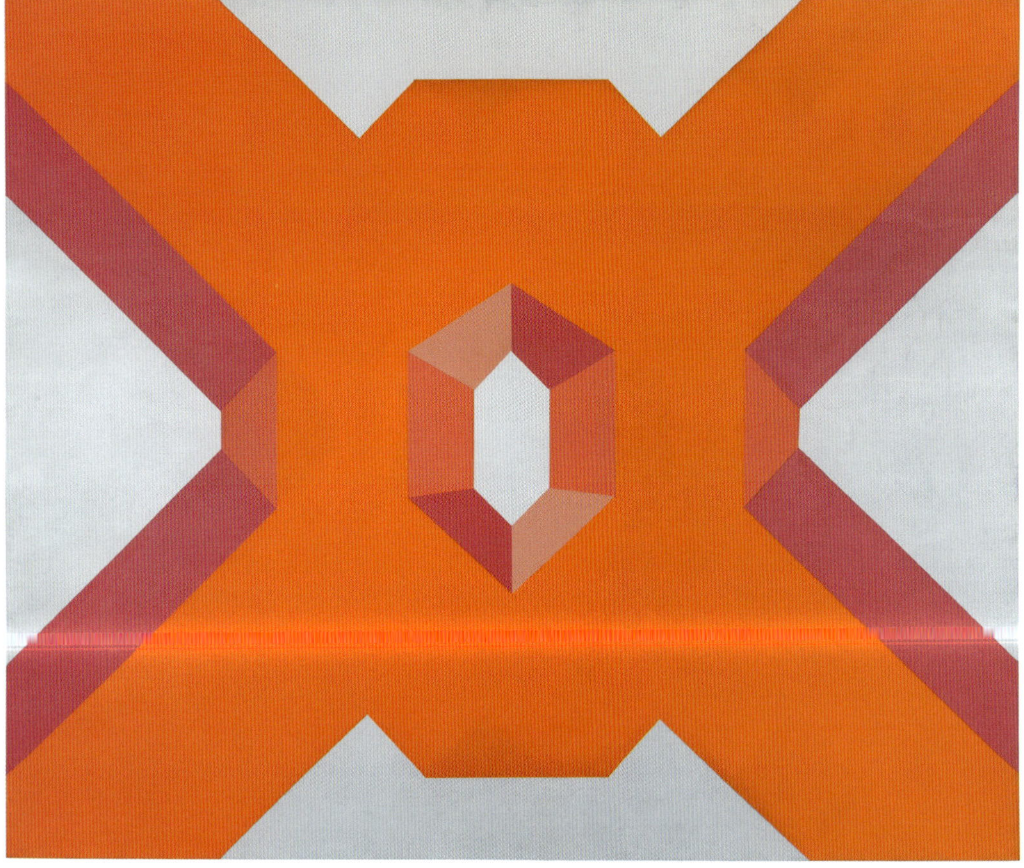

FIG. 2
Miriam Schapiro
Big Ox, 1967
Acrylic on canvas
90 × 108 in.
(228.6 × 274.3 cm)
Courtesy Eric Firestone Gallery, New York

recall the body, even its most sexual, pendulous form is capped by a red chevron that evokes a corporate logo. This geometric chevron transforms the perspective into an overhead view and recasts the figure as a car hood, signaled in large part by way of its reflecting light. The cool, polished-steel textures of *Saxon* become psychologically loaded empty mirrors in Remington's paintings beginning in the early 1970s with canvases such as *Dorset* (1972; **PAGES 107–9**). In *Dorset*, as in most of Remington's work from this fecund two-decade period, irregularity of shape asserts the organic. After all, what could these wavy lines, asymmetrical forms, and floating bits of matter be if not bark, flakes of skin, clouds? And the depicted surface (hard, flat, shiny, impersonal, industrial) insists upon the mechanical.

However, it is not just the depicted surfaces of the imagery contained in Remington's paintings but also the curiously perfected surfaces of the paintings themselves that speak to the mechanical in a poignant register. Early on, critics interpreted the ambiguous image of Remington's paintings as a television set, owing in part to the distinctive backlit glow of a cold, unnatural light. Writing in *Artforum*, critic Knute Stiles ponders, "Perhaps the actual machine which it suggests (without actually resembling it) is a TV set. The TV set is a luminous object in many peoples' darkened rooms."[13] The invocation of television was also based on television's function as an image-generating machine; its capacity to contain incongruous and incomprehensible feelings, events, and experiences ("drama, violence, tragedy, and even sexual release"[14]); and its ability—a liability, to be sure—to screen, to mediate, to, as the word *television* promises, "see at a distance."[15] But might this also be an upshot of Remington's idiosyncratic technique of painting her compositions twice, in two thin coats? In the first campaign, she would "get the painting completely—the surface completely covered and all the adjustments made, like this line here and that line here and this one is thinner and that one is thicker and pull this out and push that back, all the gradations are in, everything is done." And then she would "go back and do it all over again."[16] That is, she would repaint the painting, literally reproducing it, *screening* it. This creates luminosity, and it explains the hermetic seal of the surface, the perfect glaze, the mechanistic quality.

To the list that contains masculine and feminine, hot and cold, order and chance, dissonance and harmony, color and line, organic and mechanical, we must add: immediate and mediated. The question "How do you marry the organic and the mechanic?" is just as much about form (medium) as it is about content (imagery). *New York Times* critic James R. Mellow observed that the "untouched by human hands look" of Remington's painting style is "perfectly appropriate to her imagery."[17] The "untouched by human hands look" (a look that was resolutely made by hand, with regular bristle brushes) places Remington's paintings squarely within the most vexing issue in advanced American painting in the 1960s: the relationship that representation bears to reproduction.

The ritual art historical reference is of course Andy Warhol's method of silk screening already mass-produced photographic images in an assembly-line fashion at his studio, known as the Factory, though Photorealist painting, which emerged in the mid- and late 1960s, offers a closer comparison to Remington. Long dismissed as a too-literal elaboration of Pop art, Photorealism was understood by its detractors as painting's death rattle, a last gasp bid for skill at the moment of Conceptual art's rise and, what's more, a redundancy at the moment of the belated acceptance of photography as fine art by the academy and the museum. Distinguished by its often painstaking emulation of the surface effects of a photograph in paint, Photorealism exploited the ontological parallelism of the flatness of photography and of painting in order to give form to the flat surfaces onto which the world was being made and remade (photographs, video monitors, television sets, computer screens), and in so doing to resist or dramatize the relentless pace of reproductive media technologies via the handmade-ness of painting. Take for example Vija Celmins's *T.V.* from 1964 (**FIG. 3**). It depicts in a nondescript gray setting a black-and-white television set that displays an image of an exploding airplane (the on-screen image came from a World War II news photo rather than a television broadcast). It crystallizes the power of the photograph to dislocate events—disasters, violence, death—in order to relocate them across time and space, and the power of television to reproduce subjects as massive and common as exploding warplanes in our homes (today, in our pockets). The power of the painting, then, is that it supplies the artist—and the viewer—a medium in which to try to wrap one's mind around such gravity and banality, to make destruction of incomprehensible scale visible enough, or mediated enough, that we might actually see it, or see how we see through it. For artists like Celmins, painting in this manner allowed her to retain representation, while dispensing with illusionism.[18] Remington plays with the same dyads; however, she reproduces without representing and holds onto illusionism and abstraction alike, by attaining formal balance through asymmetry.

Where Remington's paintings are reflective—akin to a screen, as I want to argue—her *Soot Series* (1963–76) is absorptive. With one clear, late-dating outlier, *Soot 11* (1976; **PAGE 55**), the *Soot* drawings consist of a single, round-edged, horizontal shape tapering into two inward-pointing spikes or thorns at the bottom. The only materials are soot gathered from the

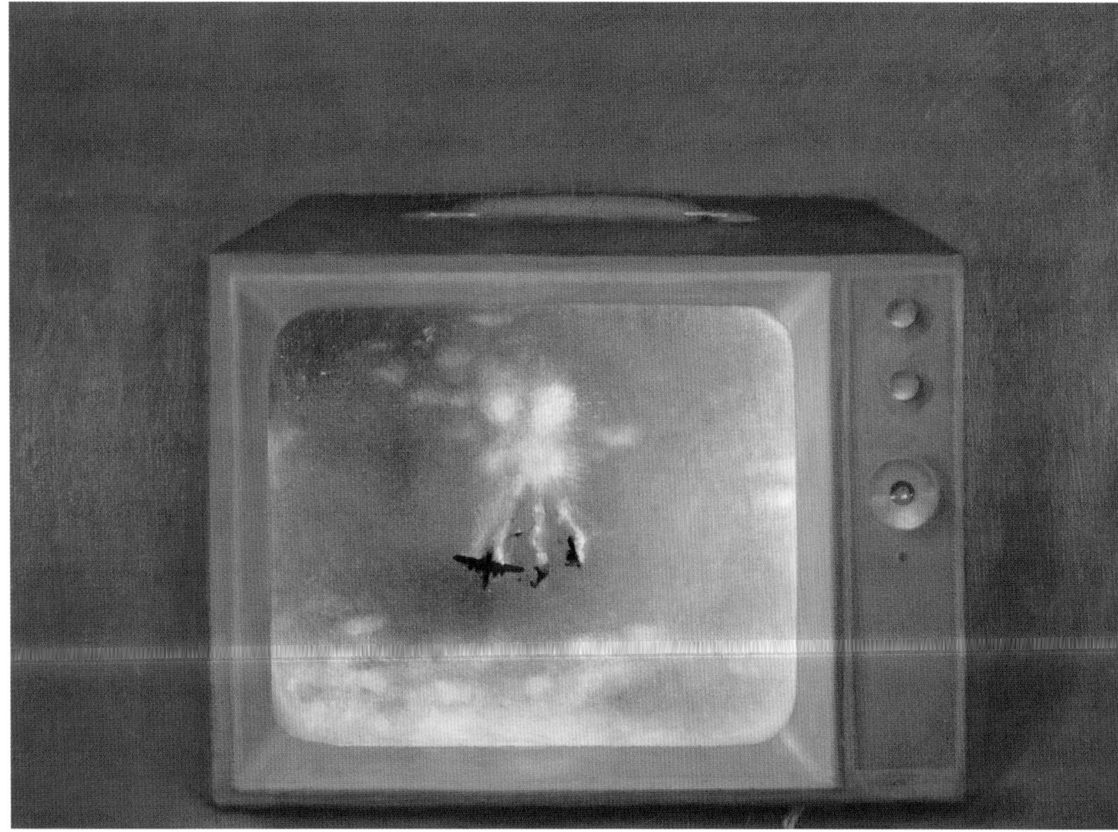

FIG. 3
Vija Celmins
T.V., 1964
Oil on canvas
26 1/4 × 36 in.
(66.7 × 91.4 cm)
Courtesy Matthew Marks Gallery

fireplace and red crayon applied to muslin and later charcoal on warm yellowy-white paper. Visual activity is contained within this idiosyncratic shape that recalls a wide-cuff bracelet, a gaming console, and the ovoid designs in carvings by Northwest Coast Indigenous artists (from here the associations flow in a now familiar associative chain, from musical instrument, to proscenium, shell, insect, appliance, and UFO). The *Soot* drawings utilize a thick, powdery black ground of light-absorbing soot for both allusion (to an outer space "scape") and illusion (to an expansive, deep space), similar to sculptor Lee Bontecou's use of the material starting in the late 1950s. While employing her oxyacetylene welding torch to mount metal armatures to the wall, Bontecou accidentally discovered that if she turned down the oxygen on the torch, soot would flow off of the flame in a plume. She tacked sheets of muslin and paper to the wall and directed the thick residue onto these supports. Bontecou referred to her soot drawings as worldscapes and, oriented in the landscape format, they suggest the distant horizon of a far-off planet, star, or moon. A soot drawing, such as *Untitled* (1958; FIG. 4), is covered entirely in plush black, indicating an ever-expansive outer space, save for the spare horizon line amid a swath of gray. Thus, both Remington and Bontecou use soot to conjure space that is far away pictorially, but quite close materially, palpable as sheer matter. Remington's paintings perform the inverse operation: the images are close to the surface but out of reach.[19]

If Remington's paintings recorded themselves, as it were, in their two coats, then the study of her drawings becomes especially illuminating; it is as if looking at the first coat of one of her paintings through X-ray vision. Her drawings were complete and independent works, neither studies nor sketches, that nonetheless bore a striking resemblance to her paintings and often anticipated her paintings' compositions by several, or more, years. The *Adelphi Series* (1963–83) drawings betray an affinity to collage, the elements akin to scraps that are layered on top of one another, on top of the support. Rather than providing the illusion of a foreign object appearing from the background, hovering, glowing, a fixed unit, as in the formidable *Memphis* (1969; **PAGE 2**), they stir an image of the artist pinning down free-floating forms against grounds that are visibly made up of strokes of the pencil, hard and dense at the top and gradually softer and sparer at the bottom, as in *Untitled* (Adelphi Series) (1963; **PAGE 65**). We can easily imagine Remington constructing this drawing in the manner she once explained about her *painting* process—as having "little slide projectors in the back of my head," such that she would stare at a blank canvas, and "at some point, sometimes only for an instant, something will be projected on the canvas. I'll get up and draw it."[20] Comparing *Untitled* (Adelphi Series) to its compositional echo, *Aryx* (1982; **PAGE 137**), dated nineteen years later, we note that what is bare, toothy paper in one medium becomes reflective metal in the other; what appears as a rip or tear in one is a scratch or glitch in the other; in drawing, what is warm in terms of color temperature, as well as vulnerability, is cold, cool, and remote in painting.

The metaphor of a projector is apt, not particularly because it gives the artist the status of a machine, but because it invokes analog media, like film. In fact, Remington's *Soot* and *Adelphi* drawings have a photographic quality, grainy and softly gradated, with focused foregrounds and fuzzy backgrounds. Looking back, we read in them a nostalgia for print in the era of screens, for in her remarkably prescient way, in the 1960s and 1970s Remington made paintings that predicted the ways in which very nearly everything in contemporary life seems to be mechanically reproduced and electronically simulated.

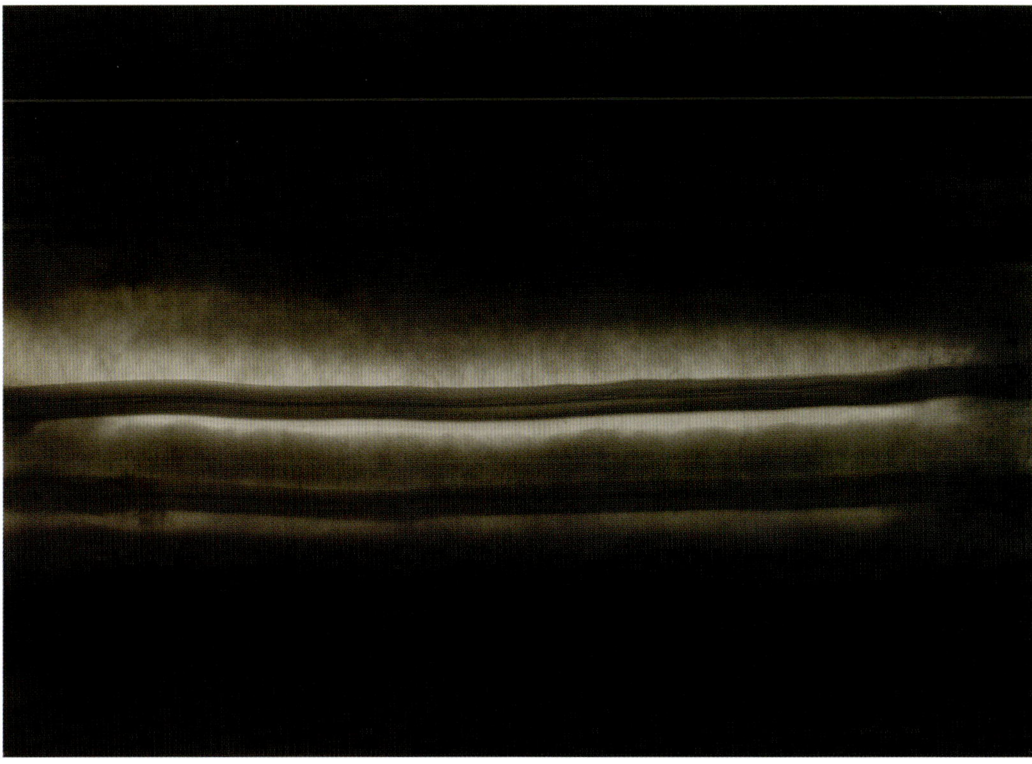

FIG. 4
Lee Bontecou
Untitled, 1958
Soot on wove paper
27 5/8 × 39 3/8 in.
(70.2 × 100.1 cm)
National Gallery of Art, Washington, D.C. Gift of Helen Porter and James T. Dyke

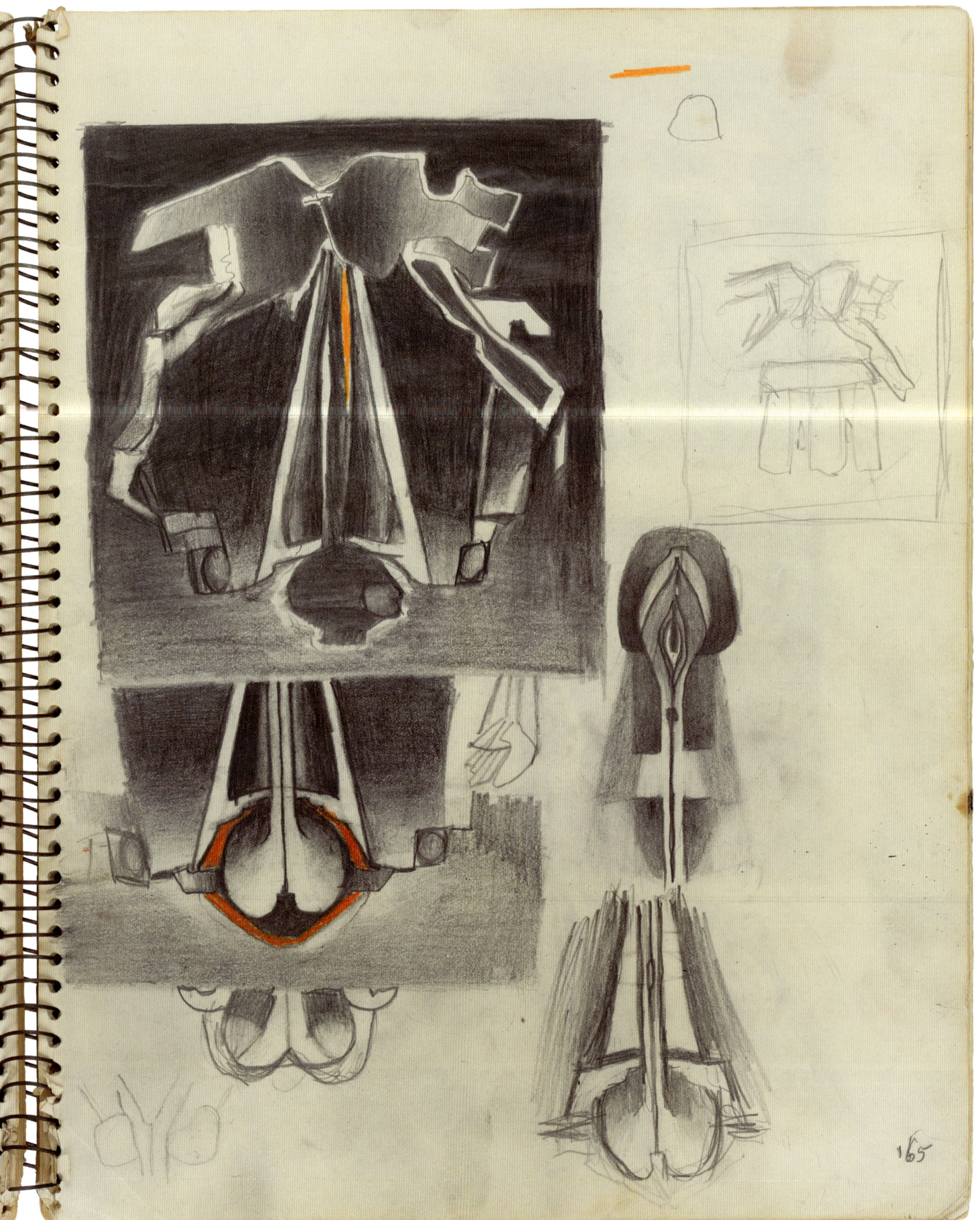

Deborah Remington: Space, Craft

CARROLL DUNHAM

Deborah Remington must have been a loner. By the time she relocated from San Francisco to New York in the mid-'60s, she had been around, both as a serious young presence in the Bay Area art scene and off on a mostly party-of-one, self-created residency in Japan, with subsequent travels around Southeast Asia and India. Remington was thirty-five when she moved to New York, full of experiences to process, eager to be involved in a larger and more challenging art scene, and with the basic tools and tactics of the forthcoming period of her work already in place. As she put it, "The images became completely isolated from the surface," by which she meant that the things she was drawing no longer touched the edges of what she was drawing (or painting) on. Her palette was reductive and limited, weighted toward black and gray with elements of red. The drawn structures were delineated by glowing edges and suggestions of heat and light painted fastidiously in beautifully gradated tones. Her work was entering a different phase. A new, somewhat crazy pictorial space appeared, and for the next ten years her interest in painterly gesture was hidden behind illusionistic layers of refinement and selection. The co-presence of twisted optics and severe abstraction was unusual and straddled seemingly contradictory positions in the discourse of the day.

Shortly after moving to New York, Remington met Klaus Kertess, the cofounder and director of Bykert Gallery, located at 81st Street and Madison Avenue, who agreed to have an exhibition at his gallery. There was something very comforting about the insularity and blithe cultural chauvinism of the New York art scene(s) of the sixties and seventies. It was by present-day standards a tiny world, composed of mutually exclusive yet interacting microclimates. Bykert Gallery briefly occupied a special place in that scene, managing to be simultaneously intellectually serious, aggressively nondoctrinaire, and cool. In this context Remington's work, although an odd fit, could be reconsidered as part of an "advanced" New York–centric, if perhaps obscure, conversation with Ralph Humphrey, Barry Le Va, Brice Marden, David Novros, and Dorothea Rockburne, or the sculptors David Rabinowitch and Richard Van Buren. This couldn't have been a better or richer context for Remington's practice.

FIG. 1
Page from Remington's sketchbook, 1965

As young artists new to New York in the early '70s, my friends and I followed the gallery's program carefully. Kertess was friendly and liked to talk about art, so we spent a lot of time at

Bykert Gallery. His choices for programming were diverse, always driven by his innate visual intelligence and feeling of personal chemistry with artists. In hindsight it's amazing how ill-equipped I was to respond to what Remington was doing back then. I have no doubt that I saw several of her shows at Bykert, but my memory of the experience is vague and generic; I wasn't paying sufficient attention to the experience for it to register clearly. Remington's paintings were always slightly at odds with other contemporary abstraction that I was already busy trying to figure out how to think about. Both the systemic thinking and emphasis on specific materiality of Humphrey, Marden, Novros, or Rockburne had little overlap with Remington's concerns. I think when I once asked Kertess about her, he mentioned that she was "from California," which I ignorantly assumed meant she was connected to artists from L.A., like Larry Bell or Ron Davis, who at that time fell outside my appreciation of what was acceptable. That association probably wasn't entirely misplaced, but my sense of what's "unacceptable" has undergone profound reconsideration as my own life and work have evolved and painting itself has evolved around me. At some point in the last decade (I'm not actually sure when or where), I saw a picture of a Remington painting from the 1970s and thought, "How did I miss how odd and wonderful this work was?"

For several years, in meticulous charcoal drawings, Remington developed a vocabulary of quasi-mechanical subjects with strong associative properties and no literal references to real objects, which followed an unconscious construction process driven by linear drawing. These subjects float free from the edge of the paper, creating the void of heavily suggestive darkness characteristic of all the paintings during this phase. *Haddonfield* (1965; **PAGE 91**) is clearly described in a sketchbook page dated the same year (**FIG. 1**). The nominal subject, the "image" in Remington's phrase, hovers detached from the edges of the field, both set off from and partially delineated by fundamental blackness. Years later, the thing "represented" in this

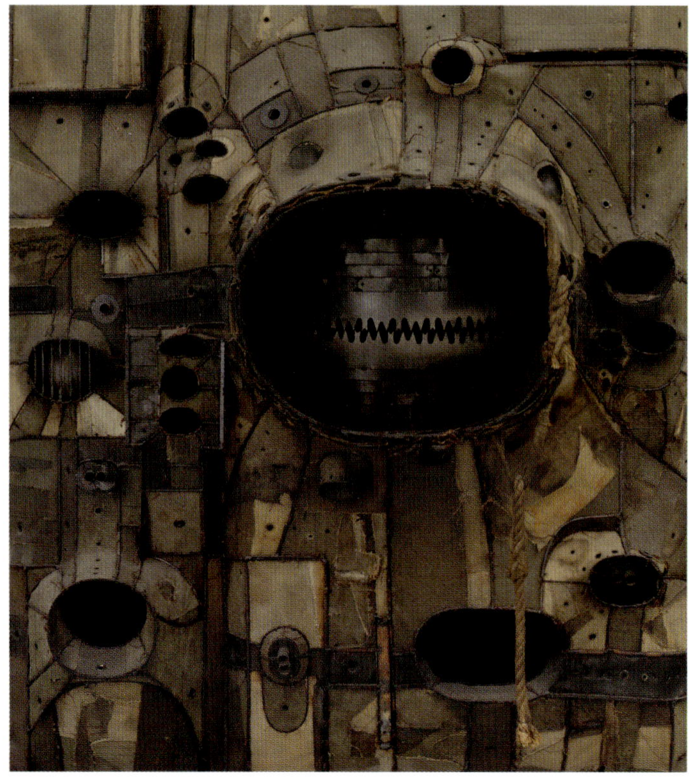

FIG. 2
Lee Bontecou
Untitled, 1961, 1961
Welded steel, canvas, wire, and rope
72 1/2 × 66 × 24 3/4 in.
(184.2 × 167.6 × 62.9 cm)
Whitney Museum of American Art, New York. Purchase

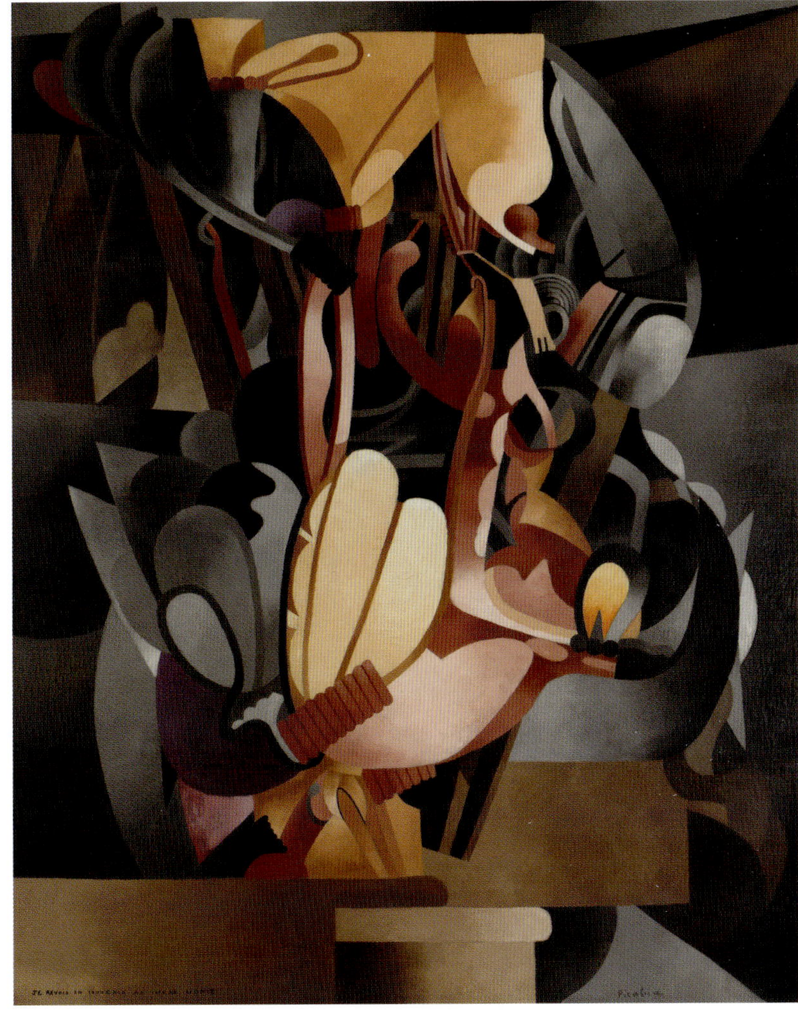

FIG. 3
Francis Picabia
I See Again in Memory My Dear Udnie, Paris, June–July 1914
Oil on canvas
8 ft. 2 1/2 in. × 6 ft. 6 1/4 in.
(250.2 × 198.8 cm)
The Museum of Modern Art, New York. Hillman Periodicals Fund

painting is still quite frightening and incomprehensible. It has aspects of a mask, an air pump, a car grille, or the shattered remains of an experimental device whose purpose we can only guess. It has qualities of a person, an animal, a plant, a machine, or a mathematical model. Its lack of interpretability is its most overpowering attribute, and in this it sets the tone for the artist's subsequent development. The hovering presence, giving the impression of bilateral symmetry while violating it repeatedly, the depiction of object-like things intermingled with spacelike things, the transformation of lines into depicted objects with physical thickness—all are elements that begin to reappear continually in her work. These confusions of category, which are imbued with her Lovecraftian sense of strangeness, would constitute her primary subject in the ensuing years. Remington's imagery and approach were jarring but not without precedent. Lee Bontecou's dark, looming constructions (*Untitled, 1961*, 1961; **FIG. 2**) share Remington's abstract ferocity and, going back further, Francis Picabia's early masterpiece *I See Again in Memory My Dear Udnie* (Paris, June–July 1914; **FIG. 3**) is an early example of uncategorizably hybrid subject matter.

As she explored this new terrain, Remington moved away from preplanning and relied increasingly on spontaneous gesture and drawing directly on the canvas to establish each painting's compositional structure by instinct and elimination. The imagery feels coaxed forth rather than imposed. In *Memphis* (1969; **PAGE 2**), there is a much less developed feeling of a thing floating before us and more a condition, a local disturbance of some deeper manifold with apertures and structures of its own. There is a vertical axis dividing the field and a roughly butterfly-shaped event unfolding—shapes, lines, and voids all defining and contradicting each other. There is an overarching feeling of stability and balance, which is odd in that every element occupies an ambiguous position in the third dimension of the optical painting space. The center of the painting gathers into a shape that is something like a presence, not quite an abstraction of something figurative but more just a place where red lines become glowing, embodied things. The slightly approximate trajectory of the linear structures in the painting makes a fascinating disconnect with the detached intensity of her painting method.

The paintings were increasingly constructed around an image of a bright geometric shape painted on a gradient from gray to white, seemingly both a reflective surface and a window onto infinite distance. In *Axios* (1971; **PAGE 103**), this mirror/window is a pyramidal triangle, a very stable form. Deployed around it are shapes that have probably emerged from gestures made on the canvas but could be the curtains around a puppet theater rendered in dark energy defined by glowing hot red lines. This feeling of energy as defining form, of shapes possessing an element of heat (the infrared) as well as light, is strong here and became of increasing interest to Remington.

What we might mean by Remington's mirror paintings is elusive. The subjects are mirrors in the way Jasper Johns's "cross-hatch" images (*Corpse and Mirror*, 1976; **FIG. 4**) are understood as such: the hatches don't actually cross. Remington's mirrors are mirrors because our mind's eye says so. Not unlike a mirror by Roy Lichtenstein (*Mirror #1*, 1969; **FIG. 5**) representing "nothing"

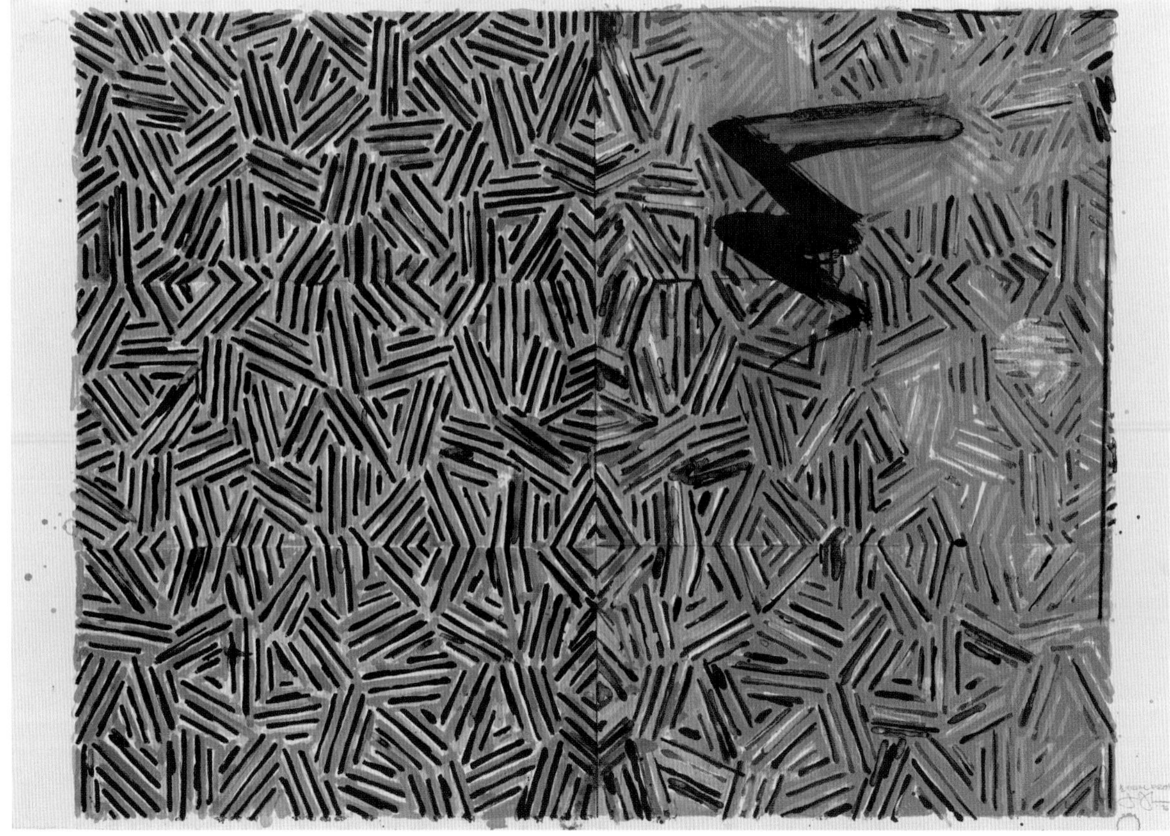

FIG. 4
Jasper Johns
Corpse and Mirror, 1976
Lithograph in black and gray on wove paper
28 3/8 × 42 in.
(72.1 × 196.7 cm)
National Gallery of Art, Washington D.C. Patrons' Permanent Fund and Special Friends of the National Gallery of Art

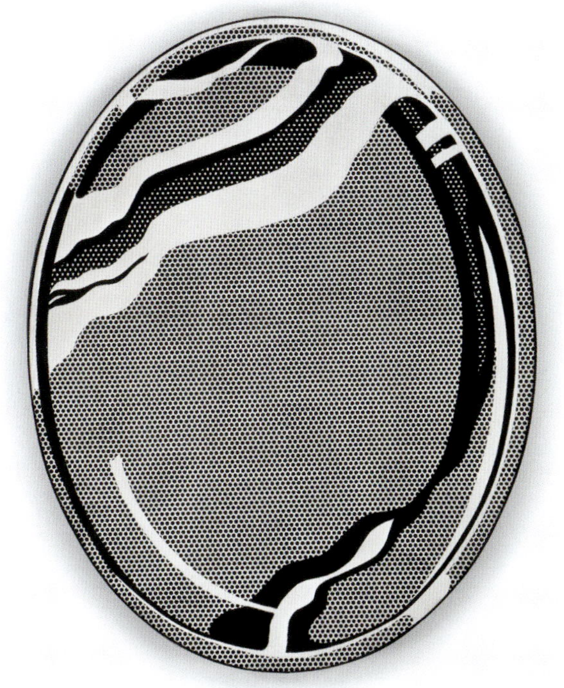

FIG. 5
Roy Lichtenstein
Mirror #1, 1969
Oil and Magna on canvas
60 × 48 in. (152.4 × 121.9 cm)
The Eli and Edythe L. Broad Collection

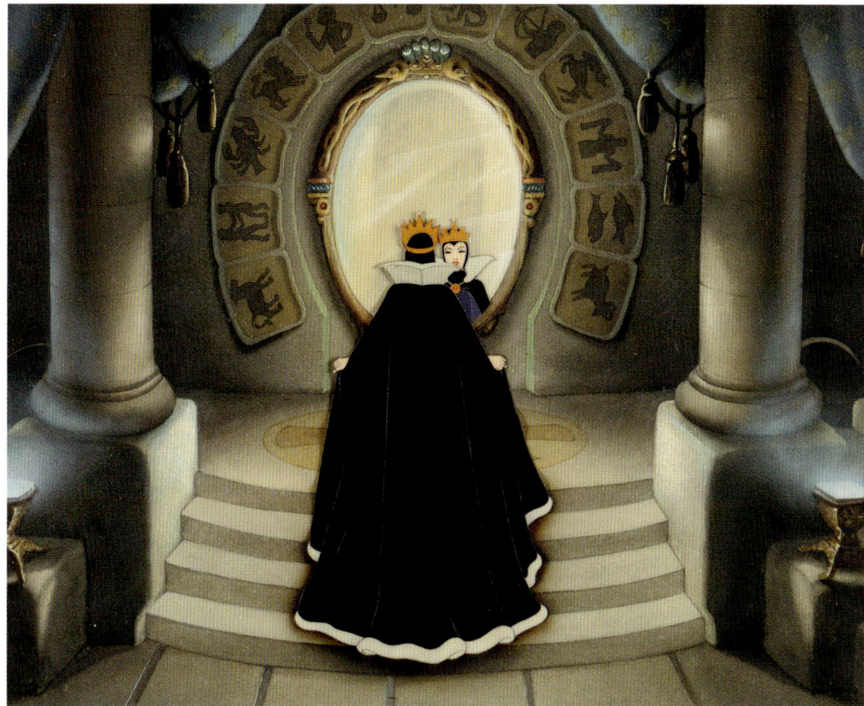

FIG. 6
Still from *Snow White and the Seven Dwarfs*. © 1937 Disney

and reflecting that back, too, they rely on simple systems for their illusions. This sort of nose-on-your-face approach to the unpacking of Remington's work avoids many pitfalls of interpretive overreach and is consistent with the way she spoke about her decision-making process. Rather than embodying specific subject matter, her paintings embody choices and decisions. The sum of her denials becomes the image, and anything in the world of objects and emotions might be drawn into this visual association system.

She was willing to let certain references penetrate the strict abstraction of her basic position. Both *Essex* (1972; **PAGE 113**) and *Dorset* (1972; **PAGES 107–9**) make clear reference to mirrors as we understand them culturally through fairytales and cartoons. The image in *Essex* is centered on a vertical mirrored shape within a frame sitting on a wall; the mirror is slightly warped, which gives everything a mildly woozy feeling. Above the mirror is a cluster of shapes that could be molds for prosthetic body parts or just further disturbances in the integrity of the optical plane. The central shape in *Dorset* immediately recalls oval picture frames and "Magic Mirror on the wall" references (**FIG. 6**) suspended in an irradiated shape that could be a giant camera staring back from the painting. There are shards of whatever material this world is composed of floating in the space in front of the putative mirror, a device Remington used in numerous paintings to complicate any understanding of object, context, or what is being posited in this precisely described world of almost indescribable specificity. In *Seneca* (1971; **FIG. 7**) there is a seemingly random strip of paint drifting in the elliptical mirror space, contributing to the complexity of its depth and destabilizing symmetries.

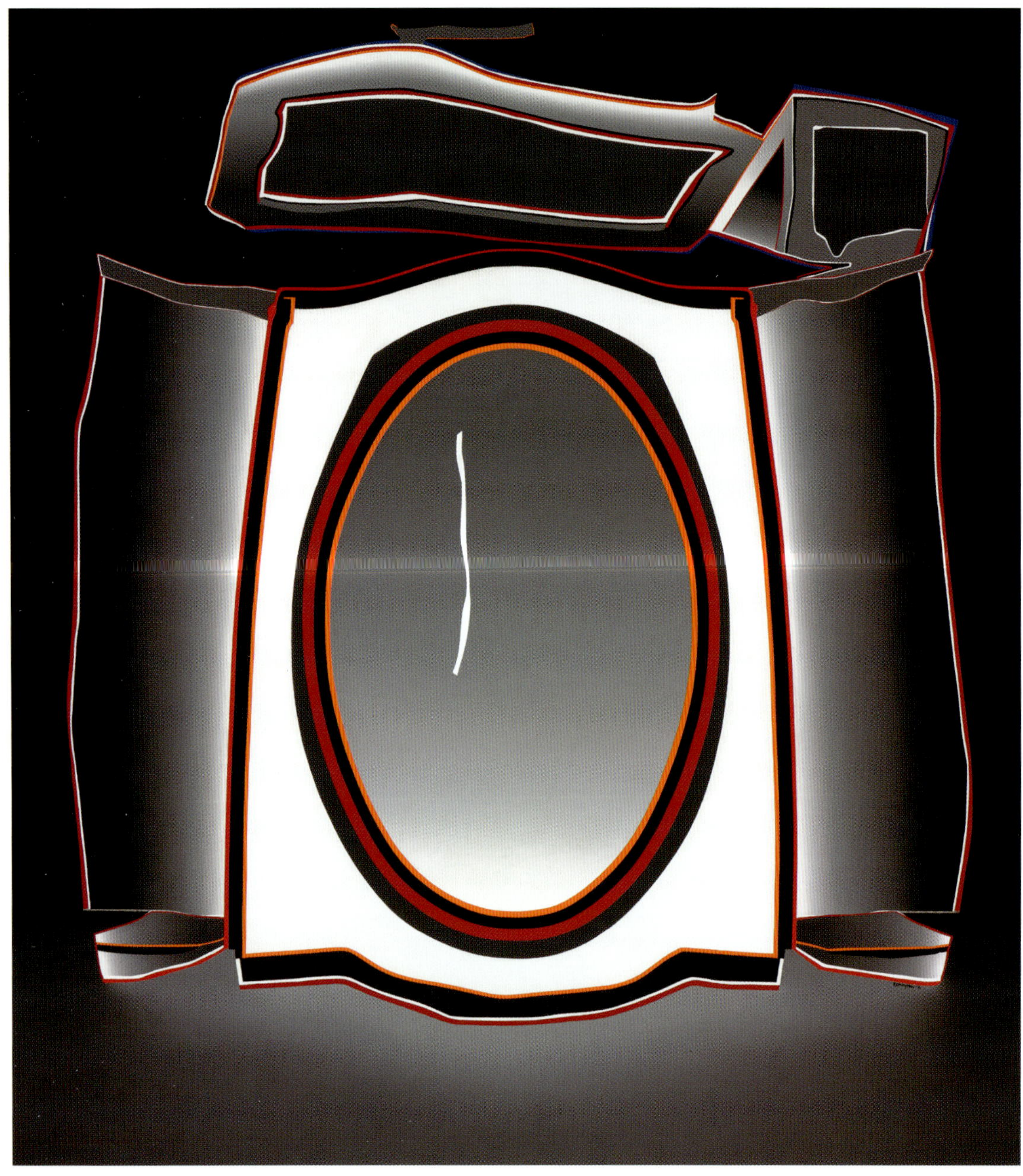

FIG. 7
Deborah Remington
Seneca, 1971
Oil on linen
50 × 46 in. (127 × 116.8 cm)
Museum Boijmans
Van Beuningen, Rotterdam,
Netherlands

Depth was of interest to Remington in several ways. Because her constructions floated free from the picture's edges, she somehow felt free to let there be space, to allow illusions of spatial depth that humans see to take over the entire visible field of the painting. This sets her very much apart from Humphrey's or Marden's notion of how a surface is conceptualized. Al Held's paintings of enormous geometric constructions might come closer, but the vibe is entirely different. It was also important that her paintings feel chromatically deep and have a rich surface. At a certain point Remington described that she began to paint her paintings twice, meaning: all over again on the same canvas after the image is fully established a first time. This is a strange thing to think about, much less to do. Embedded in each painting is then an entire trajectory of attitudes from loose gestural marks to an overdetermined singularity. The crushing together of all this energy subliminally intensifies the apparent emptiness of these places she created.

All these paintings begin in darkness; darkness is their fecund premise. One could imagine it otherwise, the situation negativized and forms emerging from a field of light. Already there are examples of both foundational premises in the earliest modernist abstraction, if one contrasts the dingy darkness of Aleksandr Rodchenko's early abstractions (*Non-Objective Painting, no. 80 (Black on Black)*, 1918; **FIG. 8**) and the white field of light on which Kazimir Malevich based his inventions. One might go in a surprising direction and invoke the late black paintings of Ad Reinhardt to find an approach as dependent as Remington's on the ultimate darkness of the planar premise underlying all subsequent developments and relationships, and there's a shared interest in things that are impossible to interpret, however different the manifestation. Remington's forms appear to us out of a gloom so dark you almost need a new word, leaning toward strange and extremely deep olives, grays, and blue-black. It's unclear whether light is a luminosity of the objects and/or events presented (presenting) to us or from an outside source. Red, and sometimes orange, plays a huge role in this drama, being a color Remington can use to convey heat and light simultaneously. There is a sensation of seeing red and infrared simultaneously that is very unusual, lines made of red-hot lava making circuits around the spatial field.

Remington spoke about her own work's development as one of emptying-out, essentializing what was already there, pushing implications to their logical outcomes. To us her paintings of this period can look almost ornate, interpreted decoratively by default, given our present dependence on information and background. But their complexity can also be seen as manifestations of the artist's refusals: refusal of gesture as an index of emotional sincerity, of flatness and surface physicality as the sources of painting's drama, or refusal of the need for a stable frame of reference when faced with content that's inexplicable. Making something that opens up an entire world, yet remains literally unspeakable, is profound.

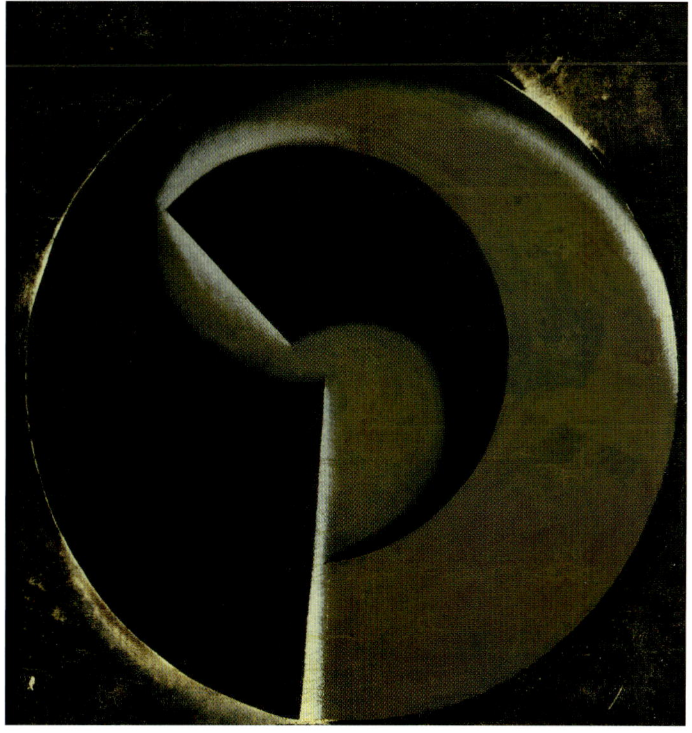

FIG. 8
Aleksandr Rodchenko
Non-Objective Painting no. 80 (Black on Black), 1918
Oil and bitumen on canvas
32 1/4 × 31 1/4 in. (81.9 × 79.4 cm)
The Museum of Modern Art, New York. Gift of the artist, through Jay Leyda

1983–2007

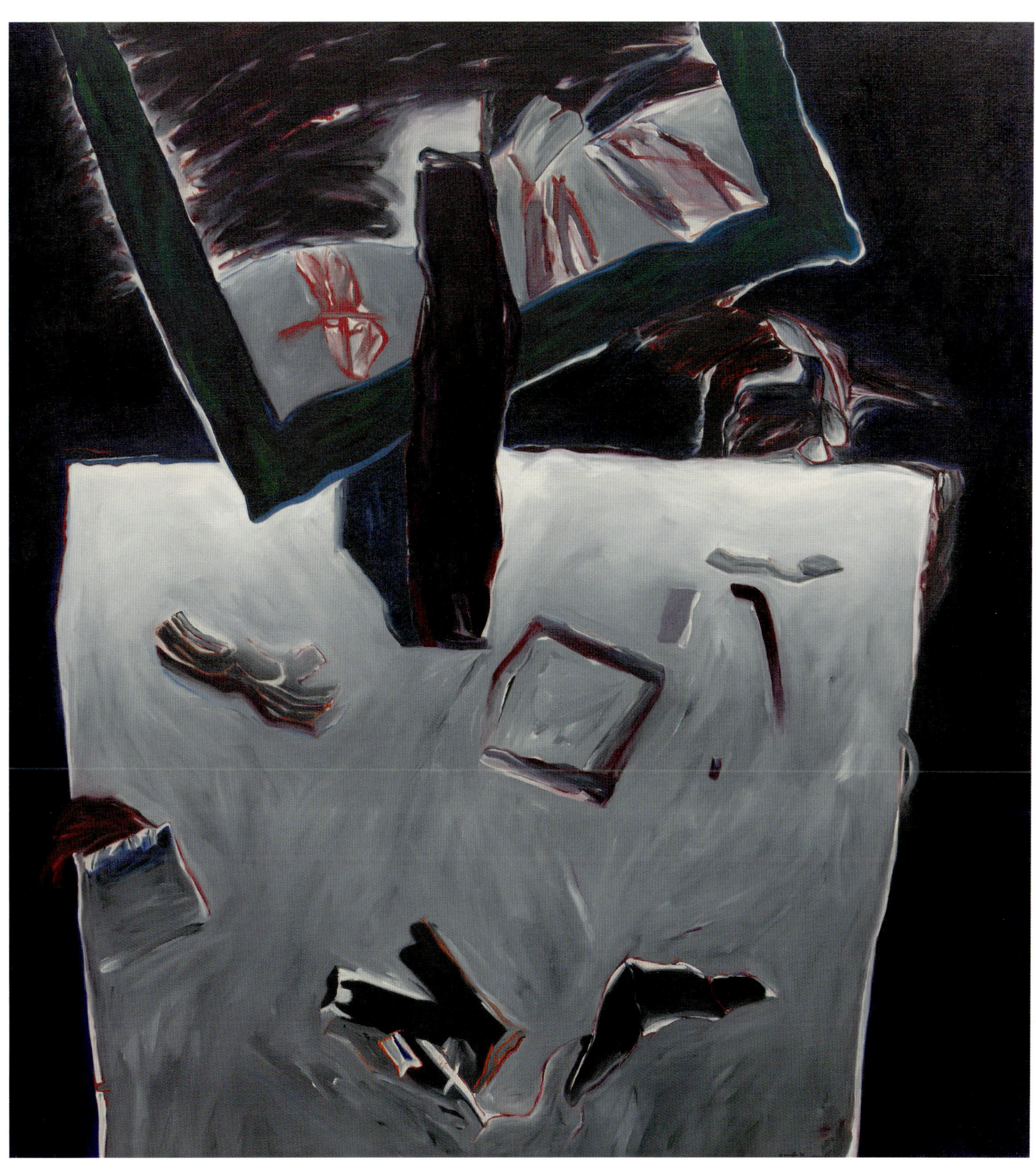

Santee, 1986. Oil on canvas, 53 × 52 in. (134.6 × 132 cm)
Deborah Remington Charitable Trust for the Visual Arts

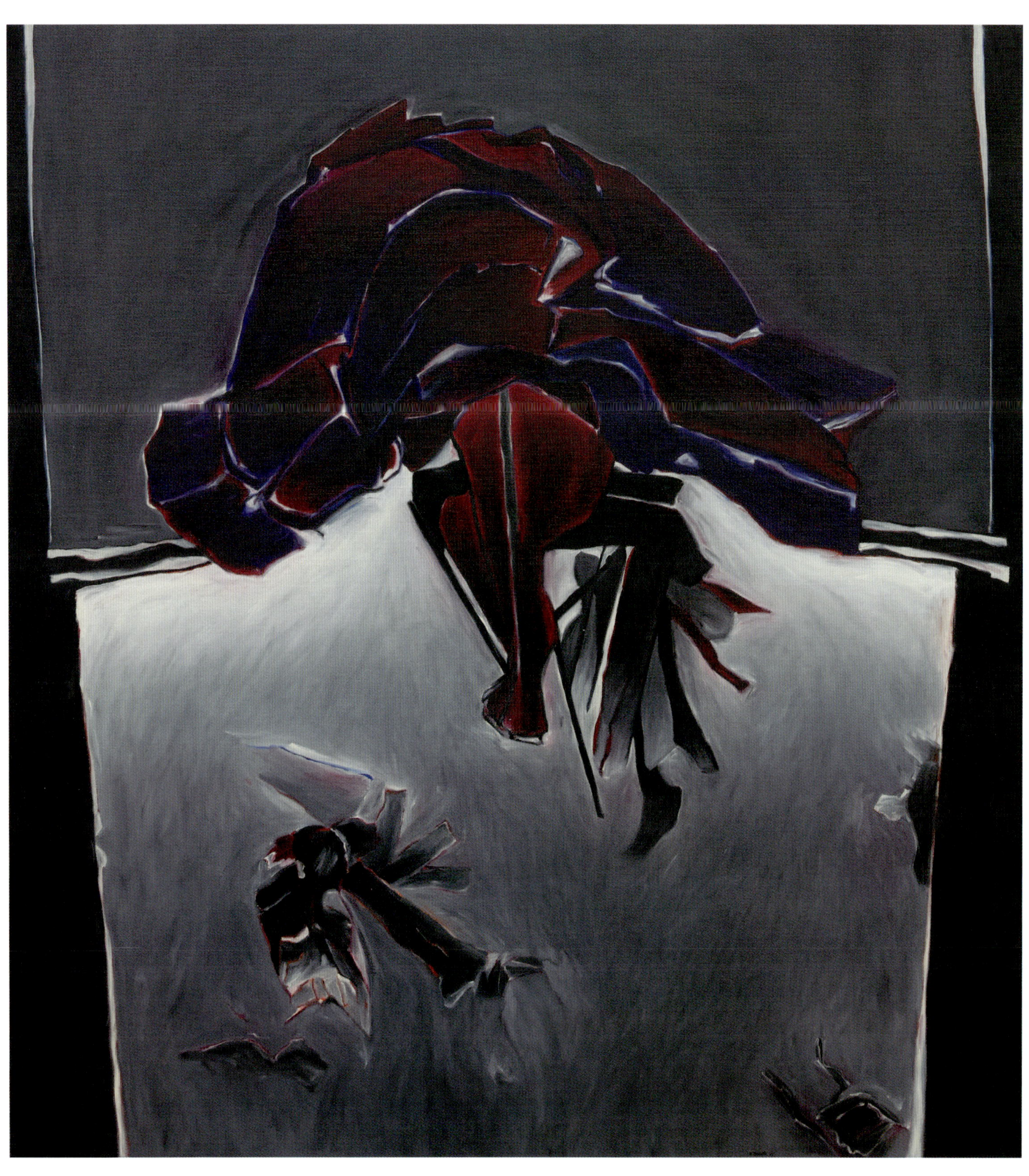

Troas, 1987. Oil on canvas, 56 × 52 in. (142.2 × 132 cm)
Deborah Remington Charitable Trust for the Visual Arts

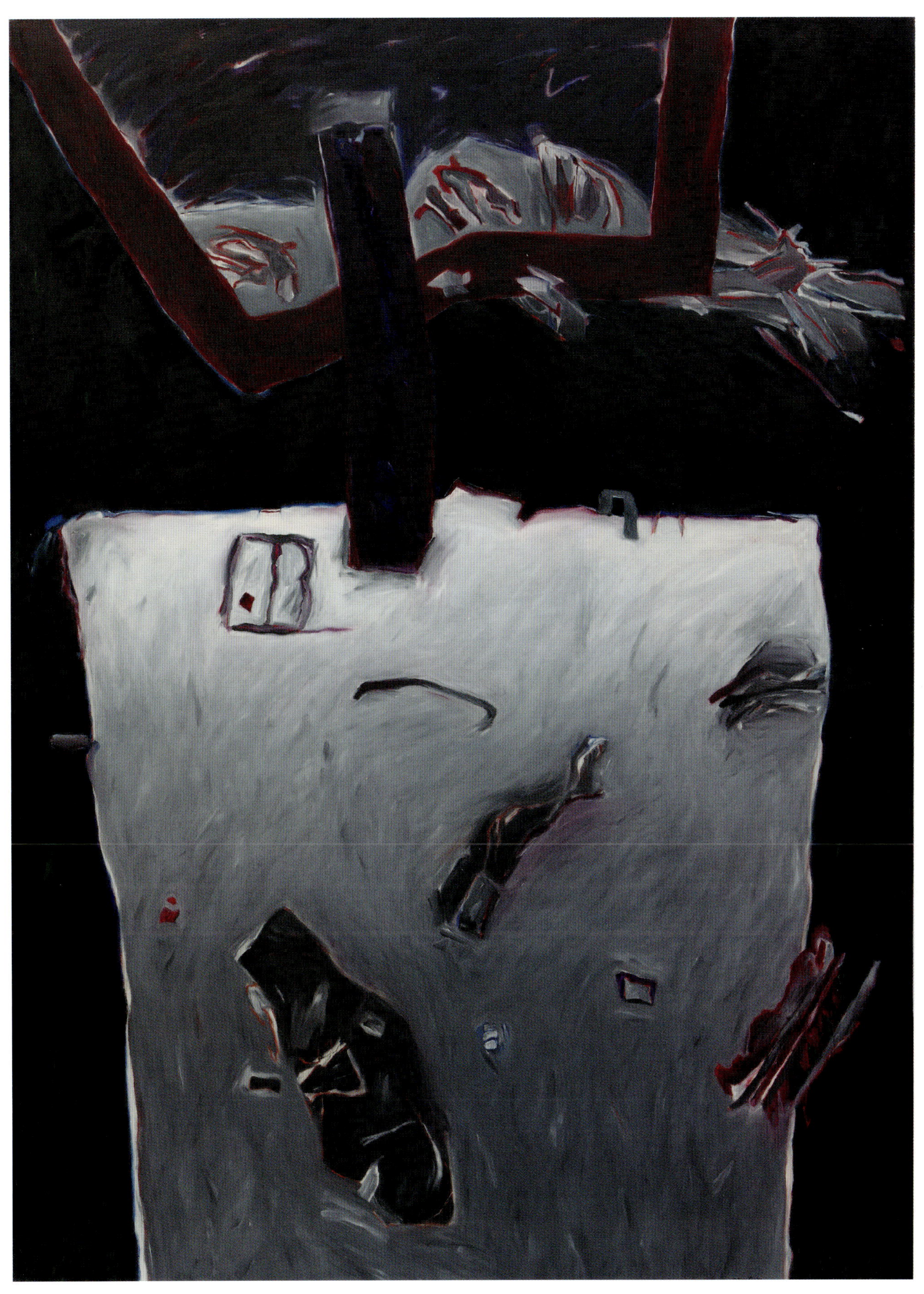

Bakh, 1987. Oil on canvas, 64 × 47 in. (162.6 × 119.4 cm)
Deborah Remington Charitable Trust for the Visual Arts

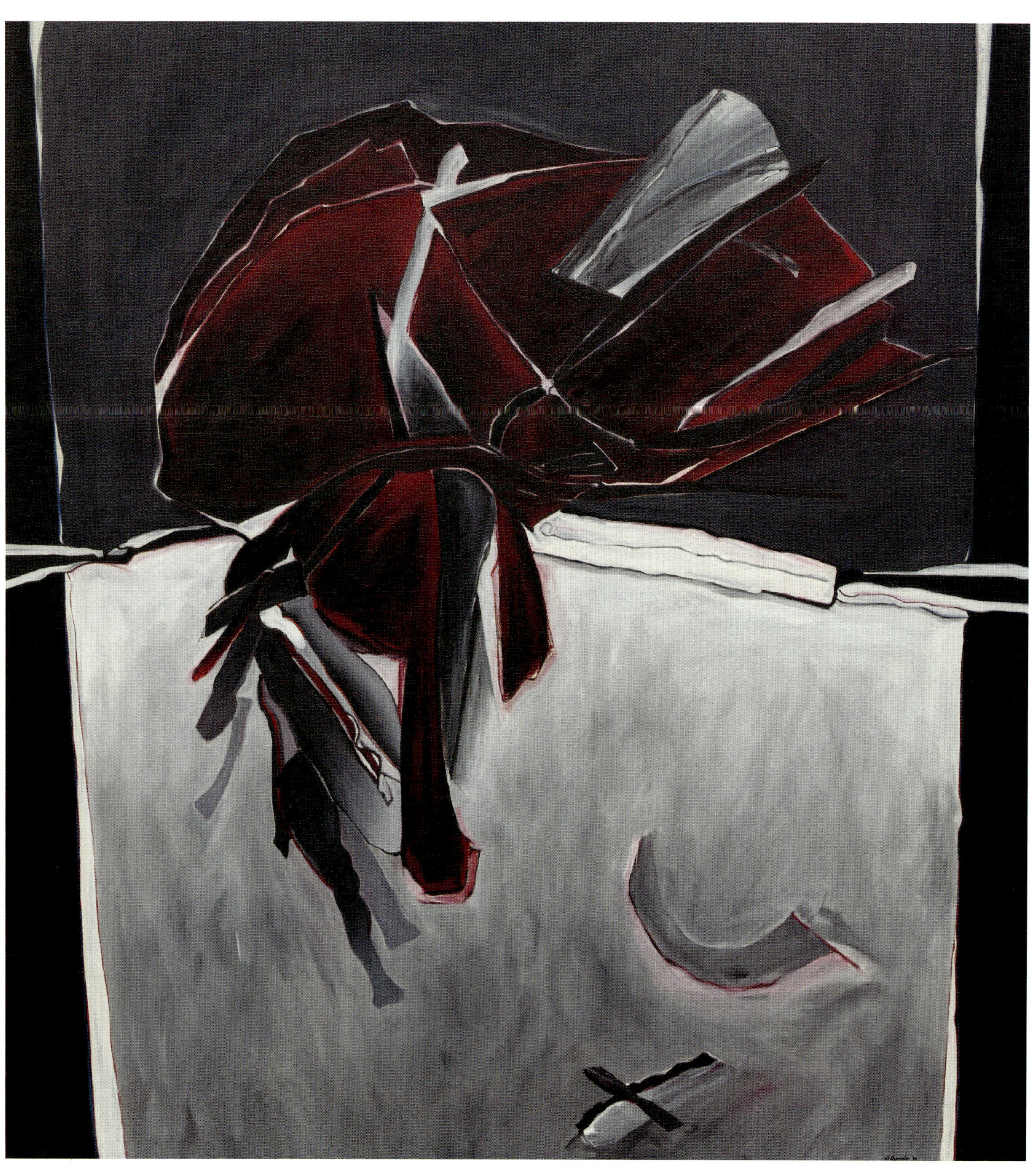

Dorado, 1986. Oil on canvas, 56 × 52 in. (142.2 × 132 cm)
Deborah Remington Charitable Trust for the Visual Arts

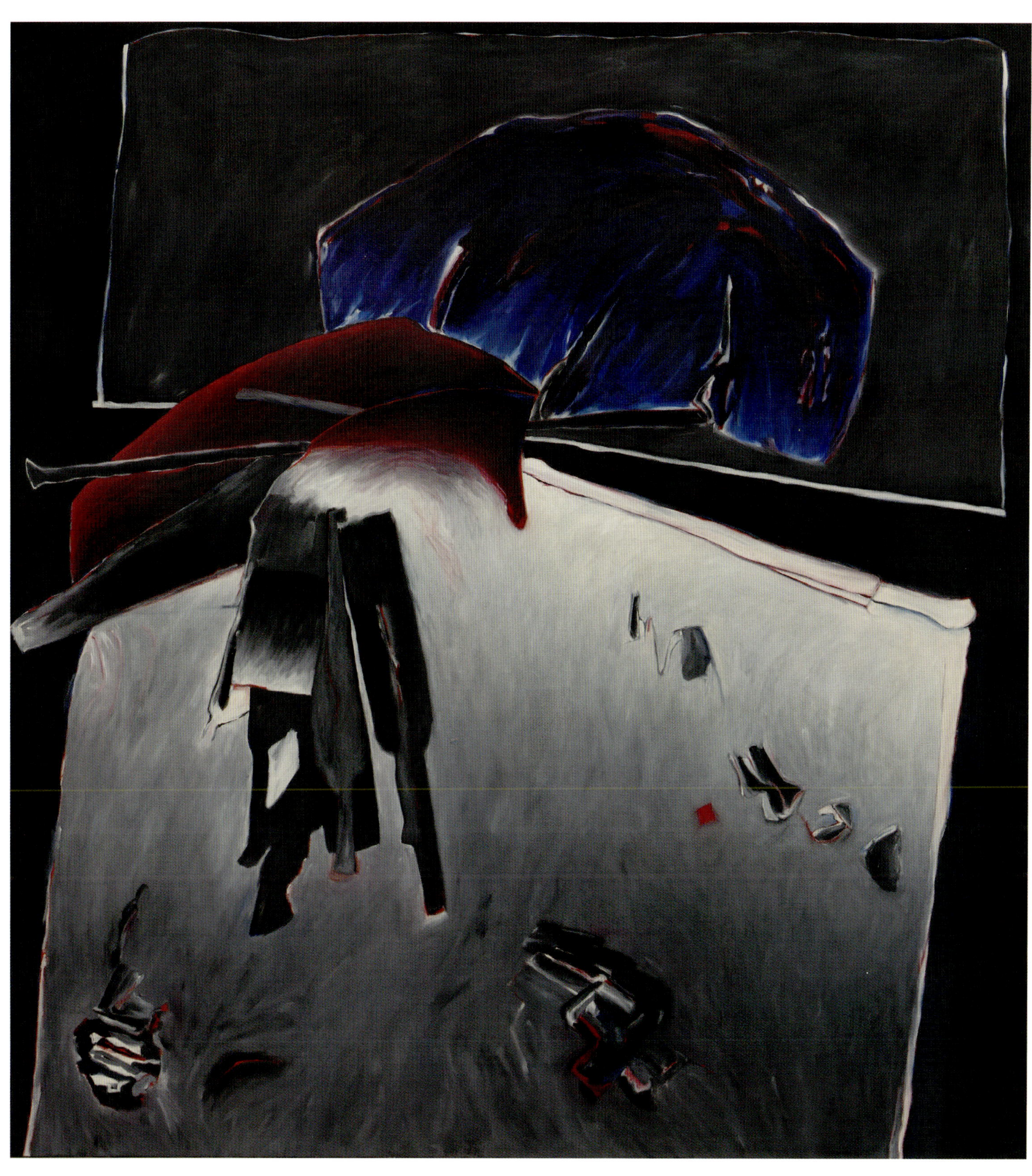

Volans, 1987. Oil on linen, 56 × 52 in. (142.24 × 132 cm)
Deborah Remington Charitable Trust for the Visual Arts

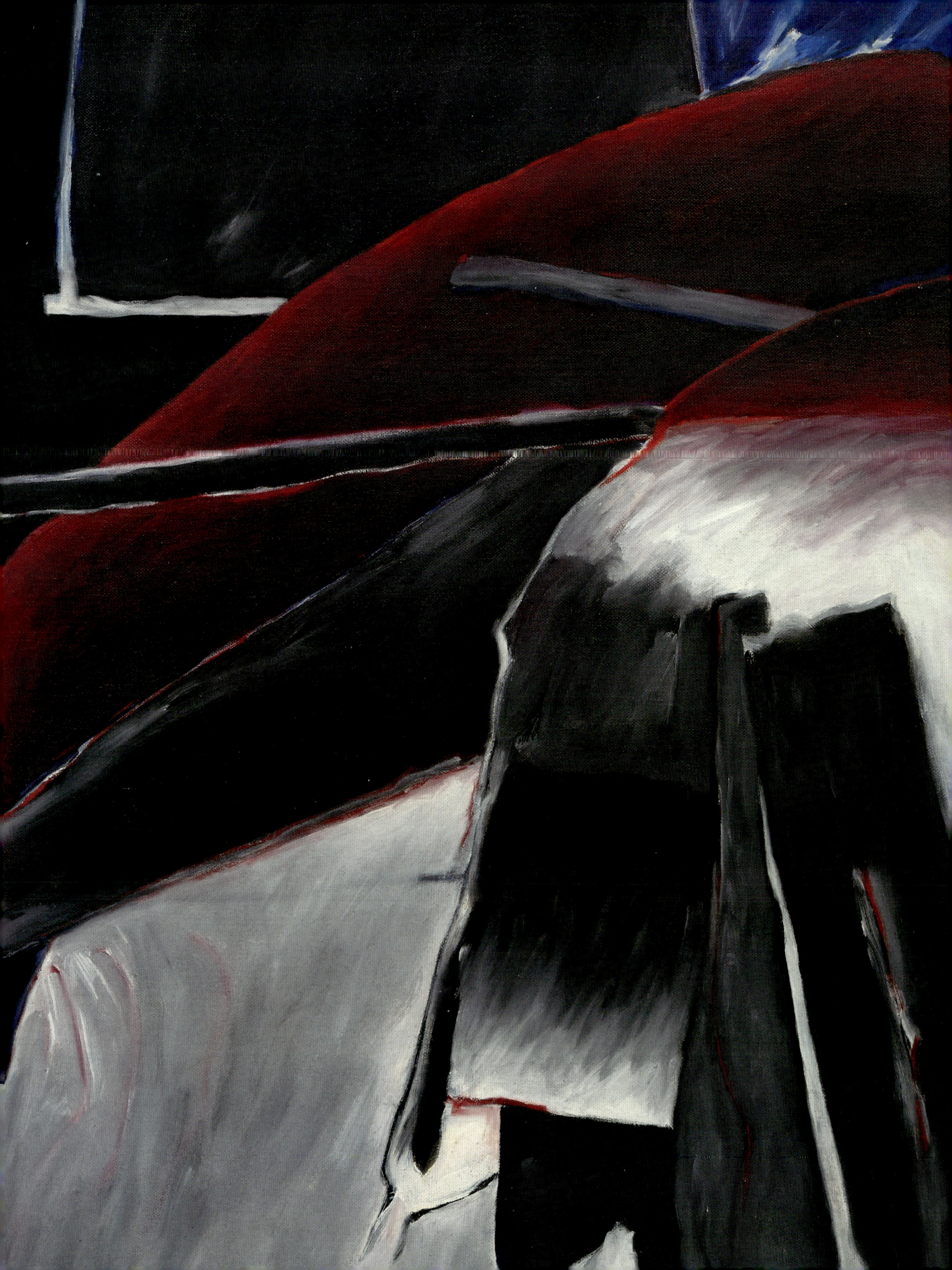

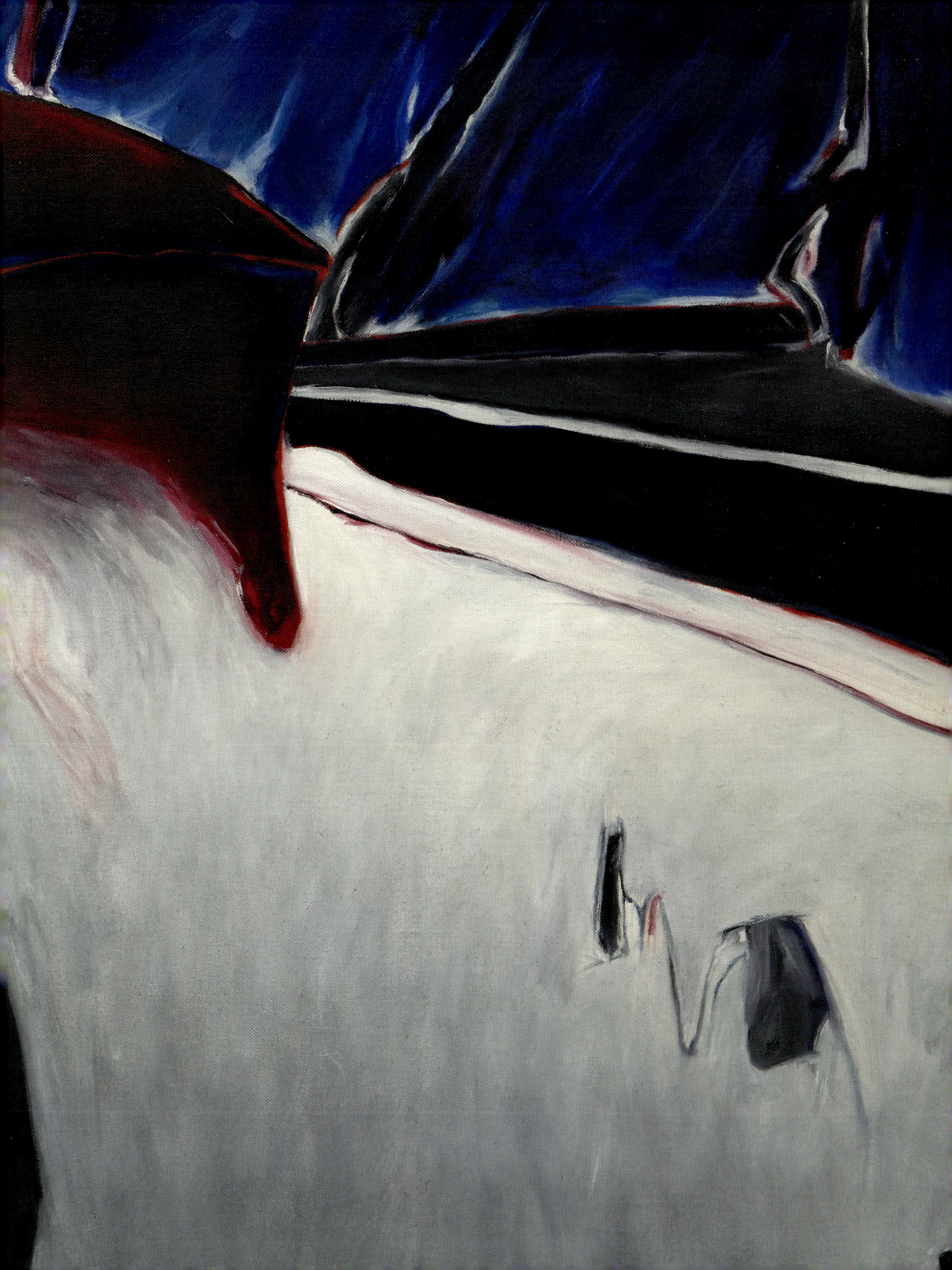

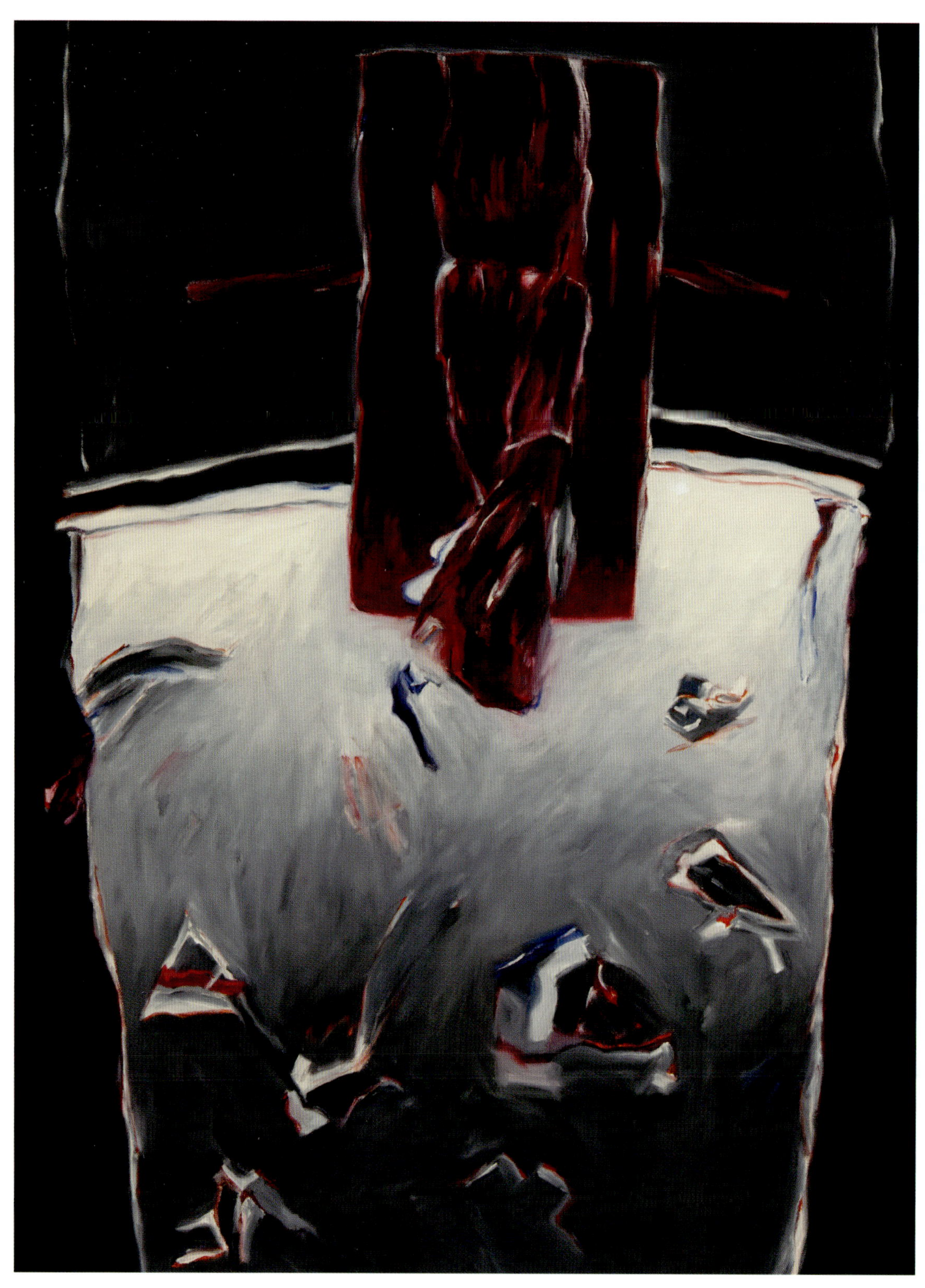

Zyra, 1987. Oil on canvas, 32 × 24 in. (81.3 × 61 cm)
Deborah Remington Charitable Trust for the Visual Arts

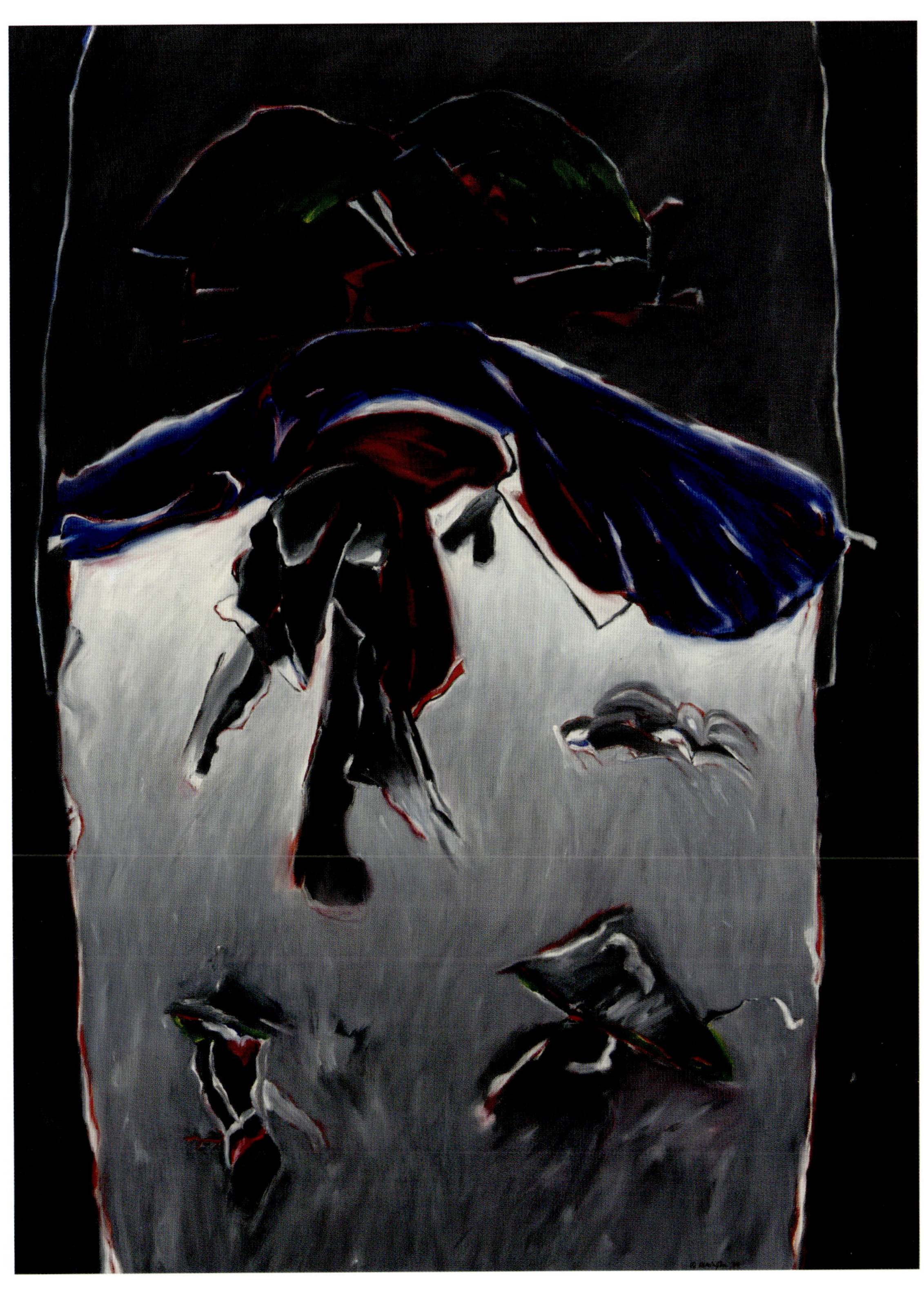

Xton, 1988. Oil on canvas, 32 × 24 in. (81.3 × 61 cm)
Deborah Remington Charitable Trust for the Visual Arts

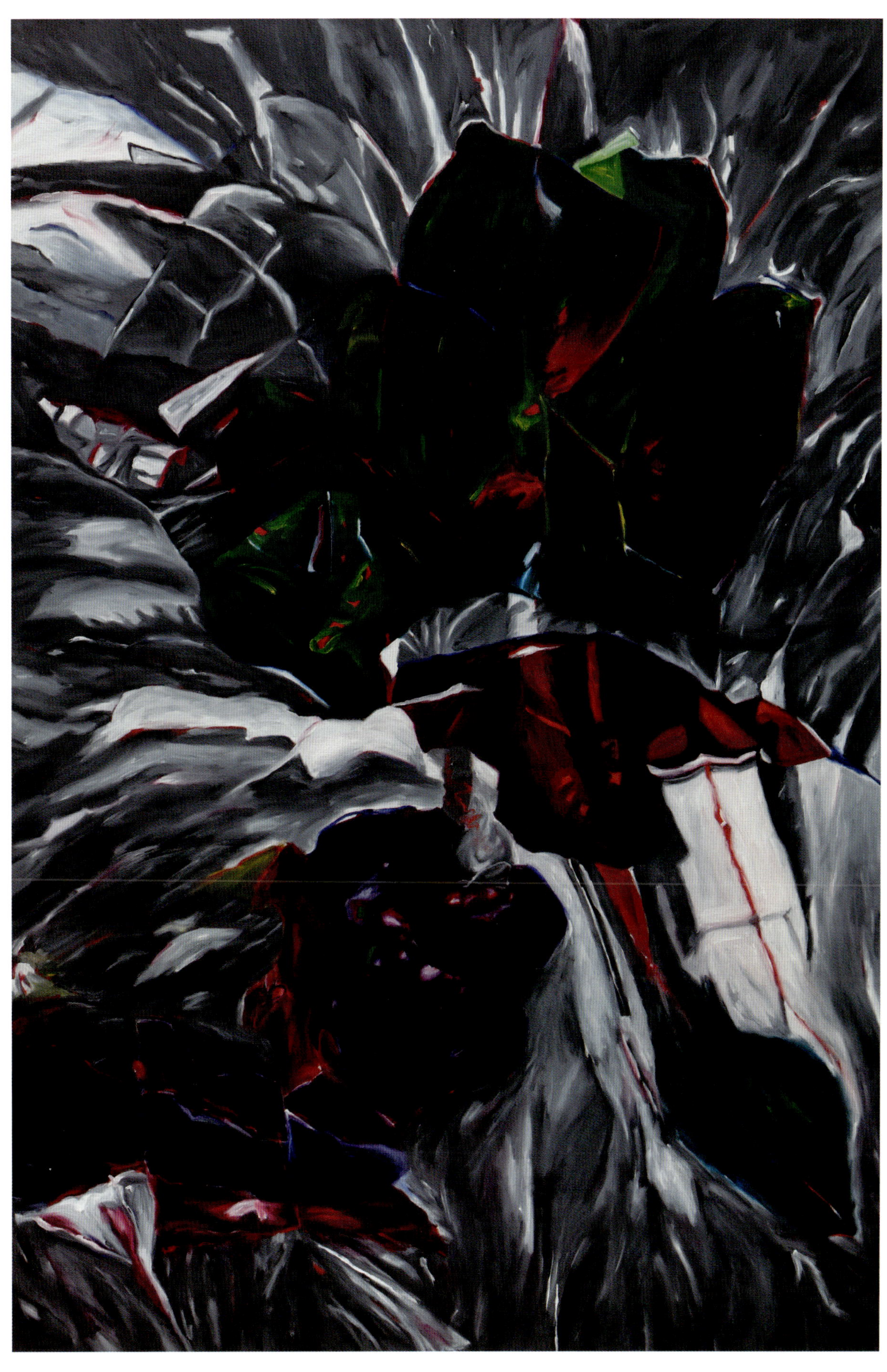

Penrith, 1989. Oil on linen, 74 × 50 in. (187 × 127 cm)
Deborah Remington Charitable Trust for the Visual Arts

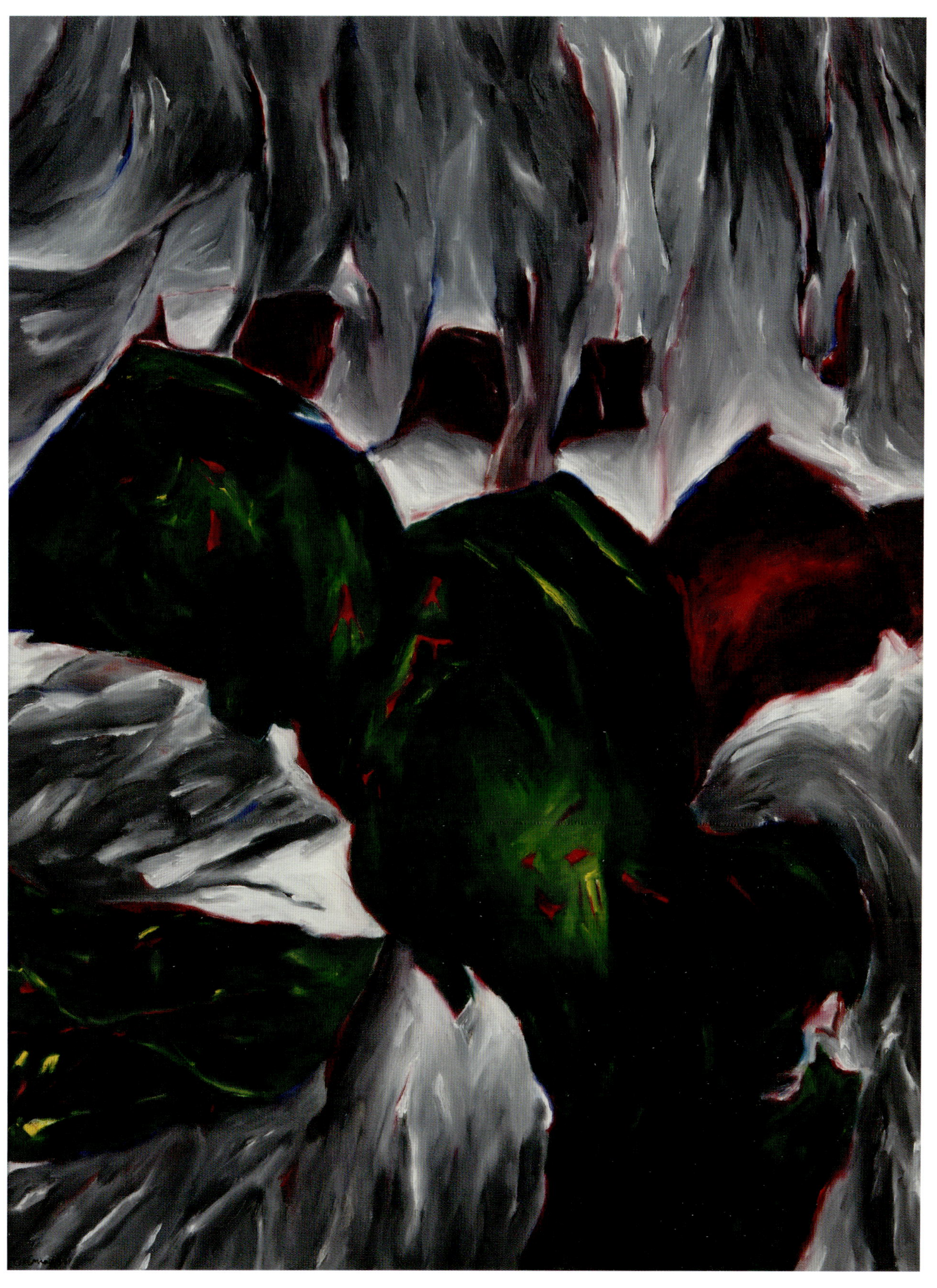

Praxis, 1989. Oil on linen, 32 × 24 in. (81.3 × 61 cm)
Deborah Remington Charitable Trust for the Visual Arts

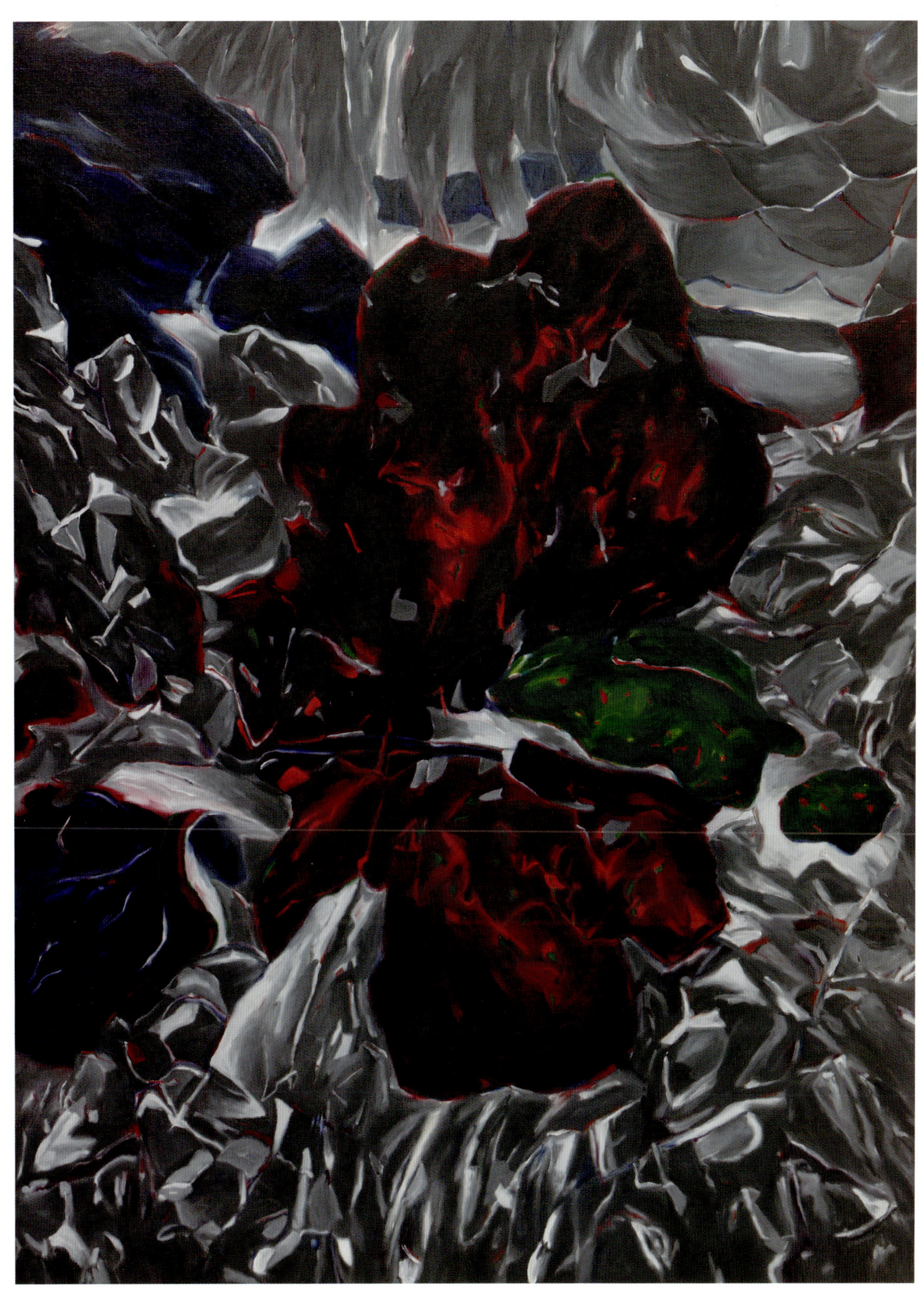

Mechelen, 1991. Oil on canvas, 64 × 47 in. (162.6 × 119.4 cm)
Collection of Timothy C. Headington

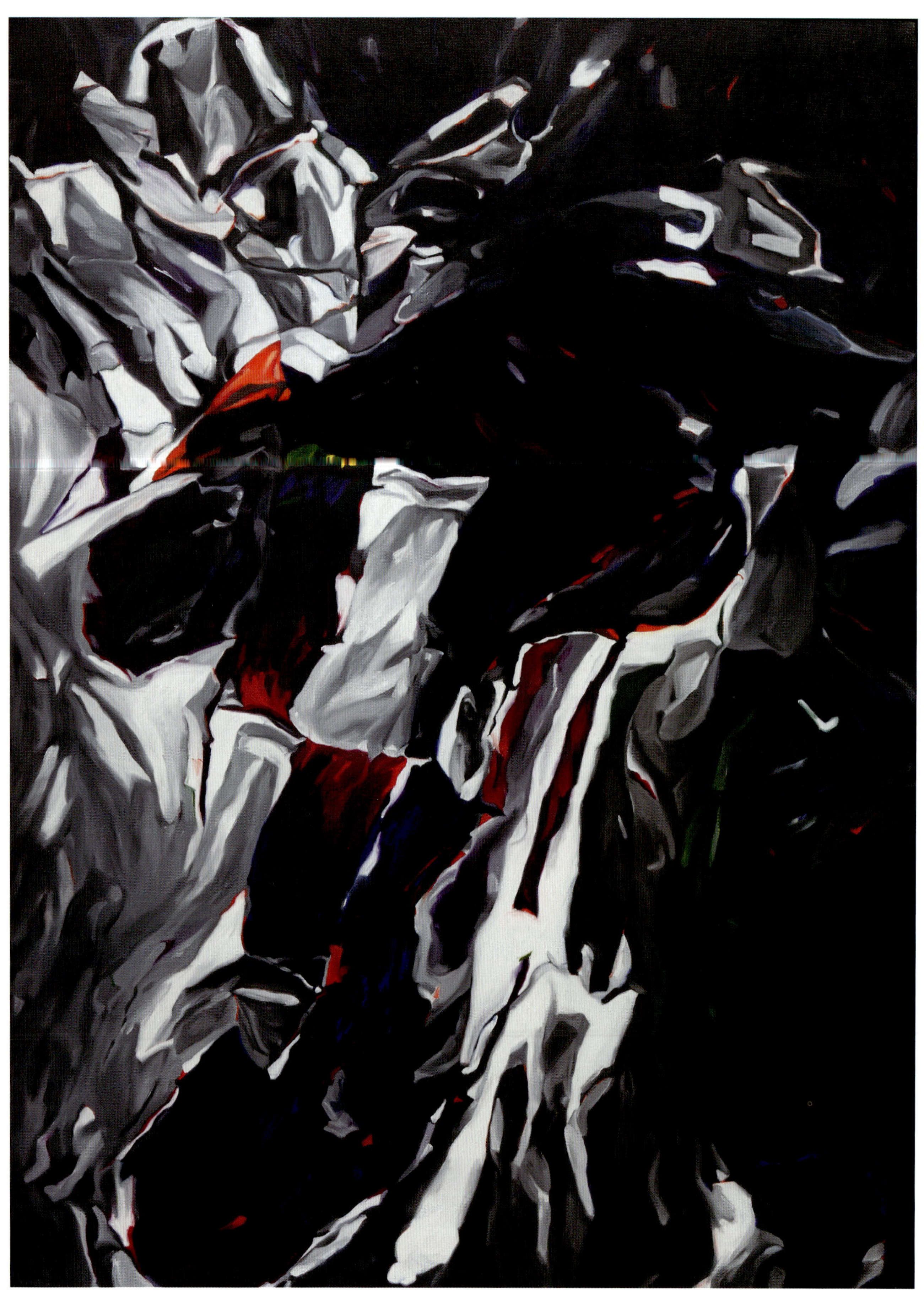

Dark Run, 1992. Oil on linen, 64 × 47 in. (162.6 × 119.4 cm)
Deborah Remington Charitable Trust for the Visual Arts

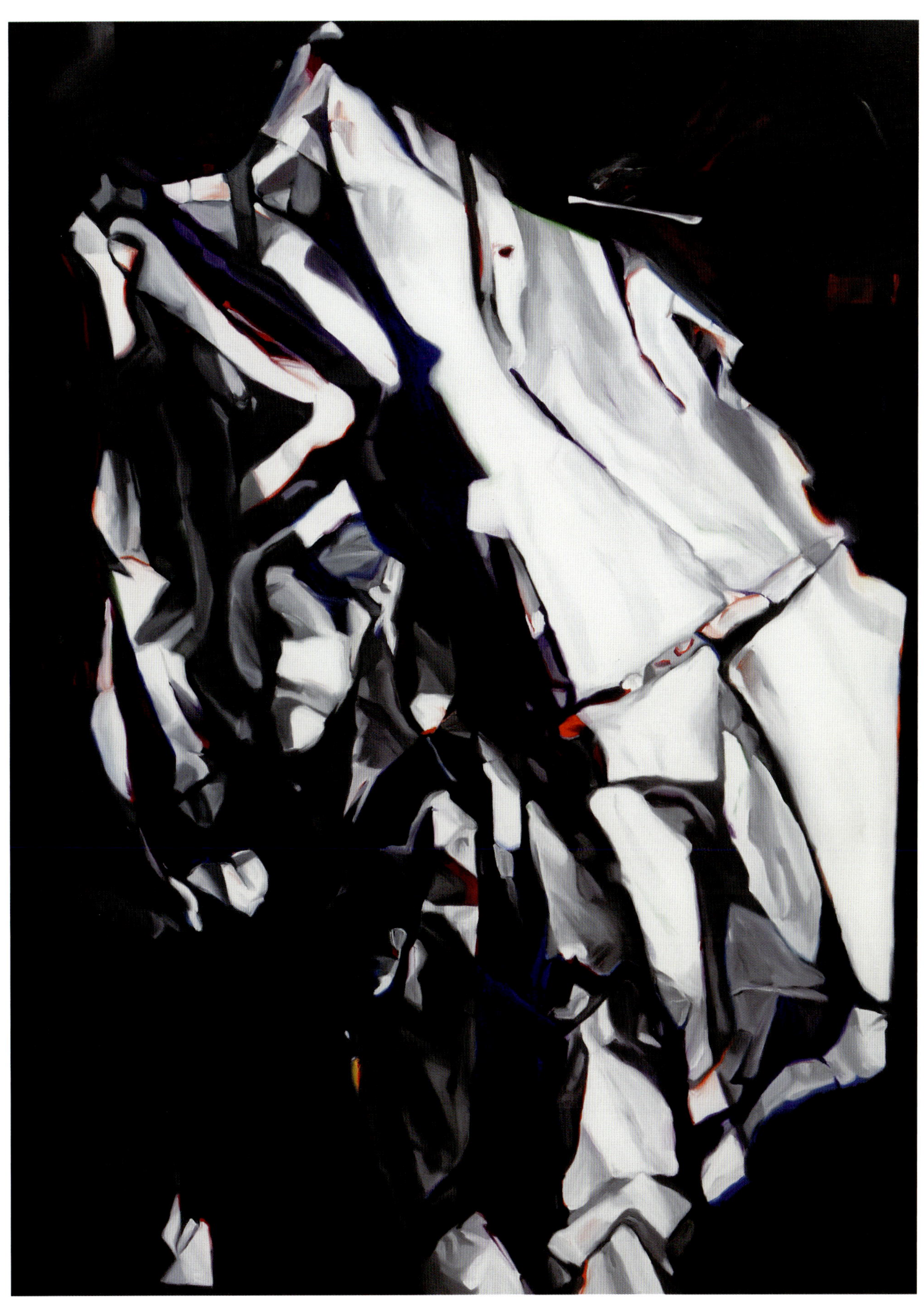

Hydrus, 1993. Oil on linen, 64 × 47 in. (162.6 × 119.4 cm)
Deborah Remington Charitable Trust for the Visual Arts

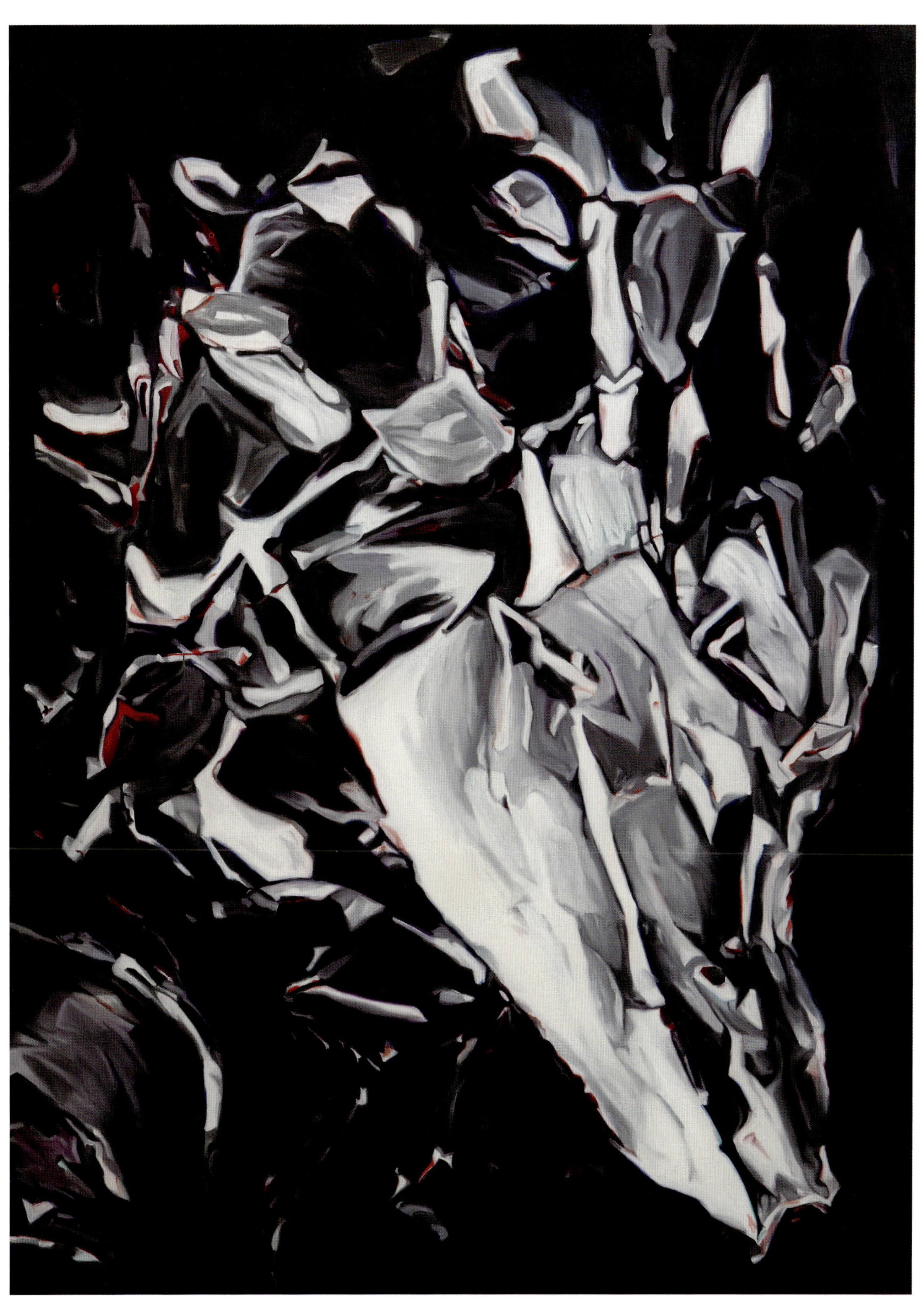

Hebsed, 1993. Oil on linen, 64 × 47 in. (162.6 × 119.4 cm)
Deborah Remington Charitable Trust for the Visual Arts

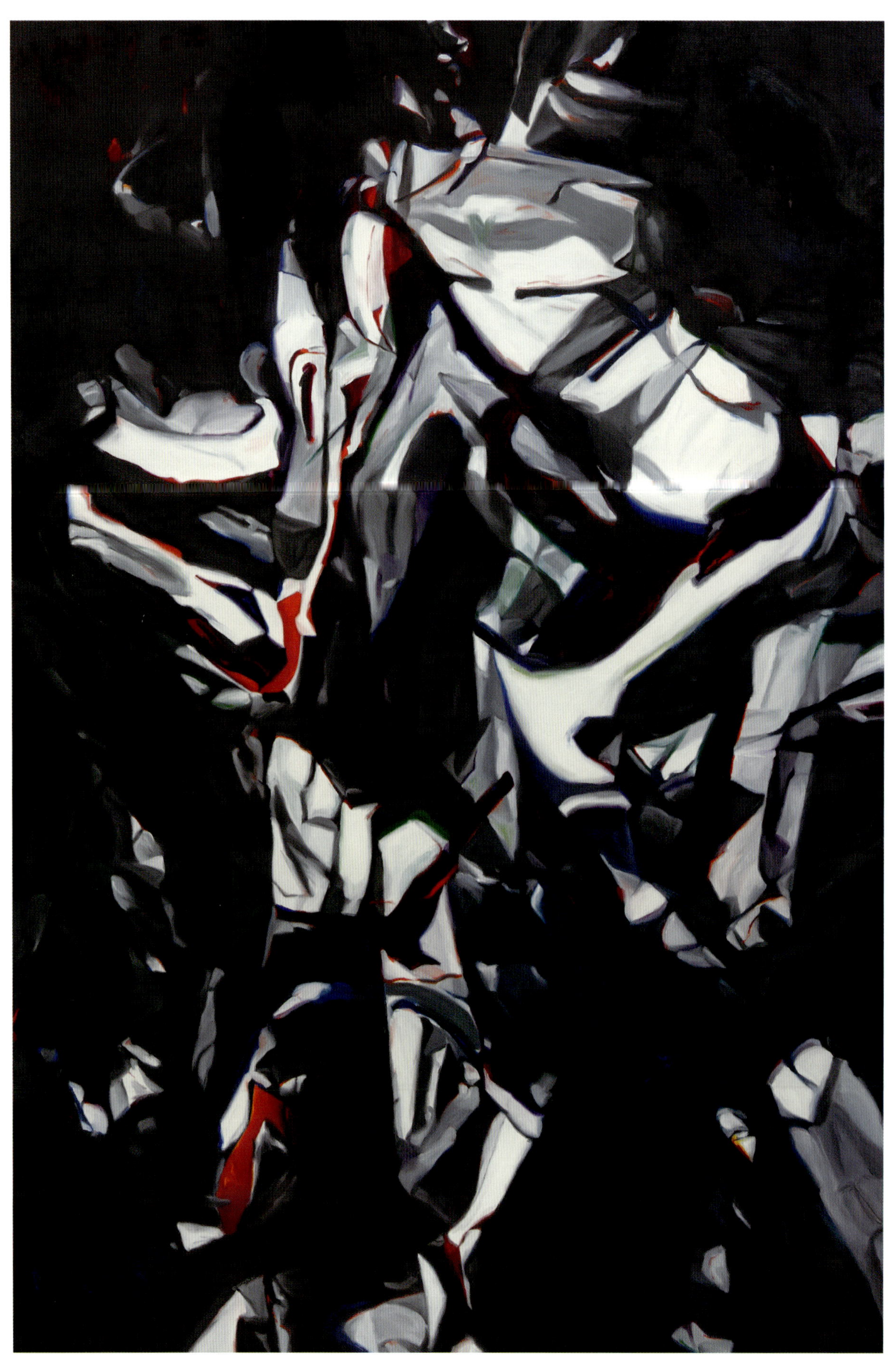

Zeno, 1994. Oil on canvas, 74 × 50 in. (188 × 127 cm)
Deborah Remington Charitable Trust for the Visual Arts

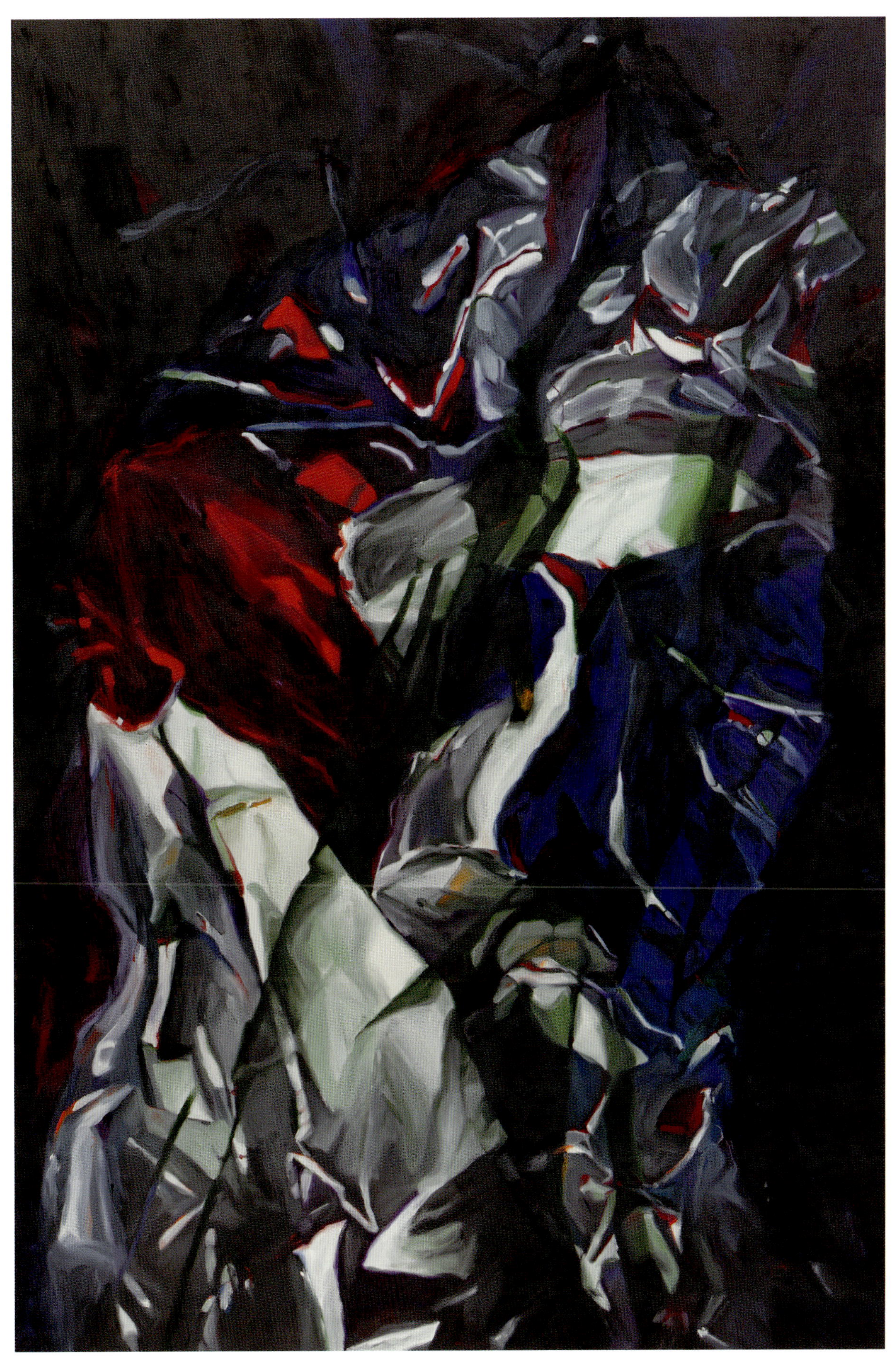

Vertum, 1994. Oil on linen, 74 × 50 in. (188 × 127 cm)
Deborah Remington Charitable Trust for the Visual Arts

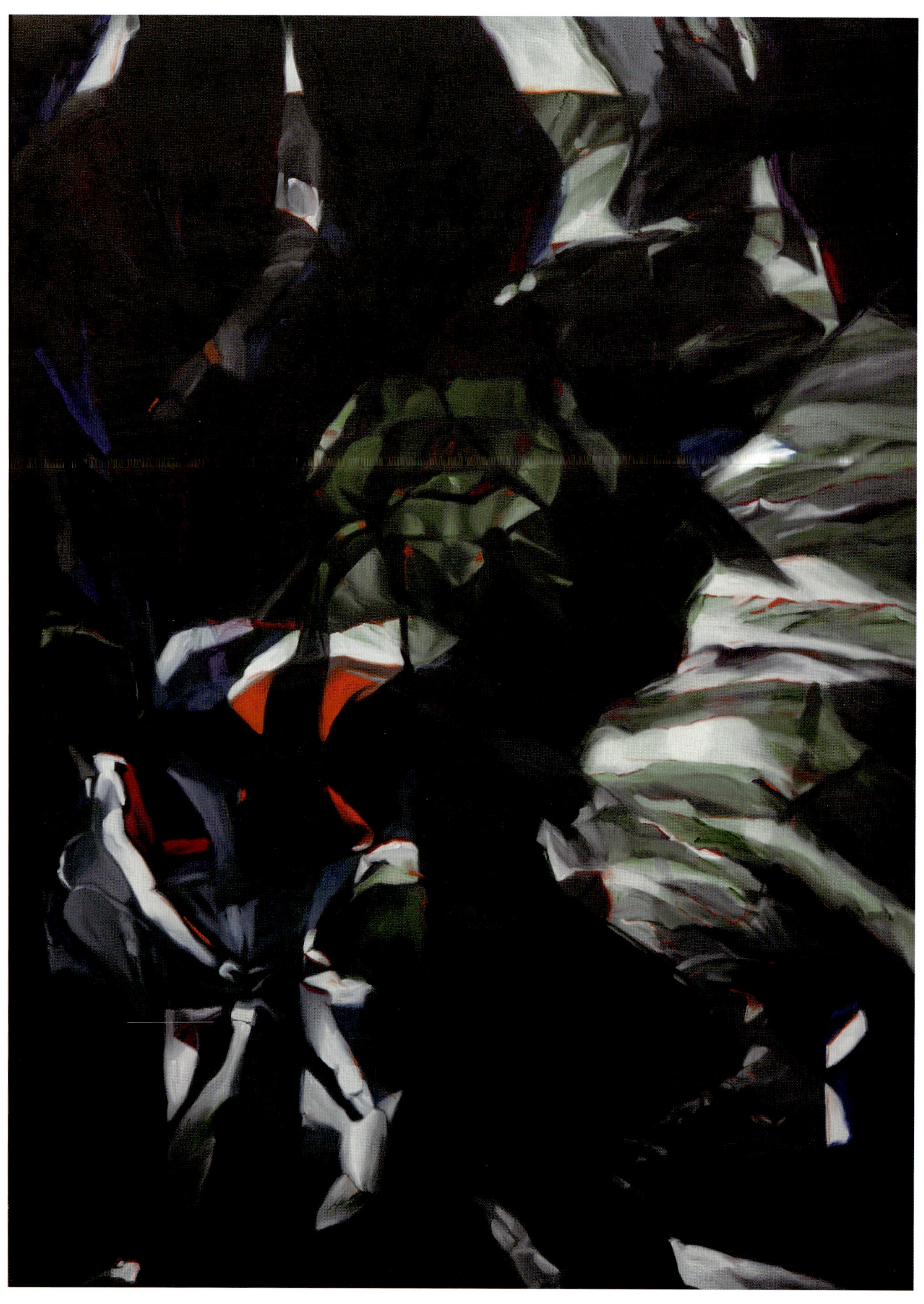

Ketu, 1995. Oil on linen, 64 × 47 in. (162.6 × 119.4 cm)
Deborah Remington Charitable Trust for the Visual Arts

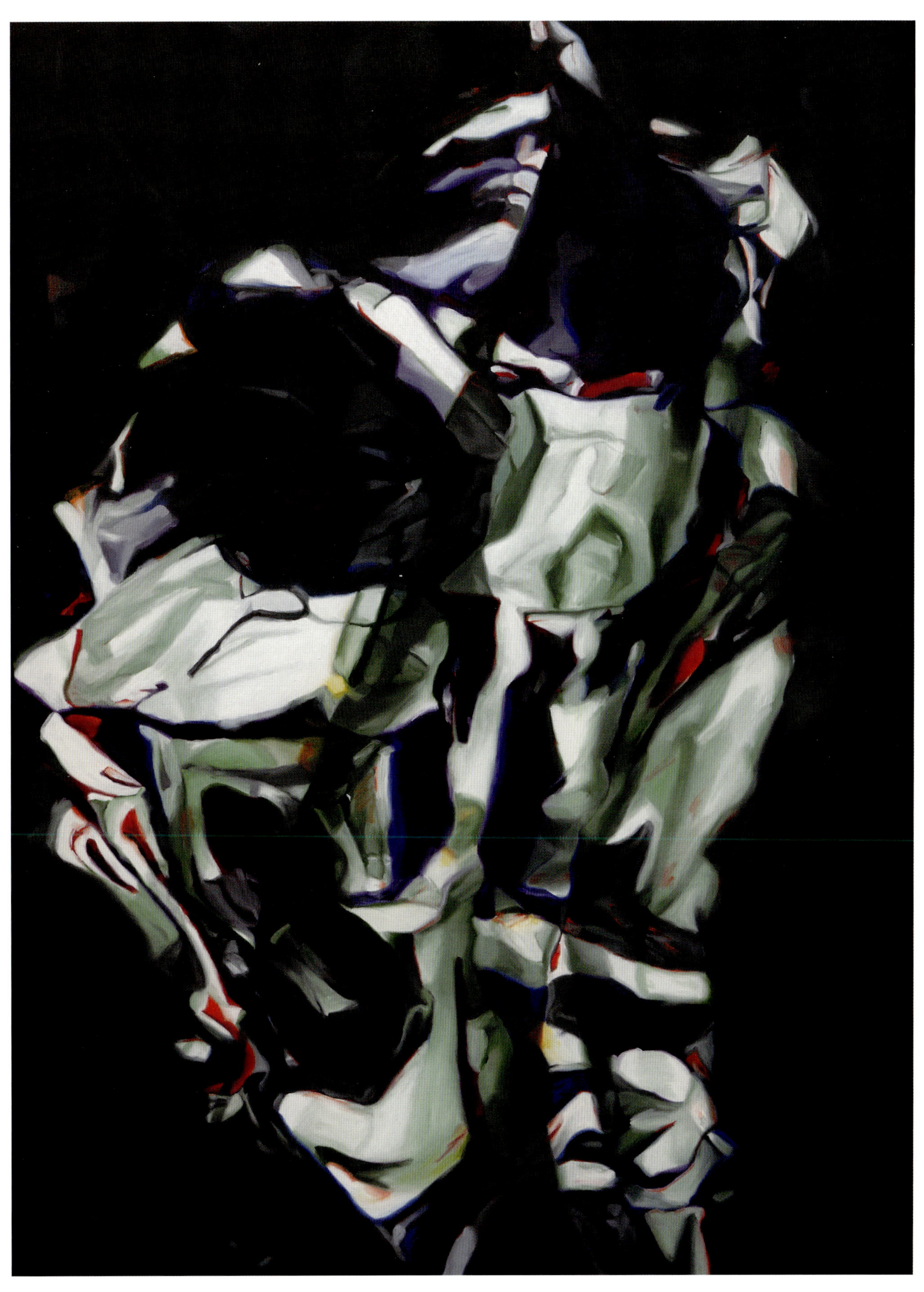

Minquas, 1995. Oil on linen, 64 × 47 in. (162.6 × 119.4 cm)
Deborah Remington Charitable Trust for the Visual Arts

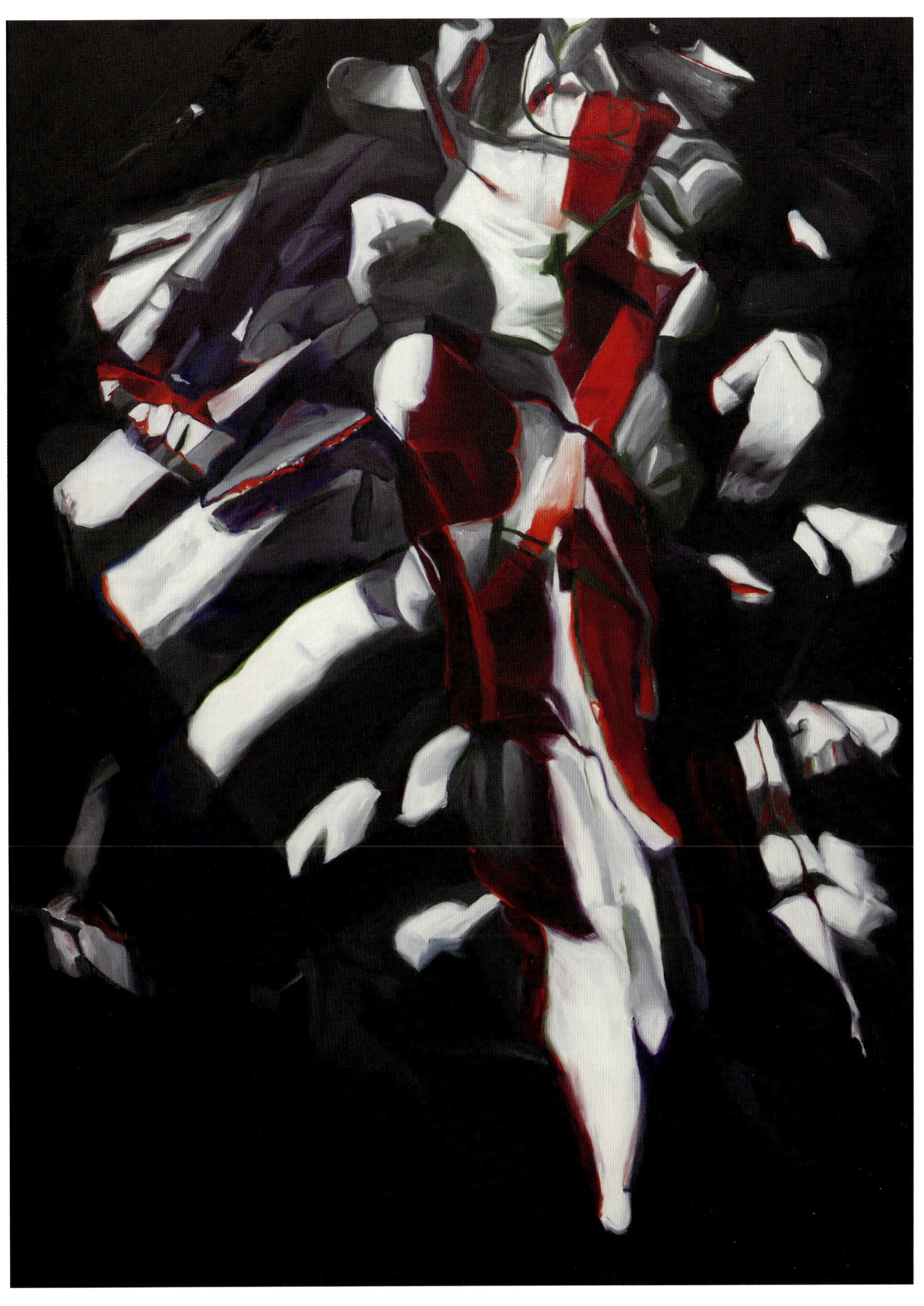

Tarx, 1998. Oil on canvas, 64 × 47 in. (162.6 × 119.4 cm)
Deborah Remington Charitable Trust for the Visual Arts

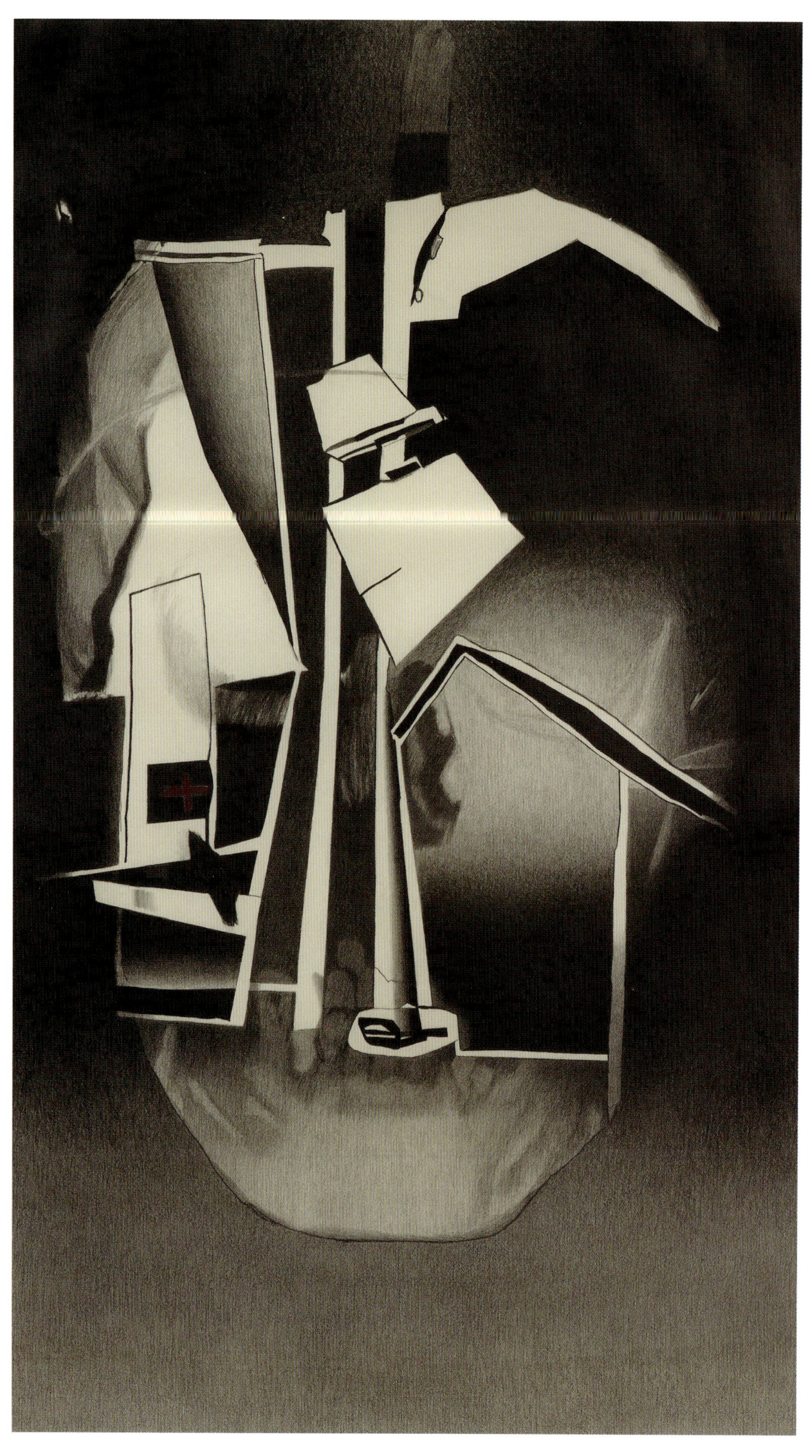

Beinen I, 1997. Graphite and crayon on paper, 72 × 42 in. (182.9 × 106.7 cm)
Deborah Remington Charitable Trust for the Visual Arts

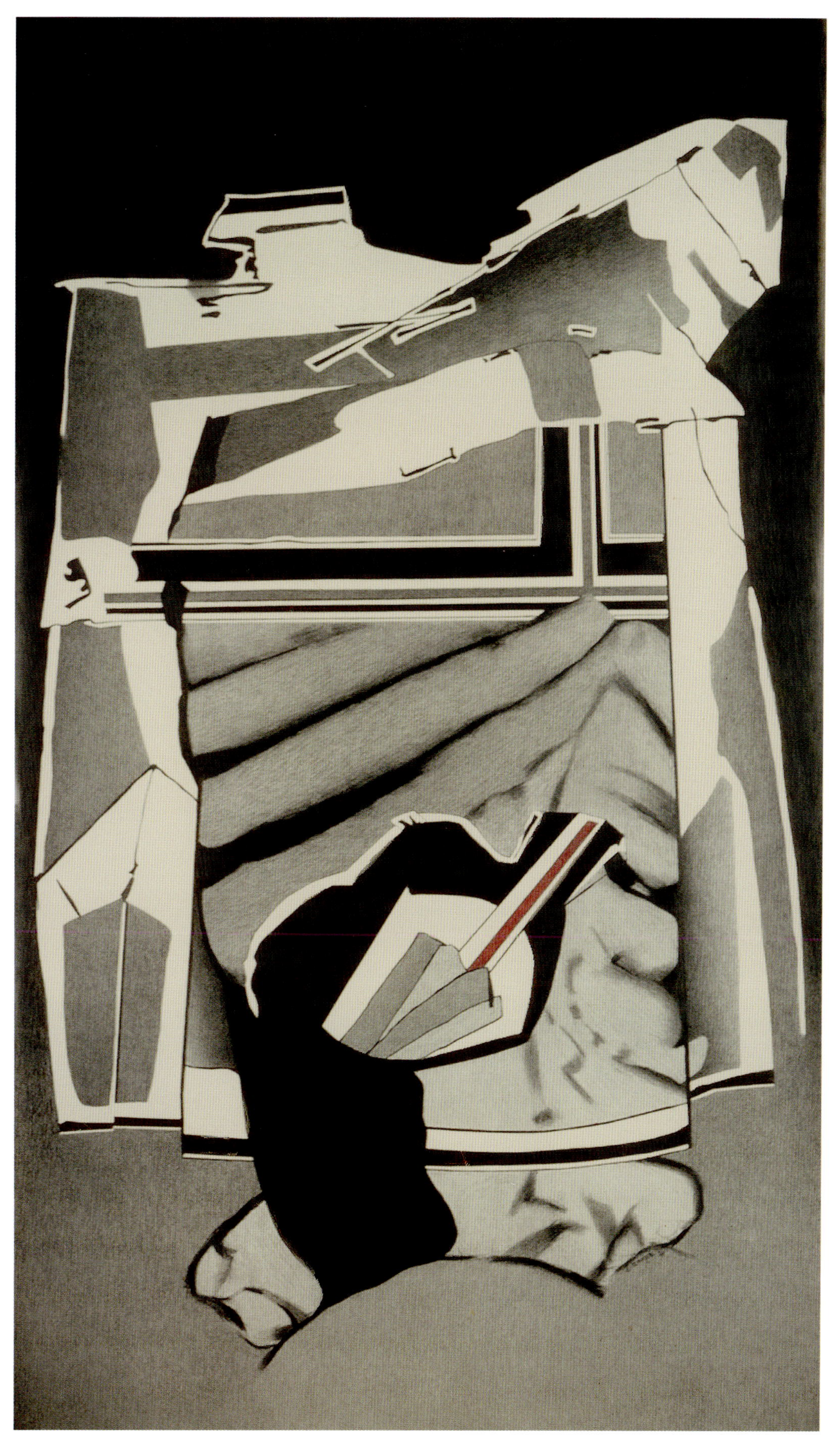

Beinen II, 1998. Graphite and crayon on paper, 72 × 42 in. (182.9 × 106.7 cm)
Collection of Beth Rudin DeWoody

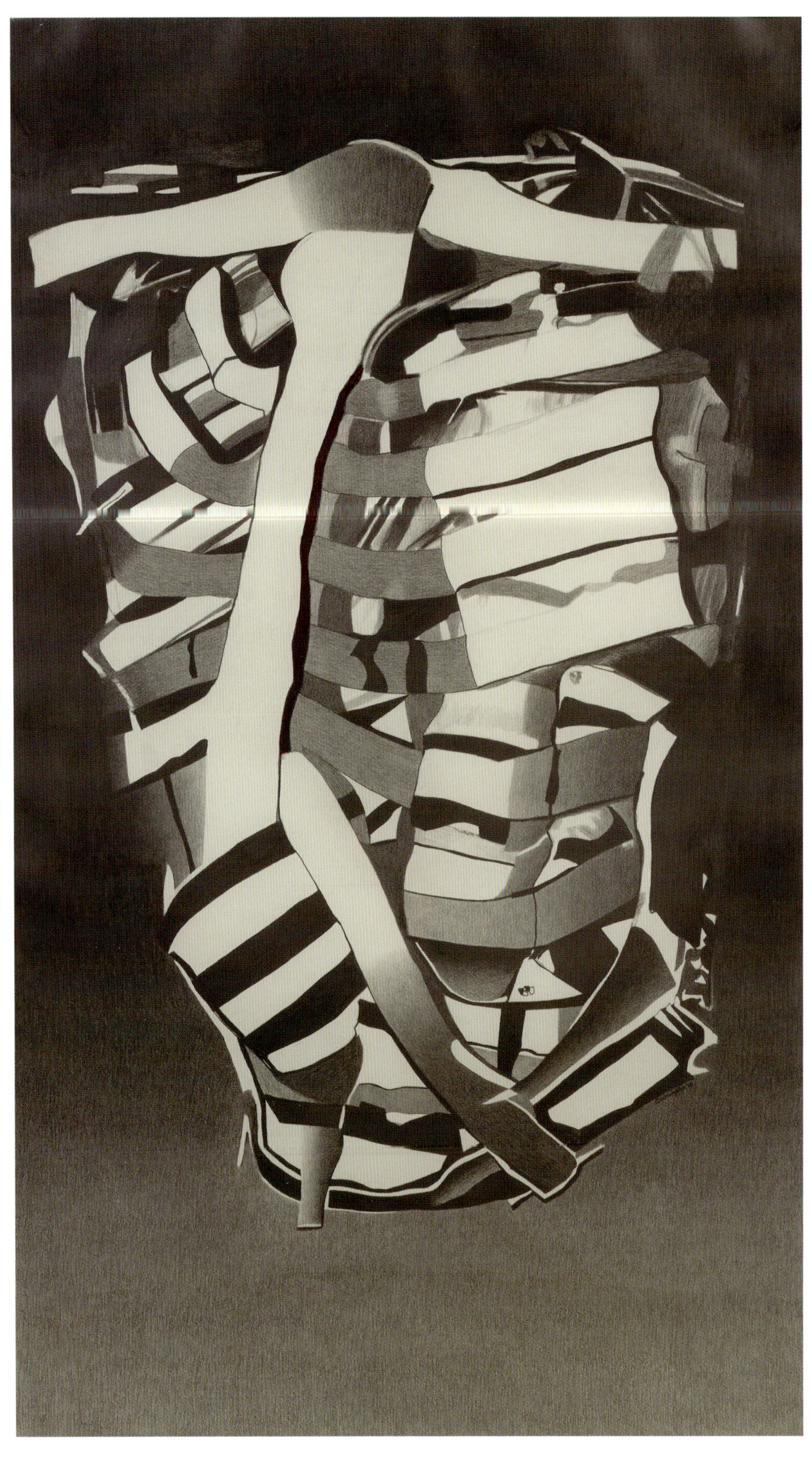

Beinen III, 1998. Graphite and crayon on paper, 72 × 42 in. (182.9 × 106.7 cm)
Private collection

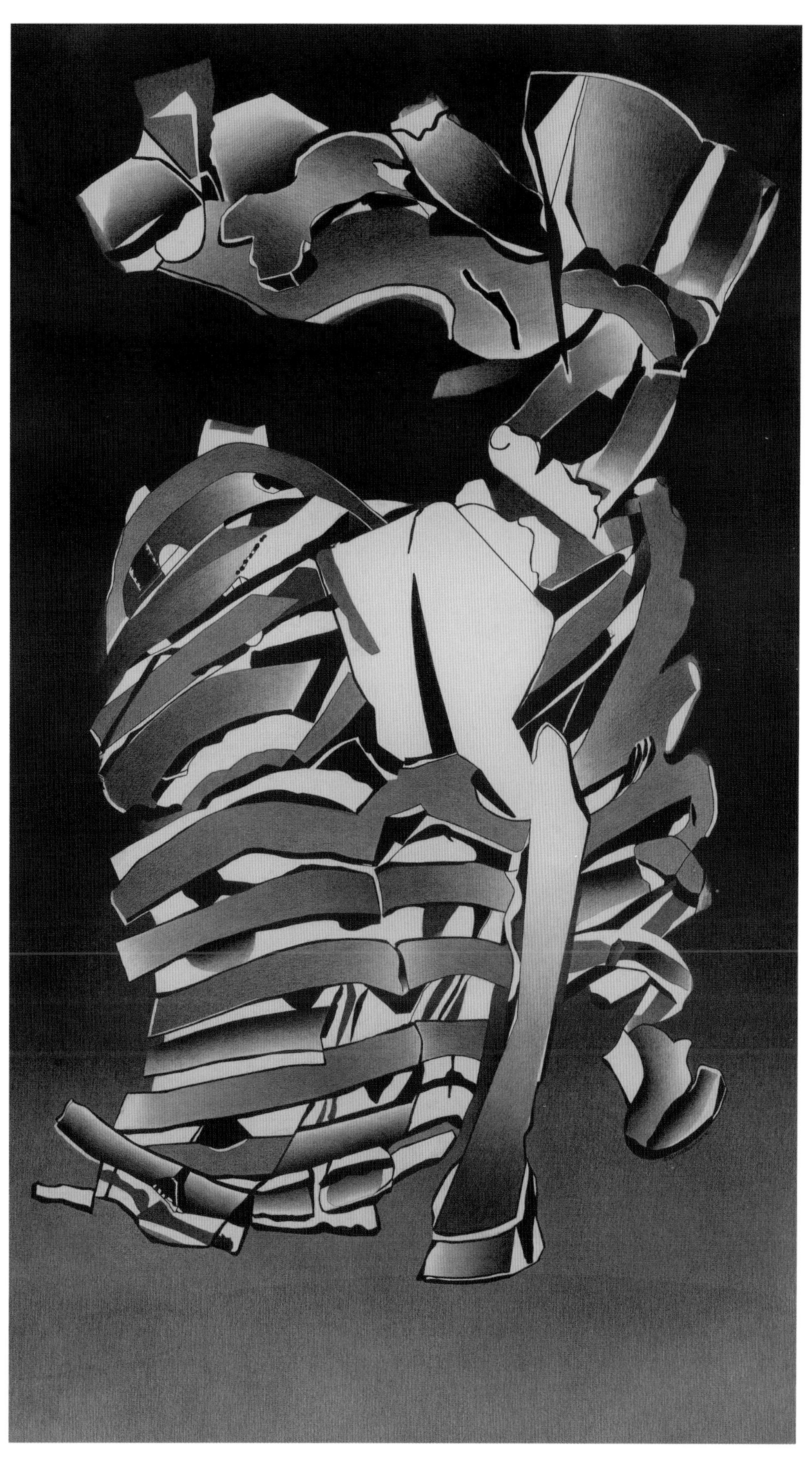

Beinen IV, 2000–01. Graphite and crayon on paper, 72 × 42 in. (182.9 × 106.7 cm)
Deborah Remington Charitable Trust for the Visual Arts

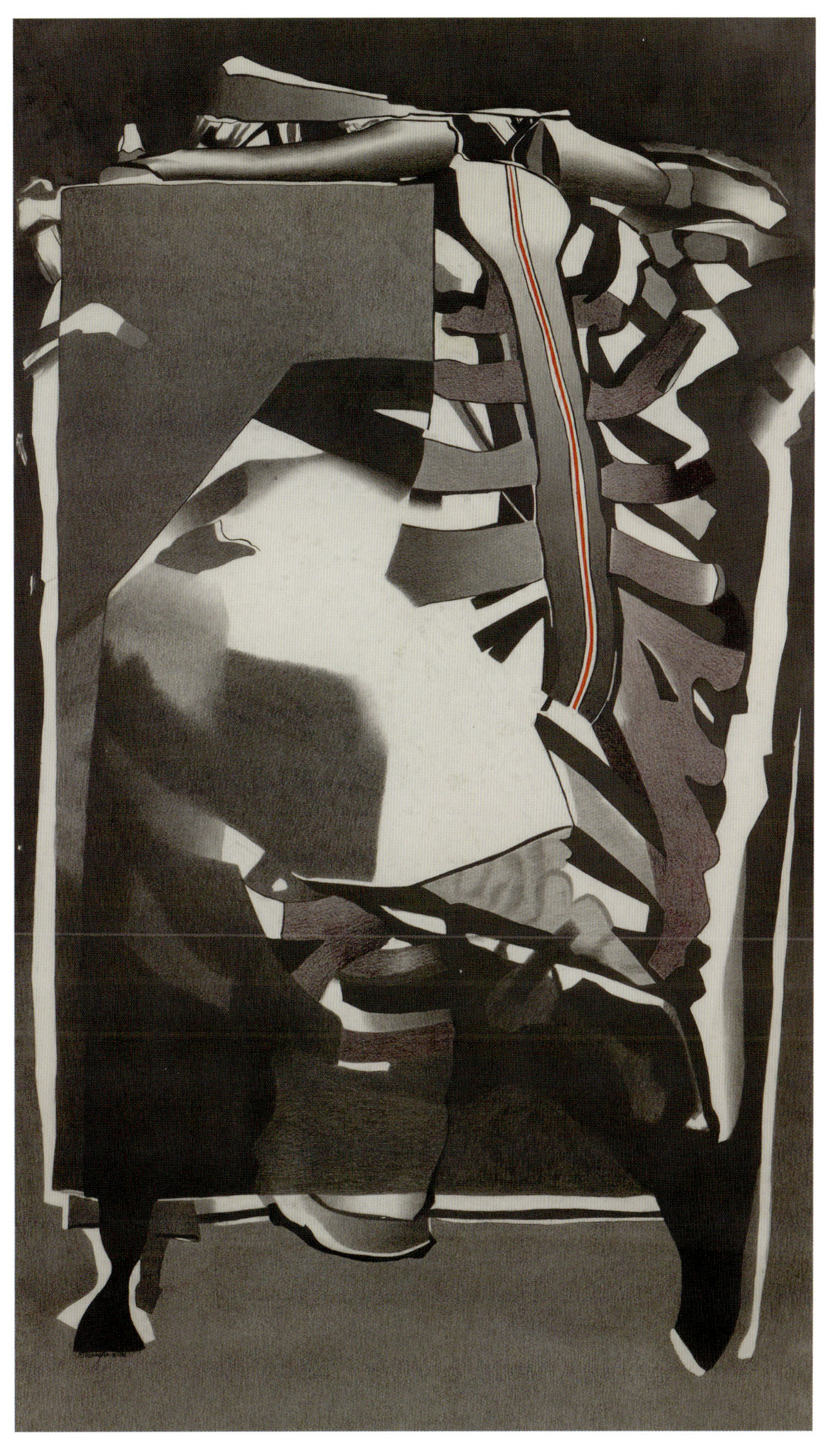

Beinen V, 2006. Graphite and crayon on paper, 72 × 42 in. (182.9 × 106.7 cm)
Private collection

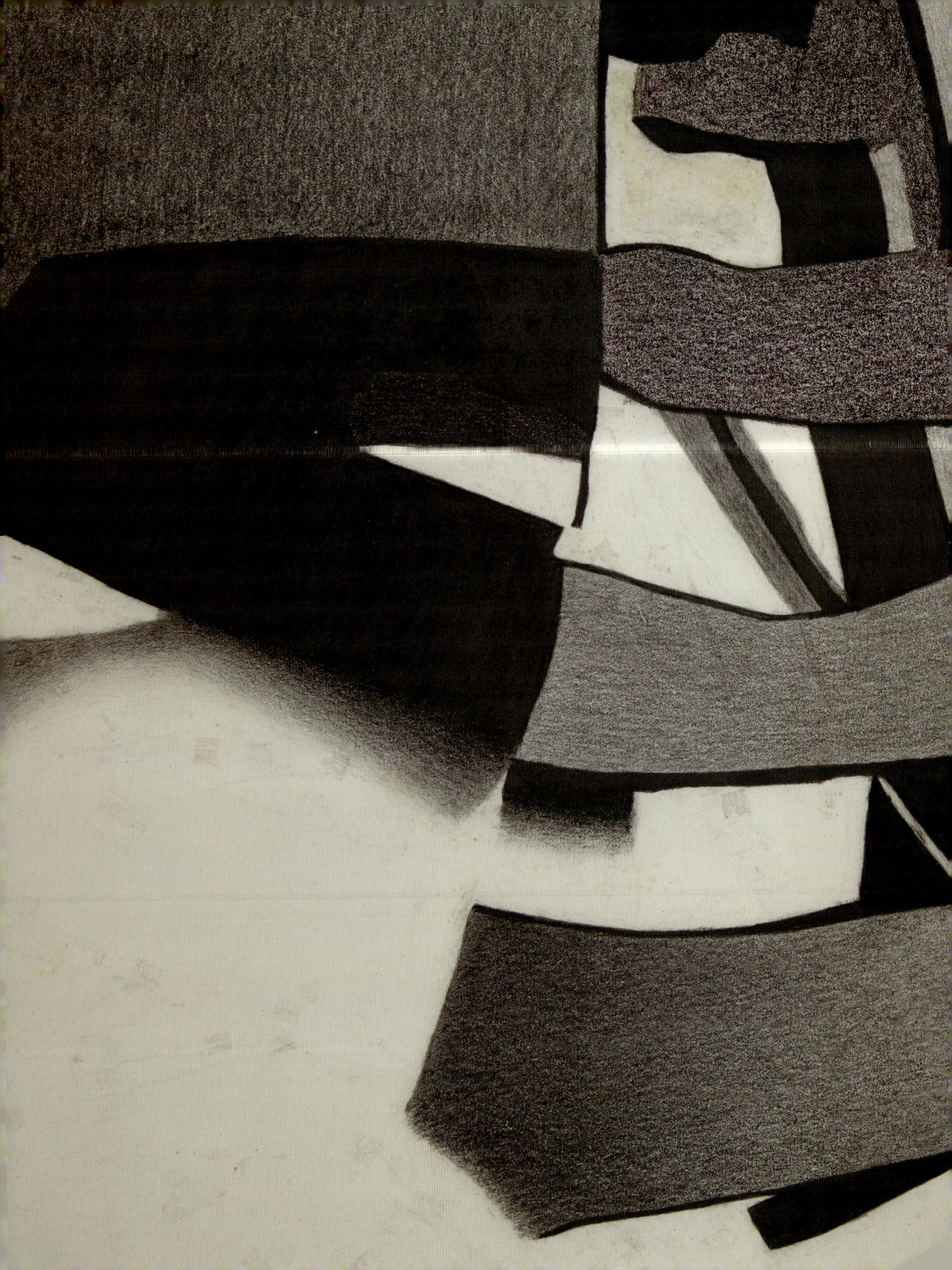

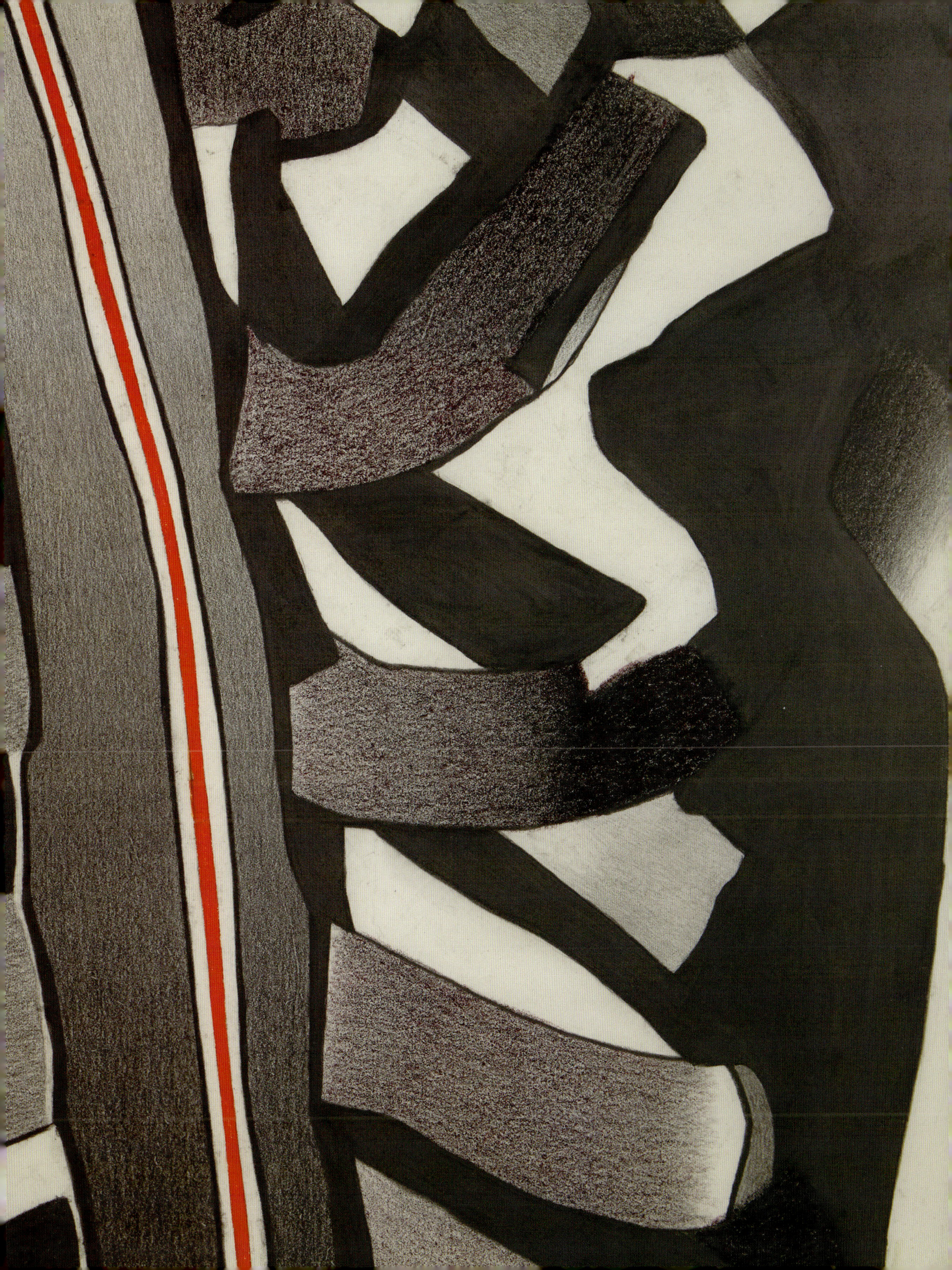

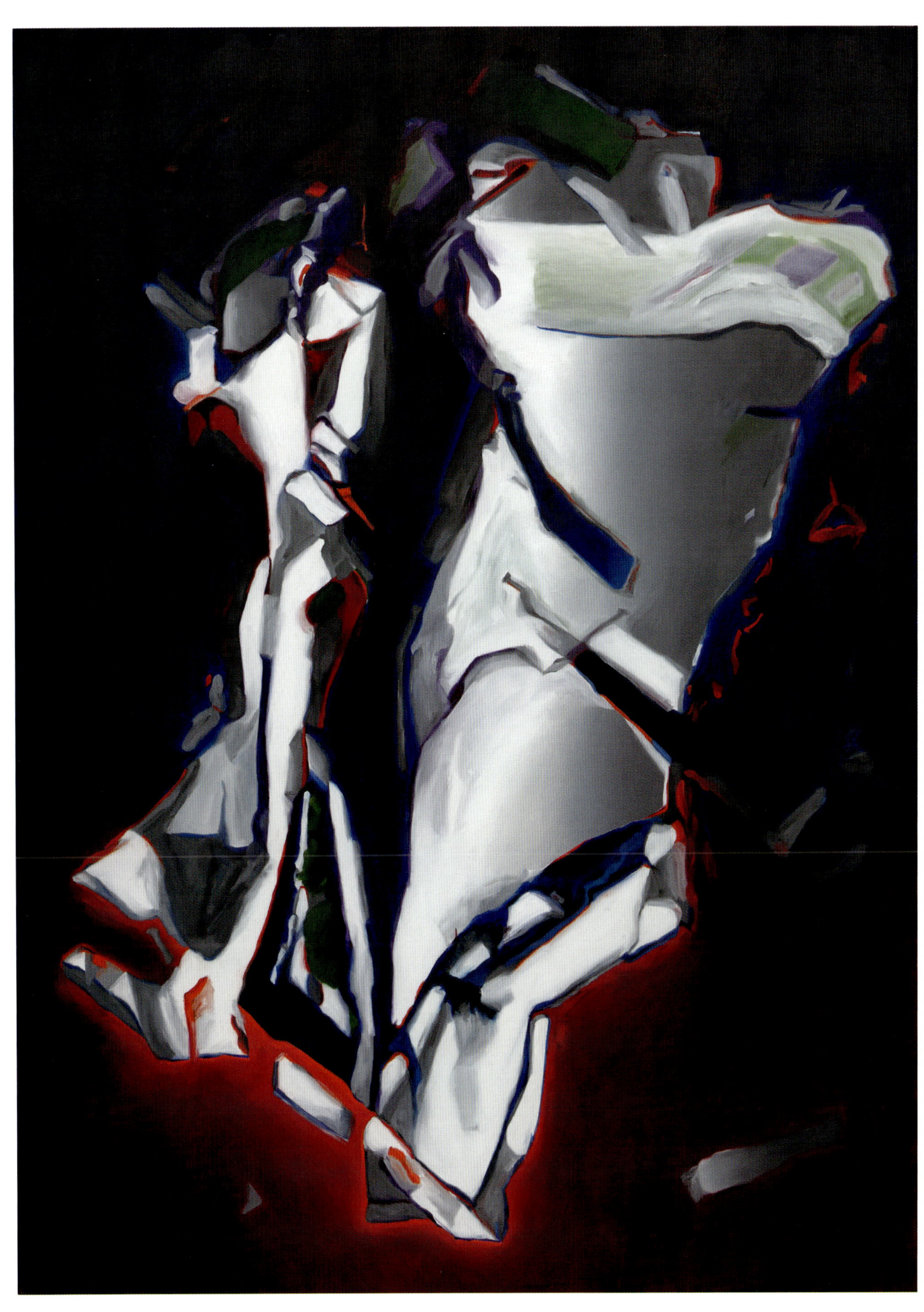

Eridan, 2001. Oil on linen, 64 × 47 in. (162.6 × 119.4 cm)
ASOM Collection

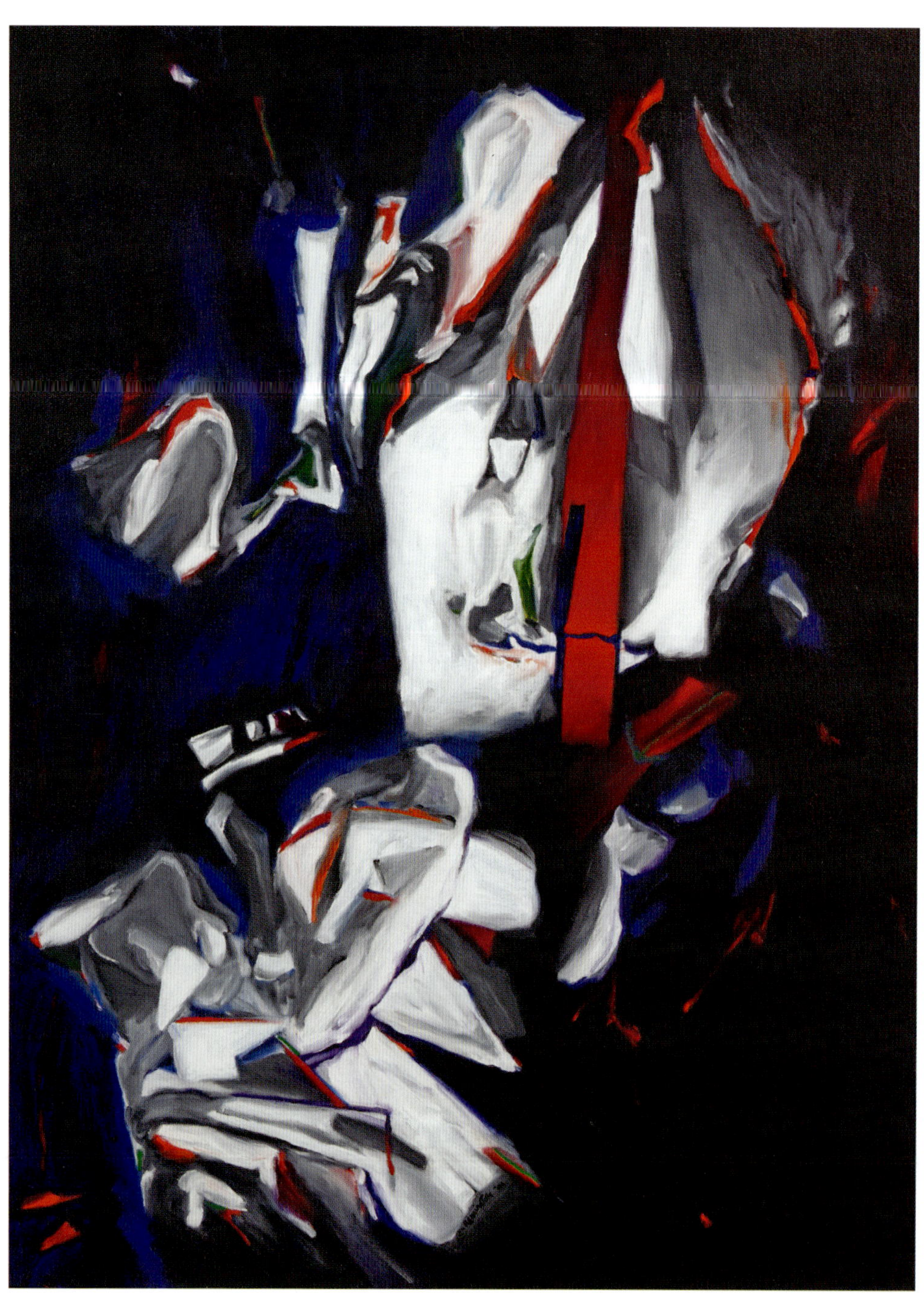

Ides, 2001. Oil on canvas, 32 × 24 in. (81.3 × 61 cm)
Deborah Remington Charitable Trust for the Visual Arts

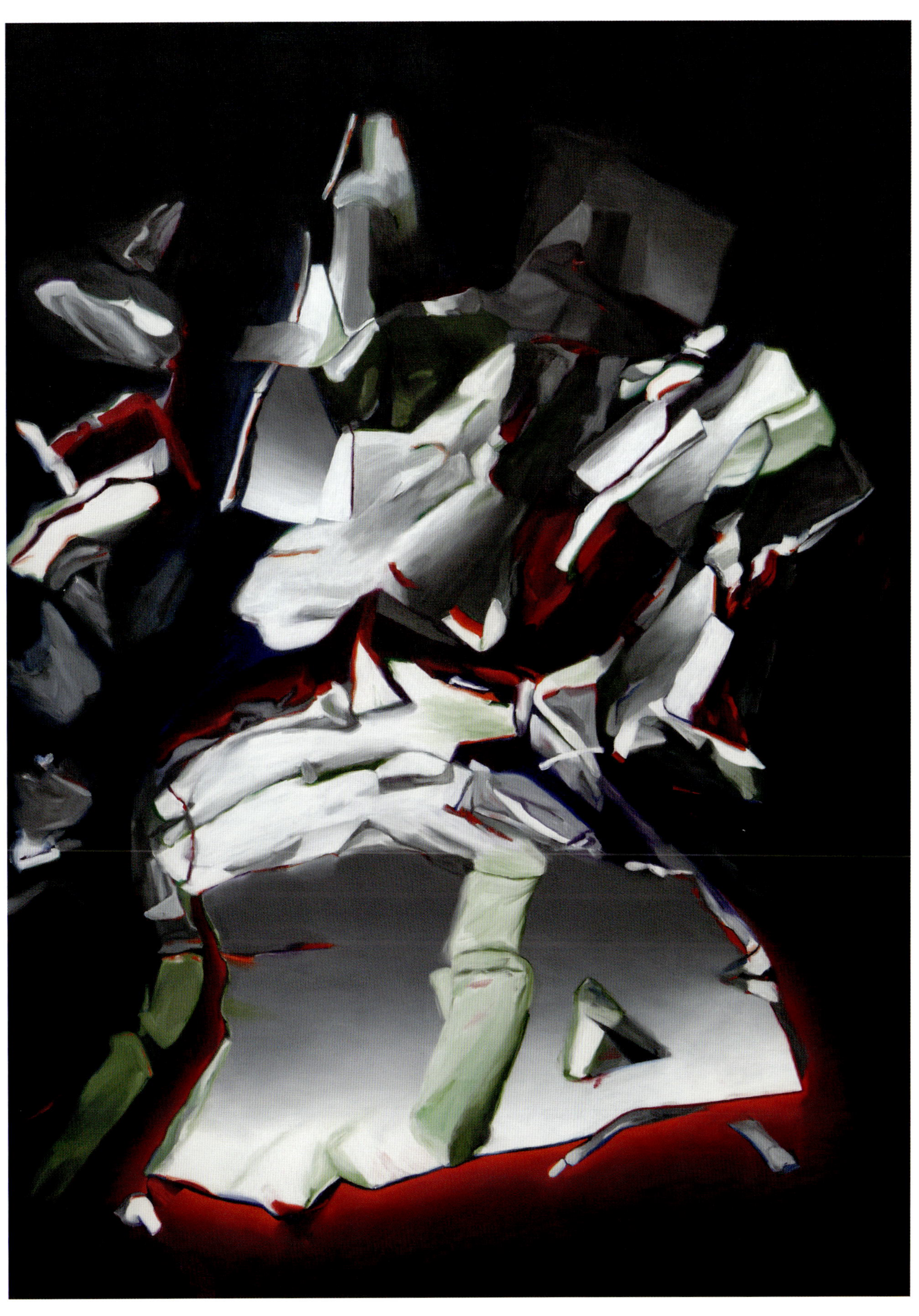

Calyd, 1999–2003. Oil on canvas, 64 × 47 in. (162.5 × 119 cm)
Collection of Timothy C. Headington

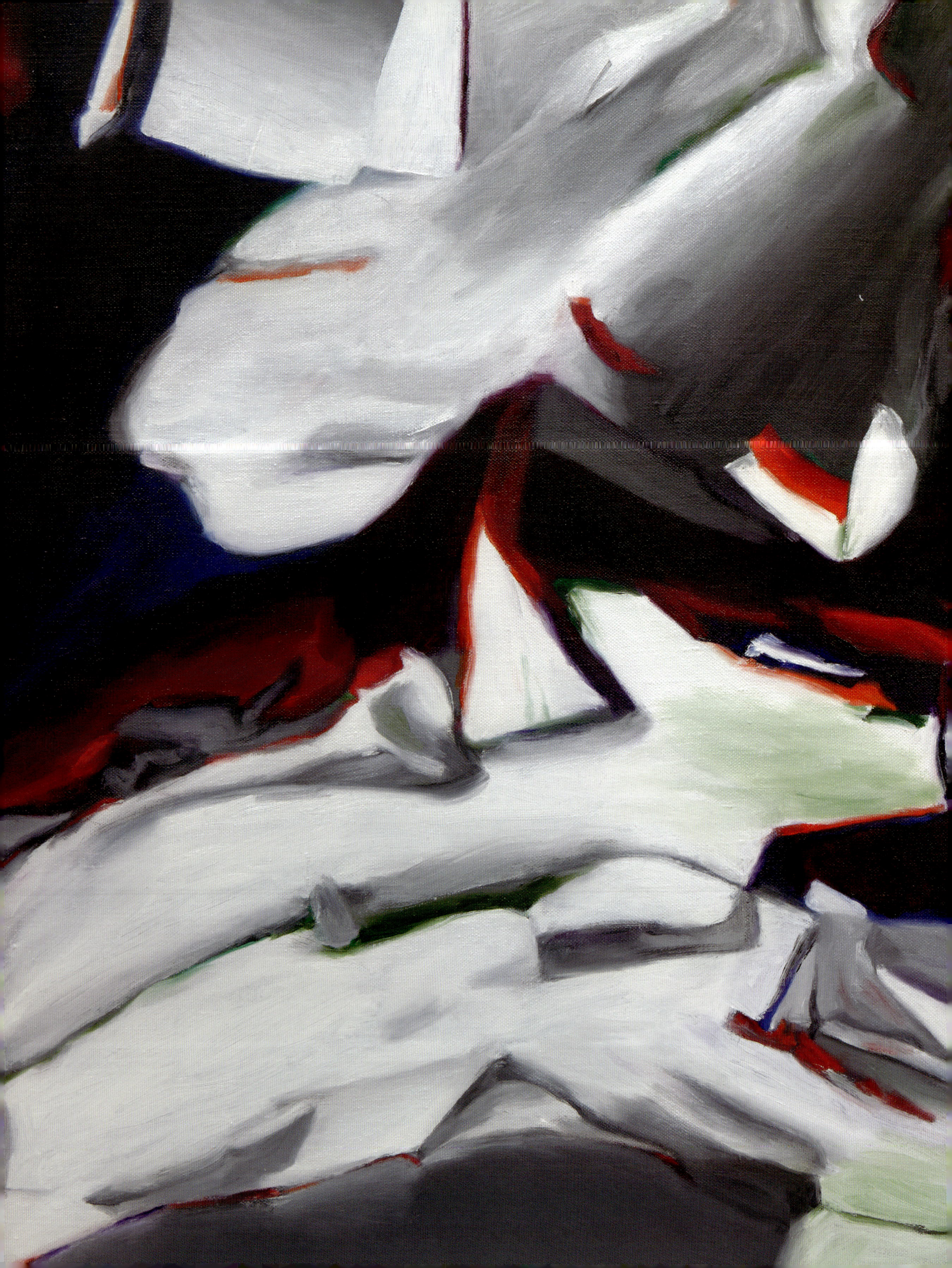

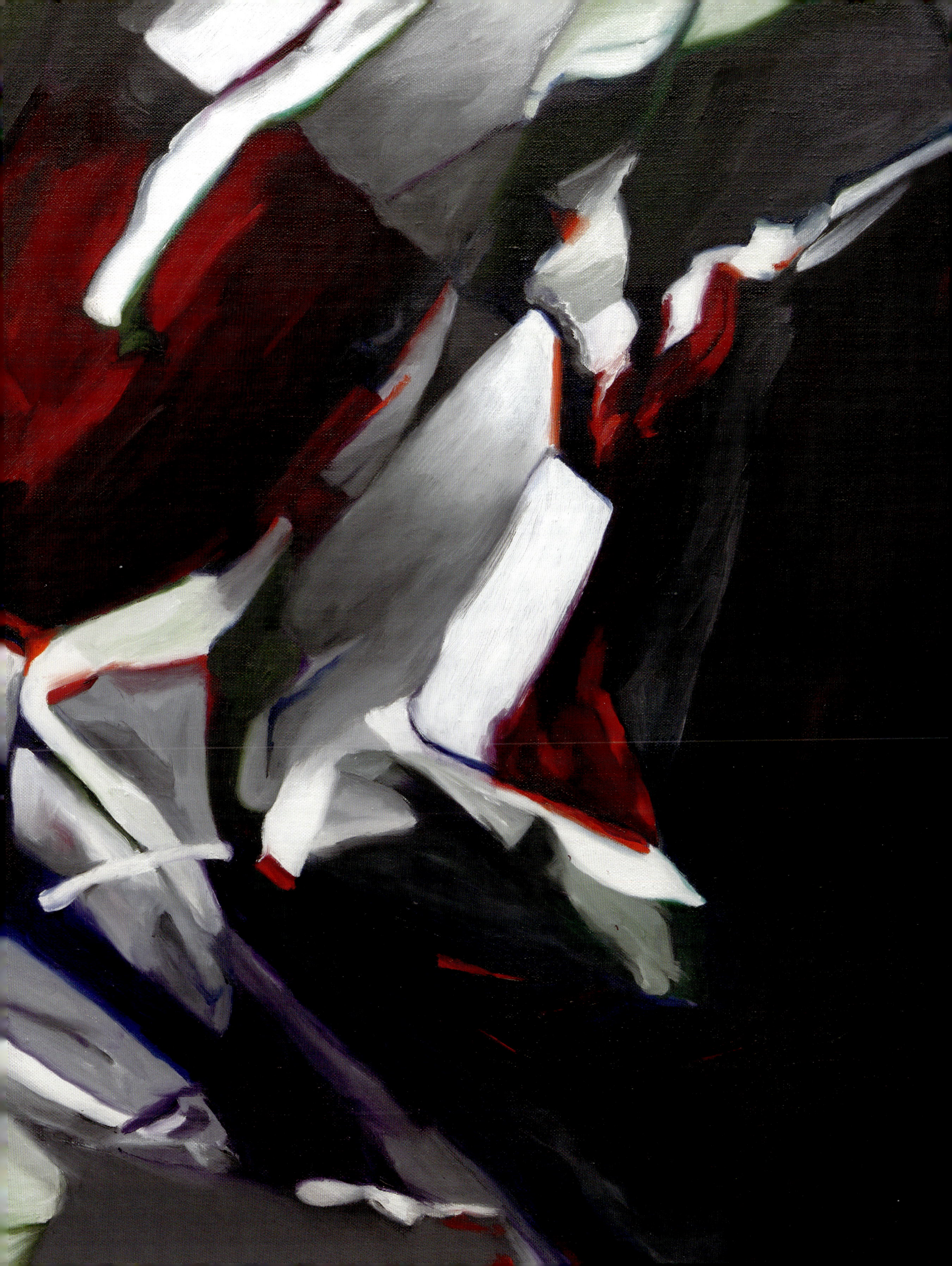

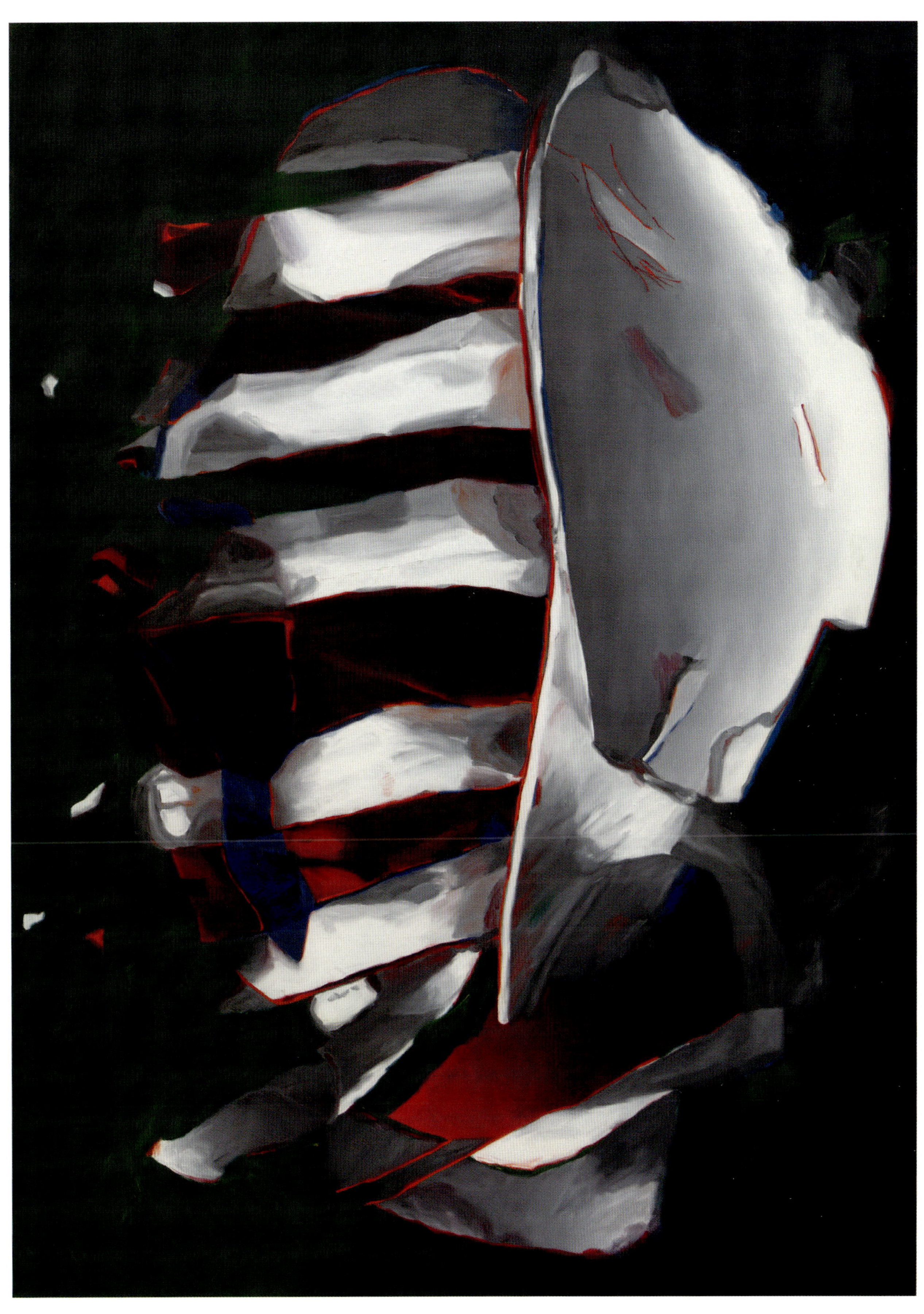

Tumulus, 2002. Oil on linen, 64 × 47 in. (162.6 × 119.4 cm)
Deborah Remington Charitable Trust for the Visual Arts

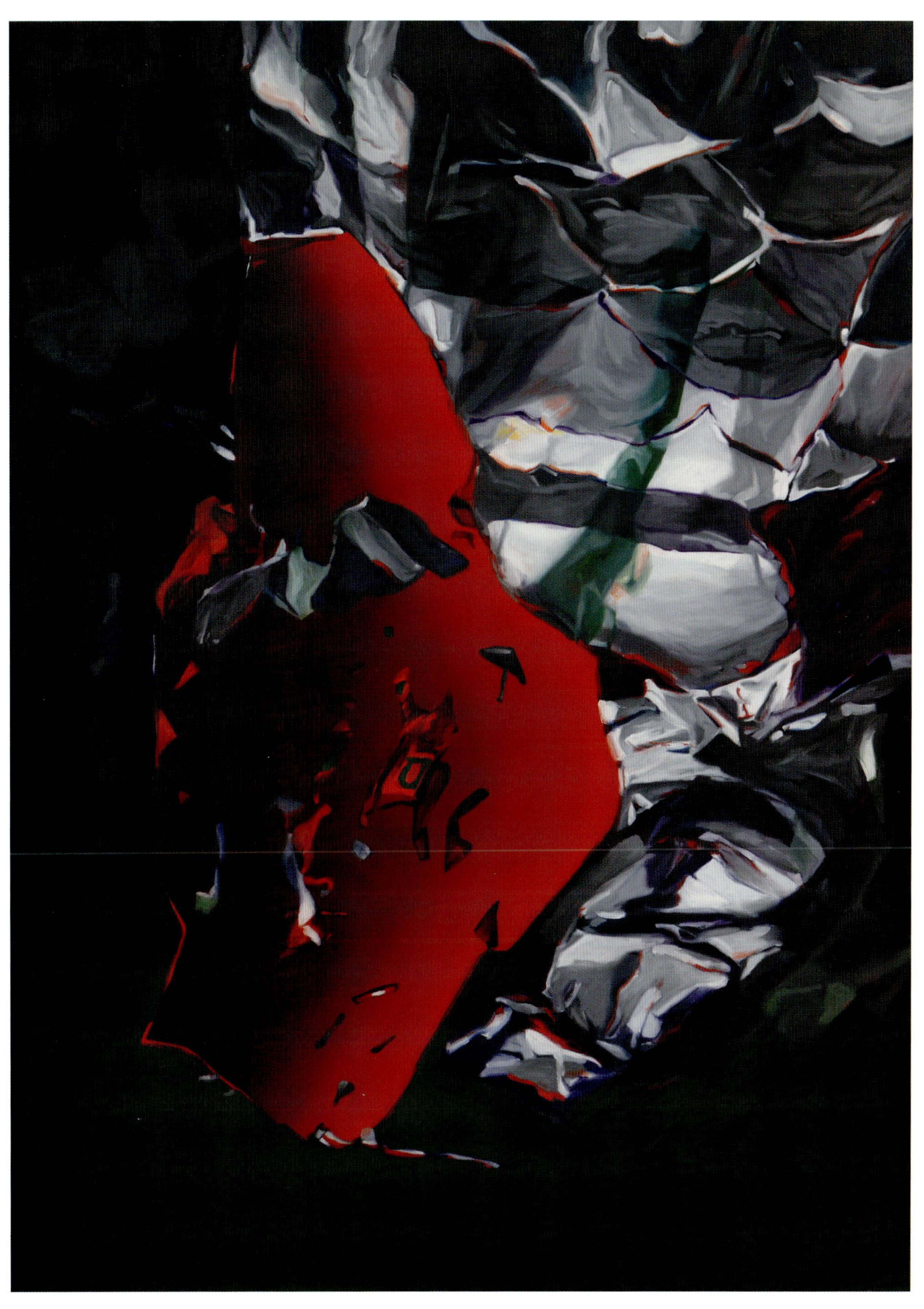

Maligant, 1996–2003. Oil on linen, 64 × 47 in. (162.6 × 119.4 cm)
Private collection

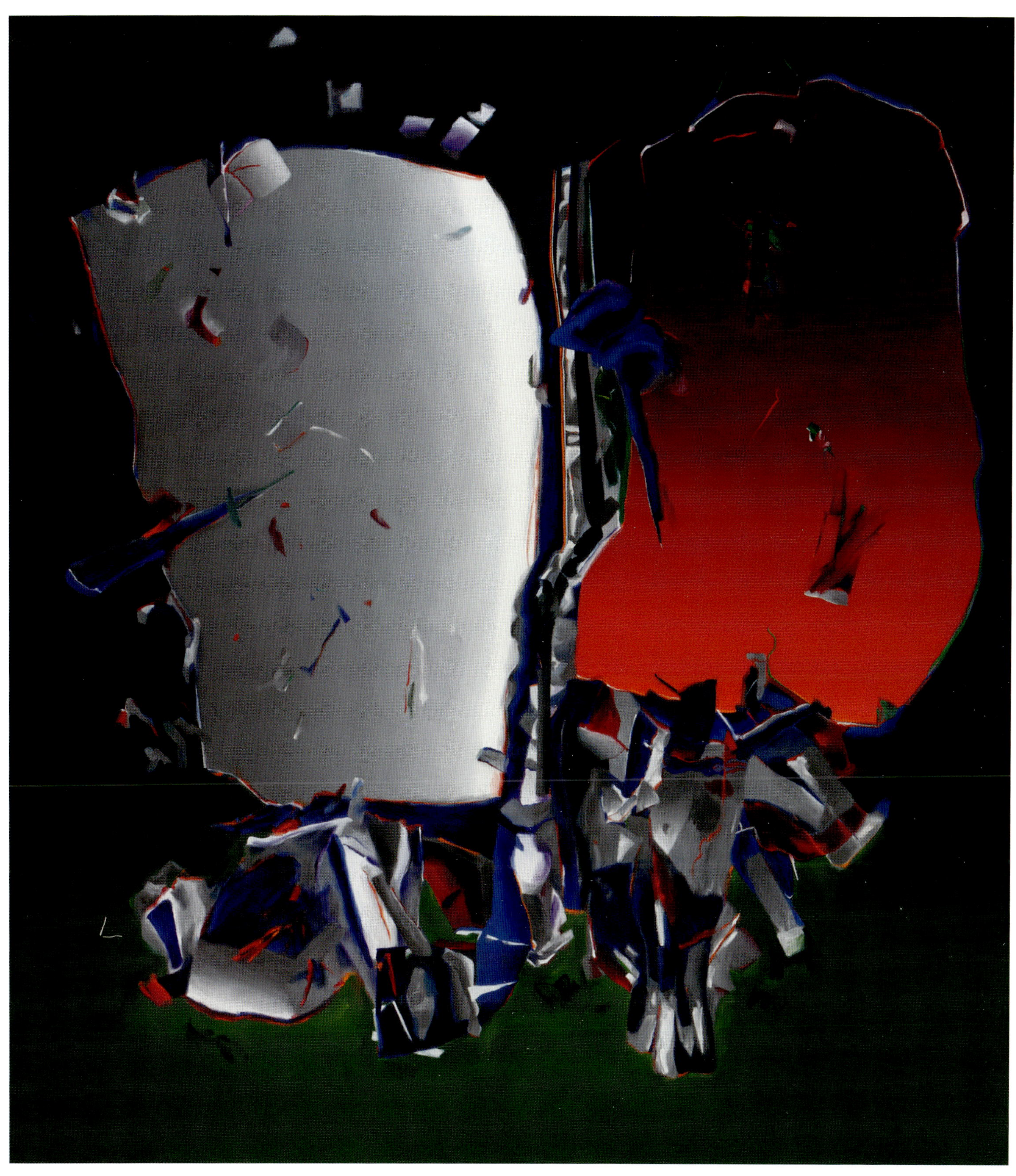

Encounters, 2007. Oil on linen, 72 × 67 in. (183 × 170 cm)
Deborah Remington Charitable Trust for the Visual Arts

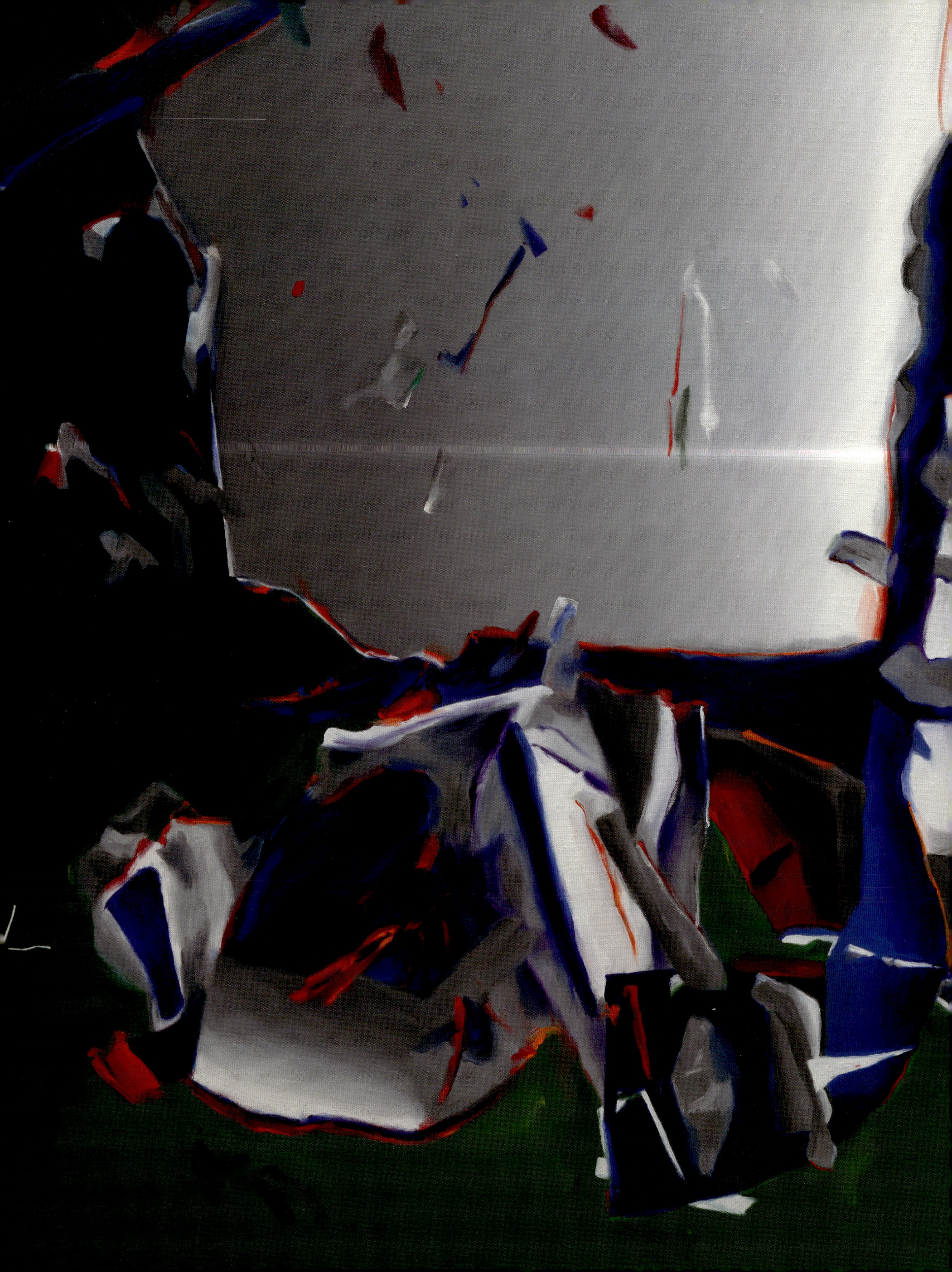

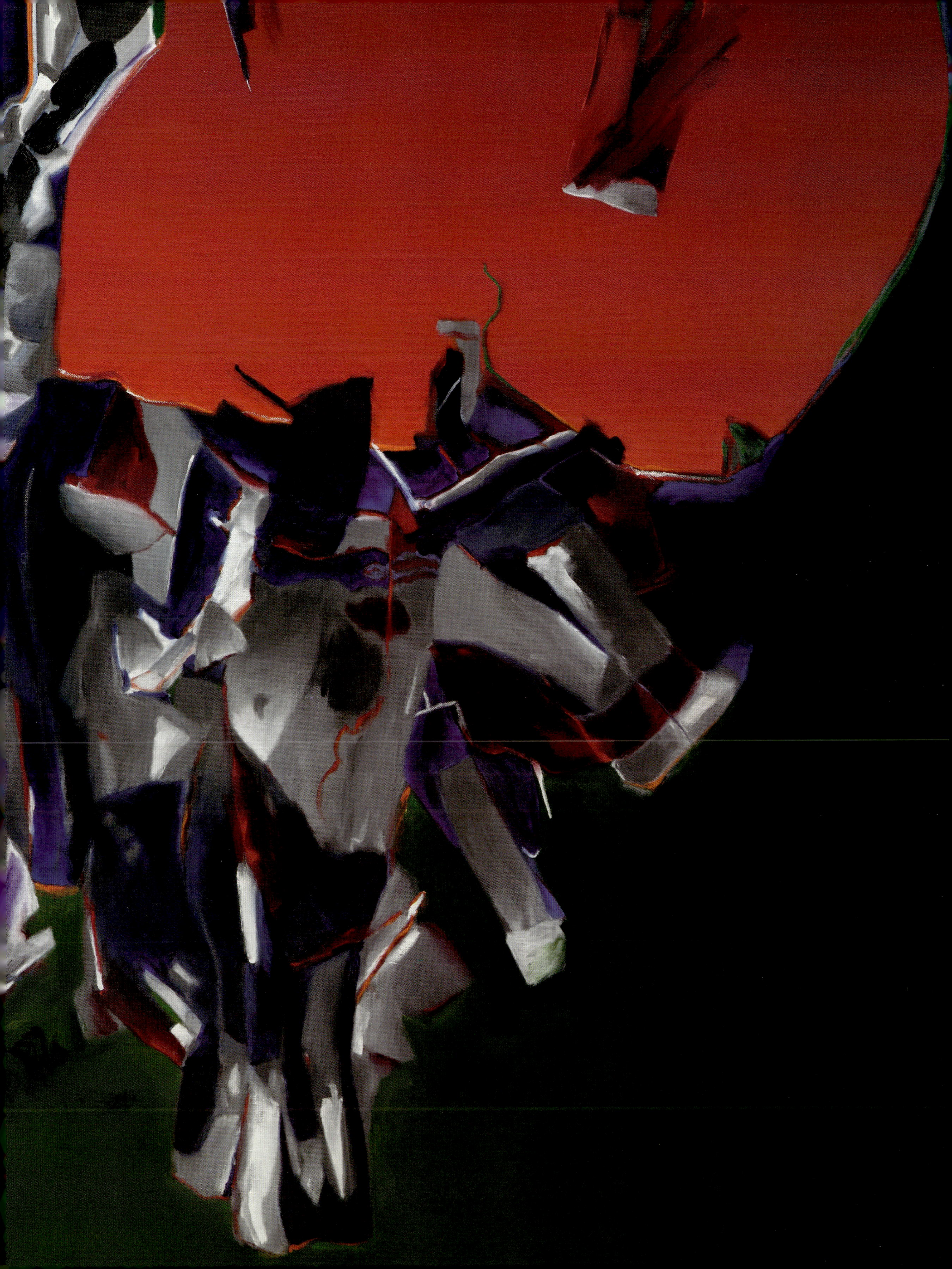

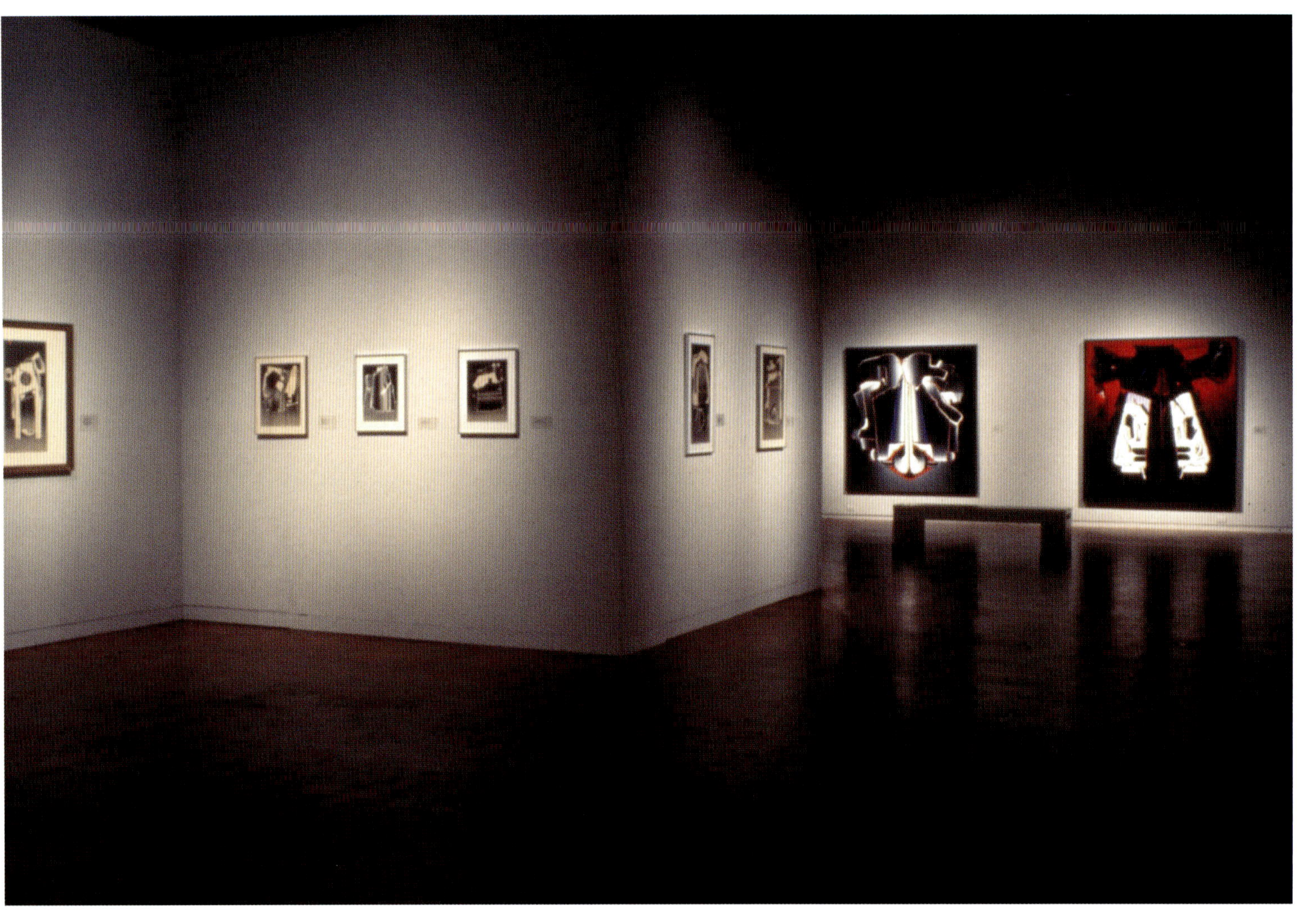

Encounters: Deborah Remington's Late Works

SUZANNE HUDSON

On December 15, 1983, the exhibition *Deborah Remington: A 20-Year Survey* opened at the Newport Harbor Art Museum in Orange County, California (**FIG. 1**). Curated by Paul Schimmel, the presentation comprised nineteen paintings and twenty-one drawings, a number of which had already been placed in public collections. It was Remington's first—yet still more astonishing, only—career retrospective.[1] The exhibition's press release emphasizes this precedent while underscoring the importance of Remington's work, which was summarized as bearing "an intense individual perspective in her commitment to painting."[2] Language in the National Endowment for the Arts Organizational Grant Application for the museum's exhibition funding is even more emphatic, casting her steadfast achievement as exemplary and the presentation of it more broadly analytical: "In a time where artists seem to change their interest, media and eventually their style with every passing shift in the art world, Remington has persistently continued to paint her own personal, mysterious forms. Not only are we seeking to better understand and evaluate her work, but also to understand and evaluate the kind of artists who are relentlessly concerned with one major concept throughout their oeuvre."[3]

Remington had established the terms for these "personal, mysterious forms" in 1963, when she completed *Statement* (**PAGE 49**): a vertical composition bearing a centered and frontally presented kimono-like image, its disembodied but oddly animate sleeves reaching edge-to-edge against the modulated ground. While the palette continues the burning crimson cut with the black of *Big Red* (1962; **PAGES 39–41**) and *Winter '63* (1963; **PAGE 43**), among others, *Statement* announced a stylistic shift from expressive handling that was thick with impasto to something less gestural. What followed were successively flattened, facture-less paintings bearing unmoored images floating in an impossible space coincident with but distinct from the picture plane. In these remarkable works from 1963 through the 1970s, Remington tempers an impulse toward autonomous painting with an imperative to locate it paradoxically within the tradition of a three-dimensional rendering (reliant on skills of manipulating light and color, shading and shadow to create pictorial illusions). Within two years of completing *Statement*, Remington describes an abiding concern "with expressing an intense and personal vision through an imagery which is particularly my own."[4]

FIG. 1
Installation view of *Deborah Remington: A 20-Year Survey*, Newport Harbor Art Museum (now the Orange County Museum of Art), Newport Beach, California, December 15, 1983–March 25, 1984

The first of Remington's paintings to enter a museum collection, *Statement* remained decisive, critically shaping her first institutional retrospective.[5] Since it was the earliest work in *Deborah Remington: A 20-Year Survey*, it appeared in the catalogue's opening spread opposite the title page.[6] In her essay for the catalogue, art historian Dore Ashton describes *Statement* as "the foundation of her career as a painter of highly emblematic, shield-shaped forms . . . personal icons drawn from her own imagination rather than the culture at large."[7] Fed by Remington's experiences, her forms were associative rather than duplicative. (In an earlier oral history interview for the Smithsonian with writer and curator Paul Cummings, Remington eschews appropriation but allows that her "imagery comes, I think, over a long, long period of years, all, everything, my travels to the Far East, every life experience one has seems to go into wherever it is. I don't know. I think of myself really as a great IBM machine of some sort, a great computer, because all the stuff just gets fed in."[8]) In relation to *Haddonfield* (1965; **PAGE 91**), named for the New Jersey town of Remington's birth, Ashton grasped the possibility for interpretative leeway and memorably found "an ancient trumpet; a modern thermometer; an insect; a skull; a mask rendered with anamorphic cunning."[9]

Nevertheless, where Ashton could log so many possible correlates in a single work (much less so across pairings or groupings of them, as with *Dover* [1975; **PAGE 123**] and *Engla* [1977]), others found a different kind of surfeit in Remington's consistency of method. Artist Paul Sutinen covered Remington's 1977 show at the Portland Center for the Visual Arts, Oregon, and he used the heading "Remington Is Redundant" for his review. Damning her determinism, he queried whether a viewer should "see some growth or progress over eight years" given the "repetitiveness of format."[10] This critical line recurred with visual arts columnist Kate Regan writing about the 1970s works in the *San Francisco Chronicle* in 1984: "Deborah Remington's consistency is her most imposing and troubling quality. Since her 1963 breakthrough painting, 'Statement,' her work has not wavered or much evolved in style of imagery. Her precisionist, richly colored abstractions have an austere grandeur that is both a limitation and a strength."[11] The celebrated constancy of her "one major concept" was now deemed a hindrance. Irrespective of valuation though, Remington, too, seems to have come to a similar conclusion, if apart from these appraisals. She was already transforming her work by the late 1970s, accommodating a fluid continuity of process that assumed the inevitability of change.

In a 1980 statement drafted for an unsuccessful Guggenheim Foundation Fellowship, Remington wrote that in 1978 her "work again began to undergo another strong change through a series of drawings. The central imagery and basic structure with which I had been working since 1963 started to break apart and disappear."[12] She included with her materials for the fellowship a selection of five drawings from the *Trace Series* (1978–80; **PAGES 132–35**) that showed a spatial mutation and dynamic reordering against the white page. Spare drawings, made with black spray paint, pencil, and graphite, the *Trace* pieces exploit tonal modulations without the interactions of color. Also in 1980, Geraldine Wojno, a perceptive contributor to *Arts Magazine*, noted a "change of emphasis" in Remington's contemporaneous paintings, charting a course from *Omina* (1978; **PAGES 129–31**) to *Auriga* (1980; **PAGE 136**): "A clear progression shows an opening of boundaries and a relaxation of tensions. . . . She now feels that the central shape can be pinched and softened, and that the surrounding elements need not be belted into place."[13]

Remington included *Zanthus* (1983; **PAGE 143**) as her most recent work in the Newport Harbor presentation, so new that it had not yet been varnished at the time of the opening.

Despite the narrative utility of 1963 as a point of origin, the date 1983 is then less precise, marking when the show opened rather than when Remington's practice shifted. Concurrent with her preparing for the Newport Harbor exhibition, Remington applied again for a Guggenheim Foundation Fellowship (this time successfully), making a case for the importance of funding on the basis of an emergent change in her work that was "looser and freer, [and] represents a major departure from the previous work over the past 20 years."[14] In 1984 she showed some of these drawings made during her Guggenheim Fellowship at the Adams-Middleton Gallery in Dallas, where the exhibition brochure emphasizes Remington's involvement "with metamorphosis, the apparent change of one thing or thought into another."[15] Later that year, she also installed examples of the new, freshly gestural graphite and mixed-media

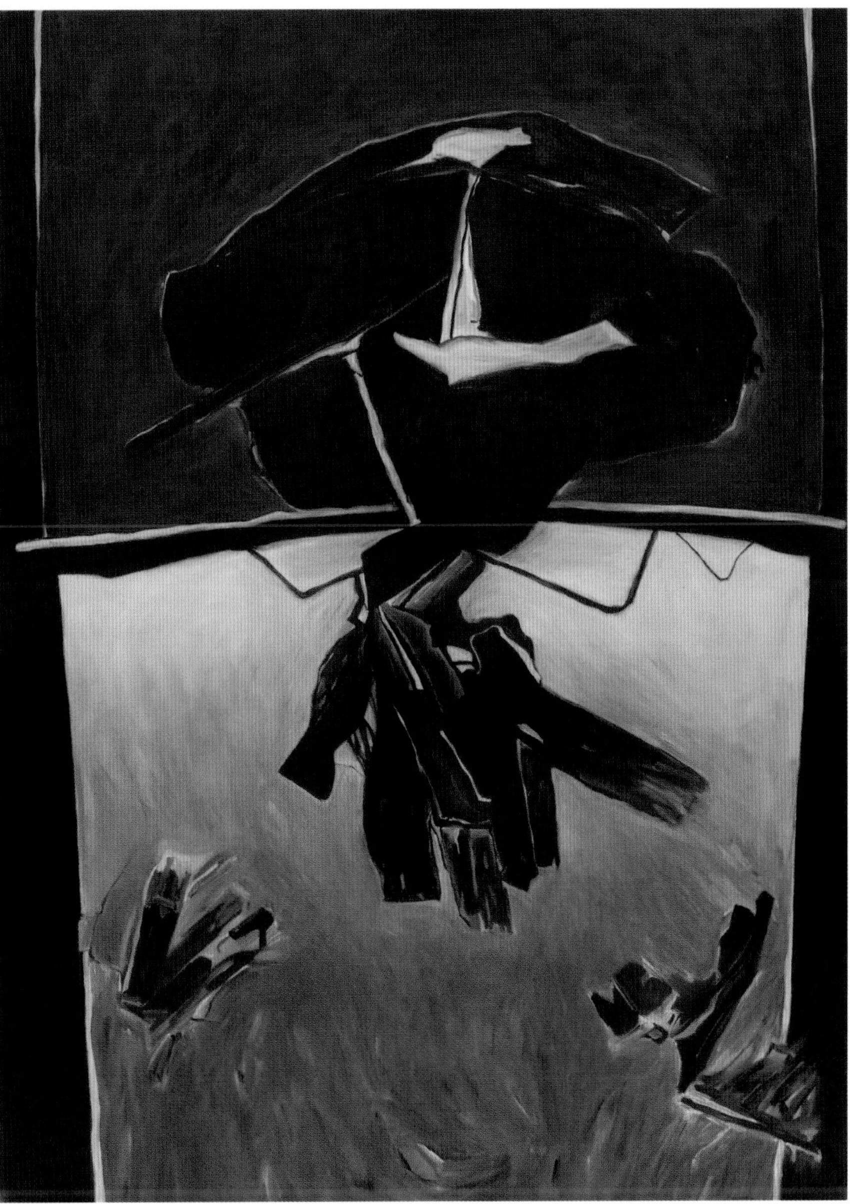

FIG. 2
Deborah Remington
Actium, 1986
Oil on canvas
64 × 47 in. (162.6 × 119.4 cm)
Deborah Remington Charitable Trust for the Visual Arts

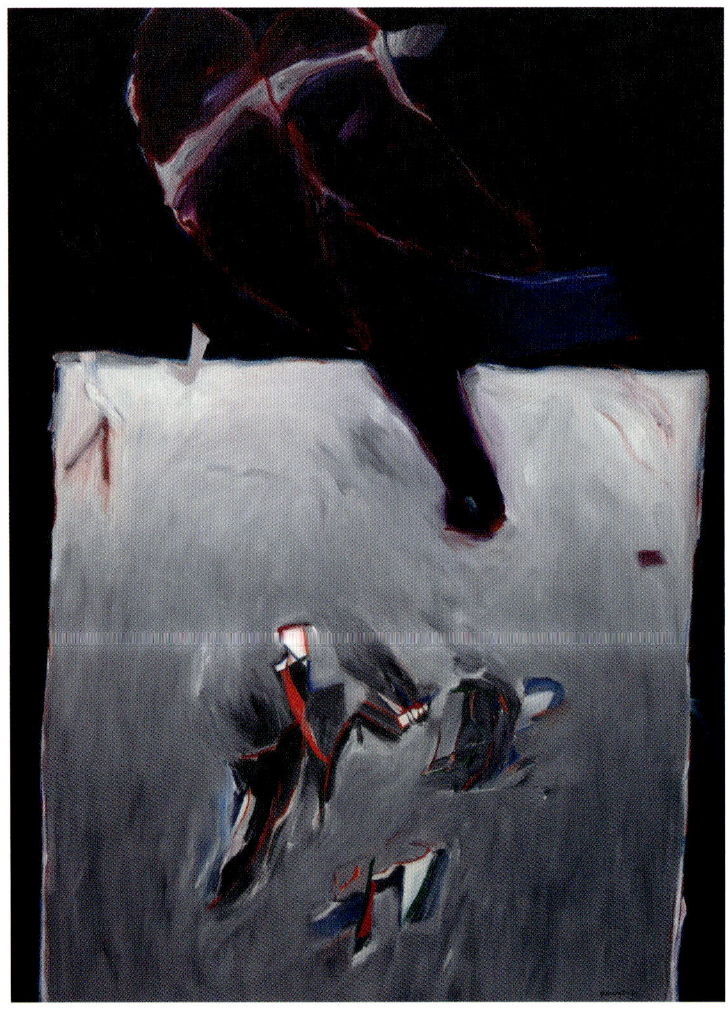

FIG. 3
Deborah Remington
Sarq, 1986
Oil on canvas
32 × 24 in. (81.3 × 61 cm)
Deborah Remington Charitable Trust for the Visual Arts

Euros Series (1983–86) at Gallery Paule Anglim in San Francisco, while *Deborah Remington: A 20-Year Survey* traveled to the Oakland Museum of California. (In the above cited review, Regan by contrast praises these recent efforts: "Remington's tough, quick intelligence is at work here, and if the final products feel less handsomely polished than those of the past, they also look infinitely more lively."[16])

In the 1985 exhibition brochure for *Deborah Remington: Works on Paper* at the Gallery at Greenville, Delaware, Victoria Manning describes the Remington retrospective two years earlier at Newport Harbor and its aftermath: "The fact that this change is taking place just as she has reached a pinnacle in her career due to a style that is recognized for its individuality, points to an inherent quality in the artist's character. She thrives on challenges and has embraced them throughout her life both on a personal and a professional level."[17] Quoted in the same brochure, Remington states, "My works reinterpret and change as I grow and change. . . . I don't respond to 'isms' that come and go, the 'Image-of-the-Month-Club,' trends. . . . I take change as one of the standards of what life is about: life and death and in the middle is change."[18] During the next year, she moved to oils like *Actium* (1986; **FIG. 2**) that make over the invention of the *Euros* works—their broad strokes layering atop uninflected monochromes, which become sketchy instead of unmodulated—as well as *Santee* (1986; **PAGE 163**) and *Sarq* (1986; **FIG. 3**), incorporating the lessons of the related drawings.

In *Santee* and *Sarq*, Remington pushes down the central void and tips the form above it off to an angle, implying a still life apprehended askew. Where her earlier paintings from the mid-1960s through the 1970s have less tension between the forms and the canvas edges, works from the mid-1980s have more—or at least draw attention to the edges as a physical seam as well as a conceptual border.

Following four years of self-imposed professional seclusion, Remington's embrace of gesture in a 1987 show at Jack Shainman Gallery in New York was declared a "rare surprise"[19] by *Art in America* contributor Walter Thompson. Art critic Vivien Raynor welcomed the exhibition as a "small but sparkling show"[20] in the *New York Times* and art historian Arlene Raven offered a fulsome tribute in the *Village Voice*, in which she compared the frontal rectangular forms to stelae. Raven connected the slabs to both Egyptian commemorative funerary practices and botany (as the "central cylinder in the stems and roots of vascular plants, is itself alive"[21]). The tombstone's memorial tenor plays against botany's vital organicism. Gardening had become a mainstay for Remington after purchasing her Coatesville, Pennsylvania, home in 1985, and the reference to Egypt is likewise astute. Her interest in otherworldliness began with her interest in the space program but led to her fascination with Egyptian conceptions of the afterlife. She had traveled to Egypt in 1980 and filled a sketchbook with visual and textual notes of tombs and dynastic genealogy, assertions of the apposition of the stele to the autobiographical text, named and inscribed with images of and prayers to the dead. Indeed, this sketchbook is resonant with Remington's longstanding interest in heraldry as a symbol of her own family history (as in the shields that manifest themselves in some of her paintings from the 1970s and 1980s, evocations of boundary stelae, symbolic but also very real thresholds) (**FIG. 4**).

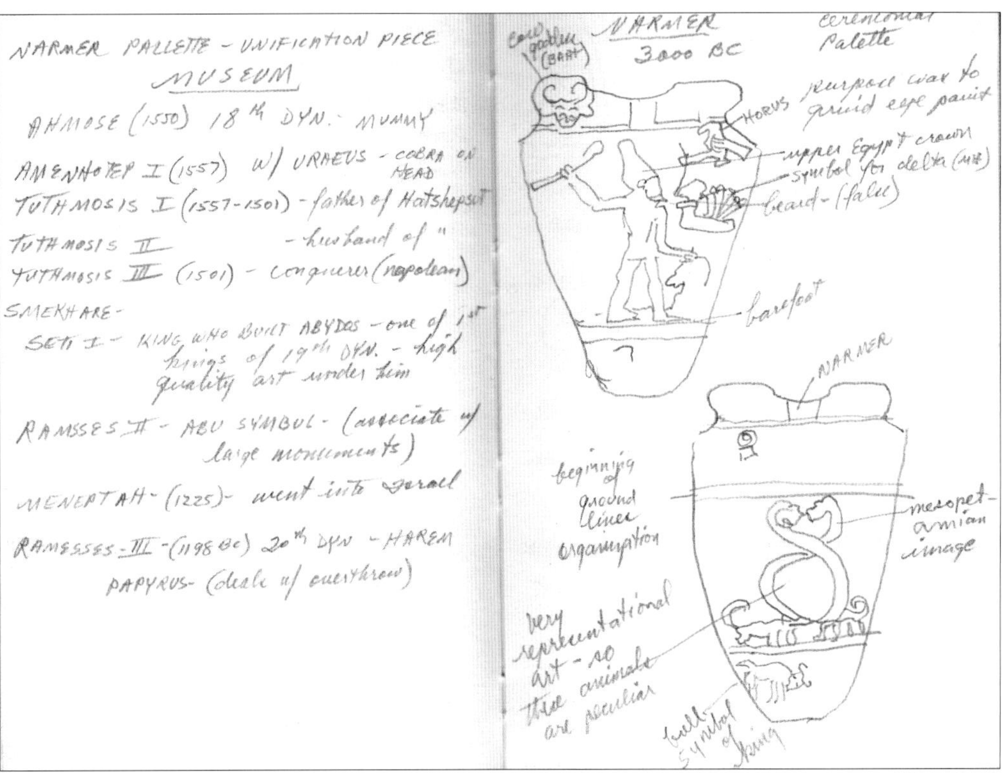

FIG. 4
Spread from Remington's sketchbook, 1980

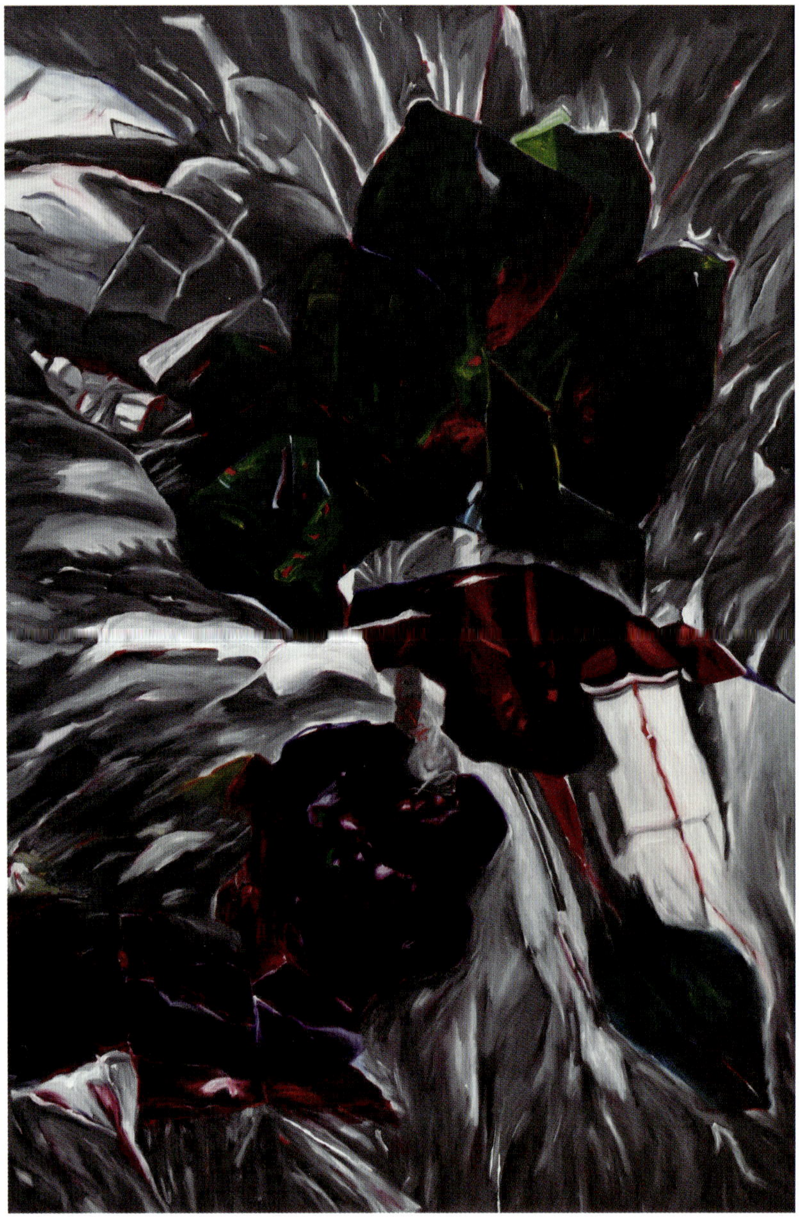

FIG. 5
Deborah Remington
Penrith, 1989
Oil on linen
74 x 50 in. (187 x 127 cm)
Deborah Remington Charitable Trust for the Visual Arts

As with the kimono references left over from her sojourn in Japan (1956–58), Remington likewise subsumed these distinct references to Egypt in her work during the last three decades of her life. Conjoining the rectangular and the organic, the affective power of their evocations of lineage and mortality remained, notably in the long aftermath of a 1983 breast cancer diagnosis, surgical intervention, and medical treatments that continued off and on through 2010 with a diagnosis of stage IV lung cancer. *Penrith* (1989; **FIG. 5**) is one of a series of gestural paintings inspired perhaps by the lushness of the gardens Remington carefully tended at her Coatesville retreat. It is a revelation: a jewel-colored mass fracturing dark grays applied with a range of brushes. Strokes, aggregating and fluttering, are the constitutive stuff of surface in related efforts from *Quanta* (1991) to *Dark Run* (1992; **PAGE 178**). These works are marked by an observational sensitivity that recalls her 1959 ink drawings of marsh grasses (**PAGES 24–25**). Even more obviously than in her mid-1980s incorporation of touch, these later works demonstrate a directness of bodily imprint, and by extension a more forthright relation to the biographical. By the 1990s, she was recovering her 1970s lexicon of emptied frames, looking glasses, and ferric windows; by 2000, they bend and warp, and as in the case of her monumental *Encounters* (2007; **PAGE 207**), none-too-subtly assume the bilaterally segmented and imperfectly symmetrical outlines of suspended, shieldlike lungs.

Her *Beinen Series* (**PAGES 188–95**)—named after a German word for bone—on which she labored from 1997 to 2006, is an expression of sheer will in six-foot-tall drawings of rib cages and carcasses, chest cavities and ambiguous interior chasms portrayed in graphite and crayon. Each drawing manifests an act of volition.[22] Undeterred by the cancer and injuries sustained in two separate falls in 1994 and 1997, Remington scaled the sheets to the span of her reach; she pinned them on the wall of her studio and in her living room, working on them over an extended period of time. Materially, they recall the *Adelphi Series* of drawings (**PAGES 62–69**) spanning 1963 to 1983.[23] Art critic Lilly Wei movingly records that the *Beinen Series* "point to human fragility and transience. They muse on mortality, on disappearance and reappearance, as if to say that in our beginning is our end, our end yet another beginning."[24] But as art writer Rachel Churner discusses Remington's works from the late 1980s onward, the existential cycle of "disappearance and reappearance" that Wei identifies may also refer to Remington's position within the institutions of the art world.[25] Churner acknowledges that "it is difficult not to read into the changes around this time a certain frustration with the then-tepid responses of the art world to her paintings," and here, she includes *Penrith*, "and to the failures of her own body."[26] She is referring to the relative invisibility Remington faced in her last decades, when she lacked gallery representation and very little of her work was shown in major museums or written about.

In letters and interviews in Remington's archive, she reveals her frustrations on this count. One finds in them indications aplenty of predatory commerce that left her demanding the money from work sold. Then there was the unrelenting capacity for misogyny expressed by people in the art world; in essentializing language, dealers indicted her for being a "difficult" artist who unduly exerted agency in a manner more befitting of a man. In one 1982 note to artist Hassel Smith, Remington concedes that the gallery system is "rotten . . . but it's the only system we have so what can one do. At present I feel that I'm doing a body of pretty important works and am feeling very frustrated in not being able to show them in N.Y. . . . there is so much visual crap being shown and touted and hyped here and all of it comes and goes in a flash."[27]

Remington's last years were increasingly difficult, knowing how ill she was and anticipating how her life and work would be remembered absent her presence to frame it. Late paintings including *Tumulus* (2002; **PAGE 203**) and *Maligant* (1996–2003; **PAGE 205**) reveal the twinning of production and legacy. Where the first—another brittle rib cage or bandaged cavity—takes its title from an artificial hillock, as over a grave, the second is a play on the word *malignant* (as in a virulent disease but also meaning malevolent). The comparatively diminutive *Episode* (2004; **FIG. 6**), made the year before her cancer returned and part of a lung was removed, plainly bespeaks a period of illness. It bares Remington's once-impenetrable order under pressure: the structure collapses, its integrated forms liquifying, or dissolving from within. Her last work was the aforementioned *Encounters*, a eulogy for breath, made as her lungs were hardening, three years before she died. The culmination of Remington's incorporation of anatomical imagery,

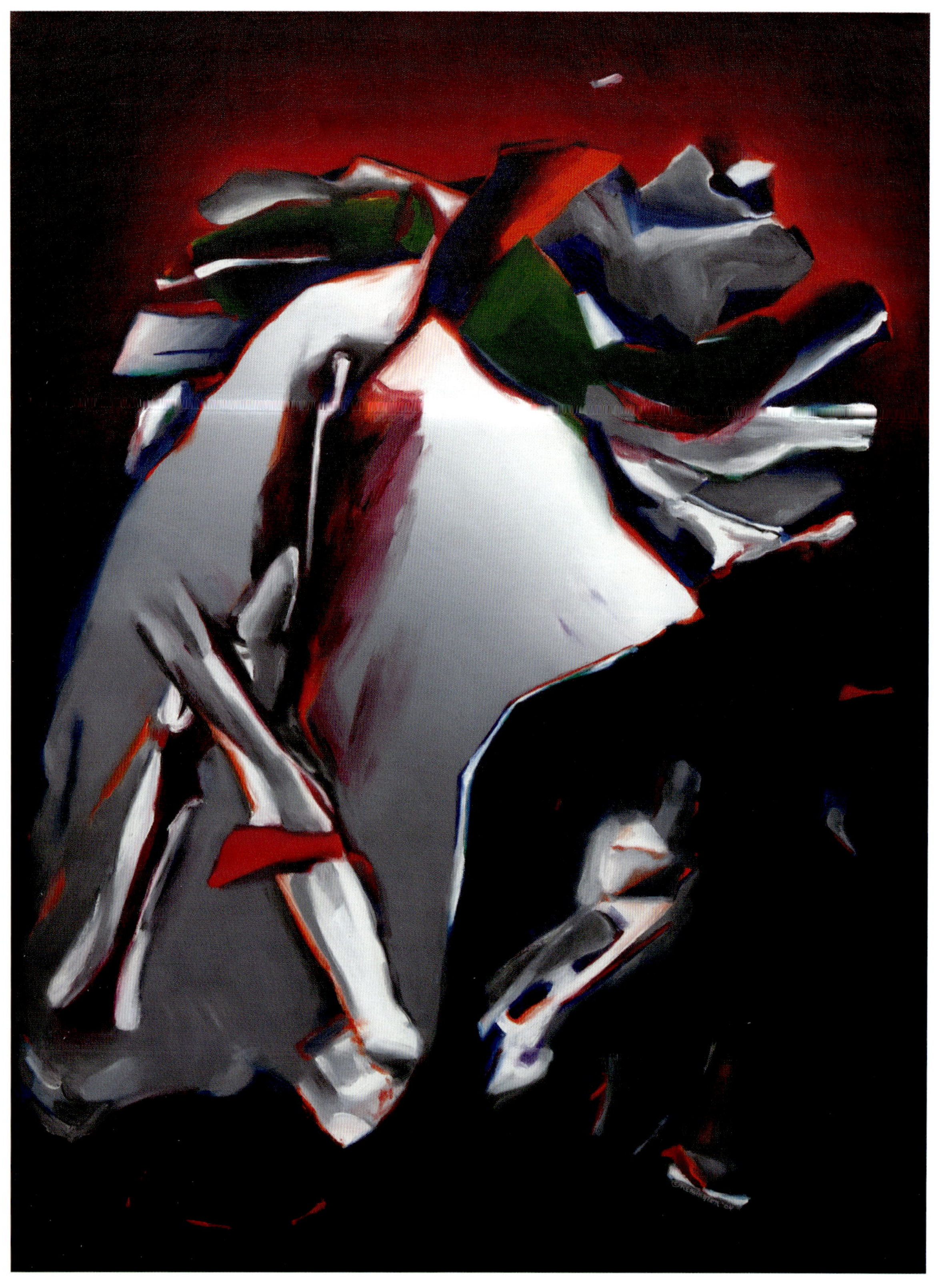

one organ shimmers silvery-gray, its near-prosthetic armoring nonetheless pierced by a cobalt shard, paint daubs raining like confetti; the other, the red of candy apples and coagulating blood, shows its capacity diminished, a fraction of the size of its double.

Encounters occupies the tradition of the memento mori (from the Latin, "remember that you must die"), a remarkable turn of the genre to self-portraiture that in no way lessens its claims to universality; if anything, the legibility of *Encounters* is predicated upon a desire for the conveyance of personal insight, of the implacable reality of impermanence, that was far from Remington's alone. With *Encounters*, she acknowledges the limits of art's ability to alter reality, while simultaneously offering the possibility of a communicative act that will survive its creator. An encounter, as this painting embodies, is an unexpected meeting, or experience, sometimes unnerving. In Middle English, the word connoted the meeting of an adversary, someone, or something foreign and unfamiliar. In this sense Remington's painting is an allegory of the challenge of studio work, the habitual practice of confronting the self before the other. Yet, Remington also effaced labor in the earlier, meticulous paintings that hid her hand, which contributed to the perfection of seemingly acheiropoietic panels. Remington's mirrors from the 1970s were always vehicles for projection, mysterious and crystalline surfaces that disclosed nothing; finally, Remington allowed for the possibility of recognition through her paintings from the 1980s and '90s. In *Encounters* we do encounter Remington, more or less literally I think, facing herself, as we do ourselves. As a pendant to *Statement*, an artwork tendered half a lifetime earlier, *Encounters* affords a declarative if more vulnerable address to the world soon beyond her.

FIG. 6
Deborah Remington
Episode, 2004
Oil on linen
32 × 24 in. (81.3 × 61 cm)
Private collection

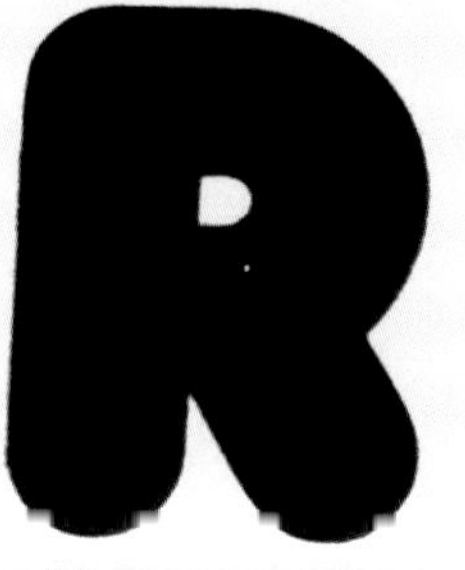

Dec. 31, 1981

Dear Paul

As the New Year approaches, I wanted to drop a note to tell you just how much your concern and support meant to me during my recent illness. The flowers were beautiful and cheered me up each time I looked at them. Thank you for being so special and so thoughtful — but mostly, thank you for your friendship.

I'm looking forward to seeing you here soon and would like to give a little dinner in your honor. I thought →

Recalling Deborah Remington's Career-Defining Survey

PAUL SCHIMMEL

This text was condensed and edited from an interview with Paul Schimmel by Nancy Lim.

Deborah Remington: A 20-Year Survey happened in the most fundamentally beautiful way. My mentor, James Harithas, who was the director of the Corcoran Gallery of Art in Washington, D.C., before moving to the Everson Museum of Art in Syracuse, New York, where I worked for him for a little bit before he moved to the Contemporary Arts Museum Houston, owned a beautiful drawing by Remington that he had acquired around 1972. I saw it in 1974 in Houston. He had bought it directly from the artist, and it's a beautiful, beautiful drawing—early 1970s, kind of perfect, gorgeous.

When I first got to the Newport Harbor Art Museum, I was working on an Alan Saret exhibition with director Cathleen Gallander, who happened to adore [gallerist and critic] Klaus Kertess, and I knew he had shown Deborah at Bykert Gallery in New York.[1] Cathleen wanted to feature more women, so I suggested Deborah to her because I knew Klaus would support the idea. This was 1981 or '82, and Klaus said, "Oh! Deborah Remington is fantastic." If it hadn't been for Deborah, Bykert would've closed because Klaus could sell Deborah's work. Klaus and I convinced Cathleen to go visit Deborah in New York, and that's how the exhibition came about. It was a very different time, and while the Whitney [Museum of American Art, New York] exhibited artists from the West Coast, most other institutions did not. We put together a very good checklist, which, to a large degree, we were able to accomplish because Deborah owned so much of her own work, although there were paintings that came from Bykert. In terms of the layout, we agreed that it should move forward like a rather traditional retrospective: chronological and by material so that the drawings would be grouped together in such a way that they followed the same order as the paintings but on different walls.

And then the tour—the tour was a nightmare. Deborah really was not happy about lots of things, but mostly about the venues.[2] There were venues that we should have approached early on, like the Neuberger [Museum of Art, Purchase, New York], which she completely rejected because it wasn't in Manhattan, it wasn't the Whitney. Eventually we tried them all, but she wasn't on anybody's list, and it had nothing to do with personality proclivities or bad reputation, both of which she had. Minimalism and its generation were not beloved at that time in the 1980s. It was expressionism and neo-expressionism that was going on. And she had no reputation in terms of the market.[3]

Letter from Remington to Paul Schimmel, December 31, 1981

In California she wanted the show to go to SFMOMA (San Francisco Museum of Modern Art), but they had no interest whatsoever. That was not their thing at that moment. They were trying to go more international. It was near the end of Henry Hopkins's tenure.[4] And then she wanted it to go to Berkeley [Art Museum and Pacific Film Archive]. I was disappointed by Berkeley. I'd sent a show there when I was in Houston, and I thought there would be interest. But Berkeley did not understand her as a woman and as a Bay Area artist. They just didn't see it as being very current; it was like old Bay Area stuff. But I really thought Berkeley would have been kind of perfect for it. Oakland [Museum of California] did it because I think they understood that this was an important part of history, in some ways a little bit like Newport back then, which was collecting and focusing on California. Oakland was a miracle. If it weren't for Phil Linhares![5]

When we opened the show at Newport, I think Deborah was happy with it because she liked the way it looked. It was beautifully laid out, and it was all the things she liked to do, which was a very dramatic spotlight. It still may be the best show of her work because it looked great, and we got beautiful things. But it wasn't L.A., and it didn't have the critical reception she hoped for, which she made clear to everyone, saying, "I only did this show because I wanted a tour, and you didn't get a good tour." And because the tour was so small, we needed to raise money and that was very hard.[6] I don't remember it being particularly successful.

She was so disappointed. I've done a lot of retrospectives, a lot of surveys, but Deborah was among the most challenging—not only in terms of satisfying her but doing what you are responsible as a curator to do, which is wanting to change the game for that artist. Maybe it was bad timing. I know it wasn't bad work—but very crystalline at a time when everything was so much more expressive. For me, the context was Minimalism, Asian influences, and artists like John McLaughlin. I don't think the critical response was great because in some cases they thought it was too polished. It's like saying Vermeer is too slick. Deborah's mirrors, while not a big body of work, were superintense and totally meticulous. I would say that her overall work was simultaneously out of step *and* way ahead of the long overdue revisionism in terms of women in the history of postwar art. Too late, not soon enough! The reception of the show was not what it would be today.

I think that scholarship in the history of postwar Northern California art is still very early. Deborah was a New York artist, but she really comes out of the Bay Area. In terms of her spirituality and the impact that Japan had on her and her sense of an almost virtuosic dedication to craft, I think she is a Bay Area artist of the '50s. Japan's influence is a mystery to me, but you can see the change in the work, and it's profound. References have been made to lacquer art and craftsmanship, and she wasn't exactly the most Zen person on earth, but there is a sense of personal, internal harmony by giving herself over to a craft that requires slowness and dedication. And then once she moved to New York, Minimalism had a profound and dramatic impact although she started doing things that maybe were too sensual and electric for Minimalism. She was kind of like Myron Stout, whose small and intimate Minimalism was so precise—one hair, one edge at a time. I had done a Myron Stout show, and he knew who Deborah was and admired her.

To me, it's the sense of the quality of her work that still compels people today. Her individuality and dedication are absolutely evident. But I don't think she's even close to being appreciated because I think we're presently living in a very provincial period. Deborah may be the dark and almost glittery version of Georgia O'Keeffe—that sense of flowers, the body, imagination, that kind of perfection, nature remade. I've also thought of her as the Vermeer of biomorphic sensual abstraction with the same exquisite finishes and intensity of experience of easel painting. Along with aspects of European modernism mainly from between the wars, Deborah's work could be described as eccentric abstraction, particularly in terms of the contrast of color and darkness coming out of the Bay Area.

I don't think her works from the late '80s, which were more gestural, were as good as the earlier works, and that may have had something to do with her health. I don't think they had the same intensity and unrelenting commitment to finish and surface, the very qualities that some people may have found overdone in her work but that I thought were their best qualities. I felt that drawing and the intensity of something very intimate and small were always her very best, even better than the paintings from her best period. I think all of her almost obsessive behavior somehow found a balance with drawing. They're not just more advanced than her paintings, but more *her*. Look at those surfaces and how she handles graphite. It's so rich. Those drawings that got big toward the end of her life, the *Beinen Series* (1997–2006)—those might be interesting. They seem a little unresolved in some ways, but they also seem very ambitious. As a curator, sometimes you don't want to put this against that. I'd love to see them isolated so that you're not judging them against what she did when she was in her thirties, but instead judging her by what she could do in that moment. For Deborah, it's important to look at her work episodically.

CHRONOLOGY

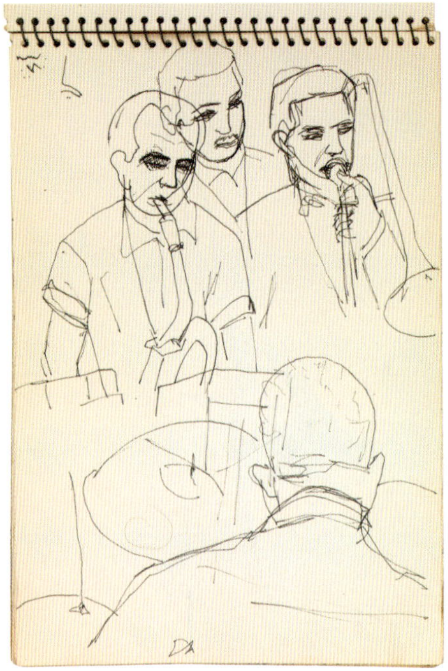

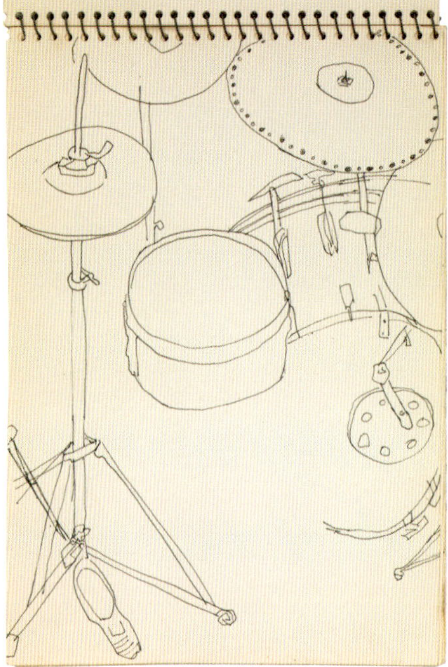

Pages from Remington's sketchbook, c. 1950

1930

Deborah Williams Remington is born in Haddonfield, New Jersey, a suburb of Philadelphia. From a young age, she keeps a notebook of drawings, stories, and poems that she calls "The Fun Book." Her mother, Hazel, recognizes her child's interest in art and hires a local tutor for private lessons.

1938

At age eight, Remington begins taking Saturday art classes at the Philadelphia Museum and School of Industrial Art (now the Philadelphia Art Alliance at the University of the Arts), where she is the youngest student; she begins drawing from a live model by age ten. After class, she regularly visits local museums with her mother and realizes that art will remain an important part of her life. "I really remember somewhere between age nine and twelve making a conscious decision . . . I am going to paint. I'm going to devote my life to that, dedicate whatever I am to that. . . . Never any deviation." [1]

1940

Her father, Malcolm, is diagnosed with leukemia; her mother cares for him until his death four years later.

1944–45

Remington and her mother spend the summer in Canada. After a brief return to Haddonfield, her mother decides to relocate to Pasadena, California, with her teenage daughter. "Before there was air pollution in California, it was absolutely beautiful," Remington later recalls. "I remember walking to school. Often in the mornings, I would look up in the mountains . . . and the mountains would be so clear. They looked two-dimensional as if they were cut out and stuck there . . . I'm sure that has carried over somewhere in my work." [2]

1945–48

Remington enrolls in Eliot Junior High School (now Eliot Arts Magnet Academy) in Altadena, California, and later attends Pasadena High School and Pasadena Junior College, California, where she befriends fellow future artists Wally Hedrick, Hayward King, John Ryan, and David Simpson. Simpson introduces her to the work of Pablo Picasso, the Surrealists, and modern art in general, all of which she eagerly embraces.

Jazz also becomes a passion for Remington and her friends. "We were fifteen- and sixteen-year-old kids, and we'd go in the bars and listen to Charlie Parker and Dizzy [Gillespie]. I first remember hearing Billie Holiday [in Los Angeles], Lester Young, all these people. Very often, I would sit there and draw. . . . Nobody bothered us. We just sat there and listened to the music and pretended we were much older so we could drink. . . . Those years were absolutely marvelous because I got to do

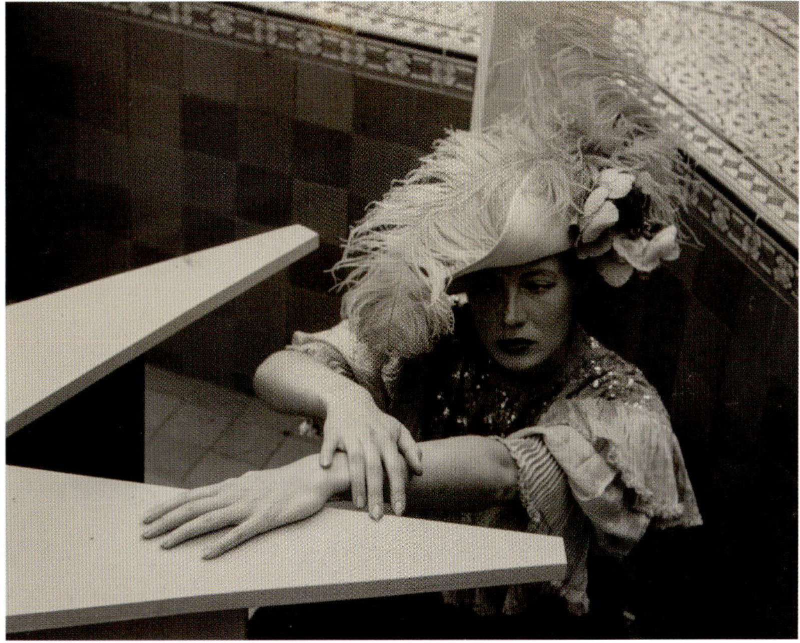

Image from a series of self-portraits, c. 1950

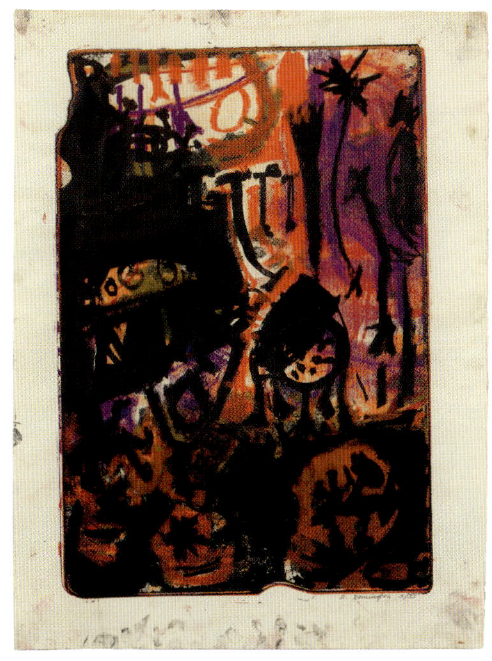

Deborah Remington
21 Thousand Leagues Under, 1955
Lithograph, 21 1/4 × 15 in. (54 × 38 cm)
Deborah Remington Charitable Trust for the Visual Arts

all those things and hear all those people. It was all part of the art thing that was developing in me, and my awareness of it, visually, it collided so well with these ideas in music . . . that were going around."[3] Remington's passion for jazz continues throughout her life.

1949

Remington, Hedrick, and Simpson enroll in a disappointing semester at Otis Art Institute (now Otis College of Art and Design), Los Angeles. "We had all decided that well, that's where we'd go. So fine, all right," Remington later recalls. "[But] it wasn't interesting enough. It wasn't revealing enough, strong enough, hard enough for kids who were really serious, as we were. We really wanted to get into this."[4]

Subsequently, they decide to enroll in the California School of Fine Arts (CSFA; later the San Francisco Art Institute), San Francisco, intrigued by its "marvelous reputation on the West Coast."[5] "[My mother and I] went to look at the school, and I fell in love with it immediately. . . . We walked into the patio, and it was raining. And I looked at all the art hanging on the walls around the patio, and a lot of it, I didn't understand. I had just walked into something called Abstract Expressionism, right straight smack in the face. It fascinated me. I loved it. I hated it. It interested me all in the first impact. . . . It was like a step into another world all of a sudden."[6] During her first year, her professors include Elmer Bischoff, Ed Corbett, and Jean Varda. Remington dives into the Bay Area's Beat scene.

1950–51

Remington creates a group of untitled black-and-white photographs that depict her posing in vintage clothing sourced at thrift shops in combination with clothes her mother sews according to Remington's specifications.

During Remington's second year at CSFA, she takes courses with professors Maynard Dixon, David Park, and Hassel Smith, among others. She wins numerous awards, including the Robert Howe Fletcher Cup for outstanding merit.

1952

Remington receives a Certificate of Completion from CSFA.

Remington marries the poet and writer Don Johnson. They leave San Francisco and move north to Healdsburg in Sonoma County. There, she stars in two local plays under the name Deborah Johnson.

1953

Remington divorces Johnson and returns to CSFA to enroll in its newly established BFA program.

Invited by the artist Jess [Collins] and the poet Robert Duncan, Remington has her first solo exhibition at the short-lived but legendary King Ubu Gallery in San Francisco, located

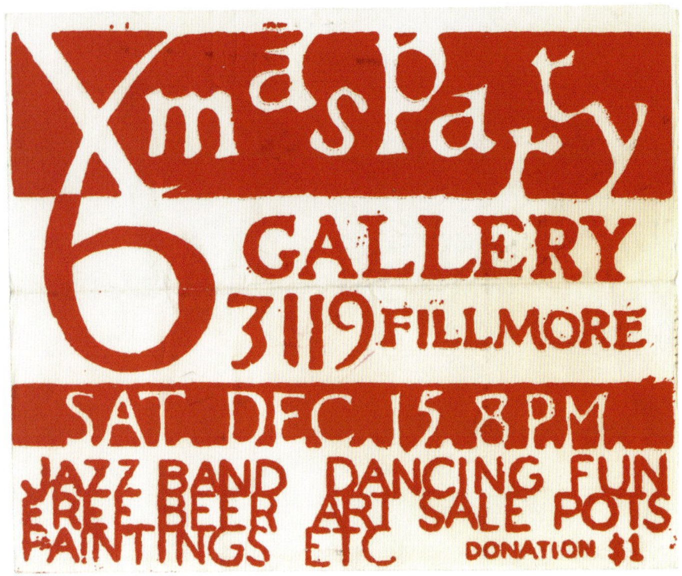

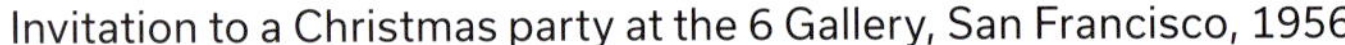

Invitation to a Christmas party at the 6 Gallery, San Francisco, 1956

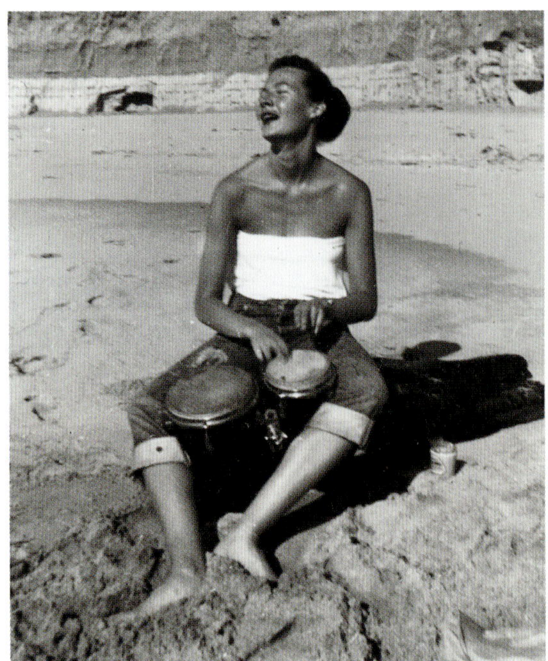

Remington playing bongos on the beach, San Francisco, 1955

in a former auto repair shop on Fillmore Street. "I didn't know what to do. I'd never had anything like that happen to me before. . . . Wally [Hedrick] helped me frame. . . . We framed stuff with strip framing, and then you'd stain the frame and paint it with one of the major colors in the painting! So if you had a painting with a lot of rose in it, then your frame was rose! Ha! We thought that was pretty hip."[7]

The Oakland Art Gallery (now the Oakland Museum of California) includes Remington's work in its *1953 Annual Exhibition of Oil Painting*.

1954

King Ubu Gallery in San Francisco closes, leaving a void where CSFA students and faculty were once able to regularly exhibit their work. Remington cofounds the 6 Gallery in King Ubu's former space with Wally Hedrick, Hayward King, John Ryan, David Simpson, and the poet and CSFA professor Jack Spicer. Its wide-ranging program includes Allen Ginsberg's debut of his poem "Howl," and the gallery quickly becomes a popular gathering place among students and CSFA faculty for evenings of art, music, poetry readings, and other events before closing in 1957. "We were the obstreperous kids of the time. We wanted to make something that was fun and good. There was a sense of anti-establishmentarianism. . . . Nobody would have us, so we had to make a place of our own. It never occurred to us that we couldn't do it. We just did it."[8]

Remington meets Lloyd Davis, a drummer for the Dave Brubeck Quartet, who shares stories of his travels to East Asia and becomes a romantic partner. At CSFA, she also becomes friends with two students of Japanese heritage, one of whom later helps Remington make arrangements to live with a family in Tokyo in an informal "exchange" program.

Fast Company, a print made in January, is featured in the *Third International Biennial of Contemporary Color Lithography* (April) at the Cincinnati Art Museum, Ohio. Under the sponsorship of the Foreign Service of USA and the American Federation of Arts, versions of the exhibition travel to Algeria, France, Italy, and the former Yugoslavia.

Remington begins Japanese-language classes at Galileo Adult School, San Francisco. She also enrolls in a Chinese-language class the following year.

1955

Remington presents work in a two-person show at the 6 Gallery in San Francisco (January–February).

Remington receives her BFA as one of a small number of students in CSFA's first degree-earning class. That summer, she works as a registrar for the school, writes short stories, and continues experimenting with lithography.

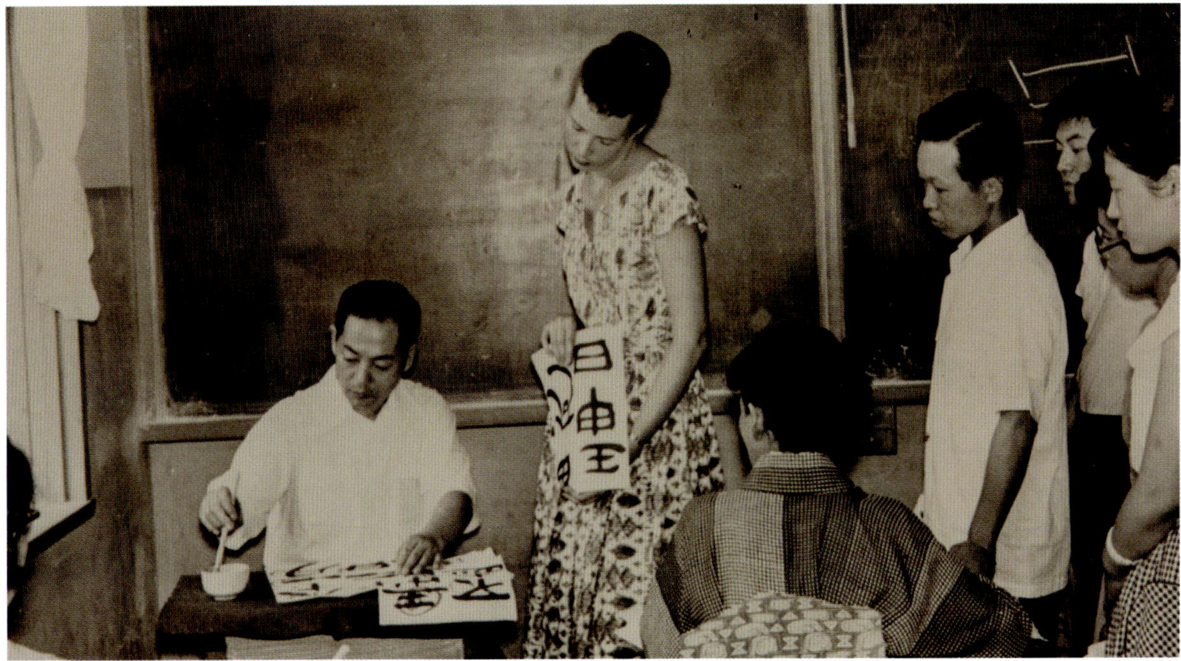

Remington studying calligraphy in Tokyo, 1956

Remington exhibits jazz-inspired color lithographs in the *Bay Area Printmakers 1st Graphics Annual* at the Oakland Art Gallery (now the Oakland Museum of California) (November–December) and the San Francisco Art Association's *Nineteenth Annual Drawing and Print Exhibition* (December–January), hosted by the San Francisco Museum of Art (SFMA; now the San Francisco Museum of Modern Art). Titles in this body of work reference her love of jazz and wordplay, such as *On the Scene* (1954), *21 Thousand Leagues Under* (1955), *Conservatory Jazz* (1955), and *Gopher Baroque* (1955).

1956

SFMA features Remington's work in its *75th Annual Painting and Sculpture Exhibit* (March–May). She subsequently participates in the 1960, 1961, 1963, 1964, and 1965 annuals.

For the next two years, Remington lives in Japan, where she studies *sumi* painting and classical Chinese and Japanese calligraphy. In later years, Remington will reference the influence of Japanese calligraphy on her work, explaining, "In [calligraphy] you develop a whole sensitivity to the relation of one stroke to another. Though what I was studying was basically line and angle, I got the feeling that nothing can be dead in a stroke—it has to have a spring to it like a twig. I got a lot of feeling for a certain movement of line and for the angles of relationships of lines."[9] Remington becomes highly proficient in Japanese and supports herself by teaching English and American slang to Waseda University students, acting in Japanese B movies, and working as a translator, comedian, and nightclub host. She also travels to Burma, Cambodia, Hong Kong, India, Laos, Taipei, Thailand, and Tibet, where she works as the cook for a team of mountaineers.

1958

In late summer, Remington boards a U.S. vessel departing from the port of Yokohama, Japan, and returns to San Francisco two weeks later.

CSFA hires Remington as an instructor of classical Japanese calligraphy.

1959

Using repetitive, gestural strokes alive with motion, Remington creates several pen-and-ink drawings (PAGES 24–25) inspired by her training in Japanese calligraphy, as well as the movement of the marsh grasses along the shores of the San Francisco Bay.

Remington takes on additional teaching courses at San Francisco State College (SFSC; now the San Francisco State University) and the University of California, Davis. She also makes jewelry and works as a server to cover expenses for food and art supplies.

1960

Finally able to better support herself, Remington moves into a spacious apartment on Pacific Street in San Francisco, where she begins a series of drawings with soot and red crayon on muslin (PAGES 53–59), purportedly using the soot from her new fireplace. In a letter to a friend she writes, "New pad's a real gasser . . . 7 large rooms, a real fireplace, huge jungley backyard, much sun, etc. & no neighbors that are a drag . . . all for $85 a month."[10]

Dilexi Gallery, San Francisco, features two drawings by Remington (July–August) in her first of several group exhibitions at the gallery.

1961

Remington continues working as a server at the Jazz Cellar, a Beat hub for poetry and jazz in the North Beach neighborhood of San Francisco.

SFSC's university gallery launches a new program of solo exhibitions and invites Remington to inaugurate the series. Her show (May–June) features four oil paintings and five ink drawings, and the gallery acquires one of the drawings for its collection.

1962

Remington's first solo exhibition at Dilexi Gallery in San Francisco opens (October), and for the next three years the gallery continues to feature her in solo and group shows in its San Francisco and Los Angeles locations. "[Dilexi] was the best gallery in San Francisco," she says later. "I got good write-ups, good critical reviews and so on. [But] the sales were meager. . . . I found this very frustrating because what I really wanted to do with my life is devote myself to a professional career in painting. . . . [Anyway] the gallery was held in high esteem by other artists, by collectors, by everybody that knew about the art world. . . . When [founder Jim Newman] chose an artist or asked an artist to become a part of the stable, he did so with great conviction and great dedication to that artist."[11]

Remington participates in *Drawings from the West Coast of USA* (October) at the Auckland Art Gallery, New Zealand. The exhibition is inspired by Auckland's show from the previous year, *Painting from the Pacific* (May 1961), whose catalogue includes a contribution by George D. Culler, SFMA's second director (1958–65). He writes that "there is a unique American idiom [that] should be made increasingly apparent with this exhibition of drawings."[12]

1963

Statement (1963; PAGE 49) is featured in *Exhibition of Contemporary Art* (December–January), hosted by the First Savings and Loan Association, San Francisco. Remington is awarded a "purchase award" of five thousand dollars by a judging panel that includes SFMA's director, George Culler, and the painting is gifted to SFMA by the First Savings and Loan Association. Remington considers this work a pivotal one in her practice. "In 1963, after three years of doing large gestural work where I was exploring and pushing several ideas toward a specific imagery, I created a seminal painting titled *Statement* which represented a significant breakthrough. . . . This work was hard-edged, more centralized, and 'cooler.'"[13]

1964

The *83rd San Francisco Art Institute Annual*, hosted by SFMA (April–May), features *Emanon* (1964; PAGE 61), which reveals a new direction in Remington's work. She "has abandoned expressionist paint-handling altogether and has substituted a tight delineation of curious, highly resolved architectural fantasies,"[14] writes *Artforum* in a review of the exhibition. Remington's friends, meanwhile, are "dumb-founded. They didn't understand what this painting was," Remington recalls. "I thought people were going to have heart attacks over this. I mean, I got phone calls in the middle of the night from friends. . . . People had just many different reactions. . . . [Some] loved it. But how much support can you get in San Francisco? Here again, it goes back to I couldn't make my living doing this."[15]

1965

The California Palace of the Legion of Honor (now the Legion of Honor, Fine Arts Museums of San Francisco) includes an *Adelphi Series* (1963–83) drawing in *Regional Exhibit of Contemporary Drawing* (February–April) and acquires the work for its collection.

In the spring, Remington's work is introduced to international audiences with *Adelphi Series 9* (1963) and *March* (1964; PAGE 71) in *Art '65 Lesser Known and Unknown Painters: Young American Sculpture—East to West* at the American Express Pavilion of the New York World's Fair (April–October).

In the fall, Remington moves to New York. "The period of years of my development out there [in San Francisco] I think was very good because there was no pressure. . . . One could be left alone to nurture and develop in one's very own individual way, and this is very important. But I got back to New York and . . . I ate it up. It was like so much food for me, and it still is."[16]

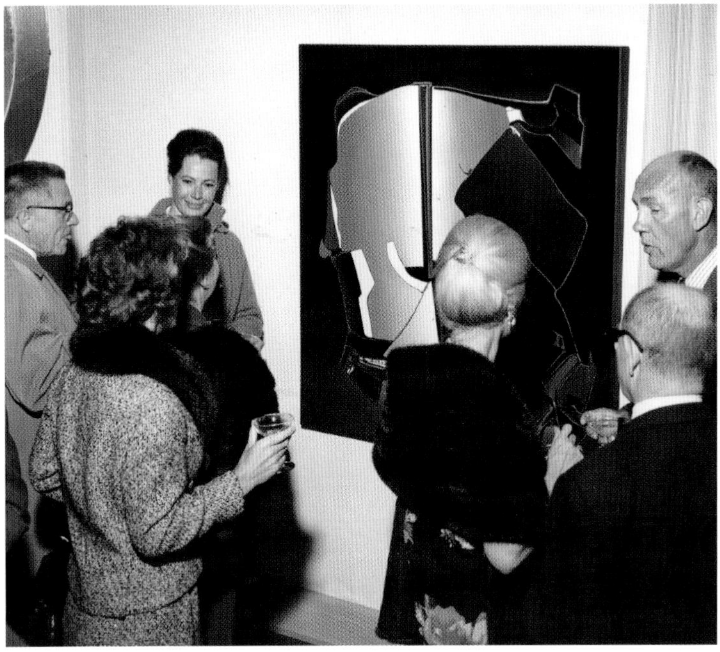

Remington with guests at SFMA's opening for *Art Across America: Western Regional Selection*, June 30, 1965

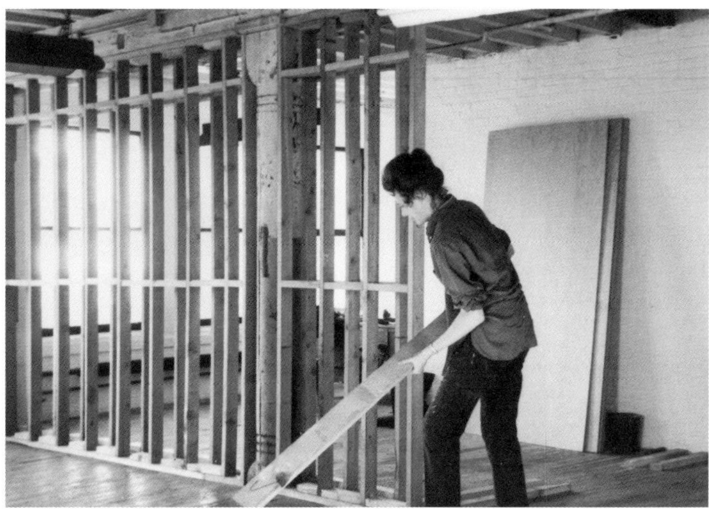

Remington renovating her new loft at 309 West Broadway, New York, 1966

After settling temporarily in a friend's loft in SoHo, she falls in love with the neighborhood and rents an apartment at 361 Canal Street for sixty-five dollars a month.

Remington's decision to move to New York results in increased critical recognition on both coasts. Her third and final solo exhibition with Dilexi Gallery in San Francisco inaugurates its new location on Clay Street (September–October). Reviewed in *Artforum*'s November issue, it features the painting *Shimo 404* (1965), which is also included in the Whitney Museum of American Art's 1965 *Annual Exhibition of Contemporary American Painting* (December–January). (Remington will again be featured in the 1967 and 1972 Whitney Annuals, which become the Whitney Biennial in 1973.)

1966

The Whitney Museum of American Art acquires *Haddonfield* (1965; PAGE 91), named after the artist's hometown in New Jersey and features the painting in an exhibition of new acquisitions. "After the Whitney purchased one of my paintings, my phone rang constantly for six weeks. Dealers, collectors and other artists—most of whom I had never met—wanted to see my work and talk about it."[17] Painting sales enable Remington to purchase a loft in SoHo in an artists' co-op, which will remain her primary residence for the rest of her life. She enters into a long-term relationship with Richard Hurwitz, a musician who plays trumpet in various Broadway shows. Hurwitz helps her renovate the new loft, complete with a soundproof room for his practice sessions, and they join Manhattan's growing downtown art scene.

Darthea Speyer, founder of the Centre Culturel Américain, Paris, invites Remington to join her new Paris gallery, Galerie Darthea Speyer, whose program will focus on American art. At Speyer's encouragement, Remington and Hurwitz divide their time between New York and Paris for the next two years in preparation for her show.

1967

Founded by Klaus Kertess, New York's prestigious Bykert Gallery hosts the artist's first solo show, *Deborah Remington* (April). "[Klaus] sold out my first show in New York rather easily. I mean, I was astounded. . . . One had, as you could understand, great trepidations about the first show and being unknown."[18] She will have three additional solo exhibitions before the gallery closes in 1975.

1968

Coinciding with the May 1968 uprising, Remington's solo exhibition (May–June) inaugurates the gallery's program, opening to enthusiastic reviews. "As we walked out the door [of the gallery to head to the dinner party at Darthea's apartment]," Remington later recalls, "every car had a collection of champagne glasses on top of it. And the sun was kind of setting. The whole street was golden and lit by this marvelous light, and as you walked down the street, the light would go through these champagne glasses. And it looked like the cars had sprouted some kind of icicle things that were catching and refracting and reflecting light. . . . Everything was very yellow and golden."[19]

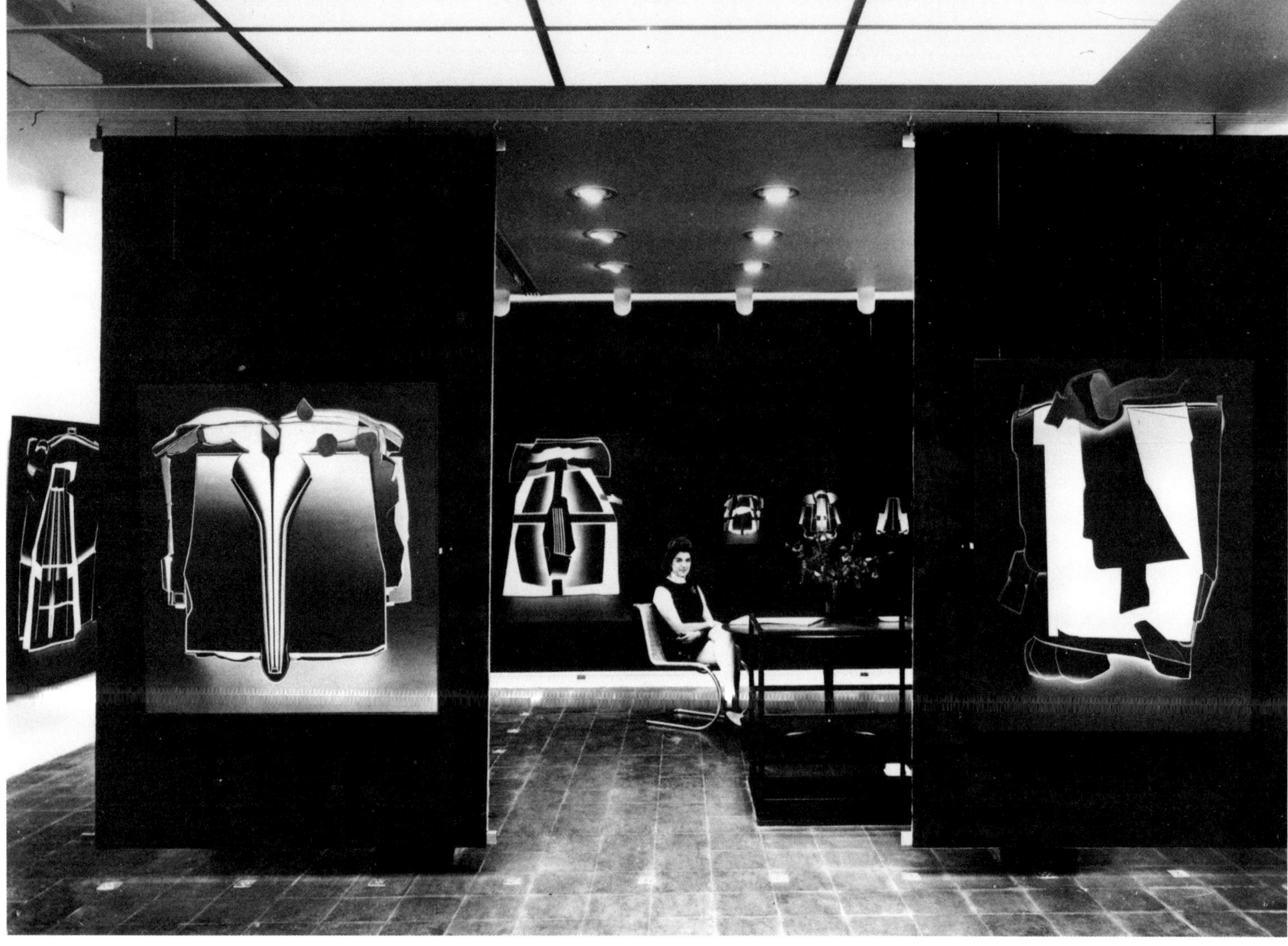

Installation view of Remington's solo show at Galerie Darthea Speyer in Paris, 1968

Speyer places work by Remington with several European museums and private collectors who are eager to add works by contemporary American artists to their collections. Remington continues showing with Speyer through the early 1990s.

1969

Remington begins a one-year visiting lectureship at The Cooper Union, New York, on Chinese and Japanese art "from the neolithic beginnings to the 18th century."[20]

1970

Remington exhibits *Memphis* and *Devon* (both 1969; **PAGES 2** and **105**), in *L'art vivant aux États-Unis*, curated by New York–based critic Dore Ashton for Fondation Maeght in Saint-Paul de Vence, France (July–September). The exhibition includes work by sixty-five contemporary American artists, including Carl Andre, Lee Bontecou, Hans Haacke, Brice Marden, and Louise Nevelson.

1971

Remington's work is included in the exhibition *Drawings by New York Artists* at the Utah Museum of Fine Arts, Salt Lake City (November–January), which features five *Adelphi Series* drawings and travels to several venues. "Drawing for me is not an adjunct to painting but rather a parallel," she explains of her approach to drawing. "It is always related to but never derived from the ideas that govern my painting. . . . It really is a separate art with a life and vitality of its own. . . . The way the drawing looks . . . the magic, the illusion, the surface matters a lot."[21]

1972

Remington's mother, Hazel, becomes seriously ill, and Remington helps to provide the nursing care for her until her death in November.

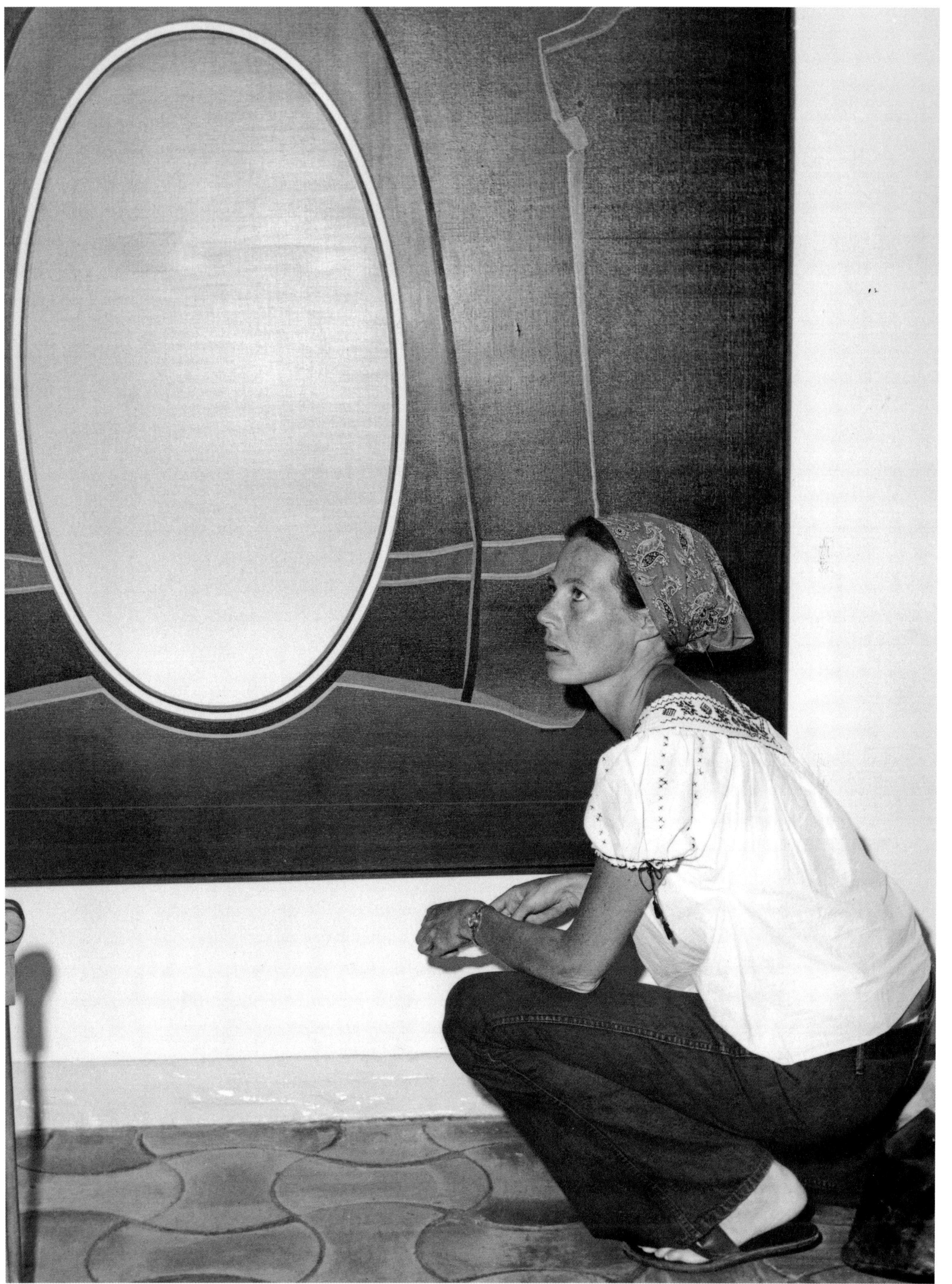

Remington installing her painting *Devon* (1969) for *L'art vivant aux États-Unis*, Fondation Maeght, Saint-Paul de Vence, France, 1970

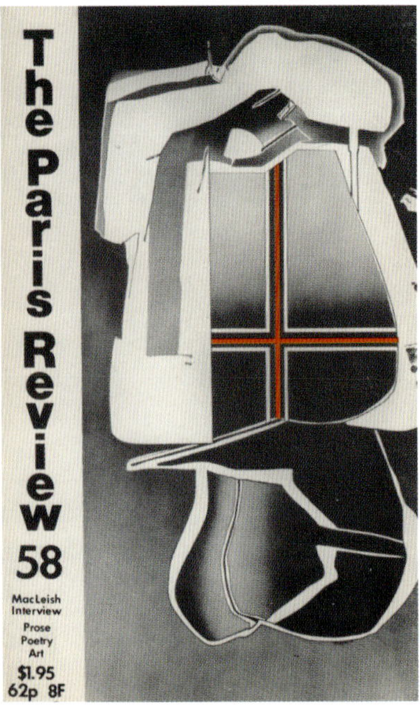

Adelphi Series (1974) on the cover of *The Paris Review*, Summer 1974

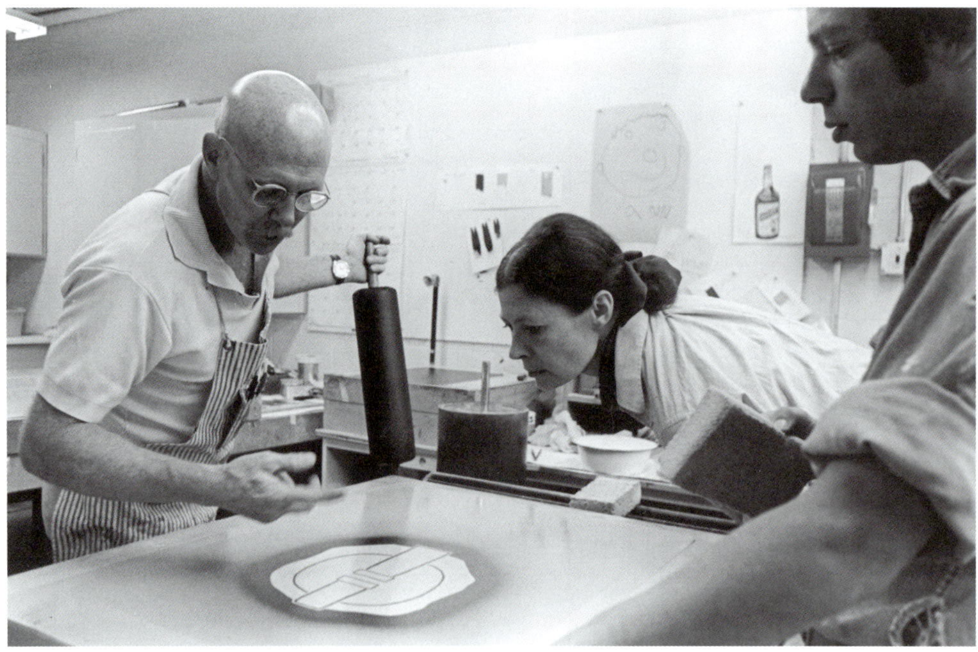

Remington with John Sommers and Glenn Brill at Tamarind Institute, University of New Mexico, Albuquerque, 1975

1973

Exhausted from caring for her mother and recovering from two debilitating medical operations herself, Remington takes a break from painting and accepts an invitation to work with master printers at the Tamarind Institute, University of New Mexico, Albuquerque. There she produces twelve editioned prints of color lithographs. "Tamarind totally re-educated me as well as re-sensitized me to the art of lithography. I was taught how to use the medium of lithography to accommodate and extend the statement of my painting and not to just make paintings in prints," she said of the collaborative process there. "The Tamarind experience will always remain in my thoughts as the most intense, challenging and rewarding."[22] She would return to Tamarind in 1975, 1978, 1980, and 1981.

Paul Cummings, director of the oral history project for the Smithsonian Institution's Archives of American Art, invites Remington to participate in a series of interviews.

1974

The Art Institute of Chicago includes Remington in the *71st Annual American Exhibition of Painting and Sculpture* (June–August).

Remington is featured in the *19th Biennial National Print Exhibition* (November–January) at the Brooklyn Museum.

Remington begins teaching advanced painting and drawing at The Cooper Union in New York. Aside from a break between 1977 and 1979, she continues teaching there until 1997.

1975

Remington's work is included in the exhibition *Image, Color and Form—Recent Paintings by Eleven Americans* (January–February) at the Toledo Museum of Art, Ohio.

Six paintings by Remington are featured in *Painting Endures* (May–June), a group exhibition at the Institute of Contemporary Art, Boston, with a catalogue essay written by Dore Ashton.

1976

The Hamilton Gallery of Contemporary Art, New York, represents Remington for the next three years and hosts a successful solo show in 1977 that includes such large-scale paintings as *Essex* (1972), *Dover* (1975), *Sussex* (1976), and others.

1978

Remington begins her *Trace Series* (1978–80; **PAGES 132–35**), made with graphite and black spray paint on paper. "In 1978 my work began to undergo another strong change through a series of drawings. . . . The central imagery and basic structure with which I had been working since 1963 started to break apart. A different spatial dialogue emerged and the color scheme became more intense."[23]

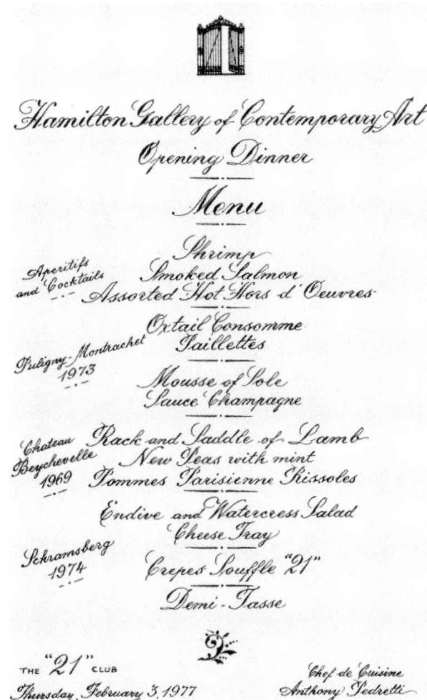
Hamilton Gallery of Contemporary Art
Opening Dinner
Menu

Aperitifs and Cocktails
Shrimp
Smoked Salmon
Assorted Hot Hors d' Oeuvres

Oxtail Consomme
Paillettes

Puligny-Montrachet 1973
Mousse of Sole
Sauce Champagne

Chateau Beychevelle 1969
Rack and Saddle of Lamb
New Peas with mint
Pommes Parisienne Rissoles

Endive and Watercress Salad
Cheese Tray

Schramsberg 1974
Crepes Souffle "21"
Demi-Tasse

THE "21" CLUB
Thursday, February 3, 1977

Chef de Cuisine
Anthony Pedretti

Menu from the dinner celebrating the inaugural exhibition at Hamilton Gallery, New York, which included work by Remington, 1977

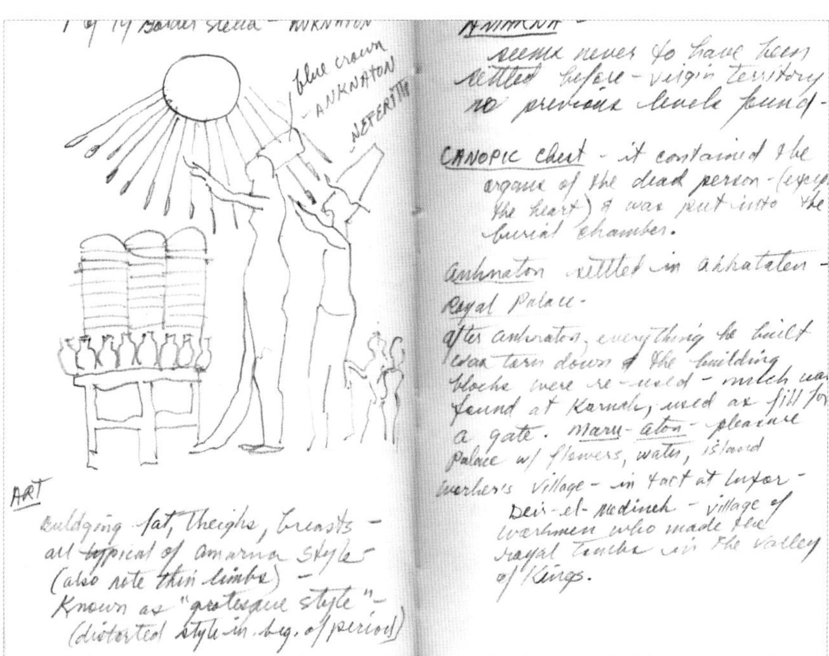

Spread from Remington's sketchbook, 1980

1979

Remington is awarded a National Endowment for the Arts grant, enabling her to continue a transition toward new imagery and expressiveness. She paints *Kamerun* (1979; **PAGE 139**), which she later describes as "the real breakthrough ptg. And things have been developing ever since."[24]

1980

In January, Remington delivers a lecture on the development of her work from 1959 to present at the Toledo Museum of Art, Ohio.

Remington travels to Egypt with a friend. Of particular interest to her are the ubiquitous ceremonial palettes, and she makes numerous pencil drawings of these in a sketchbook. "My trip to Egypt still haunts me," she says, trying to explain its impact. "Something of the experience has crept into my work . . . no, not pyramids or sphinxes . . . but deeper and more complicated . . . perceptual, conceptual, philosophical."[25]

Her detailed pencil sketches also include Egyptian gods, headdresses, stelae, and the famous Narmer Palette, whose shield-like shape potentially influences later paintings, such as *Zanthus* (1983; **PAGE 143**), *Maligant* (1996–2003; **PAGE 205**), *Tumulus* (2002; **PAGES 203**), and *Encounters* (2007; **PAGES 207–9**).

1981

Despite a variety of health issues, Remington continues to paint and show her work. Exhibitions include *The New Spiritualism: Transcendent Images in Painting and Sculpture* at the Oscarsson Hood Gallery, New York; the University of Connecticut, Storrs; and the University of Vermont, Burlington. She also exhibits drawings from the *Adelphi Series* (1963–83) and *Trace Series* (1978–80) in the exhibition *New Dimensions in Drawing, 1950–1980* (May–September) at the Aldrich Contemporary Art Museum, Ridgefield, Connecticut.

1983

Remington receives a diagnosis of breast cancer and undergoes treatment. The Newport Harbor Art Museum (now the Orange County Museum of Art) opens *Deborah Remington: A 20-Year Survey* (December–March), the artist's first major career retrospective. Dore Ashton writes the lead catalogue essay. In 1984, the exhibition travels to the Oakland Museum of California (August–October). To raise money for the catalogue, the artist produces *Praia* (1983), a color lithograph signed and numbered by the artist in a limited edition of fifty with five artist's proofs and three printer's proofs.

1984

Remington is featured in *The Dilexi Years, 1958–1970* (October–December), an important historical exhibition at the Oakland Museum of California.

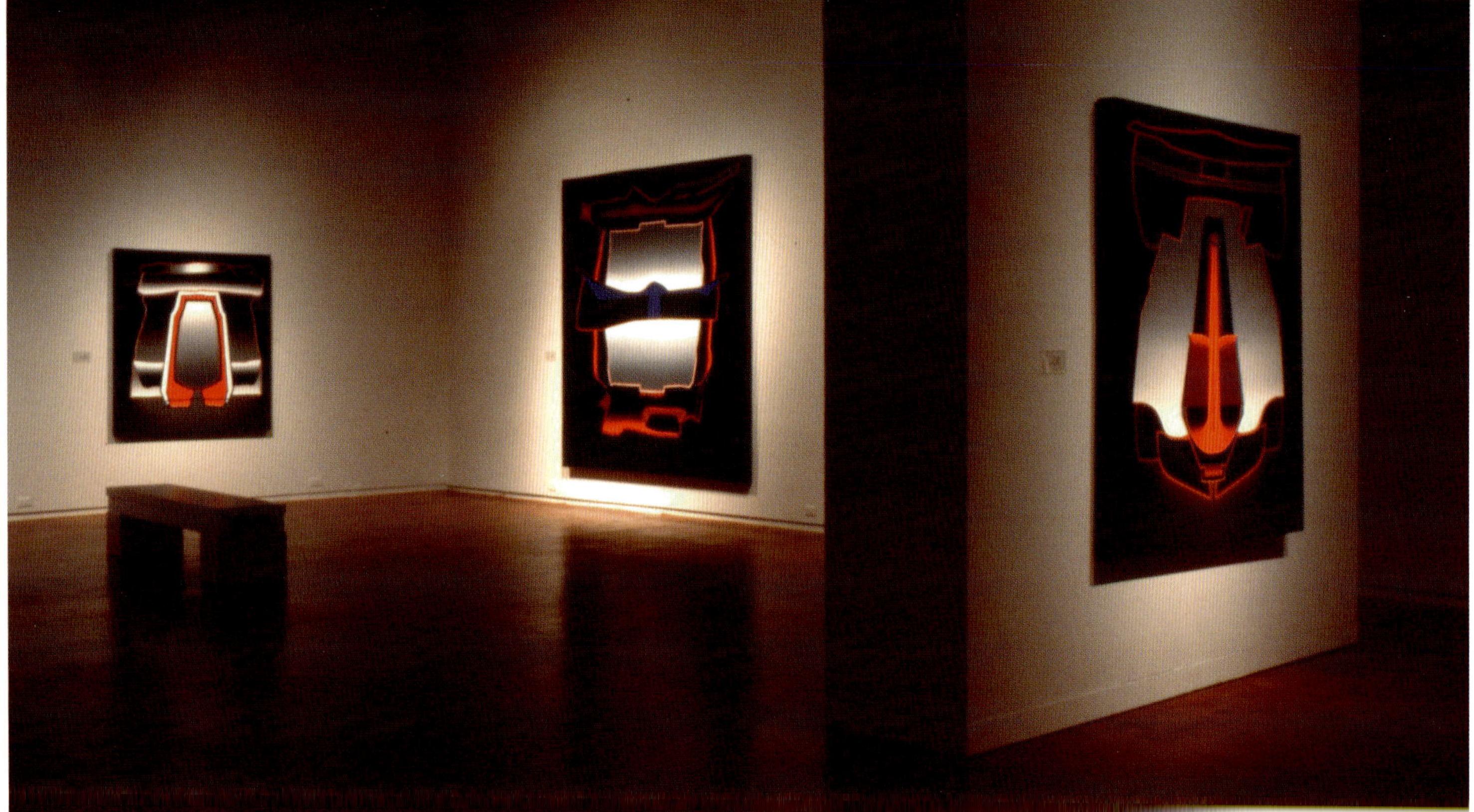

Installation view of *Deborah Remington: A 20-Year Survey*, Newport Harbor Art Museum (now Orange County Museum of Art), Newport Beach, California, December 15, 1983–March 25, 1984

Remington is awarded a Guggenheim Foundation Fellowship that leads to a new series of paintings and drawings called *Euros* (1983–86), which she exhibits in 1987 at the Jack Shainman Gallery, New York (March–April), and in 1988 at the Shoshana Wayne Gallery, Los Angeles (May–June). "My work is changing again . . . back to a little looser and more direct approach with no tape, etc. Right now I'm working on a series of large-scale drawings (6' and up) which are very exciting . . . all black, white & gray."[26] This series develops into a number of related paintings, such as *Dorado* (1986; PAGE 166), *Santee* (1986; PAGE 163), *Troas* (1987; PAGE 164), *Volans* (1987; PAGES 167–69), and *Xton* (1988; PAGE 171).

1985

Remington purchases a country home in Chester County, Pennsylvania, where she will spend her summers. Here she builds a separate studio, hires summer interns to assist with large-scale work, and grows her own vegetables, preserving them for use throughout the winter months in New York. "I'm off to Pa. for about 3½ months . . . for a fun time of gardening and making art. I'm as excited as a kid going off to her favorite camp. Have started lots of seedlings and shall be going there with over 135 little creatures which were born in N.Y. on my windowsills. Hope these street kids will get along with the country bumpkins."[27]

1989

Remington's drawings, which continue to be a vital part of her practice, are in exhibitions including *The Question of Drawing* at Miami Dade College, Florida (January–February), which travels to the Fort Wayne Museum of Art, Indiana, and the Pensacola Museum of Art, Florida, among other venues.

1990

Remington's early work and that of her Bay Area Beat colleagues is the focus of a historical exhibition titled *Lyrical Vision: The 6 Gallery, 1954–1957* at John Natsoulas Gallery, Davis, California (January–February).

Remington finds herself without gallery representation in New York. To support herself, she sells work directly out of her studio and continues to teach part-time at The Cooper Union. By the early 1990s, Remington also no longer has gallery representation in Paris through Galerie Darthea Speyer.

Throughout this decade and the early 2000s, Remington's work undergoes a dramatic transformation. After decades of disappearing evidence of her hand, Remington begins embracing again the gestural brushstrokes that she had last used in the 1950s and early 1960s. "I began trying to synthesize and unite two 'divergent paths,' which had begun in the 1963 painting titled *Statement* with which I had been working for over thirty-five years. I continue to be interested in containing images spatially but in a less-controlled manner."[28]

1993

Remington begins teaching part-time in New York University's MFA program.

1994

Remington fractures her right arm and is diagnosed with osteoporosis.

1996

Remington begins painting *Maligant* (1996–2003), completing it seven years later. Its title is a play on the word "malignant."

1997

Remington begins *Beinen*, a series of large-scale drawings in graphite and red crayon that continues her investigation of structure (1997–2001). Made in response to wrist and arm fractures in 1994 and 1999, they echo rib cages and bones. "I broke an ankle and a wrist in a fall. And I thought, 'Oh lord, bones, it's what holds us together, it's what holds us up,'" she later explains. "My work is nonrepresentational but you can still get the feelings of bones in this [series]."[29]

Remington's teaching position at The Cooper Union in New York comes to an end.

1999

Remington is awarded a Pollock-Krasner Foundation Grant and elected to the National Academy of Design.

Her teaching position with New York University ends. She becomes an instructor at the National Academy of Design, New York, until 2007.

She fractures her left wrist and undergoes surgery.

2001

Mitchell Algus Gallery, New York, features *March* (1964; PAGE 71) at the Armory Show (February) in New York, and later that year includes Remington in *Reconstructing Abstraction* (October–December), a group exhibition showing several of her large-scale works, such as *Eridan* (2001; PAGE 197). This breakthrough painting, according to Remington, presents an abstracted rib cage whose bones appear both fractured and fused.

The Worcester Art Museum, Massachusetts, includes Remington's energetic color lithographs from the early 1950s in *The Stamp of Impulse: Abstract Expressionist Prints* (April–June). The exhibition travels to the Cleveland Museum of Art, Ohio; the Amon Carter Museum of American Art, Fort Worth, Texas; and the Block Museum of Art, Northwestern University, Evanston, Illinois.

Because Remington has difficulty breathing after the attacks of 9/11, she temporarily leaves her SoHo loft for her home in Pennsylvania. There, she works on a series of drawings and paintings with body-like imagery in a more colorful reprise of the earlier *Beinen Series* (1997–2001).

2004

Remington receives a diagnosis of lung cancer and undergoes treatment.

Remington completes a small painting titled *Episode*, where the body once again appears to be dissolving—a comment perhaps on her increasing sense of fragility as she faces her own mortality.

2007

Remington's prints are featured in *Paths to the Press: Printmaking and American Women Artists, 1910–1960* at the Block Museum of Art, Northwestern University, Evanston, Illinois (September–December). The exhibition travels to the McNay Art Museum, San Antonio, Texas, and the Wallach Art Gallery at Columbia University, New York, among others. Her work is also included in *The Abstract Impulse: Fifty Years of American Abstraction at the National Academy, 1956–2006* at the National Academy Museum, New York (August–January).

Remington is diagnosed with cancer in her other lung.

She finishes *Encounters* (2007; PAGES 207–9), her final painting.

2010

Omina (1978; PAGES 129–31) is included in *Psychedelic: Optical & Visionary Art Since the 1960s* at the San Antonio Museum of Art, Texas (March–August), and travels to the Telfair Museums, Savannah, Georgia.

Remington is diagnosed with stage IV lung cancer, and she enters hospice. On April 21, she passes away in a nursing home in Moorestown, New Jersey.

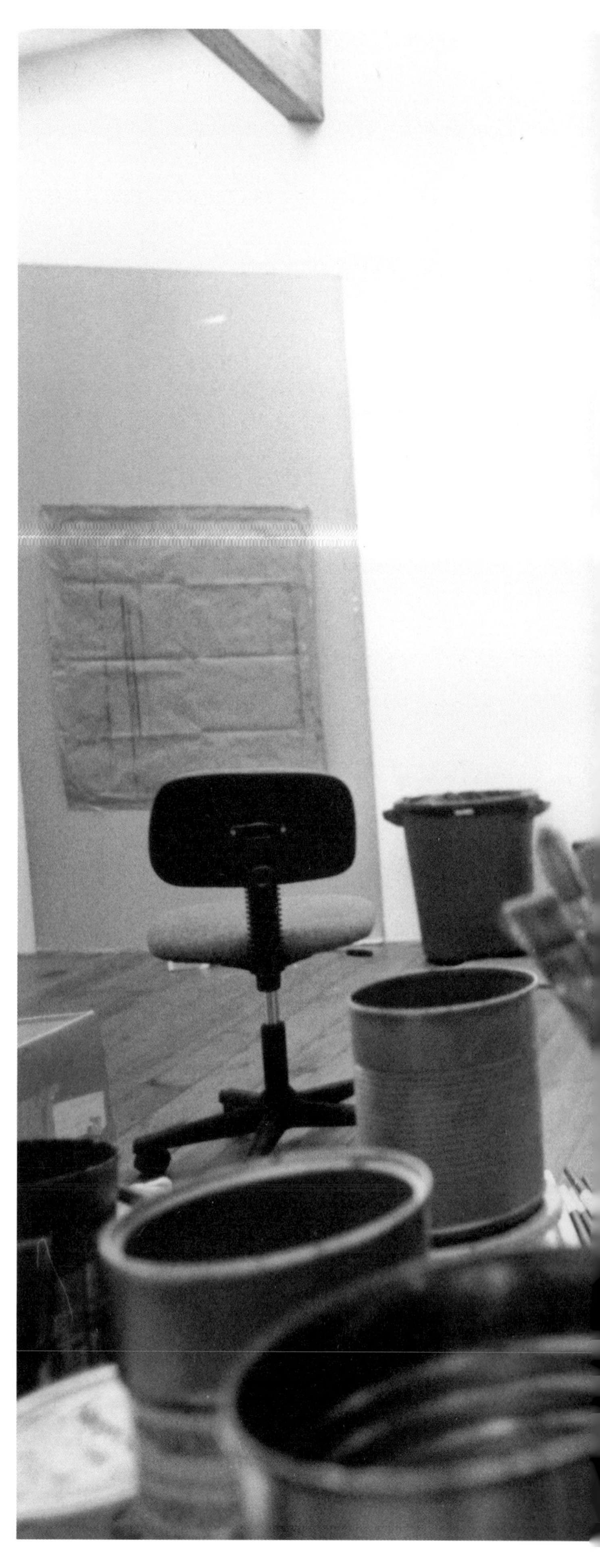

Remington in her New York studio, c. 2001

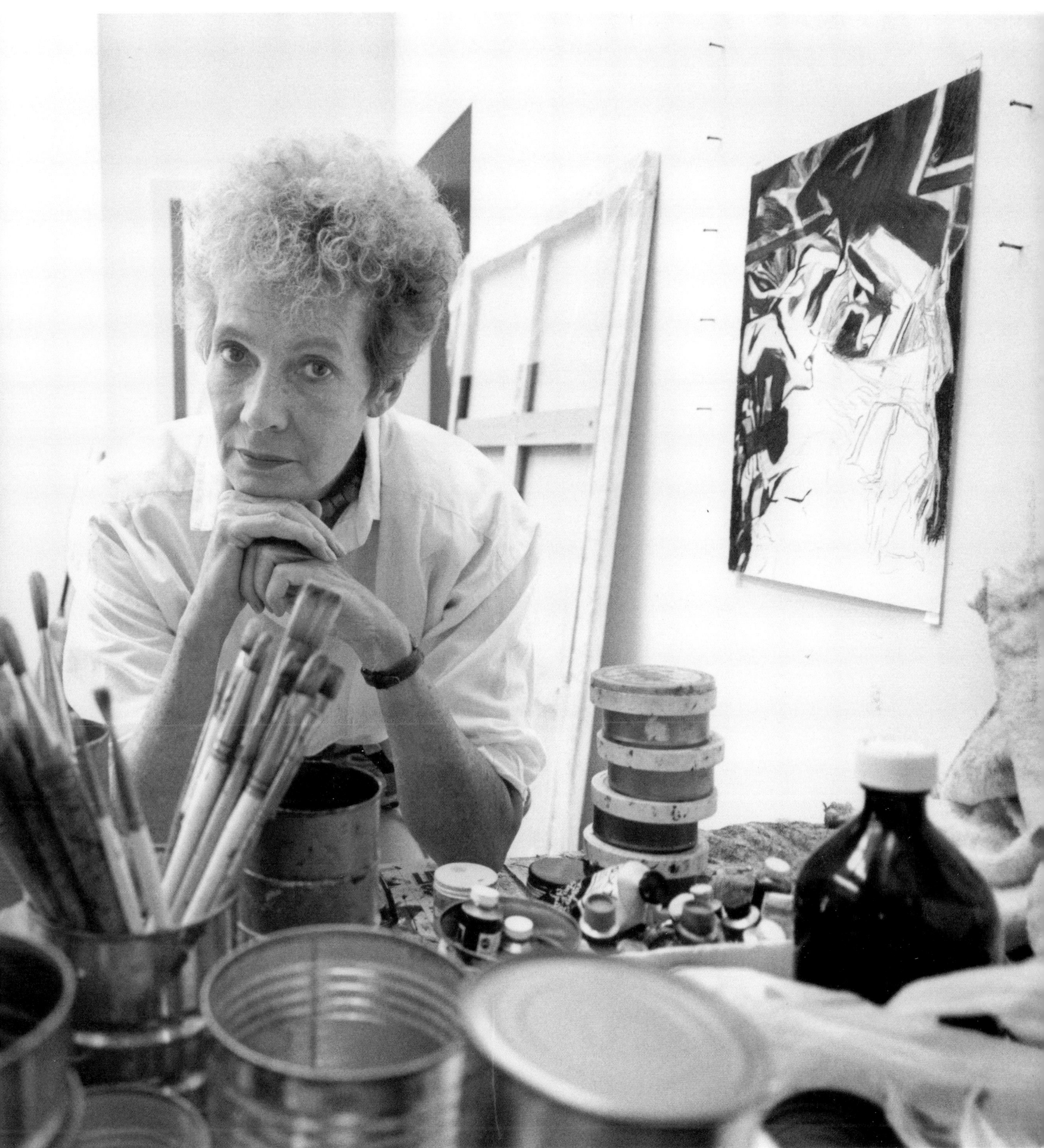

Deborah Remington R.I.P.

KEVIN KILLIAN

I read in the *New York Times* that the American artist Deborah Remington died last week, nearly eighty; what a wave of regret and desolation blew through me when I read these words. And yet I can say I had a grand encounter with her, just last year. Yes, I met her but once, and it was unforgettable.

I was writing a biography of the California poet Jack Spicer when I first heard Deborah Remington's name. She was one of the young bohemians who started the 6 Gallery in the mid-1950s, a legendary space in California art and poetry. Remington was the grandniece of the American West painter Frederic Remington and partook in something of his long view and historical sense. She came to the California School of Fine Arts (later the San Francisco Art Institute) from Southern California with a group of young friends and met Spicer there: he was their teacher, taught them history, English, and "the humanities."[1]

Teacher and students, impatient with the conventional gallery system, opened a place on the site of the old King Ubu space on Fillmore. Over the next few years, it became the epicenter for the new painting, sculpture, and what you would today call multimedia experiments. Allen Ginsberg gave a famous reading at the gallery in October 1955, premiering his controversial poem "Howl." At the time I started working on the Spicer biography, one of the "6," Hayward King, had already passed on, but I managed to interview several others of the group and put together a decent enough account of Spicer's work with the gallery. But in the back of my mind, like all biographers, I'm sure, there was always this feeling that, oh well, too bad I didn't try harder to find Deborah Remington! But she had moved to New York, I didn't have her number—oh, I had lots of half-assed excuses.

Ten years later Peter Gizzi and I edited Spicer's collected poems, and the idea was to have a reading from the book on each coast. Here in San Francisco, we had a reading at the main library, inviting a dozen poets and artists who had not necessarily known Spicer, for their number was shrinking every year, but who had been influenced by him—young, old, middle-aged, men, women, straight, gay, a little of this and that, the good old San Francisco way.

Our New York event was a coproduction of two estimable NYC nonprofits: Poets House and the Poetry Project at St. Mark's Church in the Bowery. At the Poetry Project, Stacy Szymaszek, its executive director, asked me which New Yorkers I'd like to see at the reading—now rather a grand affair with a mini-conference attached. An ancient memory awoke in me, "I always wanted to interview Deborah Remington," I sighed. "Who?" asked Stacy. I tried to explain, but Stacy soon quieted me. "Sssh, sssh, sssh, we'll find her."

To my surprise, Remington agreed to participate in our tribute to Spicer but when asked to read a poem, she wouldn't. "I would feel stupid," she said. "I'm not a poet." "Okay, so how about I interview you, live, onstage, and you could give me all your memories of Spicer being your teacher, etcetera?" "In the middle of everyone else getting up and reading his poems? Sure, why not?" She made it so easy. Maybe she liked doing something different from the others, the way she just loved being the only woman in the "6" group. I apologized for not having found her twenty years before. "You could have, very easily," she said. "I've been in the same apartment in New York since 1967."

We devised a method whereby I would "preinterview" her, by phone, and try to condense her memories into some quick zippy sound bites that would impress an audience, as we'd been scheduled for only ten minutes to complete our interview. I was nervous speaking with her on the phone. She told me that, contrary to what I thought, she was far younger than anyone else in the "6." She had graduated from high school early and was only sixteen or something when she started at the Art Institute, whereas the boys she joined up with had delayed their education by serving in Korea, so they were all much older than she. I warmed to her instantly, and after a few hours and many emails back and forth, we agreed to do our interview with bullet points, one, two, three memories; some general reflections on California art; one further memory; what was it like to be a woman artist in a benighted time for women? Perhaps one final amusing anecdote. It was going to be great.

Cut to May 15, 2009, in New York, the evening of our show, Stacy asked me if I had heard from Remington. (To preserve the secrecy of her appearance, we spoke of her in code, using code name *Remington Steele*, like the corny 1980s TV show.) "I haven't, but I'm sure she'll be here." But then doubt set in. We had scheduled her for a beauty spot: she and I were to mount the stage as the first act in the second half of the program, right after the intermission. But where was she? I didn't even know what she looked like, not really, though her website had some old photos and I owned a clutch of pictures of her from when she was young and in full Beat-queen regalia, but this was fifty-five years later—she must have changed, everyone does! A handful of old women dotted the crowd. We surveyed them with skeptical eyes. Could that old lady, with the bare feet and the patched shawl and the wild gray Brunhilda hair, be Deborah Remington? "I don't know, Stacy, I just thought she'd take care of herself better than that." "I'll ask her." "Pardon, are you Deborah Remington?" Pause. "No, she says she has no name; she's a being from another planet." "I didn't think she was her." Even the oldest of the old-timers we had gathered at the Project were too young to have known Deborah Remington: Basil King, Martha King, George Stanley, all of them had come onto the SF scene after Remington had already left for Japan. Finally, we decided maybe Remington was sick or something. The program began, and I just left it up to the gods.

The auditorium was packed, and I guess I got caught up, I kind of forgot. Wellbutrin will do that. Toward the end of the first act, I noticed hands moving in my row—someone was passing a note to me. I unfolded the paper. Stacy had scrawled, "Remington Steele has landed!"

"Pardon me, pardon me, pardon me," I kept excusing myself. Eventually, I scrambled back to the lobby. My brow furrowed once more. I didn't see any old lady. There was just one woman there, exquisitely dressed, made-up, coiffured. A woman younger than I surely, sitting in a chair directly under the most beautiful golden light. "Where is she?" I asked Stacy, frightened that Remington had come and not liked what she had seen and departed. "Kevin, this is Deborah Remington," she said, indicating the seated and remarkably composed artist. "Is that really you?" I asked Deborah Remington. She shook my hand and I started to babble. She explained that she was only able to appear for half an hour because a friend was having a dinner party in her honor and she had a car waiting outside to take her back to the party. A weak half smile, half regret, half pride, crossed her face, and I had the impression people gave parties for her constantly—why? Because she was so fabulous. She had that Lauren Bacall thing going on of ageless grace and élan. Luckily I had the presence of mind to take some pictures of her real quick. And I got her to sign my autograph book. And then up on the stage Stacy was announcing to the crowd a surprise appearance by a living legend—one of the "6" from the 6 Gallery. Stagehands had rearranged the stage to look like a talk show setup with two chairs, a little lamp, a bowl of flowers. I took Remington's hand, we walked down the main aisle like a bride and groom, we sat down in our chairs, and she killed them. Just killed them. Afterward people were like, "Oh my God," and everyone wanted to meet her, but she had slipped back into the night, into her car, and that was my meeting with her, the most vibrant and young person in the room that night.

Roberta Smith's obituary for Remington—from which you can get a general picture of her career in art—tells us that she had been lying about her age for many years, that she wasn't the teenage prodigy she claimed.[2] What can I say? I fell for her, but good. Who was it that said, "Brightness falls from the air / Queens have died young and fair"?

This text was originally published on May 19, 2010, at https://openspace.sfmoma.org/2010/05/deborah-remington-r-i-p/.

Endnotes

Nancy Lim
INTRODUCTION: A LUMINOUS VISION

1. Alexandra Anderson, "A Singular Painter Sees Double," *Village Voice*, September 6, 1976, 78, 80.
2. The Whitney Annual evolved into the Whitney Biennial in 1973.
3. Oral history interview with Deborah Remington, Archives of American Art, Smithsonian Institution, May 29–July 19, 1971.
4. Thomas O'Connor, "Remington Retrospective Under Way," *Register* (Orange County, CA), December 16, 1983.

Nancy Lim
DEBORAH REMINGTON'S EARLY YEARS

1. Remington described the education at Otis as "mediocre, pedantic. It wasn't interesting enough. It wasn't revealing enough, strong enough, hard enough for kids who were really serious, as we were. We really wanted to get into this. And it was this nonsense." Oral history interview with Deborah Remington, Archives of American Art, Smithsonian Institution, May 29–July 19, 1971.
2. Elmer Bischoff, quoted in Thomas Albright, *Art in the San Francisco Bay Area, 1945–1980* (Berkeley: University of California Press, 1985), 19.
3. Oral history interview with Remington, Archives of American Art.
4. Remington's CSFA transcript does not list coursework with Clyfford Still, but her interview with the Archives of American Art suggests that she studied with him in some capacity: "Clyfford Still, I was studying with him. . . . The comments he made to me were really projections of his own work. I mean, certain space concepts, certain ways to use bits of colors here and there, certain ways form worked. A lot of things about space and form and really how the world related to his own work." Remington's transcript also does not list coursework with Mark Rothko, who was teaching at CSFA during the summer of 1949, but his presence at the school exerted an influence on her paintings. See oral history interview with Remington, Archives of American Art.
5. This watershed event in accounts of Bay Area Figurative art and its art historical recountings are discussed in Janet Bishop, "David Park: A Picture as an Event," in *David Park: A Retrospective*, ed. Janet Bishop (San Francisco: San Francisco Museum of Modern Art; Berkeley: University of California Press, 2019), 27–28.
6. Oral history interview with Remington, Archives of American Art.
7. Albright, 26.
8. Remington, "More History of the Six Gallery," Letters to the Living Section, *San Francisco Chronicle*, March 14, 2004.
9. Manuel Neri, "Manuel Neri: A Kind of Time Warp," *Currant* 1, no. 1 (April–May 1975).
10. Oral history interview with Remington, Archives of American Art.
11. Notably, preparatory notes for a lecture reflecting on her career that Remington gave at the San Francisco Art Institute suggest that she planned to begin her presentation with a slide of the lithograph *On the Scene* (1954), narrating her beginnings by remarking that "I feel [this work] captures the essence of what I was working with in that time." Deborah Remington, letter to Fred Martin, February 8, 1981. Box 1, Folder 10, Deborah Remington Papers, Special Collections and University Archives, Rutgers University Libraries.
12. Remington later retitled this painting *Dacia*. It received institutional recognition early on, including a prize in the *75th Annual Painting and Sculpture Exhibit* of the San Francisco Art Association in 1956.
13. Oral history interview with William Wiley, Archives of American Art, Smithsonian Institution, October 8–November 20, 1997.
14. Peter Selz, "Notes on Funk," in *Funk* (Berkeley: University of California Press, 1967), 3.
15. Remington, quoted in Cindy Nemser, "Deborah Remington: Fascinating Contradictions," *Feminist Art Journal* 3, no. 1 (Spring 1974).
16. Oral history interview with Remington, Archives of American Art. Elsewhere in this interview Remington also notes, "I would hold the bottle of ink and constantly dip the pen in it because I could use pen points with wide strokes or thin strokes."
17. For further discussion of the relationship between Remington's work and the calligraphic traditions she studied, see the essay by Stephanie M. Hohlios on pages 80–87 in this volume.
18. Remington, letter to Norma and Floyd Cox, August 22, 1960. Box 1, Folder 19, Deborah Remington Papers, Special Collections and University Archives, Rutgers University Libraries.
19. Although the material support for these works is muslin, Remington considered them drawings.
20. Oral history interview with Elmer Bischoff, Archives of American Art, Smithsonian Institution, August 10–September 1, 1977.
21. Oral history interview with Remington, Archives of American Art.
22. Dore Ashton, "Deborah Remington," in *Deborah Remington: A 20-Year Survey*, ed. Paul Schimmel (Newport Beach, CA: Newport Harbor Art Museum, 1983), 20.
23. Oral history interview with Remington, Archives of American Art.
24. Remington was scheduled to teach at CSFA in the summer of 1966, but it is unclear from her correspondence with CSFA administrators whether she ever intended to return to San Francisco. See Deborah Remington Artist's File, San Francisco Art Institute Archives.
25. Oral history interview with Remington, Archives of American Art.

Stephanie M. Hohlios
FRAMING THE SELF, SEEING THE OTHER: DEBORAH REMINGTON IN JAPAN, 1956–58

1. Knute Stiles, "The Mysterious Machine," *Artforum* 4, no. 6 (February 1966), 25.
2. Stiles, "The Mysterious Machine," 26.
3. Miriam Brumer, "Deborah Remington: Fascinating Contradictions," *Feminist Art Journal* 3, no. 1 (Spring 1974): 2–4.
4. Oral history interview with Deborah Remington, Archives of American Art, Smithsonian Institution, May 29–July 19, 1971. Remington says, "[S]ome people have written about my work, critics and so forth, have seen a lot of Japanese influence in my work . . . I cannot see it. Superficially, on the surface when you look at my work, where is the Japanese element in my work? You can't point to something and say, well, that's that and that's something else. I mean, it's not there."
5. Oral history interview with Remington, Archives of American Art. Remington: "[M]y eye had such training, intense training, for two years. For calligraphy, for instance, you write a character. If the angle of a certain stroke is the slightest bit off, you're corrected, and you do it until you get it down visually perfectly, your whole sensitivity about one stroke relating to another stroke . . . what we're talking about basically is line. It's not only black and white and the certain grays that come of that, let's say, when a brush runs out of ink and you get to a marvelous gray world. But angles and relationships of one line to another . . . every stroke has a certain function in the character."
6. Oral history interview with Remington, Archives of American Art.
7. Some of her weekly language lessons are preserved in the Deborah Remington Papers at Rutgers University, New Brunswick, New Jersey. See "Japanese Lesson," 1st Week, March 1, 1955. Box 2, Folder 1, Deborah Remington Papers, Special Collections and University Archives, Rutgers University Libraries.
8. Oral history interview with Remington, Archives of American Art.
9. "I really better stand on the other side of the fence, so to speak, and look back at myself and my culture," she wrote. "It was very easy to do because . . . [t]here wasn't a chair in the house. There was not a piece of familiar paraphernalia, no knives, no forks. Everything was foreign." Oral history interview with Remington, Archives of American Art.
10. We can consider this image in connection with her series of self-portraits (1950; see page 227 in this volume), completed during Remington's studies at CSFA, which likewise draws on a visual history of women as desirable subjects.
11. Letter to Norma and Gil Linsley, December 2, 1958. Box 1, Folder 18, Deborah Remington Papers, Special Collections and University Archives, Rutgers University Libraries.
12. Oral history interview with Remington, Archives of American Art.
13. Oral history interview with Remington, Archives of American Art.
14. Hagiwara Shigeru (professor emeritus of Media and Communication Studies, Keio University, Tokyo), for example, discusses the image of foreigners (*gaikokujin*, anyone who is not Japanese) cultivated through Japanese television commercials. See Hagiwara Shigeru, "Nihon no terebi hōkoku ni arawareru gaikoku imēji no dōkō" ("Trends in the Depiction of Foreigners in Japanese Television Broadcasting"), *Hōsō kenkyū to chōsa* (*Broadcasting: Research and Investigation*) (September 2003), 77–88.
15. Kodama Miiko (professor emerita, Musashi University, Tokyo) analyzes the relationship among social institutions, practices of gender, and broadcasting culture in Japan. Kodama observes that the majority of comedians and on-screen talent involved in comedy or variety shows are male. Comedy, like other media genres, cultivates a culture of the masculine, amounting to what she calls a "feudal-style space" shaped through nepotistic, all-male lineages of masters and students. Kodama Miiko, "Hōsō bunka to jendā" ("Broadcast Culture and Gender"), *Kokusai jendā gakkai shi* (*A History of Gender Scholarship Internationally*) 7 (2009), 9–26.
16. Oral history interview with Remington, Archives of American Art.
17. See Box 10, Folder 15, Deborah Remington Papers, Special Collections and University Archives, Rutgers University Libraries.
18. Oral history interview with Remington, Archives of American Art.
19. On Sesshū's historical reception as a canonical example of East Asian ink painting in Japan, see Yukio Lippit, "Of Modes and Manners in Japanese Ink Painting: Sesshū's *Splashed Ink Landscape* of 1495," *Art Bulletin* 94, no. 1 (March 2012), 50–77. Sesshū continues to be a touchstone for ink painting and *Nihonga* ("Japanese-style painting"), in contrast with *Yōga*, or "Western-style painting," in general in the postwar years. See Matthew Larking, "Death and the Prospects of Unification: *Nihonga*'s Postwar Rapprochements with *Yōga*," *Japan Review*, no. 34 (2019), 161–90.
20. Oral history interview with Remington, Archives of American Art.
21. Sesshū Tōyō (1420–1506?), *Splashed Ink Landscape*, 1495. Vertical hanging scroll, ink on paper. Tokyo National Museum, National Treasure. Sesshū's *Splashed Ink* demonstrates the artist's ability to paint with ink in the mode of Yujian—with improvised adaption, namely, the creation of a landscape scene that begins with an uncontrolled splash of ink on the page that becomes a representational landscape scene. See Lippit, "Of Modes and Manners in Japanese Ink Painting."
22. On Franz Kline's relationship to Japanese calligraphy, see Bert Winther-Tamaki, *Art in the Encounter of Nations: Japanese and American Artists in the Early Postwar Years* (Honolulu: University of Hawai'i Press, 2001).
23. *Deborah Remington: Recent Paintings*, Zolla / Lieberman Gallery, Chicago, October 22–December 7, 1976.
24. Devonna Pieszak, "Deborah Remington," *New Art Examiner* (December 1976): 14. Box 5, Folder 11, Deborah Remington Papers, Special Collections and University Archives, Rutgers University Libraries.

25. Oral history interview with Daniel Lienau by Margaret Mathews Berenson, Santa Rosa, California, September 18, 2014.
26. Remington in Corinne Robins, ed., *Drawing Now: 10 Artists*, exh. cat. (New York: SoHo Center for Visual Artists, 1976), unpaginated.
27. Letter to Norma Linsley, May 11, 1959. Box 1, Folder 18, Deborah Remington Papers, Special Collections and University Archives, Rutgers University Libraries.

Anna Katz
DEBORAH REMINGTON, CUTTING-EDGE ARTIST

1. "The View from Los Angeles and New York: An Interview with Deborah Remington and Charles Mattox," *SFAI News* (July 1966), unpaginated.
2. Remington, as quoted in Simon Watson Taylor, "Space Machines," *Art and Artists* 2, no. 5 (August 1967), 31.
3. Remington, as quoted in Donald Miller, "Portraits of Objects in Space," *ARTnews* 74, no. 8 (October 1975), 87.
4. Oral history interview with Deborah Remington, Archives of American Art, Smithsonian Institution, May 29–July 19, 1971.
5. Remington, "Artist's Statement," in *Image, Color and Form—Recent Paintings by Eleven Americans*, exh. cat. (Toledo, OH: Toledo Museum of Art, 1975), 20.
6. Remington, as quoted in Taylor, "Space Machines," 31.
7. Remington, "Artist's Statement," 20.
8. Knute Stiles, "The Mysterious Machine," *Artforum* 4, no. 6 (February 1966), 25.
9. Corinne Robins, "Deborah Remington: Cool Fire," *Arts Magazine* 50, no. 2 (October 1975), 50.
10. Sabine Marchand, "Deborah Remington," *Cimaise* (January–February 1972), unpaginated.
11. Alexandra Anderson, "A Singular Painter Sees Double," *Village Voice*, September 6, 1976, 78.
12. Mira Schor, "Miriam Schapiro's Road to Feminism," hyperallergic.com, March 15, 2016, https://hyperallergic.com/283426/miriam-schapiros-road-to-feminism/.
13. Stiles, "The Mysterious Machine," 26. For another example of an early reference to television in the critical literature, see Taylor, "Space Machines," 30–33.
14. Stiles, "The Mysterious Machine," 26.
15. Pamela M. Lee elaborates on the meaning of the word "television" in *Chronophobia: On Time in Art of the 1960s* (Cambridge, MA: MIT Press, 2004), 187.
16. Oral history interview with Remington, Archives of American Art.
17. James R. Mellow, "Cultural Center Displays N. C. Wyeth Illustrations," *New York Times*, November 25, 1972, 23.
18. See Frances Jacobus–Parker, "Redescribing the Photograph," in Gary Garrels, ed., *Vija Celmins: To Fix the Image in Memory*, exh. cat. (San Francisco: San Francisco Museum of Modern Art; New Haven: Yale University Press, 2018), 86.
19. In a 2004 letter endorsing Lee Bontecou's proposed membership to the National Academy of Design, Remington recalled that she first saw Bontecou's work during a trip to New York in the early 1960s. Speaking of the direct impact of Bontecou's work on her *Soot Series*, Remington reflected, "I was awed by the depth and profundity of it and from the experience I had from seeing it. It had a big impact on me as a young painter and inspired me to do a series of Soot Drawings in 1963 and '64, using muslin and soot from my fireplace." Letter to National Academy Membership Committee in support of Lee Bontecou's acceptance, November 6, 2004. Deborah Remington Papers, Special Collections and University Archives, Rutgers University Libraries.
20. Remington, as quoted in Miller, "Portraits of Objects in Space," 87.

Suzanne Hudson
ENCOUNTERS: DEBORAH REMINGTON LATE WORKS

1. Likewise astounding is the difficulty Paul Schimmel had in traveling the show. Surviving documents reveal the lengths he went to contact numerous international venues and yielding only the Oakland Museum of California. (This activity is grimly tallied in an undated document headed "Remington Score Card," which lists as many rejections as possible sites.) In an August 1983 letter to Remington, where he responds to an earlier missive in which she shares concerns for the impending and yet unresolved show, Schimmel asserts that beyond remaining flexible regarding dates and fees, in his "years as a Curator I don't think I have ever sent out a more complete circulation package." Paul Schimmel letter to Deborah Remington, August 5, 1983. Orange County Museum of Art Archives.
2. Press release for *Deborah Remington: A 20-Year Survey*, December 13, 1983. Orange County Museum of Art Archives.
3. National Endowment for the Arts Museum Program, Organization Grant Application Form, 1982. Orange County Museum of Art Archives.
4. Deborah Remington's artist statement for *Art '65: Lesser Known and Unknown Painters: Young American Sculpture—East to West* at the American Express Pavilion at the New York World's Fair. She continues: "While I do not completely understand the sources of this imagery, my work contains elements, which by simultaneously attracting and repelling one another, create a tense balance which has emotional and spiritual meaning for me." She used the same statement in a catalogue for the University of Illinois Biennial at the University of Illinois at Urbana-Champaign, in 1967, and aspects of it recurred for decades thereafter in other published statements and in interviews and lectures.
5. Importantly as it relates to a history of intermittent institutional interest, *Statement* was acquired by the San Francisco Museum of Modern Art in 1965.

6. The catalogue ultimately was funded not by the National Endowment for the Arts but through the California Arts Council and with money raised by the sale of a sixteen-color lithograph, *Praia* (1983), that Remington printed with Jeffrey Sippel and Conrad Schwable at Ocean Works Press for the cause.
7. Paul Schimmel in *Deborah Remington: A 20-Year Survey* (Newport Beach, CA: Newport Harbor Art Museum, 1983), 9.
8. Oral history interview with Deborah Remington, Archives of American Art, Smithsonian Institution, May 29–July 19, 1971.
9. Oral history interview with Remington, Archives of American Art. In this, she follows the tendency recognized by Carol Donnell-Kotrozo, who, in 1980, catalogued responses to Remington's biomorphic forms, a range of imagining encompassing "machines for transcendence, surreal human organs, plant and flower openings, among other things." Carol Donnell-Kotrozo, "Dynamics of Illusion," *Artweek* 11, no. 4 (February 2, 1980).
10. Paul Sutinen, "Remington Is Redundant," *Willamette Week* (Portland, OR), November 20, 1977.
11. Kate Regan, "Remington: Past and Future: Oakland Museum Retrospective and a New Show," *San Francisco Chronicle*, October 11, 1984.
12. Guggenheim Application 1980. Box 1, Folder 49, Deborah Remington Papers, Special Collections and University Archives, Rutgers University Libraries. Remington applied numerous times between 1973 and 1983 and used almost identical language each time.
13. Geraldine Wojno, "Deborah Remington," *Arts Magazine* (1980), 10.
14. Guggenheim Application 1983. Deborah Remington Papers, Special Collections and University Archives, Rutgers University Libraries. In 1984, Remington wrote to her friend Lillian Delevoryas that her "work is changing again . . . back to a little looser and more direct approach with no tape, etc. Right now I'm working on a series of large scale drawings (6' and up) which are very exciting. . . . All black, white & gray." Letter to Lillian Delevoryas, January 13, 1984. Box 1, Folder 1, Deborah Remington Papers, Special Collections and University Archives, Rutgers University Libraries.
15. Adams-Middleton Gallery brochure, May 1984. Following this, it reads: "The paintings are classic Remington; rigorously-designed, highly-finished, fusions of natural and mechanistic forms in glowing color. The new drawings are more gestural and explosive than her previous graphic work. They indicate more of an emphasis on the synthesis of human emotion and organic form than her earlier work but maintain their metallic sheen. Now, however, these layered surfaces are more evocative of soft metal; lead, pewter or silver, rather than brightly polished steel. These drawings gained Remington one of this year's coveted Guggenheim fellowships."
16. Regan, "Remington: Past and Future."
17. Victoria Manning, *Deborah Remington: Works on Paper* (Greenville, DE: Gallery at Greenville, 1985), unpaginated.
18. Remington as quoted in *Deborah Remington: Works on Paper.*
19. Walter Thompson, "Deborah Remington at Jack Shainman," *Art in America* 75, no. 7 (July 1987), 127.
20. Vivien Raynor, "Deborah Remington," *New York Times*, April 3, 1987, C22.
21. Arlene Raven, "Night Light," *Village Voice*, March 3, 1987, 90.
22. To be sure, as with other moments in her career, drawing was essential to Remington's development as seen in drawings from the *Kennett Series* and coalescing in the rich surfaces of the paintings from this period.
23. In an unpublished interview by Carlos Villa on August 10, 2005, Remington noted: "I have done these large drawings ever since I got out of art school, since the late fifties, on and off through the years. I don't do them consistently. They are very labor intensive. In the late nineties, I started a group called the *Beinen Series* and it is based on bones. I broke a few bones and it focused me on bones. It's true. I broke an ankle and a wrist in a fall. And I thought 'oh lord, bones, it's what holds us together, it's what holds us up.' It's true; I mean we take them for granted. I started doing these drawings; well I've done four major huge drawings about bones. I mean they are literally based on bones. My work is nonrepresentational, but you can still get the feelings of bones in this work. And I'm doing another one now." See Deborah Remington artist's file, San Francisco Art Institute Archives.
24. Lilly Wei, "Drawing It Out," in *Deborah Remington: A Life in Drawing* (New York: Deborah Remington Charitable Trust for the Visual Arts, 2016), 27.
25. Rachel Churner, *Deborah Remington: Five Decades*, essay in brochure published by Bortolami Gallery, New York, 2021, unpaginated.
26. Churner, *Deborah Remington: Five Decades*.
27. Letter to Hassel Smith, June 21, 1982. Box 1, Folder 8, Deborah Remington Papers, Special Collections and University Archives, Rutgers University Libraries.

Paul Schimmel
RECALLING DEBORAH REMINGTON'S CAREER-DEFINING SURVEY

1. Klaus Kertess (1940–2016) was the founder and director of Bykert Gallery, New York, where Deborah Remington's first solo exhibition was held in 1967.
2. During the exhibition's planning stages, Remington was diagnosed with breast cancer and underwent radiation. In a letter dated July 25, 1983, she outlined to Schimmel the stress of simultaneously navigating exhibition preparations and her treatment: "Sorry it's taken so long to get this letter with the enclosed contracts off to you, but I've been in the hospital again. I'm home now but must go there every day at 10:30 AM for treatment. This will continue until they feel the disease is under some kind of control, probably for about another two months. I'm pretty devastated by all this. It's very hard on me, not only the treatments but the stress and anxiety over both my health and the museum show. All this stress is not helping the prognosis. Concerning our show, I'm feeling anxious about where everything

stands and who's doing what . . .
My energy level is not what it used to be before I got sick, so this is really taking a heavy toll on me. I hope you will help in whatever way you can, both in your position as curator and as a friend. I certainly need your help and support as never before." Orange County Museum of Art Archives.

3. In response to Remington's criticism about the lack of tour venues, Schimmel wrote to her on August 5, 1983: "Over the last two years, since we first discussed the exhibition I have written over 50 individual pieces of correspondence on a person-to-person basis relative to raising funds, approaching collectors, and attempting to sell the print. In addition to that, there have been over 30 circulation packages sent out to various museums around the country soliciting their participation. To follow this up, I have made at least 50 phone calls to different museums. . . . We have been flexible both in the dates and in the participation fees with the institutions, and we are providing them with a complete professional package, including duplicates of slides, articles, etc. concerning your work, as well as project description. In my years as a curator I don't think I have ever sent out a more complete circulation package." Orange County Museum of Art Archives.
4. Henry Hopkins (1928–2009) was the director of SFMOMA from 1974 to 1986. Following his tenure, John Lane (b. 1944) became the museum's fifth director, serving from 1987 to 1997.
5. Phil Linhares (b. 1939) was the chief curator of the Oakland Museum of California from 1990 to 2011.
6. To help fund the exhibition catalogue, Remington published a seven-run, sixteen-color lithograph, *Praia* (1983), priced at $650 in an edition of fifty. Sales were moderate and the print continued selling through the museum's bookstore for some years after. Schimmel's letter to potential collectors of the print noted that *Praia* "is outstanding, and exemplifies the perfection which is characteristic of her art. She was working here with Ocean Works for almost two weeks to achieve the delicate gradations of color she desired. The juxtaposition of shading captivates and holds the viewer. Deborah and the printers experimented with highly saturated inks for this print, creating a quality close in brilliance to her paintings." Orange County Museum of Art Archives.

CHRONOLOGY

1. Oral history interview with Deborah Remington, Archives of American Art, Smithsonian Institution, May 29–July 19, 1971.
2. Oral history interview with Remington, Archives of American Art.
3. Oral history interview with Remington, Archives of American Art.
4. Oral history interview with Remington, Archives of American Art.
5. Oral history interview with Remington, Archives of American Art.
6. Oral history interview with Remington, Archives of American Art.
7. Oral history interview with Remington, Archives of American Art.
8. John Natsoulas, *The Beat Generation Galleries and Beyond* (Davis, CA: John Natsoulas Press, 1996), 83.
9. Oral history interview with Remington, Archives of American Art.
10. Letter to Norma and Floyd Cox, August 22, 1960. Box 1, Folder 19, Deborah Remington Papers, Special Collections and University Archives, Rutgers University Libraries.
11. Oral history interview with Remington, Archives of American Art.
12. George D. Culler, *Drawings from the West Coast of USA* (Auckland, New Zealand: Auckland Art Gallery, 1962), unpaginated.
13. Remington in a lecture, date unknown.
14. James Monte, "Sculpture Steals the Show in the 83rd Annual," *Artforum* 2, no. 11 (May 1964), 23.
15. Oral history interview with Remington, Archives of American Art.
16. Oral history interview with Remington, Archives of American Art.
17. "The View from Los Angeles and New York: An Interview with Deborah Remington and Charles Mattox," *SFAI News* (July 1966), unpaginated.
18. Oral history interview with Remington, Archives of American Art.
19. Oral history interview with Remington, Archives of American Art.
20. The Cooper Union course catalogue, 1969. The Cooper Union Archives and Special Collections.
21. Remington in Corinne Robins, ed., *Drawing Now: 10 Artists*, exh. cat. (New York: Soho Center for Visual Artists, 1976), unpaginated.
22. Tamarind Artist Questionnaire, c. 1981. Box 5, Folder 21, Deborah Remington Papers, Special Collections and University Archives, Rutgers University Libraries.
23. Guggenheim Application 1980. Box 1, Folder 49, Deborah Remington Papers, Special Collections and University Archives, Rutgers University Libraries.
24. Letter to Bob (last name unknown), December 11, 1982. Box 1, Folder 8, Deborah Remington Papers, Special Collections and University Archives, Rutgers University Libraries.
25. Letter to Hassel Smith, July 26, 1980. Box 1, Folder 8, Deborah Remington Papers, Special Collections and University Archives, Rutgers University Libraries.
26. Letter to Lillian Delevoryas, January 13, 1984. Box 1, Folder 1, Deborah Remington Papers, Special Collections and University Archives, Rutgers University Libraries.
27. Letter to Joe and Eva Zirker, May 12, 1986. Box 1, Folder 8, Deborah Remington Papers, Special Collections and University Archives, Rutgers University Libraries.
28. Source unknown.
29. Remington in unpublished interview by Carlos Villa, August 10, 2005. Deborah Remington Artist's File, San Francisco Art Institute Archives.

Kevin Killian
DEBORAH REMINGTON R.I.P.

1. Deborah Remington was Frederic Remington's second cousin once removed.
2. Roberta Smith, "Deborah Remington, Abstract Art, Dies at 79," *New York Times*, May 18, 2010.

Contributors

Margaret Mathews Berenson is director of the Deborah Remington Charitable Trust for the Visual Arts. Following positions at the Philadelphia Museum of Art and the Metropolitan Museum of Art, she founded an art advisory business and worked as an independent curator. Exhibitions include *Homeland [In]Security: Vanishing Dreams* (Dorsky Curatorial Programs, Long Island City, NY, 2014) and *Women and Print: A Contemporary View* (Ruth Chandler Williamson Gallery, Scripps College, Claremont, CA, 2014). She is also the former director of the Drawing Society and editor in chief of *Drawing* magazine. She has taught at New York University, the International Center of Photography, and the 92nd Street Y, all in New York.

Carroll Dunham was born in 1949 and lives and works in New York and Connecticut. His work has been the subject of numerous solo exhibitions at international institutions including Museum Ludwig, Cologne; Millesgården, Stockholm; and Drammens Museum, Drammen, Norway. A mid-career retrospective was held at the New Museum of Contemporary Art, New York (2002–03). A retrospective of his drawings will be exhibited at the Art Institute of Chicago in 2026. *Into Words: The Selected Writings of Carroll Dunham* was published by Badlands Unlimited in 2017. He has written extensively about modern and contemporary art for museum catalogues, *Artforum*, and other publications.

Stephanie M. Hohlios is assistant professor of art history at Flagler College in St. Augustine, Florida. She specializes in the history of art, architecture, and performance in Japan and Asia. Her first book project, based on the dissertation *Coal Visualities: Labor, Gender, and Regional Consciousness in Chikuhō* (2021), examines the role of the arts in a former coal mining community in Kyushu, Japan. It foregrounds the tensions inherent to articulations of ethnicity, gender, and class within the concentric frames of region and nation. Her forthcoming article in *Review of Japanese Culture and Society* analyzes the intersection of contemporary experimental theater and social activism on behalf of working communities in Japan.

Suzanne Hudson is a professor of art history and fine arts at the University of Southern California in Los Angeles. An art historian and critic, she writes with special emphasis on the history, theory, and conventions of painting and process. She is also a regular contributor to *Artforum* and has written numerous essays for international exhibition catalogues and artist monographs. Recent books include *Agnes Martin: Night Sea* (Afterall/MIT, 2017) and *Contemporary Painting* (Thames & Hudson, 2021). Hudson is currently working on *Better for the Making: Art, Therapy, Process*, a study of the therapeutic origins of art making within American modernism.

Anna Katz is curator at The Museum of Contemporary Art, Los Angeles (MOCA), where her recent and upcoming exhibitions include *Ordinary People: Photorealism and the Work of Art Since 1968* (2024), *MOCA Focus: Eddie Rodolfo Aparicio* (2023), *Long Story Short* (2023), *Judith F. Baca: World Wall* (2022), *Pipilotti Rist: Big Heartedness, Be My Neighbor* (2021), and *With Pleasure: Pattern and Decoration in American Art 1972–1985* (2019). From 2015 to 2017 Katz was the Wendy Stark Curatorial Fellow at MOCA. Previously a Joan Tisch Teaching Fellow at the Whitney Museum of American Art from 2008 to 2013, she holds a PhD from the Department of Art and Archaeology at Princeton University.

Kevin Killian (1952–2019) was a San Francisco–based poet, playwright, novelist, biographer, editor, critic, and artist. Highly prolific and radically queer, he published several volumes of poetry and short stories, as well as four novels. He also wrote and produced fifty plays. Four chapbooks have been published of his 2,000-plus Amazon reviews, and Semiotext(e) is preparing a major collection. In 2023, Pilot Press published a new edition of his first book of poetry, *Argento Series*. Nightboat Books is publishing his collected books of poetry. With his wife, Dodie Bellamy, he edited *Writers Who Love Too Much: New Narrative 1977–1997* (2017).

Nancy Lim is associate curator of painting and sculpture at the San Francisco Museum of Modern Art (SFMOMA). Curated and co-curated exhibitions include *Creative Growth: The House That Art Built* (2024), *Chiura Obata* (2023), *New Work: Anna Sew Hoy* (2023), *Joan Brown* (2022), and *Mythos, Psyche, Eros: Jess and California* (2019). She also contributed to the retrospectives of Vija Celmins (2018) and Bruce Conner (2016). Prior to SFMOMA, Lim held curatorial positions at the Solomon R. Guggenheim Museum and the Museum of Modern Art, both in New York.

Paul Schimmel is an independent curator based in Los Angeles. In 1983, he organized *Deborah Remington: A 20-Year Survey* at the Newport Harbor Art Museum (now the Orange County Museum of Art) in California. Remington's first and only survey, it traveled to the Oakland Museum of California. Schimmel was chief curator of The Museum of Contemporary Art, Los Angeles, from 1990 to 2012, and he has organized major exhibitions on Chris Burden, Richard Hamilton, Laura Owens, Robert Rauschenberg, and Charles Ray. His numerous thematic shows include *Helter Skelter: L.A. Art in the 1990s* (1992), *Out of Actions: Between Performance and the Object, 1949–1979* (1999), *Under the Big Black Sun: California Art 1974–1981* (2011), *Revolution in the Making: Abstract Sculpture by Women, 1947–2016* (2016), and *Hand-Painted Pop! Art and Appropriation, 1961 to Now* (2017).

Acknowledgments

One of the greatest pleasures of a book project is its fundamentally collaborative nature. We would like to thank our many partners on *Deborah Remington*, whose extraordinary effort and support proved essential to realizing this publication.

Since the artist's death in 2010, the Deborah Remington Charitable Trust for the Visual Arts has been charged with establishing her legacy. We are deeply grateful to the trust for its ongoing support: Craig Remington, executive trustee; Phyllis Landau, attorney; and Cheri Smith, who was Remington's trusted friend and former studio assistant. Smith's memories of the artist's life and studio practice have been invaluable. Jeremy Adams, the trust's development specialist, undertook diligent research and fundraising oversight for this book and other ongoing projects. Along the way, Leah Levy, executive director of the Jay DeFeo Foundation, provided generous counsel, and we have benefited immeasurably from her expertise and thoughtful encouragement. We are also fortunate to have relied on the Aspen Institute's Artist-Endowed Foundations Initiative, which offers artists' trusts and foundations the opportunity to discuss key issues that impact art stewardship and cultural philanthropy.

Numerous galleries and individuals have contributed to the Remington Trust's efforts over the past fourteen years. We are especially grateful to independent curator Jay Gorney for his steadfast belief in Remington's work. In 2015, he organized a solo exhibition at Wallspace Gallery in New York that led to relationships with other galleries and to exhibitions at Kimmerich Galerie in Berlin and parrasch heijnen in Los Angeles. In 2020, Margaret Mathews Berenson began conversations with Stefania Bortolami and Evan Reiser from Bortolami Gallery in New York, who have since become indefatigable and energizing partners. Serendipitously, the gallery's first solo presentation of Remington's paintings, in 2021, ran concurrently with an exhibition of her drawings at Craig Starr Gallery in New York. Bortolami's second presentation, in fall 2024, coincides with the publication of this book. Stefania and Evan also introduced Margaret to the incomparable Wendy Wahlert, who expertly managed countless aspects of this project with efficiency, humor, and unshakable good sense. We are indebted to Wendy. In the final months of the project, Emma Thorup provided additional and much-needed assistance.

In the making for several years, this volume realizes the trust's long-held hope for a major monographic publication on the artist. Carroll Dunham, Stephanie M. Hohlios, Suzanne Hudson, and Anna Katz contributed essays that radically deepen our understanding of Remington's practice and the worlds in which she moved. Curator Paul Schimmel shared his prodigious memories of his time working on her twenty-year survey exhibition in 1983, and Dodie Bellamy generously allowed us to republish a text authored in memoriam by writer Kevin Killian. For attending to these essays and the book's many other components, we thank our stalwart editor, Elizabeth Franzen, whose exceptional editorial oversight, warmth, and frequent exhortation "Onward!" inspired us all. Amanda Glesmann has our gratitude for her critical editing in the project's last stages and for her advice all throughout. We also thank Kelli Rae Patton for the precision and speed of her copyediting. Henk van Assen and Melissa Leone at HvADesign created a beautiful catalogue that befits the indomitable spirit of Remington's artwork. For their dedication, we are grateful to the team at Rizzoli Electa: Charles Miers, publisher; Margaret Rennolds Chace, associate publisher; Ellen R. Cohen, senior editor; and Alyn Evans, production manager. The National Endowment for the Arts and the Pollock-Krasner Foundation enabled this publication through generous grants.

Individuals at various libraries, archives, and institutions have been essential to our research. At Rutgers University Libraries, Fernanda Perrone, archivist and head, Exhibitions Program, Special Collections and University Archives, oversaw the cataloguing of Remington's archives and made this rich resource available to our team of writers as well as to scholars, students, and other researchers. Jeff Gunderson and Becky Alexander at the SFAI Legacy Foundation + Archive continually offered fascinating information about the artist's years as a student and teacher at the California School of Fine Arts (later the San Francisco Art Institute). At The Cooper Union, where Remington taught painting and drawing from 1974 to 1997, Mary Mann and Dale Perreault in Archives and Special Collections readily provided access to their trove of historical documents. We also extend gratitude to Meredith Patute at the Oakland Museum of California and Amanda Seadler at the Orange County Museum of Art, who aided our research enormously.

Finally, we salute the people who have been beside us at every step. Nancy Lim thanks Bruce Wallace, a wondrous source of love, support, and ice cream; and Angelina Lim, the kind of sister few in this world are lucky to have. Ollie joined the project partway through, born into an ocean of editing. Margaret would like to thank Richard Berenson not only for sharing his expertise in book design and publishing but most importantly his wry sense of humor, which so often provided an alternate perspective and the occasional levity that sustained her throughout this endeavor.

Index

Note: All works are by Deborah Remington unless otherwise indicated. Page numbers in italic type refer to illustrations.

All works by Deborah Remington © 2024 Deborah Remington Charitable Trust for the Visual Arts / Licensed by Artists Rights Society (ARS), NY. Additional image credits, where applicable, are provided below, listed by page number:

Front cover: Deborah Remington, *Encounters*, 2007 (detail). See page 207. **Frontispiece:** Deborah Remington in her studio, New York, 1971. **Page 2:** Deborah Remington, *Memphis*, 1969. Oil on canvas, 60 x 53 in. (152.4 x 134.6 cm). Collection of Beth Rudin DeWoody. **Back cover:** Deborah Remington, *March*, 1964. See page 71.

Image Credits
Covers, 20, 23, 29–31, 37, 39–41, 43, 51, 62, 71–72, 74 (left), 84 (left), 107–9, 115, 117, 125, 126, 139, 163–88, 190–209, 213–14, 216–18: Photo: Kristian Laudrup, courtesy Bortolami, New York. **2, 54, 65, 67**: Photo: Matthew Grubb, courtesy Wallspace, New York. **Frontispiece, 6, 80, 82, 215, 220, 226, 227 (left), 228 (right), 229, 231–34 (right), 235, 238–39**: Courtesy Deborah Remington Papers, Special Collections and University Archives, Rutgers University Libraries. **10, 53, 68**: Photo: Adam Reich, courtesy Craig Starr Gallery, New York. **17, 45**: Photo: Fraser Marr. **19, 76**: Courtesy Denver Art Museum. **21, 33**: Photo: Howard Agresti. **24–25, 63**: Photo: Zachary Callahan, courtesy parrasch heijnen, Los Angeles. **27**: Image courtesy Karma, New York. **47**: Photo: Jenny Heffernon, courtesy Oakland Museum of California. **49, 61**: Photo: Don Ross, courtesy San Francisco Museum of Modern Art. **55, 56, 64, 66, 134, 152, 189**: Photo: Dan Bradica, courtesy Craig Starr Gallery, New York. **69, 91, 133**: Digital image © Whitney Museum of American Art / Licensed by Scala / Art Resource, NY. **74 (right)**: Photo: Johanna Arnold, courtesy di Rosa Center for Contemporary Art, Napa, CA. **57–59, 77, 99, 100, 111, 227 (right)**: Photo: Guang Xu, courtesy Bortolami, New York. **84 (right)**: ColBase: Integrated Collections Database of the National Institutes for Cultural Heritage, Japan (https://colbase.nich.go.jp/collection_items/tnm/A-282?locale=en). **85, 105**: Photo: Adam Reich. **86**: © 2024 The Franz Kline Estate / Artists Rights Society (ARS), New York. Digital image © Tate, London / Art Resource, NY. **93**: Photo: Yves Chenot, © Rights Reserved Cnap **95**: Courtesy Smithsonian American Art Museum, Washington, D.C. / Art Resource, NY. **97**: Courtesy Indianapolis Museum of Art at Newfields. **98**: Photo: Allen Phillips, courtesy Wadsworth Atheneum Museum of Art, Hartford, CT. **101**: Photo: Richard House, courtesy Yale University Art Gallery. **103**: Courtesy Addison Gallery of American Art, Phillips Academy, Andover, MA / Art Resource, NY. **113, 132, 136, 141**: Photo: Joachim Schulz, courtesy Kimmerich Galerie, Berlin. **119**: Courtesy Toledo Museum of Art. **120**: Courtesy Carnegie Museum of Art, Pittsburgh, PA. **121**: Courtesy Rago/Wright/LAMA. **123**: Photo: Mike Lundgren, courtesy Phoenix Art Museum. **127**: Courtesy Pazo Fine Art, Kensington, Maryland. **129**: Photo: Alayna Barrett Fox, courtesy San Antonio Museum of Art. **137**: © Worcester Art Museum, Massachusetts, USA/Bridgeman Images. **143**: Photo: Devon Johnson, courtesy Marlborough Gallery. **146**: Courtesy Estate of Christina Ramberg and Corbett vs. Dempsey. **148**: © 2024 Estate of Miriam Schapiro / Artists Rights Society (ARS), New York. Courtesy Eric Firestone Gallery, NY. **150**: © Vija Celmins, courtesy Matthew Marks Gallery. **151**: © Lee Bontecou 2024, All Rights Reserved. **154**: © Lee Bontecou 2024, All Rights Reserved. Digital image © Whitney Museum of American Art / Licensed by Scala / Art Resource, NY. **155**: © 2024 Artists Rights Society (ARS), New York / ADAGP, Paris. Digital Image © The Museum of Modern Art/Licensed by SCALA / Art Resource, NY. **156**: © 2024 Jasper Johns and ULAE / Licensed by VAGA at Artists Rights Society (ARS), NY, Published by Universal Limited Art Editions. **157 (left)**: © Estate of Roy Lichtenstein. Courtesy The Eli and Edythe L. Broad Collection **157 (right):** © 1937 Disney. **158**: Photo: Studio Tromp, courtesy Museum Boijmans Van Beuningen, Rotterdam. **159**: © 2024 Estate of Alexander Rodchenko / UPRAVIS, Moscow / ARS, NY. Digital Image © The Museum of Modern Art/ Licensed by SCALA / Art Resource, NY. **210, 236**: Courtesy Orange County Museum of Art, Costa Mesa, CA.

First published in the United States of America in 2024 by

RIZZOLI ELECTA
A Division of Rizzoli International Publications, Inc.
300 Park Avenue South
New York, NY 10010
www.rizzoliusa.com

In association with the Deborah Remington Charitable Trust for the Visual Arts
www.deborahremington.com

This project is supported in part by the National Endowment for the Arts and Pollock-Krasner Foundation.

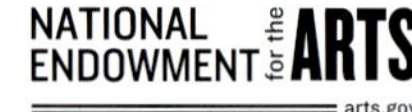

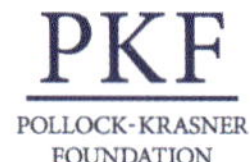

For Rizzoli Electa
PUBLISHER: Charles Miers
ASSOCIATE PUBLISHER: Margaret Rennolds Chace
SENIOR EDITOR: Ellen R. Cohen
PRODUCTION MANAGER: Alyn Evans

Deborah Remington Charitable Trust for the Visual Arts
DIRECTOR: Margaret Mathews Berenson

Publication
PROJECT EDITORS: Margaret Mathews Berenson, Nancy Lim
MANAGING EDITOR: Wendy Wahlert
EDITOR: Elizabeth Franzen

DESIGN: Henk van Assen with Melissa Leone, HvADesign, New York

2024 2025 2026 2027 2028 / 10 9 8 7 6 5 4 3 2 1

ISBN: 978-0-8478-3414-3
Library of Congress Control Number: 2024934485

Printed in China

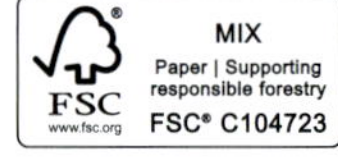